Too Long a Child

The mother–daughter dyad

Too Long a Child

The mother–daughter dyad

Nini Herman LMSSA
Psychotherapist

Whurr Publishers Ltd
London

First published in Great Britain by
Free Association Books 1989

Reprinted with permission by
Whurr Publishers Ltd 1999

British Library Cataloguing-in-Publication Data
A catalogue record for this book is available from the British
Library.

ISBN 1 86156 109 1

Printed and bound in Great Britain by Athenæum Press Ltd,
Gateshead, Tyne & Wear.

For my granddaughters, Rebecca and Katya.
In memory of their late great-grandmother, Ellen.
For her granddaughters, Ruth, Sylvia, Jenni, Becci.

Contents

PART V

ACKNOWLEDGEMENTS

My thanks to Susie Breakell-Herman, my research assistant, for some of the early chapters, and my mother, for suggestions out of her fund of folklore wisdom.

To Levana Marshall for more loving support and encouragement than can be put on paper.

To Mary Gifford-Brown, who was one step ahead of me in writing her book: *Reflections. Images of British Women in their Own Words.*

To Mirjam Hadar, Mira Hammermesh, Anthea Zeman, and others whose minds I plundered intermittently, over all of five years.

To Josef and my children, for putting up with my constant preoccupation, compulsive talk on mothers and daughters, rather terrible cooking and bouts of bad temper.

To the staff of the London Library, The Fawcett Library and the Women's Library and Resource Centre, for unfailing patience, courtesy and generous giving of their time.

To my editor, Karl Figlio, who taught me much about myself, and to publisher Bob Young, for a whole world he has set in motion.

The publishers would like to thank the following for permission to quote from published material. Every effort has been made to trace copyright owners and any omissions should be notified to the publishers.

Aeschylus, *The Oresteia*, translated by Robert Fagles, 1977, Wildwood, translated by Tony Harrison, 1981. M. Cardinal, *The Words to Say It*, Pan Books, 1984; trans. P. Goodheart, Van Vactor & Goodheart. D. Dinnerstein, *The Rocking of the Cradle and the Ruling of the World*, Souvenir Press. S. Ernst and M. Maguire (eds) *Living with the Sphinx: Papers from the Women's Therapy Centre*. The Women's Press, 1987. Euripides: *MEDEA AND OTHER PLAYS* translated by Philip Vellacott (Penguin Classics, 1963), copyright © Philip Vellacott, 1963. L. Garrett Anderson, *Elizabeth Garrett Anderson*, Methuen London, 1939. Excerpts from *The Moon and the Virgin* by Nor Hall and Ellen Kennedy, copyright © 1980 by Eleanor L. Hall. Reprinted with permission of Harper & Row, Harper & Row Publishers, New York. Published by The Women's Press, London, 1980. *Memoirs of the Life of Colonel Hutchinson* by Lucy Hutchinson, edited by James Sutherland, 1973, Oxford University Press. H.A. Jenkins, *Three Classical Poets: Sappho, Catullus and Juvenal*, Duckworth, 1982. C.G. Jung and C. Kerenyi, *Essays on a Science of Mythology*, trans. R.F.C. Hull, Bollingen Series 22. Copyright 1949, © 1959, 1963 by Princeton University Press. Printed by permission of New York University Press from *Beyond Their Sex: Learned Women of the European Past*, ed. Patricia H. Labalme. Copyright © 1980 by New York University. D. Lessing, *Landlocked*, 1972, and *The Four-Gated City*, 1978, Grafton Books a division of the Collins Publishing Group; excerpts from *The Four-Gated City* by Doris Lessing, copyright © 1969 by Doris Lessing Productions Ltd, reprinted by permission of Alfred A. Knopf Inc, New York. J. Liddington, *Respectable Rebel: The Life and Times of Selina Cooper, 1864–1946*, Virago Press, 1984. J. Manton, *Elizabeth Garrett Anderson*, Methuen London, 1965. M. Milner, *The Hands of the Living*

INTRODUCTION

My proofs derive from experience and . . . not from reference to
authorities . . . It is not title and eloquence . . . nor the reading of
many books . . . that are required of a physician . . . but the
deepest knowledge of things themselves and of nature's secrets and
this knowledge outweighs all else.
(PARACELSUS)

HOW RARELY it will come about on the benches of our childhood that our intuition, the love-play of imagination, receives an affirming wink. Willy-nilly we are herded, who do not know how to resist, into what one poet (Roethke, T., 1937) called the 'hutch of reason – that dreary shed'. We are taught to honour 'facts' rather than to live at ease with 'the wax and wane of doubts'; with a humble confidence that we have enduring stocks of all the spirit needs within; which places us in a position to maintain a pristine eye.

Accordingly some of us have tuned into a foreknowledge that woman is perhaps not kept in her old bedevilled place, stripped of her sovereign power, by patriarchs in conspiracy, but finds herself at the mercy of archaic transactions indigenous to the core of the mother–daughter dyad. That it is at this connection that her growth and greater freedom are continually aborted in a subversive two-way traffic to which we have, in the past, turned a curiously blind eye.

A preface, as Jacques Derrida tells us, is, of course, another lie. It is written with hindsight. Or perhaps there are two: one which sends us on our way and is subsequently scrapped in favour of the second version.

Let me start at the beginning. I set out on this adventure, with little thought what it would cost me over all of five years, shortly after the end of a long analysis of which I have written elsewhere (Herman, N., 1985). For all the many benefits which it had bestowed on me I felt that my relationship to my mother, then in her eighties, still left much to be desired. My career as a daughter and a mother of four daughters had, to say the very least, been patchy and fraught, much visited by tragedy, the roots of which, I was aware, ran back by several generations.

But beyond the personal I felt stranded with a feeling of dislodgement from the past, of being disowned in some sense. I began dimly to sense that this ahistoricity of my feminine connectedness had played a part in all these traumas. Such were the apprehensions which sent me searching for the sphinx who guards the mother–daughter theme to hear it spoken in her words.

On this particular track I slowly grew to understand why many an adopted child pursues an urgent need to know the story of her antecedents – to take her place in their ranks, even if, as in my case, it may well turn out to be an altogether different one from that which I had occupied in airy-fairy make-believe of membership of some elite. If I discovered on this journey that my true mothers were poor, undernourished and exploited, in many instances slaves, at least I knew where I belonged and could admit with much relief that it was something I had always known. I sensed that I was coming home.

So much for an initial preface, although it has already strayed into the area of hindsight. Yet 'undernourished' and 'exploited', the status of a lifelong slave, did not entirely belong to some *Uncle Tom's Cabin*. This was also myself and most of my woman-friends, including the well-known and famous, in heart-to-heart confessionals. Neither, as I recognized, had I left that furtive skivvy altogether behind on the daily nine-year couch. She was the product of my childhood in the keeping of my mother. In the working of this book she slunk away and dissolved for reasons still in part unknown.

Not knowing is familiar. Had anyone, I ask, prepared me in the course of years of training as a psychotherapist for the discovery that my woman patients would not so much reveal a different sex as amplify a different order of being on those long explorations leading into the unknown? Where each endeavour was concerned I had the distinct impression that two were settling on the couch. Where a treatment ended well, I found myself bidding farewell to two human entities. How can I say two separate people, when I remain in grave uncertainty over whether mother and daughter *ever* achieve the separation our theoreticians would approve; or whether it is in their nature to accomplish such a feat:

In Serato, a particularly dry and arid region of Brazil, a few trees trained in the shape of bushes grow. When one tries to uproot them, one discovers their roots are stronger and thicker the deeper they go into the ground. If one

*persists in digging them up, one finds they communicate with neighbouring
bushes and that they converge in one thick stem that descends even farther
while thickening, making its way finally as an enormous single trunk which
bores into the earth like a sharp instrument. One understands that this is in
fact an enormous tree which has buried itself twenty or thirty yards below the
surface in order to find water. I was one of those bushes. But deprived of the
trunk which drew the water from the depths, I was going to die. (Cardinal,
M., 1984, p. 123)*

So the author, halfway through her legendary analysis, perceived her
predicament: the travail that lay ahead: a universal category for the
mother–daughter dyad. How she, in time, resolved the issue we will
come to later on.

Freud had already decreed early in this century that the sexual role
we live by owed no obedience to the facts of our anatomy. Sex became
a state of mind rooted in phantasy, smelted in that crucible of earliest
development where nature and nurture merge inextricably, for life.
The sexual drive shall acknowledge no inevitable object, nor bow to
any 'natural' aim:

*In conformity with its peculiar nature, psychoanalysis does not try to describe
what a woman is – that would be a task it could scarcely perform – but sets
about enquiring how she comes into being. (Freud, S., 1933, p. 116)*

This enquiry would eschew every contamination by extraneous
disciplines. But it is my personal belief that there cannot fail to be a
network of relationships between the psychic and the social, as with
the biological. Each must supplement the other. Each has aspects to
contribute which the other cannot speak.

It has been argued with much passion that if woman could enjoy
equal opportunities with the other half, with men, she would come in
from the cold, from her present banishment from the hub of affairs,
cast her dreamy vagueness off, rise to the challenge avidly, seize
worldly power with both hands and never look back again.

Yet anyone who, like myself, has studied woman in some depth,
both herself as a patient and subsequently, over years, numbers of her
fellows too, is bound to come to the conclusion that what keeps
putting back the clock in the progress for women lies in crucial *inner*
stalemates which are active at the core of the mother–daughter dyad.
These we will examine later. They operate in each of us.

If in the working of this book I cast my 'furtive skivvy' off, that statement should be amplified. I became something other than I previously had lived. It is best exemplified in lines from H.D.'s poem 'The Master', in which she expressed her new-found status after two episodes of analysis with Freud:

> *She is a woman,*
> *yet beyond woman,*
> *yet in woman . . .*
> (H.D., 1981)

The Greeks have a word for 'in search of Greekness': it is *Romiosini*. How would they remain themselves under the heel of Rome? Could we follow their example and coin a term, 'womanness', to encompass this constituent whose experience of herself is liable to shift and change in the act of undergoing a very plethora of functions? The term 'femininity' bears too many stale accretions. It lacks a workshop atmosphere: smacks of the helpless and romantic.

It is with womanness in mind that I pursued this odyssey, but I will have no innovations just for innovation's sake. I have employed words like 'subject', like 'authenticity', in their dictionary meaning. That leaves ground under my feet even if that ground is quaking, as we are all aware, at the end of the twentieth century, in its drive to make the word submit to new experience and meaning.

Changes will, of course, occur in the outer, social world which woman will utilize to her temporary advantage. As we shall shortly see, mothers in the Middle Ages who belonged to an elite eagerly took up the option of attaining to a role of power in the status of abbess within the monastic system. Once they had secured this gain they helped the next generation – a daughter or a niece – to raise herself to that position. If I called this temporary it is because I believe that until our awareness of the many-fold subversions to woman's authenticity within the mother–daughter dyad becomes more robust and astute, womanness remains subject to perennial regression.

If this is the case the theme demands closer inspection, since its configurations account, in my considered view, for more sorrow and wastage, more frustration and backtracking in countless women's lives than any equivalent conundrum the hapless male can inflict. Whatever powers he may wield in holding woman back today, her obstacles to womanness lie largely in her collusion with the patriarchal edicts, even if at an unconscious level. We can even see this issue as a *folie à deux*. Its object, as we shall see, since a *folie à deux* always has a deeper object which defeats bilateral growth, is for each sex to deny the woundedness we have to carry through the course of our life once we tear down the illusion of mother-as-a-part-of-me: the blissful dream of symbiosis.

Certainly separation as the primal issue within the mother–daughter dyad clearly became the single thread running through its history. Once the Ancient World began to recognize this central theme, it gave us momentous myths upon and around this subject. If, something of the order of twenty-five centuries ago, Demeter and Persephone underwent the ordeal of being wrenched apart by a growing consciousness of the Law of the Father, we still painfully lack our modern equivalent: a version of that agony which can speak to us today in our monstrous isolation in front of the television screen with its charter of smooth texts. The creation of myths may very well require a potent oral tradition and the scope to address itself to a living multitude.

Meanwhile, separating out of a mother from her daughter, and the other way round, still continues to loom as a paralysing threat over the life-land of the mother, and the future of the daughter. If she leaves that body-home which nurtured and instructed her for virtually two decades in the maternal circuit, will the mother not proclaim: if you dare to make a move I shall exercise my right to take back the life I gave you? And if the daughter persists and makes that far-reaching bid for a life of her own, will the mother not feel the very ground give beneath her tired feet: her power and existence threatened with abject redundancy?

And yet, paradoxically, the girl must remain put for an anxious length of time in the maternal circuit. Through the years of adolescence she has nowhere else to go while she needs to consolidate an identification with the maternal role. Feminists may be outraged that this is putting back the clock. But we need to bear in mind that, to the daughter as a child, woman *is* a mother. In that role she will be judged as sufficient or as wanting to the exclusion of all else. Whatever else the girl becomes once she is set on a path of differentiation, it has to be envisaged, first, as a separating out from the maternal role as exercised by her mother, only later to become its creative reconstruction on her individual terms. For this project to succeed she must first identify, she must know herself as *someone*, even in phantasy, before becoming someone different with sufficient confidence.

But the maternal shelter serves a second essential purpose. It provides an opportunity for the girl to elaborate her intuitive possession of a good inner space in which 'life can be brought on'. Omitting a reference to babies is intended to suggest that this sanctuary is required in due course to incubate all forms of creativity. Since the girl, unlike the boy, lacks external evidence of sound (pro)creative organs, time itself is of the essence in a dreamy testing out of an optimistic credo that such an inner space exists. If these notions seem archaic, clinical experience confirms their veracity with a deep sense of conviction.

The time has come to recognize that the vociferous bid for *equal* woman status may not serve the truest interests of emerging womanness. There *are* vital differences in the psyche of a woman with which she needs to come to terms to validate her personhood as confidently on those grounds as any which she holds in common with the psyche of the male. If we are correct in thinking, in accord with Lacan, that man's self-regard is a phallocentric one from which focus woman is an object of his phantasy, I incline to the belief that the reverse applies as well: that it is conceivable that each woman, and each man, is his/her own signifier at some deep unconscious level, so that each relates to the other primarily on a level of primitive phantasy. This, of course, presupposes that there is evidence for *primary femininity*, experienced not as pure lack but as the difference of a something at which we will be looking when we meet 'Emily' (below, pp. 18–19).

At the present time we have only the scantiest knowledge of how woman and man are constituted in unconscious dynamics while in the interim the sound and fury of this discourse is propounded in the voice of man. My impression is that women have learnt these awkward texts by heart in order to pay lip service like good little girls unwilling to be left behind, although they have failed to reflect their experience of themselves in their own womanness. Here I may of course be wrong, or simply envious.

I do not, as I said, share the belief that the phallus is the exclusive signifier. True, it is spectacular. It can emit silver fountains heading like arrows for the sun to fill our hearts with excitement, the thrill of a spectacle. In comparison with such vivid exhibitionism the vulva which leads into the dark, the mysterious heartland of procreative cavities, may seem of secondary importance, but that is to lose the point. For in the presence of the feminine as signifier in her turn, be it a valley or a nest, a quiet little earthen pot or her cultivated garden, we become enfolded in so profound a container that its role as signifier will all too readily be lost.*

How could it be otherwise? Spend a morning in that great museum in Heraklion surrounded by Cycladic art, and phallocentricity quickly falls into perspective. If psychoanalysis, in the person of Mrs Klein, gave us mammocentricity, here we still encounter woman split horizontally with the lower half relegated to a daemonium. We are still without a term which begins to define woman in her total potency.

Derrida (Derrida, J., 1976, pp. 173–4) ponders on how Rousseau postulates in his 'Essay on the Origin of Languages', that 'Pity is a voice. The maternal law is a voice.' Is there then a 'natural writing' which is that of the heart and stands in opposition to a writing without pity which is that of reason, he considers at length. What is at issue here is whether womanness will not have to integrate the two, namely *caritas* and *logos*, in her every undertaking, instead of being this good girl who hereby does violence to the true nature of her psyche. We said that the recurring theme within any history of the mother–daughter dyad emerges very clearly as the one of separation, but implicit in that is woman's struggle to come into possession of her unencumbered truth.

We are still a long way off from any such conception. Even the thorny question of woman's true love-object, whether she does or does not change her deepest allegiance to the man, is fated to remain obscure as long as man remains arrested in a phallocentric stance: that of the misogynist. As long as he is not open to her specific openness, at which we shall be looking; as long as he confiscates her ancient, honourable right to unitary experience; as long as he exploits the core of her vulnerability, which is also his own, she reaches out to find her mate hatefully disappointing. Then the only way back is to the maternal circuit: the only way forward that of the medial who is neither man nor woman in the most auspicious sense, but lives in the wilderness as a sibyl or a sphinx. If woman is to learn her truth she

* I owe these ideas to Martin Wright, Department of English, Warwick University.

requires a partnership, that haven of mutual trust from which both can face the world without their backs against the wall. A world which helps her to organize her multifarious self-fulfilment in an equality of shared responsibility for major human concerns, including that of parenting, while she is free to establish the nature of her difference.

These pages can provide no answer, but they seek to throw some light on how at least her awareness of this project, as of her need, has gradually come about in so far as we can now define its scope and nature, if only partially. Its primary workshop is the dyad which has grown increasingly aware of its own archaic pitfalls.

How was the decision taken whom to include and whom to leave out from such an enormous canvas? Criticism has been levelled only fairly recently that 'Thou shalt not use the biographies of a handful of exceptional (usually upper-class) ladies to describe the experience of the majority of (necessarily lower-class) women' (Stone, L., 1985). Noble sentiment, agreed. The obvious difficulty is that Hellenic palaces, Roman villas, Saxon halls, castles and the manor house, convents and monasteries, were generally built of stone, and stone was chosen to endure, long after mud and lath have yielded to the elements and thatch to the busy birds. The life stories which I chose illustrated the main themes of separation and the ongoing quest for woman's authenticity in a basic chronology, but there were also women who, willy-nilly, stole my heart. Was I not, I thought, entitled also to enjoy myself on this long and lonely trail through all of ten millennia?

I determined from the start that I was going to remain within my own, ancestral culture whose mainstream courses through my veins. Within the Graeco-Judaean stream I might avoid such surplus errors as I would be bound to make should I attempt to cross the Nile or drift down the mighty Ganges. My sisters born along those banks are far better qualified to string their myths and phantasies into patterns of their own making.

Central to every woman's life – as doubtless we have always known, but hidden from our consciousness so that the theme becomes uncanny – is the relationship between her mother and herself, between herself and her daughter. In this nexus I discovered in my own analysis, as in my work with other women, the hidden, central reason why women are where they are, obstinately marking time in archaic formations in some compartment of themselves. But here also

lies concealed the world's greatest love-affair, rapturous entanglement
and deathtrap to development, in madness or in suicide; the
wellspring of enduring strength or festering wound through which
faint lives drain into oblivion. Only love on the grand scale, when it
feels cheated or undone, can be subverted to the hatred where
infanticide and matricide become ghostly denizens in that sun-
drenched, golden land.

If this conviction is true, then the subject must deserve the most
patient explorations, of which the present expedition is but a single
one. Each may have set sail alone to find, once we get under way, that
we are part of a flotilla drawn from countless coves and inlets – but
unique to our own day.

> *I have a daughter fair,*
> *And none so loved as she!*
> *Not all the Lydian land,*
> *Nor Lesbos' lovely strand*
> *can weigh her worth to me.*
> (Sappho, around 800 BC)

PART I

1 A CENTURY ON THE COUCH

*The heart has reasons of which
reason knows nothing.*
(PASCAL)

*We knew, of course, that there had been a preliminary stage of
attachment to the mother, but we did not know that it could be so
rich in content and so long-lasting, and could leave behind so
many opportunities for fixations and dispositions.*
(FREUD, 'Femininity')

THROUGHOUT his four betrothal years Freud had a problem on his hands: by what tactics could he wrest his beloved from Mamma? Martha, as his future wife, had, the youthful doctor stormed, to change her allegiance from the Bernays camp to his without a single reservation. From being a good Jewish daughter who presumably lit the candles on the Sabbath, she was to be transformed into his 'comrade in arms'. 'Eli little knows what a heathen I am going to make of you' (Jones, E., 1953, p. 127). Passionately Freud confirmed that bourgeois sensibilities and orthodox protestations were to be swept away to the last and final crumbs of this unleavened bread.

But Mamma retaliated! When in 1883 Martha and her sister Minna were duly both betrothed to men whose work tied them to Vienna, she chose this moment to return to her beloved native Hamburg. Perhaps she hoped her Martha might at such a distance still be weaned from her penniless suitor with his unsavoury ideas and helter-skelter tendencies. Her daughters had no choice but to follow. Minna and the two young men launched into healthy protestations, calling her a 'selfish old woman' (Jones, E., 1953, p. 125) to no discernible effect. Martha followed like a lamb, knowing that she must now endure spells of cruel separation.

Martha's own attitude to her mother was one of devotion and strict obedience; her mother's resolute will was to her not selfishness but something to be admired, and not questioned. Her sister Minna, on the other hand, was quite frank in her criticism of her mother; it was the first bond between her and Freud. He neatly characterized the contrast with psychological acumen: 'You don't love her very much and are as considerate as possible to her; Minna loves her, but doesn't spare her.' (Jones, E., 1953, p. 122)

Already Freud had stumbled on how ambivalence breeds guilt and how guilt in its turn fosters masochistic submission.

By the time they were married Freud had clearly won his battle to outer appearances:

The only sign of war recorded in all the ensuing years was a temporary difference of opinion over the weighty question whether mushrooms should be cooked with or without their stalks. (Jones, E., 1953, p. 147)

But we know that marriages asphyxiate in such a 'peace'! At the time Freud failed to ponder all the deeper implications of this divergence in the nature of the two Bernays sisters for that 'dark continent of female sexuality'. It would take three decades until we read the later thinker:

When a mother hinders or arrests a daughter's sexual activity, she is fulfilling a normal function whose lines are laid down by events in childhood, which has powerful, unconscious motives, and has received the sanction of society. It is the daughter's business to emancipate herself from this influence and to decide for herself on broad and rational grounds what her share of enjoyment or denial of sexual pleasure shall be. (Freud, S., 1915b, p. 267)

Interestingly enough, despite the reference above, the word 'daughter' is missing in Volume 24, the complete index of the *Standard Edition of the Complete Works of Freud*. All references are to 'girl'. Were even Freud's editors, at some unconscious level, seeking to steer clear of the darker implications of the mother–daughter tangle? Freud's repeated attempts to batter the incubus of the feminine enigma into monistic submission – nice, precise parallels with male development – would consistently fail, to his lifelong exasperation. In this area, palpably, the shadow of the husband fell on the path of the explorer. The second sentence above – that a daughter ought to free herself from the influence of her mother – carries distinct undertones of marital exasperation rather than clear-headed thought from the mind which insists in every other sphere on the power of the unconscious.

If Freud had won his Pax Romana – a perfect marital truce, according to Ernest Jones – we hear in 1933:

A woman of the same age, [about thirty] however, often frightens us by her psychical rigidity and unchangeability . . . as though, indeed, the difficult development to femininity had exhausted the possibilities of the person concerned. (Freud, S., 1933, pp. 134–5)

Did Martha Freud, *née* Bernays, then fall into this category? Did she after all remain firmly in the mother-camp? Had Freud ultimately failed to wrest his wife from Mamma?

There can have been few more successful marriages. Martha certainly made an excellent wife and mother. She was an admirable manager – the rare kind of woman who could keep servants indefinitely. (Jones, E., 1953, p. 148)

So speaks Freud's *alter ego*, not Ernest Jones the analyst. It sounds as though Freud had married Mamma Bernays, in the end. We are left with a feeling, which we can neither contradict nor fully substantiate, that this 'excellent wife' was imperceptibly phased out from the centre of the stage and relegated to the wings. Minna was a different story, more the 'comrade in arms' he was always yearning for until he found a later version in his daughter Anna. The two sisters, we have seen, had a very different relationship to their mother. Was this the departure point, the quintessence of the issue which would colour their lives, like the life of every woman, in a decisive manner? Is then this relationship between mother and daughter the crux or the watershed of some parting of the ways for a girl's development, where one path leads to freedom, both of mind and of body, while another slides downhill to deep inhibitions in the two spheres or in either one? Is this the question at the heart of our investigation?

Of the countless women who in their ever-growing numbers enter psychotherapy most are in the deepest trouble, in some profound dislocation, where the enravelment with their mother is concerned. Some will say so very clearly when they first arrive for help. Sometimes they may be aware of a whole geology, a lifetime of buried pain, which will need to be unearthed if they are to thrive, while at the same time they admit to feelings of dread and terror as to what lies hidden there: what monster-visions will emerge.

But other women, when they come for that initial interview, seem to gloss over the fact that they even had a mother. One might conclude that they sprang, like Venus, straight out of the waves. For them this issue is so threatening that it may take months of work before they can tolerate any reference to the subject, until one day the therapist locates a breach in the resistance, perhaps with the aid of dreams or from other 'material' clearly pointing motherwards in the transference. Until such time they maintain: 'I had a very happy childhood. I can't think why I feel disturbed.' Or, 'I've forgotten everything: sorry, I cannot remember.'

It is by now a century since the discipline which Freud began, of exploring the unconscious and human sexuality, smoked and smouldered and erupted into its famous controversies like an unquiet volcano. But none of these has held the centre of that daunting stage as obstinately unresolved as the chameleon issue of female sexuality. No other topic exercised Freud's thinking so defiantly. None refused so stubbornly to yield up its story of secrets until the master labelled this inaccessible interior 'the dark continent'.

'*Was will das Weib?*' he asked himself. 'What is it that the female wants?' he pondered time and time again, as successive followers have puzzled by the generation. Yet, like a spider's web, that intricate issue, riddled with dark phantasies, is delicately interwoven with everything we undertake; while at the centre of this network hovers our connectedness to that image we call mother. The image may gravitate from the phantastical towards reality in time. Then, as adults, we emerge as from the dressing-room of a fabled prima donna who finally, to our amazement, has removed the masks and veils, the paint and wigs which we provided with our infantile phantasies, to stand before us as a woman wrapped in no greater mystery, no powers or attributes more baffling, magical or threatening than her womanly complexity. But this relief may be denied us. We may also go through life merely altering the costume in new and self-defeating ways, adding halo, horns or feathers from some endless costume chest, wounded or exasperated, goaded by some expectation which will never be fulfilled.

What *is* it that woman wants?

The answer which seems to emerge in the majority of cases during psychotherapy, sometimes after years of work, is in effect: to be myself, to live my life as I desire, by my own personal design – without offending my mother, without antagonizing her or hurting her own views and feelings; without thereby having to make an enemy of her, because I need her as a friend, a comrade and beloved sister, as a lifelong all-in-all.

Now that sounds sensible enough: a sane and realistic project. But try to put it into practice! A hundred obstacles at once break into a hideous chorus. A clutch of witches seem to burst out of some smouldering inferno. Will we ever escape to attain some *terra firma*, with the help of a support group, solitary ruminations or our psychotherapist? Or will the passing of the years, the procession of the generations, modify this burlesque?

In 1911, when Colette was thirty-eight, about to enter on her second marriage, a self-supporting individual by temperament and life experience, this conversation, which she transposed into *La Naissance du Jour*, was, quite possibly, her last with her enigmatic mother, Sido.

'You like this Monsieur X a lot?'

'But Maman, I love him!'

'Yes, yes, you love him . . . you don't need to tell me that you love him.'

She thought a bit, trying to hold back what her celestial cruelty was forcing her to say, and then burst out:

'Ah! I'm not pleased!'

I lowered my eyes with false modesty, trying to shut out the image of the handsome, intelligent, enviable man with his bright future, and answered softly: 'You're being difficult.' (Sarde, M., 1981, p. 184)

Sido died shortly afterwards. Colette, for whatever reasons, did not attend the funeral. She married her Monsieur X, the Baron Henry de Jouvenel, and threw herself into her first experience of 'the blind happiness of a woman in love' (Sarde, M., 1981). It was as though her mother's death had somehow set her free after long twilight years of domestic unhappiness – free not only to love, but also to bear her only child, the daughter called 'Bel-Gazou'. A decade was still to pass until Colette set to work dreaming up her mother Sido, who was finally to step from her daughter's inner world into those enduring pages that would see the light of day in the late 1920s, when she was coming up to sixty (Colette, 1966).

As her mother had predicted, the marriage to Monsieur X, like the previous one to Willy, drifted on to fatal rocks. But it is 'Minet-Chérie', Sido's pet name for her daughter, who blossoms in our memory – the maiden who is all her mother's in those halcyon summer days, until that hour when she is 'abducted' by a 'stranger' into marriage. Until the rape that will wrench the enchanted circle of the dyad apart for an eternal winter. Here is but another version of

Antiquity's great myth, Demeter and Persephone, re-enacted time and again in agonized perplexity: a theme with endless variations.

But Freud, the nineteenth-century man – and, what was more, a man of 'science' – still wanted what was nice and tidy. All around him, day by day, among the linen tied with ribbons, the hats with artificial flowers, the veils and household minutiae – all the sacred rituals of a frumpy Victorian world – winked pieces of that jigsaw puzzle from some highly suspect boudoir, when one portion of his genius was to hanker all his life after the laboratory over which he once presided.

Furthermore his self-analysis, that extraordinary feat by which the Oedipus complex first saw the light of day, was the work of a *man*. Freud, at the time, was still determined to apply to that elusive minx what seemed true of the boy. The only difficulty was that since the little girl was 'already castrated', what did *she* have to fear? What terror caused the dissolution of the complex in *her* case? And what was he to make of Dora, his famous hysterical patient? Should not the amorous advances of the fatherly Herr K have turned this young woman on? But Dora did not oblige. She insisted from the start that her seducer's embrace, in which she felt his hard penis pressing against her body, had utterly disgusted her. What was Freud to make of that? He had only recently been subjected to the blow of seeing his seduction theory, so to speak, go down the drain. Was this, in turn, to be the fate of that latest great discovery? Was Dora, a mere girl of eighteen, going to deal a further blow?

Scrutiny of the case, which continues unabated, meanwhile rests at the conclusion that it was in fact Frau K, the seducer's wife, who was the true object of the girl's romantic love and deeply enacted passion. According to this line of thought, because the girl must change her object – from her mother to her father, from woman to the man – she runs the risk of remaining fixated in a lifelong indecision, unable to 'define herself as a man or as a woman because she cannot finally choose between her father and her mother . . .' (Kohon, G., 1984, p. 81).

Female sexuality clearly did not lend itself to any nice and tidy answer. From the twenties to the forties a number of psychoanalysts tried to thrash the matter out in one of those great debates which punctuate that discipline. J. Lampel de Groot sided readily with Freud. Others, like Helene Deutsch, Ruth Mack Brunswick, Marie Bonaparte, Josine Muller and Karen Horney – and also Ernest Jones

– made distinctive contributions which need not concern us here. Here it is relevant that, as gradually emerged, the oedipal drama has earlier and deeper layers than the stage of the process where Freud's spade first struck gold. Triangulation can be traced to the early months of infancy, as subsequently came to light in the work of Mrs Klein. How else could that ecstatic tangle of symbiosis be resolved, growth put out its shoots unhampered?

Winnicott postulated that the 'father' is introduced as a joint creation on the part of the dyad, to facilitate a space which initiates separation. The notion of the 'symbolic father' is, furthermore, a kingpin in the thinking of Lacan, to which we will be returning.

What is it that the female wants? In every likelihood it is a paradoxical package: a close identification with the person of her mother and her loving permission to separate and go her way into full autonomy as a sexual and creative woman in her undisputed right. This will surely imply that as healthy symbiosis moves towards its natural end, she wants a protecting father to lead her out towards a beckoning world and thereby strengthen her resistance against regressive backsliding into the maternal circuit, once that phase needs to come to a time-appropriate conclusion. Did not Olympic Zeus, father of Persephone, cause the many-bloomed narcissus to flower in the Nyasan Fields and draw his daughter towards it, away from her possessive mother, Demeter of the glowing corn, to meet her adult destiny in the marriage embrace?

But before we get to marriage, can we offer any answer as to what pulls the girl back into the maternal circuit where she has 'to learn the art of fighting among women so as to dodge the maternal persecutory presence and bring him [the father] close to her' (Zak de Goldstein, R., 1984, p. 183). Not a very happy picture – one which at the best of times is universally clouded by extreme ambivalence, from which in turn the girl escapes into what Freud's patient, Anna O, called 'the clouds' of daydreaming, for as often and as long as opportunity permits, to the irritation of her mother, who complains bitterly that all the work is left to her! Yet the girl must stay put for reasons which we outlined earlier: her need to elaborate a (pro)creative inner space to her growing satisfaction.

This project has a nebulous and rather dreamlike quality in keeping with the girl-woman's diffuse erotogenic body-image, with her tremendous appetite for narcissistic supplies – in other words, for being loved and told that she is beautiful. For these supplies the daughter must enter willy-nilly into competition with her mother. Where the latter proves to be excessively narcissistic, craving endless topping up, like Snow White's stepmother, painful conflicts lie in store. Not every 'queen' will act out infanticidal impulses to have a hunter take the child into the forest and bring back vital organs as the proof of her demise; but bitter battles may rage, built upon phantasies where such a mother has failed to mature in this respect, to feel secure in her marriage and modify her own demands for admiration and attention, as her daughter grows up and prepares to take the stage.

On the subject of woman, of feminine sexuality, Freud finally bowed out with: 'If you want to know more about femininity, enquire of your own experience of life, or turn to the poets, or wait until science can give you a deeper and more coherent information' (Freud, S., 1933). If that sounds philosophical or even charmingly resigned, he none the less remained enraged by the Gioconda smile which met his thrusting explorations. Woman, he retaliated, had 'an inferior superego . . . showed less sense of justice . . . and was weaker in her social instincts' (Freud, S., 1933). That such a keen observer of the human scene passed such patent misjudgements suggests personal disappointment. As by every new religion, woman was once again willy-nilly relegated to second-class citizenship: a credo which, once ingrained within its ideology, is difficult to eradicate.

Towards the end of his life Freud gave deeper thought to the girl's earliest and evidently close attachment to the person of her mother: 'Our insight into this early pre-Oedipus phase in girls comes to us as a surprise, like the discovery, in another field, of the Minoan-Mycenean civilization behind the civilization of Greece' (Freud, S., 1931, p. 226). Had Freud been reading Bachofen, whose ideas we are coming to? Or have we here one more example of contemporaneous intuition, so mysteriously at work throughout the history of ideas? 'Everything in the sphere of this first attachment to the mother seemed to me so difficult to grasp in analysis – grey with age and shadowy and almost impossible to revivify – that it was as if it had succumbed to an especially inexorable repression' (Freud, S., 1931, p. 226).

As he had earlier asked himself repeatedly why the oedipal girl should turn away from her father, the ageing Freud says instead: 'Our interest must be directed to the mechanisms that are at work in her turning away from the mother who was an object so intensely and exclusively loved.' That she *did* turn away Freud, of course, never questioned, even if his Martha remained in the maternal circuit, as far as we ourselves can judge.

Finally, in 1938, while Freud was waiting to leave Vienna in the midst of dark anxieties for his wider family, propelled by a demonic urge to leave his lifetime's labours tidy, he returned a final time to this enigmatic topic, to that background of 'Heil Hitlers' resounding through his beloved city. In *An Outline of Psycho-Analysis*, composed under these grim conditions and published posthumously, he reaffirmed his belief that whatever stood in doubt in subsequent development, there was no uncertainty that 'a child's first erotic object is the mother's breast' (Freud, S., 1938, p. 188). This meant that autoeroticism, as an early objectless state, was given its marching orders by the dying master's mind. Earliest anxieties grew, as he was now convinced, from a central sense of loss. Loss was linked to separation from an object – the breast. And so the stage was clearly set for the next act of the drama, initiated by the person of Mrs Melanie Klein. From her workbench in Berlin this mother of three, analysand of Karl Abraham, began with his encouragement to focus specifically on Freud's 'earlier Minoan civilization', a highy mammocentric one. Its historical counterpart is, as we shall see, the contested rule of matriarchy. She now began to analyse small children who, in certain cases, had barely reached the age of three. Instead of free associations the children's phantasies emerged through the medium of play. Into this she would enter both as participant and as studious observer to make interpretations in the strict Freudian sense. The psychoanalytic stance and its rigorous setting were, in all respects, maintained.

Her findings in due course confirmed Freud's own intuition at the end of his life: that the infant related, from the time of birth, to the mother's breast as a so-called 'part-object', before the sense of a whole person has begun to set in, in a mêlée of drives and their primitive defences. Here, she found, was a balance sheet most precariously poised between the powers of life and death, survival and annihilation, passionate love and wild aggression, stability and mental health or fragmentation into madness.

Let us take a bird's-eye view to obtain a basic outline of the concepts she evolved from her clinical experience in the consulting room. Where intrauterine life offers the foetus optimal conditions, growth as effortless bliss, so in the course of pregnancy the mother is sensitized to be able to provide the nearest possible thing to its continuum. In this all-responsive, 'postnatal-womb' environment the infant learns to adapt gradually to life outside while contained within this sanctuary of 'postnatal embryonic life'. This supreme adaptation on the part of the mother, known as maternal reverie, will be gradually phased out, mutually and by consensus, by what Winnicott termed 'graduated environmental failure'. But as Mrs Klein confirmed, the most perfect breast-mother cannot hope to replace that precision masterpiece in the shape of the placenta through the medium of which oxygen and nourishment were effortlessly pumped in, and waste matter carried away without the slightest discomfort. In the infant deprived of this sensitive regulator, exposed to changing temperatures, with the best will in the world elements of frustration will inevitably arrive to create fear and terror. Words can barely do justice to this sense of nameless dread: of relentless persecution experienced as a consequence. It is in response to this that the earliest defences will now be mobilized by the unintegrated infant psyche. They operate at a time when the infant still relates to the breast as a part-object before the relationships to so-called whole objects come into ascendancy in the later months of the first year.

Through defences known as splitting the breast is at first divided into extremes of good and bad in terms of satisfaction or frustration. The bad gives rise to feelings of hatred, the good may paradoxically, given certain constitutions, give rise to primary envy, according to the work of Mrs Klein. Since these feelings are unbearable, the fragile psyche rids itself of these dreaded attributes through the process of projection. But it may not stay at that, for projection escalates into projective identification. This means that the breast at first, and later also the whole object at the receiving end, will now be experienced as hating, envious or murderous, greedy, biting or devouring, as the case may be. Here are the roots of paranoia.

These defences operate against the early background of infantile omnipotence, meaning a conviction that whatever tricks the mind may play can achieve the desired result – freedom from anxiety. Omnipotence is a defence: one of denial of such utter helplessness, which implies abject dependence. The important issue here is that these primitive defences negate inner psychic reality, while they operate, during the first months of life, a phase of development which Mrs Klein called the paranoid-schizoid position. This is not to imply that infants are psychotic, since this state of affairs will gradually be modified. Where this modification fails, the so-called 'fixation points' for later serious illness, which we know as the psychoses, will be traced back to this time.

Here, then, is a picture of the most tenuous existence where any premature awareness of its precariousness is optimally kept at bay with good-enough maternal care, where by maternal reverie resultant anxieties are adequately contained. Where the mother underwrites the essential delusion of a blissful unity, she maintains a time capsule which is resilient enough for her infant to discover, by the laws of his own pace, that shattering reality that here is neither a placenta nor a servant-breast, as an extension of himself; but in fact a separate person not under his own control, who – what is even worse – has to be shared with others.

This excruciating lesson, as it painfully seeps in, where everything goes well enough and where the infant's own constitution is sufficiently sound, will gradually dismantle a state of healthy symbiosis. The learning of it is approached precisely with the defence of splitting, where good and bad experience can be safely kept apart, to be enshrined and envisaged as two strictly separate breasts: one wonderful and idealized, the other all bad. In benign circumstances the two will slowly integrate towards a capacity to tolerate ambivalence: in other words, the admission that these two breasts are one – and, moreover, that they belong to a whole person, namely mother, who is both hated *and* loved.

With this profound and painful discovery the existence of the deeper drama belonging to the inner world dawns on the infant mind, where it will begin to press for growing acknowledgement of awesome complexity. Here, then, lies that watershed, across which development moves during the first months of life, gradually, with ebb and flow, in a forward direction. What we termed the paranoid-schizoid position, with its daunting part-objects – ruled by splitting and denial, projection and omnipotence, linked to a belief in magic – will become modified by a growing capacity for ambivalence and for concern, to usher in the advent of Klein's depressive position. Here the task is no longer one of basic survival, but centres on the maintenance of a good inner object. Now the urge for reparation of damage caused in phantasy by destructive impulses assumes urgent proportions. Here guilt and concern have their tentative beginnings. Here the anxieties that attacks made in phantasy on the mother, both her body and her mind, have resulted in damage greater than can be repaired may lead to self-doubt, despair and self-destructive impulses.

But why the mother's mind? Elaborating Klein's concepts, Bion focused on the crucial interplay of the maternal mind with the mind of her infant. He found in the transference of certain psychotic patients evidence of a process, very steadily at work, which went closely hand in hand with that other nutrition which took place at the breast: a process quite as subject to satisfaction or frustration, profound enjoyment or starvation, as the digestive process of the alimentary tract. He first discovered it in consequence of its default in his more disturbed patients. And to this specific function, whereby the mother's mind contains her infant's terrors which arrive by the process of projection, detoxifies and then returns them, Bion gave the name 'maternal reverie', referred to earlier. The actual capacity for this decontamination Bion termed 'alpha function'. This is the main ingredient a good-enough analyst provides, and it lies at the heart of all good infant care. For just as the mother will bathe away bodily mess to restore confidence and comfort, so with alpha function mental messes are mopped up as a crucial prerequisite to growth and mental health. Since, however, frustration, intolerance and primary envy are aroused by excellence, the infant mind may attack this essential operation, if to a varying degree based on constitutional factors.

This may be rather heavy going, but an understanding of these basic issues will help us towards an insight into some of the most tragic failures in the mother–daughter partnership. For where a mother is disturbed, either in her own right or by a particular infant, or perhaps by the circumstances surrounding that infant's birth, insufficient alpha function may leave the infant deprived and in a most precarious state. There may either be the fear of having driven mother mad with excessive needs for containment, and/or a dread in later life of owning any needs at all. This can lead to extremes where all needs will be repressed, together with a desperate bid to achieve unrealistic excellence, to be accepted at long last – in other words, to be contained. One such patient, when she came for her first interview, assured me that she had perfect, white Madonna lilies growing from all her body openings, implying that she had no needs: a perfect, funerary daughter.

Where things go well enough, however, slowly, over weeks and months, the infant will 'internalize' what she has experienced as maternal reverie and develop her own capacity for alpha function. Such a child will be able to reflect about herself in positive and caring ways – in other words, learn to enjoy intimacy with herself, as a basis for peace of mind. It means that she can exercise appropriate self-criticism when the ensuing sense of guilt arises in a milder manner than the merciless attacks which a cruel superego launches against the self in various forms of severer mental illness. Furthermore she will anticipate her own eventual motherhood with greater security and fewer anxious forebodings; fortitude which her mother will, in turn, experience with relief.

From this bird's-eye view it follows just how closely interwoven mother-mind and mother-body have initially to be with their infant's counterparts to secure not just survival, but integrated forms of growth; while we can see that miscarriage of these highly complex factors is always hovering in the wings.

If we now turn our attention more specifically again to the mother–daughter dyad, we can readily envisage certain deep anxieties now subsumed under the heading of female castration anxiety, as they will afflict the girl. For she will dread retaliation from her maternal object for attacks which she has launched in the realm of phantasy, out of envy and the hatred generated by frustration. These attacks have been directed against her mother's mind and body, including 'all her inside babies', always waiting to be born as usurpers to her claim for exclusive possession. In the most bloodthirsty games enacted in the playroom, Klein discovered how detailed and sadistic these phantasies can sometimes be, so that the girl may expect cruel attacks on her own babies and all enjoyment of her own sexuality. Since her organs in question – unlike those of the boy which lend themselves to inspection – remain hidden from sight, the onset of menstruation may only serve to confirm the sense of dreaded inner damage. Such anxieties can stoke an incipient paranoia and contribute to precarious and declining states of mind, to poisoning the relationship so that it becomes subverted to a murderous contest. Where, through ineptitudes on the part of either party, these crucial difficulties fail to be modified, the adolescent girl enters the sexual rivalry with her mother at a hazardous disadvantage. Then the daughter cannot fight for her essential share of narcissistic supplies with which she might heal the wounds of her earliest frustrations. Instead, she may pursue her quest for adult sexuality, bristling with aggression and a hostile urge for triumph which are rooted in despair, knowing that this hostility is experienced and directed against the very person on whom she must still depend, and who must serve as a model for her feminine self-image. For it will be from this pivot that she must balance and sustain her creative undertakings and the close relationships of her later, adult life, including that to her own daughter.

It goes without saying that her mother's own attitude and her deeper states of mind about herself as a daughter are of great significance in this rather fraught arena. If the mother can win through her own ambivalence, to which we will return later, to express her loving feelings; if she is secure within herself and within her marriage; if she can let her daughter enjoy a close relationship with her father and her brothers; if her own envious feelings towards this young competitor, who will in time occupy and share the centre of life's stage, are relatively minimal because she feels herself fulfilled, and for that reason less threatened; the prospects will be brighter for the daughter's development and for their crucial, lifelong bond.

But where the daughter has cause, for inner or for outer reasons, to doubt her mother's deeper love, she may linger at the stage where she has a need to please, in order to obtain reassurance that her destructive phantasies and her hostile impulses have not caused lasting harm. Then she may turn out to be excessively preoccupied with making herself beautiful, because a beautiful body is felt to serve as evidence that all is well inside it, too. Provided such anxieties do not amount to despair, they encourage sublimation, such as her work at school, which is gradually replaced by new creative interests. All these will be directed, to a certain extent, to repairing the damage done and mastering anxieties by gaining mother's approval; even if they exist in their own creative right as well.

If, throughout these years of conflict, she is blessed with a father and a mother who are close, loving and intimate, for all the usual ups and downs of human reality; who can share these attributes readily with their child, warmly and spontaneously; who can be supportive when she may seek encouragement or open admiration; who show confidence and trust in her emerging womanhood; then she will feel optimistic about her own good qualities, her future as a creative woman: that she will, in time, enjoy rewarding work and motherhood, her own sexuality in all its manifestations, just as her mother does.

When such good fortune prevails the daughter's image of her mother will tend to be realistic – of a woman of complex personality, composed of weakness and strength, of certain faults and certain assets. This picture is very different from one of crass idealization which invariably conceals the opposite, archaic image of a destructive, envious mother, the witch of the fairy tale, who may break to the surface if mental illness strikes, as we will illustrate when we come to Sylvia Plath.

Melanie Klein has left us in possession of a fuller picture of the girl's development in relationship to her mother, within its whole chronology. In time the passage of decades will reverse the position, when the ageing mother may become the dependent baby. Where the relationship was wanting, the daughter may confront this phase with a sense of total horror:

Maman had an open hospital nightdress on and she did not mind that her wrinkled belly, criss-crossed with tiny lines, and her bald pubis showed ... But I turned away and gazed fixedly into the garden. The sight of my mother's nakedness had jarred me. No body existed less for me: none existed more. (de Beauvoir, S., 1969, p. 18)

The emphasis which rises here, of despair and deep depression, is less of illness and old age than, essentially, of damage and the horror it instils. With this de Beauvoir's account of her mother's death is permeated, as to some degree are her life and much of her opus, in their deepest resonance.

If Klein has partly clarified anxieties which draw the girl back into the maternal circuit, a final question still remains: what precisely are the forces which will lure her away? And how far will they replace the early, intricate involvement with genuine and deep conviction? Will her sojourn with the male, her life-phase of procreation, carry her into *his* world, as the ritual proclaims, or will she tarry matrilocal in the most enduring sense? Or will she, like Persephone, find ways to divide her time between husband and mother, a mother who – in myth – threatened to starve the world if her daughter could not spend half of every year with her? And what happens in our time, as choice appears to grow wider to the superficial eye?

Does, we have to ask ourselves, her mother actually remain the girl's true love-object through life? Or can she negotiate a root-transfer to the man and the father of her children which stems from her gratitude for this gift of the baby which her father withheld, together with the adult status which motherhood may confer in inner as in outer terms? Is there a compromise solution with a lifelong oscillation, or are there clear-cut categories? Is it not only now, when more women have achieved seemingly realistic choices where adult status can be reached by other pathways of endeavour to claim social recognition, that we can confront these questions with some degree of fearlessness, a growing measure of unflinching?

A boundless complexity of socioeconomic changes, far beyond our present scope, have hijacked women to a position where they can start to formulate their own depth psychology, as a group and as individuals; to clear the ground of superstitions and threadbare negativities, and thereby inch their own way forwards to learn to love themselves free. We can only indicate mere landmarks of that heroic march through some ten millennia from a vantage point which is even now obscure.

This overview, a barest outline of psychoanalytical thinking as it relates to our subject, still begs an important question: is there or is there not in the experience of women, however buried and obscured by cultural and other factors, a concept of primary femininity, present from infancy to slowly ripen and mature to a full exultation of its potency in time? Freud believed, as we know, that the sense of femininity develops only in response to feelings of disappointment and castration phantasies, based on lacking a penis – and resultant hatred of the mother. This seems patently absurd, while we have to bear in mind that psychoanalytic theories were and continue to be drawn from findings in *ailing* women.

While our female patients on the couch exhibit sequences of grudges and life-poisoning resentments against their mothers, and by extension the world at large, we surely only need to step out of our consulting rooms to gain an impression of exuberant, often joyful women facing life's difficulties in a resourceful mood and style which looks altogether different from their sisters who are cowed in various masochistic postures. Even in the Old Testament, that stronghold of the patriarchs, we meet the most ebullient women, who were hardly the product of exclusive disappointment; who, we cannot help but feel, were buoyed by a profound conviction of some inbuilt primacy.

Some of the latest thinking puts a truer face on it based on what Emily, at twenty months, had to say on the subject of sexual difference: 'and Mummy has a vulva ... but Mummy, Daddy has something funny in his vulva!' 'Emily,' the author continues, 'like Freud's prototypical little Hans, has made a simple assumption about the nature of genitals: "everyone must be like me." ' From this it follows, she suggests, that castration anxiety in men or in women is anxiety over losing that genital which is actually possessed (Lloyd Mayer, E., 1985, pp. 331–47).

We must remain alert to new evidence of the existence of primary femininity. Its sources are doubtless complex and still open to much debate. One line of thought has this to say:

In other words, a girl's conviction that she is a female comes from her parents' conviction, but that part of her awareness of being a female which comes from sensing her genitalia will vary according to the anatomy and physiology of these tissues (but will not vary to the degree that she does not believe herself female). (Stoller, J., 1974, p. 270)

Today we can only wonder that so much Freudian thinking still continues to ignore such evident postulates. If parental 'conviction' plays a decisive part, as it undoubtedly must, the lion's share of this depends on maternal imprinting. If by using this word we trespass on the domain of recent ethology, I make no apologies. We will return to the importance of maternal imprinting, subsumed under 'mirroring' in the preverbal phase, of mother–infant interaction. Now we need to consider quite the strangest and most baffling phenomenon which was encountered once my research lifted anchor from this more familiar ground to head for the open sea. Let it speak for itself.

2 THE CONSPIRACY OF SILENCE

Yet this relationship has been minimized and trivialized in the annals of patriarchy. Whether in theological doctrine or art or sociology or psychoanalytic theory, it is the mother and son who appear as the eternal, determinative dyad.
(ADRIENNE RICH, *Of Woman Born*)

ROADS IN CERTAIN PARTS of Europe, until fairly recently, had a way of petering out, with or without warning. In Spain, still, in the mid-1950s, after a fair stretch of asphalt had begun to raise one's hopes, a notice would decree '*Obras*' (Road Works), whereupon the surface yielded or simply ceased entirely.

This was not anticipated with the present expedition until initial reconnoitring could leave little room for doubt. The Old and New Testaments, sources of the Middle Ages, Shakespeare and contemporaries, all seemed equally at pains to draw a veil over our saga. Fathers and daughters, mothers and sons, brothers and sisters in abundance. But mother/daughter – who were they?

Even scholars, when consulted, showed dismay and grew uneasy on discovering such a blank. They had, it transpired, found no occasion to give the matter previous thought. But there it was, confronting us in the most derisory manner: mother/daughter, the material dried up, as will an honest well, wherever witchcraft is at work. From Adam and Eve to the Borgias, with the skimpiest exceptions, silence blanketed the scene. For six and a half millennia the Judaeo-Christian culture is proverbially mum.

It seems uncanny and absurd.

In his paper on 'The "Uncanny" ', Freud defined the term like this: 'The uncanny is that class of the frightening which leads back to what is known of old and long familiar ... in what circumstances the familiar can become uncanny and frightening, I shall show in what follows' (Freud, S., 1919, p. 220). Here we find ourselves in difficulty with the indifferent translation of the standard works of Freud. The word which Freud used in the German, '*unheimlich*', should translate 'unhomely', which the Oxford Dictionary defines as 'un-homogeneous'. In meaning it comes closer to 'ambiguous' or 'ambivalent'. In other words, the uncanny is that which is ambiguous or ambivalent in a familiar area where this was not to be expected.

Freud then proceeds to explore certain familiar words, which on closer scrutiny carry a double meaning. 'Homelike, belonging to the house, intimate, friendly, . . . something withdrawn from the eye of strangers, something concealed, secret . . .' is the first of these examples:

In general [he goes on to say] we are reminded that the word heimlich *[homely] is not unambiguous, but belongs to two sets of ideas, which, without being contradictory, are yet very different: on the one hand it means what is familiar and agreeable, and on the other, what is concealed and kept out of sight. (Freud, S., 1919, p. 224)*

What is it, then, that is concealed when we start to feel uncanny? Freud concludes that the feeling fundamentally 'proceeds from forms of thought that have been surmounted', and that the uncanny is due to those elements which play a part 'in the production of infantile anxiety from which the majority of human beings have never become quite free'.

Following this train of thought, what precisely is 'uncanny' in this conspiracy of silence, as with our subject which it shrouds? What infantile or primitive anxieties could be at work? What is frightening? What leads back to what is old and long familiar about the mother and daughter which we conspire to conceal, so that we know, yet do not know, and for that reason remain silent: silent during certain epochs as opposed to others when, as with the Ancient Greeks, the subject is readily brought into the light of day?

The chroniclers, of course, were men. With the exception of Sappho it would appear that not until the fourteenth century did women first obey an urge to take to ink and pen and paper for any purpose other than that of copying the Scriptures. When they in time initiate a tradition of personal authorship, those writers such as Christine de Pizan (1363–1431) and Margery Kempe (1373–1438) remained reticent, not on the subject of their mothers so much as on their deeper feelings and, above all, on their grievances. Despite a trickle here or there, these floodgates did not really open until the twentieth century.

Yet as we shall shortly see, poets and dramatists of Ancient Greece were fascinated by their women and how they stood with one another. After that the curtain fell, and although in the Bible we find no lack of mighty women, we come across scant reference to their pivotal connection in the mother–daughter sphere. Is this change perhaps due to certain crucial distinctions between a matrilineal and patrilineal social order – to the laws which govern how property shall be passed on: from a father to his sons, or a mother to her daughter, as in the Ancient World until the end of matriarchy? Another flower-head of truth. But must we not expect to find some other, deeper explanation, besides the material one? What is it that we do not know?

The single track we have to guide us is this sense of the uncanny, experienced by my scholar friends after they had been alerted by my uneasy questioning. They soon returned to their own subjects with a sigh of relief and a shrug which seemed to say: 'Rather you than me, my dear: but all the luck in the world.' 'What a fascinating subject', others would encourage me, while maintaining a safe distance. There is no doubt that they too had shuddered at a foreboding sense of standing before the famous gate leading to an underworld: a dark and secret inner venue reluctant to open its maw and yield up some time-old secret. This feeling is one of *Verboten* which, unlike its English counterpart, carries an implication of Teutonic punishment: some archaic retribution belonging to the dark domain of infantile anxieties which relate to intrusion on the parental couple.

Our intuition would suggest that here we have another 'couple', some new creative intercourse which we have always known about but also chosen to ignore, at the heart of this enigma. What is it that we must confront? What ejaculates this sense of horror and makes us want to turn our back rather than pursue the matter?

In feminist literature we find resounding hymns of praise for the ancient matriarchies as a sort of Golden Age when the women's group thrived, intertwined in peaceful collaboration with the men kept in their place: nasty, dirty warmongers with names like 'bad breath' or 'smelly'. Then one day, the story goes, these unsavoury beings turned the whole scheme upside down when they got their revenge and the women their comeuppance.

It all sounds nasty and simple, except that nothing ever is. What is it that women share like some secret religion? What is this elixir, tasted in communion, as they crouch together in the sunshine, rest a little in the dusk, or guard the winter's fireside, listening, listening to some heartbeat murmuring in the universe that lies within them and without? Why can they remain so proud in circumstances of repression which should by all rights leave them cowed, so calm and upright in the presence of the master and the boss, prey to every human weakness, as they have ample cause to know? Do we approach the mystery when the lamenting song rejoices in the familiar selfsame breath:

> *She never cared for fashion's style,*
> *Her jewels and treasures*
> *She found them in her baby's eyes . . .*
> 'My Yiddishe Mama' [Song]

But that is not the total story. Not merely, or entirely, in her sexuality, punctuated by giving birth, does her secret satisfaction lie, of which we know and do not know.

In chapter 1 I made passing reference to the French psychoanalyst Jacques Lacan, who directed his *École Freudienne* in Paris from 1964 until 1980. In the English-speaking world he has never quite caught on. This may partly be due to his linguistic acrobatics, but maybe also to an implicit claim that here is the true son of Freud: unlike the faithless, he does not keep returning to biological destiny, thereby dirtying the purity of Freud's unsullied unconscious, which is to be carried like the Ark.

For our present purposes, Lacan evolved two ideas. The first is that we all suffer, men and women equally, from some urgent desire as a continuous distress, whose object remains mythical even if it is called a phallus, which is not the organ penis. Sanity, he claims, must rest in our renouncing the myth that satisfaction resides in one particular performance or anatomical point, as once, in infancy, it lay between the mouth and the nipple. Neurosis, he claims, is our pretence to perpetuate the myth of the phallus as signifier, where the man represents it and the woman plays the lure, with both misreading their desire, thus to remain at odds and disappointed. This repetition compulsion, so life-thwarting *par excellence*, will nullify prospects of integral relationship rooted in *jouissance*. 'The life instinct, or sexual instinct, demands activity of a kind, that in contrast to our current mode of activity, can only be called play', Norman Brown reiterates in his own substantial plea (Brown, N., 1959, p. 307). In other words the two agree that once we shake off stale assumptions to take a new, unfettered look at the question of desire and its proposed satisfaction, labelled sexuality, then the way we see ourselves and our so-called opposite number might undergo a wholesome change. This view of our sexual destiny as an experience set above biological insignia derives directly from Freud in the famous *Three Essays on the Theory of Sexuality* (Freud, S., 1905), but Lacan elaborates on the unconscious implications and redirects our understanding towards a closer alignment with new, emerging attitudes.

Once we dissolve the emphasis on the mythical phallus, once we agree with Lacan that the central issue is to move from infant to adult, from auto- to allo-erotic states of mind, where everything else is left open, we arrive at his second concept: that of *jouissance*. The word is derived from *jouir*, a slang expression for 'to come', but Lacan removes it from established sexual arenas and in a single clean sweep offers us nothing less than sensuous rebirth as women: an option which presumably is offered equally to men willing to become disciples. Thought is *jouissance*, he says. There is a *jouissance* of being, and for woman there exists a domain of *jouissance* beyond the phallus as signifier, which of course she has always known, whether in giving birth and suckling, planting, harvesting or cooking, provided that these blissful tasks are not imposed on her experience in their institutionalized forms as commands from above, but rest safe in the domain of spontaneous expression of her creativity.

From these ideas it surely follows that where a woman is lacking, she cannot say what she wants, while when the opposite is true and she is brimming in herself, she does not know that she has it. Even so she may try to divert or please the 'experts' by faking one punctilio, to supply them with the version of the female orgasm to which their theories and statistics, their dreary kudos, subscribe. Such a woman would, of course, have neither cause nor inclination to consult Dr Freud.

Mystics know about *jouissance*, as Lacan then continues:

They're all at it . . . It is the same for St Teresa . . . You only have to go and look at Bernini's statue in Rome to understand immediately that she is coming, there is no doubt about it. And what is her jouissance, *her COMING, from? It is clear that the essential testimony of the mystics is that they are experiencing it but know nothing of it. (Mitchell, J. and Rose, J., 1982, p. 147)*

Next, Lacan propounds a question of the utmost importance for our hypothesis: 'Might not this *jouissance*, which one experiences and knows nothing of, be that which puts us on the path of ex- istence?' (Mitchell, J. and Rose, J., 1982). In that case, we ask ourselves, is 'there', wherever it may be, woman's natural habitat? Furthermore, how would this realm link to the 'reality' which is ruled and occupied by men? Where do these meditations leave us in our wish to throw some light on the conspiracy of silence?

We have said that we encounter 'it' – this self-styled exit, to ex- istence – in a period in which women, with certain notable exceptions, had a minimum of power in the conventional sense; that only those who secured this dubious commodity have come down to us through time as subjects worthy of man's interest. Where they have attained to it – in other words, where they have entered material 'reality' – it seems respectable and safe to record their undertakings in a world where they exist. Whereas the great majority, while they remained precluded, seem to disappear from sight.

Where do they disappear to? The answer is that they ex- ist, even if this begs a question of baffling immensity.

Clearly, they exist as well as helpmeet, labourer or slave. This has never been in question as the main clarion call of the feminist movement. Here, they were denigrated and exploited, hardly given a look-in, as we are constantly reminded so as never to forget. But was it not this ex- isting which sustained their morale in epochs of banishment from the sphere which we call action? And did half the human race have to live this banishment to keep 'something' alive, in the way that Christianity, that great source of *jouissance*, wherever it was genuine, was nurtured through the Dark Ages? What is more, was this not accomplished, and officially to an extent, by women who in secular respects were barely even in the wings, but found within Christianity, Mariology and mysticism a sanctuary where they could transform rigid Pauline didactics into a potion for hope and life; an offering easily adapted equally for 'The White Goddess', Magna Mater, Triple Goddess, or Great Goddess, as you wish.

What we are pursuing here is an elusive butterfly. Nor must we be heard to be in favour of woman's banishment to some realm of pure ex- istence for the great majority. But we need to recognize that if we have two factors here, two distinct modes of being, disempowered reality and a secret affirmation, which require interpretation without demeaning either one, then both have first to be defined and for that purpose isolated.

A man, as Lacan instructs us, may be able to make love, in other words to undertake a poetic experience with a woman, partaking of her *jouissance*, as he did earlier with his mother, as his only respite from that machismo world where the phallus is the signifier he is supposed to carry, even if he has no wish to. The phallus as opposed to what? Presumably to *jouissance*, the life-affirming principle in all its polymorphous grace, its spiritual as well as corporeal infinity of expression, the one experience which can heal certain age-old dualisms between body and mind, masculine and feminine, clitoris and vagina – even between rich and poor, if these represent a choice. Have these categories not all been hopelessly fossilized? Have they not served to rend apart that which needs to be united if the species shall survive? Once these splits are integrated, are we not in a position to shed fanatical allegiance to one or other so-called 'side'?

If this thinking is of value, is it not conceivable that the feminists are now barking up a leafless tree? Could men, when all is said and done, really have succeeded in subjugating half the race without significant collusion – at some deep, unconscious level – unless somewhere along the line this tyranny had served some purpose in psychological terms? Does it not seem possible, if we can keep an open mind, that we needed 'two camps' – someone to carry our projections of, for example, 'strength' in the man and, conversely, 'weakness' in woman – until we had reached a vantage point from which to integrate these splits? But to let the old divisions drop, to declare them redundant, requires a brand of fortitude, of humility and awareness which we are only just approaching at our more enlightened best. Nor have we been in a position to contemplate this 'marriage' while trudging the tremendous march to secure some mastery over the environment to a point where man and nature could, *if* we are sensible and modify our mindless greed, sensitively coexist.

If we look at it more closely, the history of *jouissance* is of its unceasing persecution wherever it is manifest. Where minorities are persecuted, is it not on the grounds of the majority's suspicion that some secret inner joy must sustain them in the face of their disadvantages, which are all too evident? To a lineage of men – which ran from Orpheus to Jesus, Blake, Walt Whitman and D.H. Lawrence, to mention only a few – this persecution applied. Lawrence, you remember, wrote of his wife's – Frieda's – breasts that they were 'like Dijon roses'. 'Not every man has gentians in his house', he exulted loud and clear, from between the beloved breasts. And Connie, Lady Chatterley, leaves Sir Clifford and Wragby Hall, as Frieda left her professor, not, as the censors screamed, 'for sex', but for something more important: unitary experience: wholeness of body and of mind and, we need to add, of spirit, which perhaps is born only as a *jouissance* which overcomes the age-old dualism.

Once we think along these lines the concept of *jouissance* begins to draw closer to the Kleinian possession of a 'good inner object'. It would seem to be true that we envy and persecute individuals and groups who we suspect possess a better or more powerful inner object than ourselves, or who, we phantasize, have succeeded in taking better care of it through all the ups and downs of inner exigencies, wrought by hate and love. While there are minorities who with fanatical zeal boast of this accomplishment only to create a stick for their own battered back.

If this seems something of a detour, let us return to our point – the conspiracy of silence born at its deepest level of masculine misogyny. Since paternal prohibition severs the little boy from the beloved maternal body – where his sister may remain, to his envious perception, in safety and perpetual bliss – would he then attribute feminine *jouissance* to that blissful advantage and attack it on those grounds until he rediscovers it in his own, happy marriage, where he partakes of it once more, after a period of painful exile? But where that exile is prolonged, even lifelong in some cases, we find, as is common knowledge, the most savage of misogynists, even if these feelings are to some extent, at least, disguised. It would be within this context that the mother–daughter bond tends to be eliminated by masculine chroniclers, unless they can attribute it to material connections, the handing on of property established in the Ancient World in epochs of matriarchy. For as we shall shortly see, the grievances of Electra focused, certainly at a rational level, on her outrage that her mother offended against her rights of matrilineal inheritance. This did not prevent the genius of the three dramatists Aeschylus, Sophocles and Euripides who tackled the subject matter to explore the painful issues in a deeper sense, as well. Once they had begun to exercise their gift for insight there was, it seems, no stopping them.

If we now return to our mother–daughter dyad, where does their relationship exert its baffling potency within this mysterious nexus? Intuition suggests that in one of its aspects their union revolves around keeping *jouissance* alive in the most adverse conditions. This argument can be attacked, at a superficial level, on the ground that mothers have sided as subversive agents for a patriarchal order throughout the course of history. That they have stifled their daughters in compliance with its edicts. That they have reined them in to serve and to obey their masters, to live as self-effacing shadows at the larger feast of life.

But as with everything called truth, this is but one face of the coin. For where such reasoning is upheld, a very much subtler aspect of the transaction is ignored. Long before the spoken word, before mores and norms are dictated as commands, mirroring and imprinting of the preverbal phase exercise their influence to make an enduring impact.

Naturally there are mothers who are so broken and so cowed that infant daughters at the breast, and later at the toddler stage, will sadly read their mother's eye in hopeless negatives to be cast down for life as hardly better than trash. To modify such an assumption in later psychotherapy, or even in the face of affirming life-experience, may prove near-impossible. But what is more surprising is the extent to which mothers have, through the millennia, surmounted prevailing negatives to mirror to their infant daughter that she is a source of joy before cultural interdictions make their secondary impact. Such an experience is not easily wiped out by messages the spoken word can subsequently instil. Even in slavery are we not surprised to find many proud and upright women, whereas among the most favoured, both in a material and an ideological sense, we encounter others lacking pitifully in self-regard, in essential *jouissance*?.

Although Freud insisted that the mother–son relationship is the one which is most free of painful ambivalence, it would seem self-evident that despite its complexities it is within the mother–daughter dyad that love may be experienced and risked at its most intense.

It is, of course, common knowledge that human beings are afraid of the power of their hatred and of their aggressive feelings. We are, however, less aware that many of us live in fear that the expression of our loving feelings is extremely dangerous – that we may eat the other up, in a cannibalistic sense, or even burn them to cinders. Where a mother is cold or undemonstrative such fears will tend to be confirmed. However, where she is responsive a capacity for loving in a complete and rapturous sense has every chance of taking root. Then, as the jargon goes, the ego will not fear the id, while a kindly superego will permit their alliance to flower to the heart's content. Here is certainly one source of Lacan's *jouissance*.

This, for sure, is nothing new. Freud defined the uncanny as 'that class of the frightening which leads back to what is known of old and long familiar'. That the mother and her daughter may share this jubilant advantage is knowledge as old as the hills. Nowhere in the literature is this more perfectly expressed than where the mature Colette exults in the ecstasies that her small self, as Minet-Chérie, drank of deeply with her mother, as the latter confirms:

I can still see your graceful little form wandering about in it [the garden], while you dreamed of a thousand and one things . . . Yes, you were my golden sun. I used to tell you, too, that when you came into a room where I was you brought more light into it. And your golden hair that fell as far as the ground! (Colette, 1966, p. 12)

So wrote Sido to her daughter a few months before she died. Her letters brim with a *jouissance* which could bring the dead to life:

You've inherited some of my tastes, my beloved treasure. You like cataclysms, the sound of wind in the trees, the love of beautiful trees, rivers, the sea . . . All that is truly beautiful. I shall die without having drunk my fill of so much splendour . . . The swallows arrived at four o'clock this morning; I was able to witness their arrival. (Colette, 1966, p. 17)

So these letters sing and dance to the very gates of death, these letters of an aged woman. And Colette, writing of the happiness of her childhood: 'But my felicity knew another and less commonplace secret: the presence of her who, instead of receding far from me through the gates of death, has revealed herself more vividly to me as I grow older' (Colette, 1966, p. 19). The woman who wrote these words was already in her seventies. Colette's relationship to Sido had known dark skies and stormy seas, partly on account of Sido's fierce possessiveness. Why, yes why, should her daughters marry and tear the rapture of those bonds between a mother and her she-child:

'I've had enough of this perpetual anxiety over my daughters. Already the oldest has gone off with that man . . .'

'How, gone off?'

'Oh, well, married him if you prefer it. Married or not married, she has none the less gone away with a man whom she hardly knows.' (p. 41)

Sido refused to see that the marriage of her daughters could be other than 'abduction' (Colette, 1966, p. 42). Already she was 'one child short' throughout Colette's adolescence. And sometimes, in the depths of night, Sido, like a mother cat, would carry her sleeping kitten to a room beside her own, plagued with nightmares of loss which she would one day suffer at the hands of some 'stranger'. She never quite forgave Colette for her first two marriages and at the time of her third, Sido was already dead and thereby spared further heartache.

Men had very little place in Sido's passionate scheme of things: 'And after all, you, what have you to do with me? You aren't even a relation!' (Colette, 1966, p. 42), she would throw at her husband, for all their mutual devotion. For Sido, as for Clytaemnestra, blood-bond rather than bed-bond drew the ultimate allegiance for her matriarchal heart. No, there was no room for men in this summer-long embrace between Sido and her daughter, between Minet-Chérie and her mother, entwined in a perfumed garden of two feminine beings whose lives grew rooted heart to heart:

The Upper Garden overlooked the Lower Garden – a warm, confined enclosure . . . where the smell of tomato leaves mingled in July with that of the apricots ripening on the walls . . . and the massive lilacs, whose compact flowers – blue in the shade and purple in the sunshine – withered so soon, stifled by their own exuberance. (Colette, 1966, pp. 23–4)

What other love-affair, in truth, can come within an inch of this enchanted enravelment? We may denigrate this rapture by calling it 'unresolved symbiosis', to suggest that it is 'sick', but that will cut little ice with the living experience. We will be told to go away and kindly mind our own business while these lovers delight in the suns of their alliance, from which they draw the strength each needs through the coming years of exile decreed by the daughter's marriage, and on the day the axe will fall on one or the other's death.

Popular belief may enshrine a notion that the birth of a son

THE CONSPIRACY OF SILENCE

embodies the supreme achievement which perpetuates the seed, but does the heart of a mother underwrite this consensus? All the evidence remains highly ambiguous.

We find that once the curtain falls on the matriarchal age we must traverse eras of silence. These are shattered in their turn by a theme which deafens us with crescendo grievances where separation is acknowledged, punctuated here and there by a reference to bliss. Both extremes are uncanny. Both conceal and reveal a familiar yet frightening truth of an age-old alliance of the greatest poignancy yet doomed to wild ambivalance born of bilateral disappointment once symbiosis is dissolved. Here the overriding passion rooted in giving birth to a perfect replica surfaces uncannily, like variations on a theme throughout the lifetime of the dyad. It confounds the negative, where assumptions of a merger constantly come to naught in the face of the reality of two separate entities, if sanity is to prevail. None the less the poets sing with a veritable siren's song that the pains of separation can be readily undone by a painless reverting to a time when two were one.

Shall a morning not break when even psychoanalysts and a range of other pundits will tune into such songs as these, compiled by Tillie Olsen (1985)?

> *I felt my stomach turn when she moved in her crib of*
> *   seaweeds.*
> *'Last month, at this time,' I said,*
> *'You and my heart swam together like a pair of mackerel.'*
> (Jeanne Murray Walker, p. 10)

> *'My dear, what you said was one thing*
> *but what you sang was another, sweetly*
> *subversive and dark as blackberries*
> *and I became the daughter of your dream.'*
> (Marge Piercy, p. 28)

I gaze at her fine, pink face, glowing in the window light. Her dark hair has small, tight tight tight waves. They glow in the light. Everything glows. I am aglow with the rapture of the revelation that she is the most beautiful in the whole world, my mother. I am too young to ask, 'Why me? How come I am chosen?' I belong to what is given. (Adele Wiseman, p. 29)

Backward, turn backward, O Time, in your flight,
Make me a child again, just for tonight!
Mother, come back from the echoless shore,
Take me again to your heart, as of yore;
Kiss from my forehead the furrows of care,
Smooth the few silver threads out of my hair,
Over my slumbers your loving watch keep, –
Rock me to sleep, mother, rock me to sleep.
(Elizabeth Akers Allen, 1860, p. 36)

. . . in our hands
In our breasts
Round rolling hills
Blue veined breasts
Blue rivers caressing the earth
Of my breasts
    our breasts
Legs,
Our famous Davis legs: long and thin . . .
. . . My body is yours Momma.
I am a carbon copy.
(Laura Davis, p. 39)

A mere handful of examples chosen from a multitude, where the passion and nostalgia, a plangent longing and desire, are at last out in the open. There is no need, now, for disguise. The silence seems to have been broken, the uncanny exposed, in this lifelong feast of love. But we must not be deceived. The road to consciousness is never open. It is an obstacle course. Our scholars obfuscate the issue to the very final ditch.

Like the Gioconda's smile, so the poetry of Sappho continues to tantalize, while leading scholars by the nose. Here the issue is the only complete poem to have survived: subject to countless translations, commentaries and surmise:

Elaborate-throned immortal Aphrodite, child of Zeus, weaver of wiles, I entreat you, do not overpower my spirit, lady, with pain and anguish; but come hither, if ever before you heard my voice from afar and hearkened to it, and came, leaving your father's house, yoking your golden chariot. Fair swift sparrows brought you over the black earth, with rapid fluttering of wings, from heaven through the middle air. Swiftly they came; and you, blessed one, smiling with immortal face, asked me what had happened to me now, why now again I was calling, what in my frenzied spirit I most wanted for myself: 'Whom now am I to persuade back[?] into friendship with you? Who wrongs you, Sappho? For if she flees, she shall soon pursue; if she does not accept gifts, yet shall she give them; if she does not love, she shall soon love even against her will.' Come to me now also, free me from harsh anxiety, accomplish what my spirit desires to accomplish, and be yourself my ally. (Jenkins, H.A., 1982, p. 7)

'Formally it is a cletic or "summoning" hymn containing a prayer for aid. It is', the author continues, one which follows a 'regular pattern' from a suppliant 'addressing the god whose help he desires'. But 'Sappho's poem', he continues, 'has a private and personal quality which makes it unlike the hymns written by any other early Greek poet; none the less, it adopts the conventional form' (Jenkins, H.A., 1982, p. 8).

The author has become aware of a certain ambiguity. Deeper levels of his mind are pricking up some inner ear. He begins to scrutinize the subtle language of the poet, brimming with innuendos and startling notes of evocation. He draws our attention to the opening words, which

set the tone of the whole poem and conjure up an atmosphere that is at once splendid, intimate and gently humorous ... Aphrodite in this poem is opulently and delightfully ornamental ... Whether or not Sappho's original audience sensed a double entendre ... the very first word of the poem suggests Aphrodite's dual character: on the one hand she is an Olympian deity, on the other she is Sappho's subtle and teasing friend. (p. 9)

Jenkins is following some scent; a half-forgotten memory leads him on, like a dream, on some threshold to awaking. With the coaxing *'lissomai se'* a tone of dire entreaty reverberates through the lines. He is puzzled and half afraid: 'Aphrodite has to come from afar' ... with 'the golden chariot passing over the black earth', his commentary almost shudders. 'She is described as "smiling with immortal face" ... and yet the goddess's smile, as Sappho describes it, is so radiant, so entrancing, that paradoxically it seems to be entirely "human" ... ' 'Page' – he now pursues his trail – 'compares her to a mother with a troublesome child, and the comparison is apt, for no one can be more lovingly solicitous than a mother . . .' (Jenkins, H.A., 1982, p. 10). So near the truth, yet still so far rests the mind of the scholar, filled with academic dust.

Having come as far as this, let us go a little further. Sappho loved her mother, Cleïs. The two, we know, were very close. Sappho was not beautiful. Her nose was seemingly too long, her skin too dark and her stature remained exceedingly small, the body of a lifelong child. The girl was in her early teens when Cleïs, her mother, died:

. . . the loss of her mother meant personal desolation. It took Sappho years to overcome the effect of her mother's death. Without Cleïs, Sappho was lost . . . her longing for Cleïs is expressed in the fragment of a poem she wrote later:

> *So like a child, after its mother, I flutter . . .*
> (Goldsmith, M., 1938, p. 38)

In the years of her childhood, Aphrodite, the Goddess of Love and of the beauty of women, had been her favourite of the gods. She loved her because 'the humble sparrow, so often neglected when more beautiful birds were to be seen', was sacred to her (Goldsmith, M., 1938, p. 24). Was not the ugly little girl once her mother's beloved sparrow? Had Cleïs not reassured her that she had charm and conspicuous talent, so never mind the quest for looks, mere outward appearances?

Later, when Sappho wrote the poem – even if at a conscious level she was entreating the goddess, prostrate over her recurring loss of maybe Atthis or Erinna, the gifted poetess of Rhodes – surely the crucial loss is that of the beloved mother, which left her inconsolable. Is not the sense of loss 'displaced', as psychotherapists would say?

The theme of 'fluttering' recurs. She herself, the little sparrow, will draw the golden mother back, even over the black earth of the hated Underworld, to her childish, grieving heart. How hard it is to crack the code of the conspiracy of silence! Men have, through the centuries, worried at this enigma to turn away, time and again, from that passionate embrace between mother and her daughter: the being closest to her heart in time-old mutuality.

Did the early Christian Church, on its hunt for infidels and orgiastic excesses, pick up that underlying secret of the poet from Lesbos when around AD 380, and seven centuries on from there, it burnt the body of her work? But early in our century, scholars who were excavating Graeco-Egyptian cemeteries at Oxyrhynchus in the Fayûm, and in other parts of Egypt, 'found that the coffins of the period were made of papier-mâché, in the composition of which scraps of old books and letters had been used . . . including several pieces of Sappho' (Weigall, A., 1932, p. 312).

Out of the dust of Egypt there came one beautiful fragment after another to justify the opinion previously held. The only disconcerting fact was that the newly discovered love-poems were addressed to women, not to men; and thus those arguments which had sometimes been put forward to explain away the use of the feminine gender in the two important poems already known, were proved to be untenable. It should be remembered, however, that the tendency in certain men and women to be stirred emotionally by persons of their own sex was not considered by the Greeks to be reprehensible in any serious degree, and that, therefore, all modern censures are out of focus. (Weigall, A., 1932, p. 313)

That the one of her own sex, in the person of her mother, may, from the very first to the last and final breath, marriage and childbearing notwithstanding, remain the object of her deepest passion, is still one of our best-kept secrets and constantly subverted truths.

'What is it that the female wants?' Half a century after Freud's death, the poets, just as he had forecast, especially among us women, are jubilating a response: to find my wholeness in my mother to do with as I choose to please. Small wonder that this butterfly was obliged to extend a dreamy chrysalis ex- istence by a few millennia in a rhapsody of silence: but for what deeper purposes we have yet to define.

This line of thought must not permit us to be blind and unaware that what we have been celebrating is only one side of the coin. Ambivalence guarantees a darker and distorted side wrought of frustration and disappointment. Early Freudians believed that it lay in 'penis envy', a general umbrella term for the girl's simmering resentment that her mother fails to supply her small, imperious person with every gratification which phantasy can devise, including a penis and/or baby.

There is no doubt some truth in this, which we find substantiated in many individual cases – even if the penis is a symbol for power and exemption from the denigrated status of second-class citizen. But there is a deeper truth, belonging to a different loss. Even if the boy is exiled from mother's embrace by paternal prohibition, he is permitted to return and take possession of that body in the person of his wife. Then no holds will be barred – phantasy receives full rein, later, in his marriage bed, while the girl must make the best of a hard and hairy other, so different from the soft embrace, scented sweetly of ambrosia, for which she continues to long, plangently, as a wife. When she is misunderstood and snubbed by some unexpected difference, every fibre of her being longs for that familiar comfort, which she has to deny in these painful circumstances. Only where the early father closely shared in parenting will the transfer to the male prove deeply acceptable.

We shall pursue our search for truth by sifting through shards and fragments very much in the manner of the archaeologist:

In an old National Geographic *there is a picture of Mary Leaky on her hands and knees in the Olduvai Gorge region of Africa looking for signs of primitive life by working the parched earth with a toothbrush. (Hall, N., 1980, p. 67)*

This assembling of the signs, taking apart and reassembling, will surely never know an end, but that should not deter us as we solemnly approach the earliest human artefacts with some bearing on our subject. Let us use them as pegs on which to hang our speculations, enlivened with more recent insights where this seems relevant.

These, our artefacts, begin with the ancient Great Goddess:

She is beautiful in ways we have almost forgotten, or which have become defined as ugliness. Her body possesses mass, interior depth, inner rest, and balance. She is not smiling; her expression is inward-looking or ecstatic . . . If, as very often, there is a child at her breast, or on her lap, she is not absorbed in contemplation of him (the 'Adoration of the Virgin', with the son as the centre of the world, will come later). She is not particularly young, or rather, she is absolutely without age. She is for-herself . . . (Rich, A., 1977, p. 93)

Here the author has prepared us with her poetic incantation that in turning back the clock, by some ten millennia, we must leave our preconceptions where we leave our shoes before approaching a shrine in which we expect to be addressed profoundly and movingly in a half-remembered tongue.

When we take our leave of her, of that hypnotic embrace, knowing that she lives inside us; our earliest configuration of a maternal object, as she grows and evolves from a part-object status; we move on and stand in awe – our archaic memory trembling – before a new representation which brings tears to our eyes. Seemingly a single being from her shoulders down, known as the Double Goddess, she owns two distinct and separate heads, poised on that single body. Something is separating out in the region of the mind, even if corporeal destiny remains undifferentiated.

It sets all our alarm bells ringing, the struggle that is here foreshadowed, in which, some ten millennia on, we are still enravelled as so-called 'liberated' women. At some dark, mysterious level we confront a double portrait of ourselves and our mother, exerting some tremendous pull throughout our inmost, darkest ages, back to fusion and the womb, as onward to some giddy height. Here lies the paradox which conjures up the uncanny in self-styled 'liberated' minds.

Later, we will tear ourselves away to the mother–daughter myth. The tale of Persephone and her abandoned, grieving mother has surely never been surpassed as statement and as metaphor. Here we read the transformations which are levied in the dyad; of that lifelong make and break which constitutes the inmost body of the discipleship of procreativity – an older wheel than any other.

All these configurations have carried their inhabitation of the woman's psyche forward to this, our embattled present day, so that we find ourselves addressed profoundly and movingly as half-forgotten strings are plucked, in this shadowy museum, that they may invigorate the wellspring of poetic purpose in our own impoverished time.

But is it so impoverished, or are women slowly finding old, mysterious, semi-dreaming channels, coves and lilting inlets back to some enchanted playground, quite as polysensuous as any 'sexuality' of which our mentors approve, back to a mother–daughter Eden?

3 THE GREAT GODDESS CREATRIX

The first knowledge any woman has of warmth, nourishment,
tenderness, security, sensuality, mutuality, comes from her
mother. That earliest enwrapment of one female body with
another can sooner or later be denied or rejected, felt as choking
possessiveness, as rejection, trap, or taboo; but it is, at the
beginning, the whole world.
(ADRIENNE RICH, *Of Woman Born*)

Crossing a major mental threshold, palaeolithic males began to
worship womanhood (Mother Earth) looking upon the opposite
sex as the intermediary between man and nature's mysteries.
(AMAURY DE RIENCOURT, *Woman and Power in History*)

The scholar must be able to renounce entirely the ideas of his own
time, the beliefs with which these have filled his spirit, and
transfer himself to the midpoint of a completely different world of
thought.
(JAKOB BACHOFEN, *Myth, Religion and Mother Right*)

WE, EARTH'S OCCUPANTS TODAY, who walk on asphalt, drive in cars, or fly, like birds, in jumbo planes at many hundred miles per hour; who can split the atom, reach the moon to gaze down from outer space on our revolving Mother Earth to see a luminous blue flower – how are we to turn the clock of our imagination back by ten or more millennia? How shall we identify with those early forefathers: 'weak, relatively defenceless, and more or less isolated in small, scattered groups ... increasingly capable of abstract thought ... afraid of nature's mysterious displays of grandiose power'? An era in which 'the male stood in awe of the female, as he did of all natural phenomena – storms, lightning, earthquakes, volcanic eruptions' (de Riencourt, A., 1983, p. 18).

Bachofen did precisely that, even if we still dispute the implications of his findings. Working only from inscriptions he chanced upon on Roman tombs before the sites of Helen's Troy and Pasiphaë's Crete had been closely dreamt to light, this scholar of Roman Law, a jurist by profession, took a breathtaking leap into the Neolithic era to exhume in his mind's eye a fabled society. Its essence was womanpower and magic control over nature intricately interwoven in the mind of early man. For even in the realm of hunting, then a strictly masculine preserve for essential food supplies, woman saw the hunters off, standing briefly in their midst, hands raised to the rising sun, muttering her essential spells on which success would depend: nothing less than survival.

What clue had he alighted on among the mossy remains of Mediterranean centuries in that unlikely cemetery? Certain striking oddities in the law of property right, as ordained in Ancient Rome, that stronghold of the patriarch, had sparked off a train of thought which is still controversial. For here and there he came across provisions for inheritance, a will chiselled into stone, not from father to son, according to the classic rule, but from a mother to her daughter.

Weaving symbol and myth into that 'different world of thought', Bachofen provided us with his own groundplan for the earliest human social patterns, reaching to the very dawn of *Homo sapiens*. Accordingly, in the beginning were the nomadic hunter-gatherers, newly emerged from the forests to the more exposed savannahs, over whose sexual habits *ius naturale* prevailed. There was motherhood without marriage; unregulated hetaerism; no agriculture and no home beyond a temporary shelter; total promiscuity where woman was at the mercy of the lust of stronger males, before the incest taboo, that cornerstone of civilization, became a universal law. This epoch, which he relates to the conditions in a swamp, he named the tellurian.

Into this marauding scene the advent of agriculture, based on edible grasses and conceivably spurred into being by woman's angry discontent as object of the brute strength of these unsavoury hunters, came as a ray of hope, together with exogamy. So arose the lunar period, to govern Neolithic times: an era of matriarchy strictly ordered and ordained by the Demetrian principle of the mother goddess. Here the pattern gravitated towards conjugal motherhood and legitimate birth, even if paternity was not yet consciously acknowledged, except through animal symbolism.

In place of the nomadic swamp a settled mode of life evolved, centring upon the hearth and domestic implements, presided over by the woman and her invention of the pot, that inestimable milestone. Such basic property, rudimentary at first but growing in complexity at an almost dazzling speed, was, it would seem, handed down from the mother to her daughter, ensuring for her a status whereby she need not sell her body as in the bad old days, marred by manifold abuse.

Such is her background, then, whose brooding bulk looms over those shrouded millennia at the beginning of our tale, known to us as the Great Goddess. She will be our starting point in the Neolithic culture in that south-eastern part of Europe known to scholars as 'Old Europe', where 'the great northern plains are strewn with Aurignacian remains which indicate the prevalence of a female-orientated worship.' Here has been bequeathed to us a rich legacy of artefacts of bone and stone, and ceramic, in whole inhabited sites where a homogeneous culture testifies to fertility magic.

It would, however, be wrong if we jump to the conclusion of masculine adoration in a more modern sense of, say, Mariology. For 'prehistoric man worshipped the little goddesses, but probably more in superstitious fear than in adoration.' Indeed, shattered remains of female statuettes testify to vandalism and 'bear witness to deep-seated male antagonism' (de Riencourt, A., 1983, p. 20), throwing considerable doubt on prevalent wishful thinking of a golden and untroubled era of feminine supremacy: an age of plenty and of peace, of integrated harmony.

As we survey this mother-image of our earliest beginnings – massive, still, and inward-brooding – our eye takes the substance in with disbelief and revulsion which only gradually yield to growing tenderness and awe. How difficult it is for us, trapped in idolatry of science, to crawl through dark and endless tunnels to reach our silent foremothers. And yet, as we stand our ground, a shudder of recognition runs through that thin veneer of our latter-day sophistication, once the spirit of enquiry restores us to our prehistory. What overwhelming sense of smallness, the most abject helplessness in a mystifying cosmos, form the precarious backdrop against which the living mother, accompanied by her daughter, would drag the burden of her terrors to the feet of the Great Goddess for her magical redress. But even such a phantasy fails remotely to grasp the prevailing states of mind. How could any of these women have acted independently of the entire women's group: a homogeneous female matrix, where magic, ritual and dance set the entire tribe in motion, like some fluid entity? For in the initial phase of the cult of the Great Goddess we are still millennia from human individuation, as from any notion of laws of cause and effect; coitus and fertility; the concept of paternity. This will dawn to underpin higher cultural organization during the later phase of Demetrian matriarchy, when the concept of the father, of boundaries and separation between mother and daughter, gradually emerge as subject for the early myths. For the daughter, at this time, womanhood still implied unconscious containment in the primordial relation to the mother – not, as today, in infancy as the first and earliest phase, but extending throughout life, long before any glimmering of human personality as we envisage it today.

That shudder of recognition to which we referred earlier doubtless has certain roots in what Jung called the collective unconscious, in the intimations of our infant origins that stir to some dreamlike echo of our symbiotic past. For where the image of the Great Goddess may strike us as horrific, with those accentuated buttocks, sedentary thighs and breasts, are we not re-entering the ghostly realm of part-objects, when the dumbfounded mind first gasps and struggles for the air of meaning? There must surely be links between the development of the individual mind, as we have come to understand it in Freudian and post-Freudian terms, and the evolution of the psyche of the human race. And would they not illuminate notions of lost utopias of a matriarchal age of harmony and peace and plenty, dear to feminist constructions, like slumbering memories of infant bliss at the breast, before the trauma of weaning exiled us from Paradise?

The Great Goddess belongs to the end of an era of the harsh vicissitudes of nomadic wanderings – a time when a new range of skills began to emerge and multiply on the face of Old Europe, as though they had but lain in waiting for this opportunity in a settled mode of life, so dear to a woman's heart. A rudimentary agriculture, the knotting, weaving and dyeing of a growing range of fabrics, an elaboration of pottery, for ritual and domestic use – all these constituted a steady progress which evolved mainly in the domain of purely female expertise. Mother would pass on the know-how of such production to her daughter in their conjoint day-to-day life, half waking yet semi-steeped in assignments of magic; while the men could only marvel at such consummate skills as they gradually transformed a harsh, inhospitable world.

Only within such a context can we try to understand the worship of the Great Goddess, the feminine principle in awesome supremacy, as she brought in new harvests, wrought the comforts of the home and ensured a progeny from the fullness of her being, where woman and Goddess stood in temporal confluence. And whatever was to follow, however heavily the foot of patriarchal eras might come to rest on woman's back, in her soul she would remember, through dark millennia to come, that she had once been instructed in such profound significance. This would be the revelation stored away in the psyche and passed on to her daughter, in wordless *jouissance*, even if the spoken word would, for centuries to come, be unequal to the task, or superimpose harsher edicts in obedience to her Lord and Master at a shabby second-hand.

How can we take the matter further in the silence which prevails in this awesome museum? In an important study, in which he transposes the Great Goddess into the Great Mother Archetype, a Jungian psychologist ascribed two distinct characters to The Feminine – Elementary and Transformative – and rightfully attached to them an eternal relevance:

The Elementary represents the Feminine as the Great Round, the Great Container [that] tends to hold fast to everything that springs from it and to surround it like an eternal substance. Everything born of it belongs to it and remains subject to it; and even if the individual becomes independent, the Archetypal Feminine relativizes this independence into a nonessential variant of her own perpetual being. (Neumann, E., 1974, p. 25)

This Elementary Character is typical of matriarchy in its historical and psychological setting, where we find it active in the possessive and controlling mother who cannot let her daughter go and seeks to entangle their two beings inextricably. It 'becomes evident wherever the ego and consciousness are still small and undeveloped and the unconscious is dominant ...' and is 'the foundation of that conservative, stable and unchanging part of the feminine which predominates in motherhood' (Neumann, E., 1974, p. 26).

Neumann steps fearlessly into this archaic sleep, like every psychoanalyst on a rescue attempt where such a state of dark affairs has precipitated a psychosis. Here he is describing what today we would call regression: 'in the relation between the ego and the unconscious, a "psychic gravitation" may be observed, a tendency of the ego to return to its original unconscious state' (Neumann, E., 1974, p. 26).

Neumann lifts the spell which belongs to every matriarchal state, if it remains unmodified and at risk of dangerous regression, by postulating the intervention of an essential counter-charge which derives, as we shall see, from the Father Principle. Here psychological absence spells serious mental disarrangement to the mother–daughter dyad which, if properly acknowledged, is bound to cut sharply across utopias of matriarchy. Matriarchy *must* eventually be drawn towards 'The Law of the Father', as Lacan postulates, for it will be only the father (or masculine principle where it is integrated in the mother) who can offer the daughter access to a wider world beyond the mythopoeic circle, as becomes evident in the Persephone myth.

In early matriarchy, then, the Elementary Character remains in the ascendant, maintaining eras of stagnation and virtual prohibition of autonomy and growth. It is this poignant evidence in the artefacts of the Great Goddess that tends to make our blood run cold, for 'unconsciousness means non-differentiation. There is as yet no clearly differentiated ego, only events which may belong to me or to another. It is sufficient that somebody should be affected by them' (Neumann, E., 1974, p. 83). It is for this reason that in confronting these images, a shudder of intuition from our earliest infancy, as it contaminates our childhood and our later adult years alike, reminds us with a stab of fear how narrowly we each escaped into our autonomy; how easily we could sink back into what the Jungians call 'participation mystique', that state where the precarious ego, 'responding to psychic gravitation, sinks back into the unconscious or circles as a satellite around the Archetypal Feminine' (Neumann, E., 1974, p. 28).

With what sense of relief do we turn from these psychic quicksands of the Elementary to 'The Transformative' Feminine Character. This one Neumann describes as initiating 'the tendency towards amplification and change . . . from preserving what exists in an unaltered form' (Neumann, E., 1974, p. 29). Here we arrive at a concept which is close to Winnicott's 'graduated environmental failure', when a mother will initiate, once the moment seems right, that sensitive *pas de deux* of mother–infant separation in which we recognize today the prospects for maturity and all that spells human well-being.

This psychological momentum inherent in the transformative

stands at that historic frontier of farewell to the Great Goddess, where we must prepare ourselves to meet successive thunder gods. It could, of course, not have occurred before socioeconomic changes within the settled mode of life offered possibilities for a rudimentary surplus so that feeding ceased to be a central preoccupation. But once this surplus was achieved with the help of early agriculture and new skills in pottery which provide great storage jars, we find concrete evidence of this second character at work. Suddenly our attention, numbed by an endless array, by the brooding stasis and self-obsession, of the Great Goddesses, is startled, as by a clarion call, at the sight of an innovation nothing had led us to expect. All at once, we stand transfixed in the breathtaking presence of the 'double' or 'two-headed' Goddess.

In this prophetic apparition we see foreshadowed a first crack in the mother–daughter unit. In stone and marble she confronts us, half bemused by our amazement at this intrepid step into opening horizons. Sharing a single body are two distinct and separate heads, even if they seem to be quite undifferentiated. None the less there are two. What sense of awe overtakes us as we surmise that we here witness a momentous transformation: clear evidence of separation from the symbiotic mulch. However it first came about, whatever were its fraught beginnings in some secret chrysalis; as we gaze on it, in stone, we are bound to recognize what heroic feats have been accomplished, furtively in the mists of some prehistoric night.

The single body may show breasts, one or two pairs on occasion, as it may have one or two pairs of arms. The two are generally joined from the shoulders downwards and sometimes still by the head, as by some element of doubt whether a single state of mind must, after all, not serve them both. Mute and silent they must wait for the next transformation, which, when it comes, may permit a further thrust of separation. The silent stone seems to convey both the impossibility and the possibility within a single, speechless silence. How strangely similar, as it hangs trembling in the atmosphere, to the silence of our consulting room, when the task of separation moves slowly to the fore, often after years of labour, if it is to be achieved.

We know that time is of the essence, and we bow our heads before this truth. We anticipate that in our museum millennia will still slip by. Coming to the fifth century BC we ponder the marble stele – found in Pharsalus, in Greece – of Demeter and Kore, to whom we will come presently. Superb in the complexity and richness of the symbolism of their achieved differentiation, they present to our eye a momentous parting of the ways within that knit relationship, the cradle of procreation, that each may turn the wheel of life – fated, if in double harness, still to the single yoke.

If we rest for just a moment in that Roman cemetery in which Bachofen discovered the Demeterian concern of a mother for her daughter, we reflect and are amazed. He informs us that Berenice II, wife of Ptolemy III of Egypt, insisted on a dotal law which enabled a daughter to sue for payment of dowry if the mother had died before she had found a husband (Bachofen, J.J., 1967, p. 96). These provisions of the age, instituted by women, came under what was known as 'the virtue of thoughtfulness'.

While the Roman legions marched to extend the Empire; while the Eagle flew aloft in the high barbarian skies, far from the clang of battle, the make and break of history's fortunes over self-important heads; in the shade of a cypress tree, we meet the mute concern of women for their female progeny. Only the quiet heart testifies to the momentous. Here, at feminine insistence over many centuries, tellurian promiscuity and the hardships it imposed on women yielded to the law and order of Demetrian concern; a prolonged dialectic between the wiles of hetaerism and conjugal matrimony, which in the view of Bachofen would become the central issue of myths, like that of Oedipus and the drama of the *Oresteia*, where we will return to it.

Here we have already struck, at the dawn of our tale, the bedrock of the central issue of the relationship between mother and daughter: how the dyad is caught in that archaic conflict between the Elementary and the Transformative Character of The Feminine – then, as it is still today. The difficulty seems to be that

The Transformative Character drives toward development; that is to say, it brings movement and unrest. Consequently it is not experienced by consciousness as purely positive any more than the Elementary Character is experienced as purely negative. Both characters are vehicles of the ambivalence that is typical of the Archetypal Feminine as well as the Great Mother . . . (Neumann, E., 1974, p. 31)

Movement, then, and unrest, a tentative step forward, threatened by a gravitation when the ego 'sinks back into the unconscious or circles as a satellite around the Archetypal Feminine' (Neumann, E., 1974, p.

28), is the spiral of the epic we would wish to pursue.

To a certain degree the outcome of the interaction between these two characters will always hang in the balance to colour the relationship, just as it quivers poised between progress and regression in the wider human scene. Maternity, we must remember, is idealized as often in a reactionary as in a liberating sense, throughout the course of history.

As we move on to the myth we are willy-nilly carried to 'the metamorphosis of the concept of cosmic creation – from the universe born of a goddess without a spouse, to that born of a Great Goddess in need of a male consort . . .' (Neumann, E., 1974, pp. 38–9). If we pause to glance ahead, the momentum of this concept travels on until the day when in the biblical account, which was heavily revised to conceal matriarchal currents, the universe is created by the male godhead alone: in the beginning was the Word, from the Lord of the Storm. She, the Goddess, was banished. But as with every revolution, whose true stage is the human mind, that which has been overthrown mocks so crude a victory by deftly slipping underground to return reincarnated.

In Greece the Olympic gods would marry female deities who had resided in the land, its oceans, mountains and clear streams, in earlier supremacy. Even in Palestine, to the displeasure of the prophets, the goddess survived successfully well into the Christian era, only to be resurrected by popular demand in the cult of Mariology which would spread like a wildfire through a goddess-thirsty world.

If the patriarchs exiled pagan idolatry with fanatical zeal, Isis, Ishtar, Cybele, Diana, Venus-Aphrodite reappeared here and there to mock masculine intransigence in successive incarnations. The human heart, born of woman, refused to be comforted by the arid spectacle of a male deity deemed to rule on his own. The psyche could not sustain so profound a deprivation, except intermittently. Its androgynous essence refused to be pacified, then as in our present day, until we give our full consent to our fundamental nature.

The first millennium BC, in which we now find ourselves, may stand poised at the gates of the patriarchal revolution, but matriarchy still had a crucial task to accomplish before going underground, to leave a poignant legacy in the Eleusinian Mysteries. The Double Goddess was a phase, an interlude in a long labour. It has to move towards a birth and the cutting of the cord between mother and daughter, between her who gave life and her who in turn received it, where each unit in the cycle, while dependent on the other, achieves a separate entity.

This consent to separation must initially be levied, by hook or by crook, from the homogeneous substance of the dyadic matrix. The different, the paternal presence may stand ready in the wings, but can safely beckon to accomplish a new good only once the symbiotic bonds have loosened by their own volition, however stormy be that loosening; for failing that he is abhorred as the sadistic ravisher of Demeter's experience, and the daughter becomes the instrument which terminates the mother's life. Nowhere will we find this rending and its painstaking restitution, on a new and hopeful basis, for the whole of humankind more exquisitely defined than in the myth we now describe.

It follows that the final task for matriarchy to accomplish is at this juncture to ensure that such a separation may prove species-syntonic – in other words, may be achieved in a spirit of co-operation which minimizes paranoia. This element of safety, of an essential benison, will, we shall see, be ritualized in the Eleusinian Mysteries. Only then can the Great Mother's Elementary stranglehold be sufficiently relinquished for the Transformative to liberate fresh energies for new values and connections: 'dynamic, aggressive willpower' on the part of the Hebrews, and 'emancipation of the discursive intellect, of logic and reason' (de Riencourt, A., 1983, p. 93) on that of the Greeks; in other words to commence the struggle for a new component of the psyche's equipment: the 'godly' attribute of spirit.

The potency of the myth, its unique contribution at the gateways of change, lies in its ability to reward the devotee, like the labourer in the field of psychoanalysis, with a flash, now and then, that he has 'become the truth' (a concept of Bion's). Even if moments later darkness closes in again, faith remains that the experience will in its own good time return, provided we maintain our vigil and stance of fidelity.

4   PERSEPHONE ABSCONDS

Oh, Woman:
. . . That you may have cause again
to seek yourself, to go out among the flowers crying
'Kore! Kore!', knowing

the king of Hell
also has you . . .
(CHARLES OLSON, *The Moon and the Virgin* [Nor Hall])

. . . from this adultery committed,
the plant that provides, Corn
that at Eleusis Kore brought
out of Hell, health manifest.
(ROBERT DUNCAN, *The Moon and the Virgin* [Nor Hall])

MAJESTICALLY OUR CURTAIN rises on a momentous overture. Where there was one, enthroned alone, there emerge – bleeding, broken, torn – shadows destined to become, in their separate meaning, two; contained in their dividing skins; feet set in distinct directions. The myth is harbinger of change, straddling the future and the past: forsaking while it ushers in that which it would have us know in farewell as in greeting.

Yet with the myth, the modern mind is on the high road to misunderstanding. Has not the gift of fantasy, the wellspring of imagination, been vilely vandalized and plugged in our sweatshops of 'education'? Are we not in danger of effecting gory mistranslations? Might the temptation to exploit its legacy of deeper meanings to fit in with our latest theory not carry us far astray? For once we lift component parts out of their organic nexus we distort them instantly, however winsome our intention. Besides, we show a tendency to pick the fragments which may suit us, while we throw the rest away. Was Freud himself perhaps not guilty of being such a raiding party with a degree of disregard for the minutiae of those cultural seasons?

Some decades before the maestro appropriated the Oedipus myth to dress it in the full regalia of infantile sexuality, Bachofen had this to say concerning that constellation:

The religious ideas underlying the mythical figure of Oedipus (swollen foot) are self-evident. The swollen foot from which he takes his name shows him to be an embodiment of the male fecundating principle, which in its tellurian-Poseidonian aspect is not infrequently associated with the foot or shoe. The Neptunian significance of the chariot that caused the swelling is well known. Hygenus called Oedipus 'impudens' (shameless), quite aside from his relation to his mother. This is an allusion to the exuberantly sensual fecundating principle prevailing in the unregulated tellurian sexuality of the swamp, and it is this 'shamelessness' that gives the swollen foot its meaning . . .

The Sphinx is an embodiment of tellurian motherhood; she represents the feminine right of the earth in its dark aspect as the inexorable law of death . . . In the riddle whose solution will put an end to the Sphinx's power, man is considered only in his transient aspect, mortality; the downward path to the tomb is the sole and ultimate idea of his existence. This is the stage of mankind which knows only mother and no father . . . once it is understood, once its utter hopelessness is recognized, this law will be at an end. (Bachofen, J.J., 1967, pp. 180–1)

The question of the Sphinx was this, we might usefully recall: 'What goes on four, then two, then three legs?'; to which the answer was man, who crawls, walks upright and grows old to walk with the aid of a staff, until he is laid in the grave: a sequence which offers him no hope or any prospect of transcending his purely material nature.

The ensuing despair was giving birth, at the time, to a range of mystery cults concerned with rebirth and with resurrection. Like the Eleusinian Mysteries connected with Persephone, their initial focus was on the vegetal cycle, but accomplished a gradual shift to redemption of the human soul. Did Persephone with her infant, Brimos, the son she carries on stage among the flames and thunder, wrought by the hierophant, but a few miles from Athens, not presently reappear as the Virgin, who in the course of time would become the Queen of Heaven?

Jung, as we know, saw incest as man's search for his soul, the masculine principle in quest of its feminine counterpart, of integration and wholeness. Endless are the layers of meaning. Deep, indeed, is the well of the past. Let us approach it reverently, knowing that we are bound to err, inconsequential as we are on the dial of sun's time.

In the Introduction to the *Larousse Encyclopaedia of Mythology* Robert Graves proposes that 'myth has two main functions. The first is to answer the sort of awkward question that children ask, such as: "Who made the world? How will it end?" . . . The second is to justify an existing social system . . .' (Graves, R., 1959, p. v). But myth is also an attempt by man to come to terms with change at times of crucial transition linked to growing consciousness in our human evolution. When a four-year-old asks: 'Mummy, tell me about me when I was still a little baby. And then all about me now, and how I first learned to walk and hurt myself when I fell down', central to his urgency are psychological changes; why, despite pain and hurt built into every transformation, growth had to forge ahead, in search of certain rewards, even if at the time they remain nebulous, seeing that a part of us would still prefer to be carried, ever more a babe in arms. To help us through these growing pains, threatening chaos and confusion, the implications of the inner are overpainted and iconized by actual, outer events, to become incorporated into the individual as the collective myth. 'With myth, we are putting meaning together', as Kerenyi confirms (Kerenyi, C., in Jung, C.G. and Kerenyi, C., 1949, p. 3).

Our avowed purpose is to evaluate this myth for clues intrinsic to our subject matter: the earliest mother–daughter dyad and its gradual evolution into the complexities of that relationship. We will catch its images in a sequence of frames, not losing sight of the whole which is also in motion, aware that we may be caught wrong-footed where we misread crucial changes battering the bedrock of the time.

Firstly: the Olympian gods were approaching a terminus of their omnipotent bravado in human phantasy. Secondly, matriarchy was beginning to yield to the Law of the Father, to an epoch of patriarchy, because, as Bachofen points out, 'feminine right of the earth in its dark aspect as the inexorable law of death' had, in time, to be transcended by a transformative hope. Such are the momentous issues which we need to bear in mind as we return to our task, at the point where we had encountered the Double Goddess. Could she represent, as was suggested, a chrysalis of symbiosis yielding its earliest crack to fledge a new life-form? And in that case, what is its nature: by what name does it emerge?

How touching are those first examples. Often still joined by the head, or more often by the shoulders, in dumb stone they speak to us of our distant past as women, ever present in our today. How hard, how painful is the task of separating out, mother–daughter from one another, from that original cocoon which seemed to promise lifelong bliss. Of crawling out, like a larva from some dim totality to be pierced by a name which has yet to reveal its meaning. Gazing on these replicas, each different and yet the same, and finding our gaze returned from secretive, age-old sockets, we find ourselves confronted by a question of identity. For these earliest examples addressing us through the millennia move towards a culmination in that touching marble stele 'Demeter and Kore(?)'. That we are witnessing an electrifying psychological development, albeit cast in stone, we have, for sure, nothing but our inner heart-drum to guide us, as it misses a beat. Yet if we leave those earliest versions to contemplate the later work of the fifth century BC and ponder that question mark inserted after 'Kore', which is the Greek word for maiden, we recognize that we have found the answer we are looking for: that Kore is indeed the name by which she, this being, has emerged.

That in turn begs the question: what is the nature of her kind in its full significance? What powers has she assumed during her long dormancy? We experience them with apprehension, the thrill of some profound excitement of a great discovery, of a shock of recognition – of something we have always known.

Before we return to this key issue, let us refresh our memory by looking at the myth in outline and at the same time bear in mind the matter we left unresolved while we were 'on the couch': namely how and why the girl resolves her attachment to her mother. For the answer to this question, in its deepest religious meaning, lies buried in this myth, as in some excavated site to which so far no one has come with this single, burning question.

Demeter's daughter by Zeus, the maiden Persephone, who brightened her mother's days, was picking flowers in a field with her virginal friends when an astonishing narcissus caught her youthful eye. As she ran to pick the bloom, the earth opened at her feet. Hades, God of the Underworld, carried the maiden off. Disconsolate, in dark despair, the grieving mother wandered far and wide to seek her daughter and her joy. When the search was not fruitful she threatened to put an end to all and every growing thing, as it was in her power.

Faced with this catastrophe, Zeus was compelled to intervene. He sent his messenger to Hades to conclude the famous pact that Persephone divide her time between her husband and her mother. When mother and child were reunited Demeter's happiness was dimmed on hearing that her child had eaten certain pomegranate seeds which her husband offered her. Now her daughter would never belong to her as before. During the time they were together vegetation would thrive, to die back every year during their separation. Such is the outline of the myth as it has made a deep impact for almost three millennia.

Now let us turn to further details with which to fill in the story. They stem from the 'Homeric Hymn to Demeter' (Hall, N., 1980, p. 70) from the seventh century BC:

I begin to sing of rich-haired Demeter, awful goddess – of her and her trim-ankled daughter whom Hades rapt away, given to him by all-seeing Zeus the loud-thunderer.

Apart from Demeter, lady of the golden sword and glorious fruits, she was playing with the deep-bosomed daughters of Oceanus and gathering flowers over a soft meadow, roses and crocuses and beautiful violets, irises also and hyacinths and the narcissus, which Earth made to grow at the will of Zeus and to please the Host of Many [Hades], to be a snare for the bloomlike girl – a marvellous, radiant flower. It was a thing of awe whether for deathless gods or mortal men to see: from its root grew a hundred blooms and it smelled most sweetly, so that all wide heaven above and the whole earth and the sea's salt swell laughed for joy. And the girl was amazed and reached out with both hands to take the lovely toy; but the wide-pathed earth yawned there in the plain of Nyasa, and the Lord, Host of Many, with his immortal horses sprang out upon her – the Son of Cronos, He who has many names.

He bore her away lamenting, heard by Hecate in her cave, and also by her mother:

Bitter pain seized her heart, and she rent the covering upon her divine hair with her dear hands: her dark cloak she cast down from both her shoulders and sped, like the wild-bird, over the firm land and yielding sea, seeking her child. Then for nine days queenly Deo wandered over the earth with flaming torches in her hands, so grieved that she never tasted ambrosia and the sweet draught of nectar, nor sprinkled her body with water. (Hall, N., 1980, pp. 71–2, quoting Homer)

On the tenth day she met Hecate and together they went 'to Helios, the sun, "who is watchman of both gods and men", and inquired of him: what happened to Persephone? He asked queenly Demeter to cease her loud lamenting, thinking Hades no unfitting husband for her daughter.'

Again Demeter wandered on, disconsolate, for nine days, with only two stopping places. One was the Laughless Rock, the other the omphalos, that mythical connection to the Underworld, possibly the very spot where her child had disappeared. And still there was no news of her when she came to Eleusis. There she sat herself down beside the Maiden Well,

from which the women of the place were used to draw water . . . And she was like an ancient woman who is cut off from childbearing and the gifts of garland-loving Aphrodite, like the nurses of kings' children who deal justice, or like the housekeepers in their echoing halls. (Hall, N., 1980, pp. 71–2, quoting Homer)

There the four daughters of Celeus, son and ruler of Eleusis, saw her:

'*Old mother, whence and who are you of folk born long ago? Why are you gone away from the city and do not draw near the houses? For there in the shady halls are women of just such an age as you, and others younger; and they would welcome you both by word and by deed.*' (Hall, N., 1980, pp. 71–2, quoting Homer)

Demeter tells them a story of having been carried off by pirates 'over the sea's broad back', and abandoned at this spot. Would there by any chance, she asks, be work in the master's house? By reply she is invited in and employed as a nurse for their newborn baby brother.

Inside, Demeter

would not sit upon the bright couch, but stayed silent with lovely eyes cast down until careful Iambe placed a jointed stool for her and threw over it a silvery fleece . . . A long time she sat upon the stool without speaking because of her sorrow, never smiling, and tasting neither food nor drink. (Hall, N., 1980, p. 73, quoting Homer)

Offered red wine, she declined it but asked instead for a drink of meal, mixed with water and mint.

In charge of the infant boy, whose name is Demophoön, she places him in the fire by night to make him deathless, like the gods. His mother, catching her at this, puts an end to these methods in a tremendous rage. The Goddess then reveals herself and speaks very angrily:

'Witless are you mortals and dull to foresee your lot . . . For now in your heedlessness you have wrought folly past healing: for – be witness the oath of the gods, the relentless water of Styx – I would have made your dear son deathless and unageing all his days . . . but now he can in no way escape death and the fates.' (Hall, N., 1980, p. 73, quoting Homer)

This said, she stormed from the palace. To appease so great a wrath the people built her a temple, where she sat angrily and alone. It was from there that she threatened, after an interlude, to curse all living vegetation. In deep alarm, and only then, did Zeus himself intervene. From this version of Nor Hall's a crucial detail is omitted, which concerns the interlude just before the famous threat. Before the Goddess left the palace, Demeter taught the oldest son, whose name was Triptolemus, to harness oxen to the plough and sow the furrows for fair harvests. Furthermore she gave to him a winged chariot, drawn by dragons, so he might travel far and wide across the surface of the earth to teach her art to mortal man. Only when Zeus still shilly-shallied, and did not return her child regardless of repeated pleading, did she in the full fury of her maternal frustration threaten the dire famine unless her child was restored. And only then is Zeus the father finally drawn into the conflict, with his famous adjudication, openly for the first time.

Before, in obedience to the paternal decree, Persephone leaves her husband in the Underworld, he gives her the fateful seeds. As the pomegranate is cut the bright red juice is spilt; blood as the symbol that the Kore-Maiden has been killed, has undergone a transformation. The seeds themselves represent indissoluble union, or marriage between man and wife. He also promises his wife that here beside him, as his queen, she shall be a great power and mistress of her own domain and rule however she may wish. Reassured and gladdened by these words, Persephone then takes her leave to spend some time with her mother. The sources differ on just how the time is to be divided, nor does it seem to matter greatly since the time is here a symbol for two allegiances.

This is our material, then, from which to extract meaning relevant to our theme. For this purpose we must first explore the significance of the term Kore or Maiden, for we are bound to recognize, if we meditate on this, that daughter and Kore carry distinctive shades of meaning. Wherein lies this distinction?

Maiden goddesses are more typical of Greek religion than boy-gods or even, perhaps, divine youths. Divine maidens are in fact so typical of this religion that it cannot be called either a 'father religion' or a 'mother religion' or yet a combination of both. It is as though the Olympian order had thrust the Great Mother-Goddess of olden times into the background for the sole purpose of throwing the divine Korai into sharper relief. (Kerenyi, C., in Jung, C.G. and Kerenyi, C., 1949, p. 148)

Persephone's childhood friends, with her on that fateful day, were also classified as maidens. One of these was Athene who, as Pallas Athene, shared dominion with her father Zeus more closely than his spouse, Hera. Although adored as 'Mother Athene' in the Peloponessos and by the Athenians, she is surely an androgynous figure and in essence pure Kore. Indeed, 'the coins that bore her name were known as Korai in Athenian parlance' (Kerenyi, C., in Jung, C.G. and Kerenyi, C., 1949, p. 149).

This aura of maidenhood was seemingly related to intellectual and spiritual, to strictly non-material power, and free from sexual connotations. Whether it was Artemis, Athene or Persephone, this all three had in common. This virtue of the non-material shines in bright contrast to the earlier dark, telluric swamp where the Great Mother Goddess, as the primitive Great Round, maintained possession of her offspring – elementary, enfolding, determined never to let go.

In that negative aspect, destructive as it surely is of any separating out, she would later evolve into a Gorgon or Medusa: a terrifying female monster whom Perseus finally slew by decapitating her with the use of a sickle. Her head he significantly then presented to Athene, who wore its image engraved on the breastplate to her armour. Was it not for Athene that the hero had set out to conquer the appalling monster? Must every Kore not stand in relentless opposition to this entangling aspect of the mother who would wind her coils about her and never let her go? And indeed, it was Athene who, when the Medusa defiles her temple with her lecherous seductions, changed the hair of the offender into coiling snakes and serpents, as a just punishment for her vile habits of the swamp. We must remember that Demeter, in her old-age, grieving aspect and disguised in her dark cloak, when she is seeking her daughter, wears the Medusa's mantle to be described as 'The Black One', or Demeter Erynis: a paranoid, destructive force. These deep and mythical meanings are confirmed in Corfu, where in the temple to Artemis the killing of the Medusa is commemorated in stone on the pediment. Here the classical figure of Persephone, the Maiden, rises beautiful and pure from the scene of the carnage, while stylistic features which Perseus and Hades hold in common suggest that the latter had a share in the assassination, that he might win and keep his wife.

This still leaves the question open how in her innerness the Kore differs from a daughter. Let us postulate that a daughter has her being as a Kore during certain phases of the mother–daughter saga. True, in Greek mythology Athene symbolized a Kore who remained one all her life – to all appearances, at least. But she had never had a mother, seeing that she had sprung straight from her father, Zeus. Artemis, the other maiden, had asked her father, as a child, to be given bow and arrow in the place of finery, and was chaste all her life. Neither of these two examples had seemingly identified, like Persephone, with a mother. Both remained under the spell of an all-powerful, highly charismatic father, as a *'puella eterna'*, in Jung's terminology. They constitute a category which need not concern us further for our present purposes. Of the three much-sung maidens only Persephone is briefly poised in that role *vis-à-vis* her famous mother, as we now return to her in the Nyasan Fields on the brink of succumbing to abduction and rape.

This tremendous event, at the opening of the myth, was possible only because the Maiden had strayed some distance from her watchful mother. It suggests that she displayed signs of a mind which was her own, pointing to a dissolution of the symbiotic bonds, at least on the daughter's side, even if Zeus, her father, clearly had a hand in things. True, it might be claimed that the scent of the narcissus had stupefied her senses, or that to stray so small a distance does not imply autonomy or a mind of her own. But if we take the total myth in its many-petalled meaning it would seem that she was drawn into the 'paternal circuit', from the maternal one, not nearly as unwillingly as a more conventional and superficial reading would have us believe.

True enough, there was terror. Is marriage not for every girl initially felt as a rape, fraught with deep, archaic fears at this unknown penetration, where she was intact before, even if in part denied? But this in no way negates the deeply desired aspect.

We look and see Persephone at that moment *briefly poised* in her unfolding as a maiden and celebrate the elusive form, before its loveliness is killed, or undergoes transformation.

The Kore is a creature destined to a flower-like existence which cannot be better described than by one of the poets mentioned:

> *. . . a little torrent of life*
> *leaps up to the summit of the stem, gleams, turns*
> *over round the bend*
> *of the parabola of curved flight,*
> *sinks, and is gone, like a comet curving into the invisible.*
> (D.H. Lawrence, quoted by Kerenyi, C., in Jung, C.G.
> and Kerenyi, C., 1949, p. 151)

The Kore, then, represents a flowering instant of ideal beauty. She lingers for an inkling moment on the brink where becoming meets with dissolution, suspended between what went before, her seclusion as a daughter, and that other beckoning, where touched by death she stumbles on her true fulfilment and dominion. Only then will she be worshipped, with the solemn, oval face of countless statuettes: Goddess of the Underworld, Persephone as Queen, with the sign of wife and motherhood in the ascendant, her making in her mother's arms flowing back into the past: 'Here, then, is our Persephone: a creature standing UNSUBDUED on a pinnacle of life and there meeting its fate – a fate that means death in fulfilment and dominion in death' (Kerenyi, C., in Jung, C.G. and Kerenyi, C., 1949, p. 152).

How, we can now ask ourselves, does the Kore in her inmost meaning differ from the earlier daughter? What is this essence of a being that hangs suspended, unsubdued, poised over an age-old abyss? The bonds and bindings of a previous, abject dependency, tinged with fearful submission, rocked by ambivalence, have slowly been dissolved and severed. Some inner anchor has been lifted, almost imperceptibly. Hidden engines that were idling through the years of preparation are firing, as a growing swell in the harbour testifies. The vessel shudders on the slipway, waiting only to be named before she launches her making into the open sea. The state of mind is readiness for an imminent departure that has already taken place, that no mother and no daughter, as defined until this hour, has the power to call off. The harbour will remain the harbour. Its lights and the harbour wall will remain a well-loved port of call. But that point on the horizon where the sky rests on the sea is the setting on the compass, from now on, irreversibly. Such are the symbols for a phase which extends from the menarche to 'a moment of rape' – by its nature, brief indeed: a phase which, we must remember, fails in countless instances, where instead of a flower opening into fragrant growth, a blind bud atrophies. For where the symbiotic fusion fails to be untied, where the Gorgon Medusa aspect of the 'Terrible Mother' achieves its object of subjecting and possessive holding on, by the 'virtuous' rationale of a thousand guilty pretexts issued by God or man, there is no maiden and no marriage in the true and deepest sense: for this the Medusa must be conquered, or better, conquers herself, as does Demeter in the myth after painful tribulations.

Certainly the Kore-phase brings the Medusa out to some extent in every mother, force against counter-force, as the maiden is seized by invisible currents drawing her away to her separate destiny: 'Why, why, why! Weh, Of Weh! I'se so silly to be flowing but I canna stay!' (Spoken by the daughter Nuvoletta to her mother Livia Plurabelle, in *Finnegans Wake*; see Hall, N., 1980, p. 84). What a tearing and rending in this separating out, what awesome convulsions in the psyche of the mother and the daughter equally. To label these rites of passage 'teenage problems' at the one end and the 'change of life' at the other is no more than our attempt to subdue such upheaval with the magic of a word, to shrug off our awareness that the very life-foundations of both participants are quaking during this momentous phase. How often each may blame the other for the painful unrest and, blind to mutual benefits of new freedom and release for further creativity, see only abandonment and desolate rejection: the pangs of redundancy and, on the other hand, a being thrown to the wolves, in the wild woods of reality, far from the protection of the warm maternal circuit, which seemed a prison at the time. At this mother–daughter moment, full of promise of new freedom each feels condemned and persecuted by the prospects of change.

What happened to Persephone, when the earth had swallowed her? When she had been carried off by Hades to the Underworld, known as the place of shadows, where the former living lost all but the faintest semblance of their individual features? What transformation lay in store for this much-guarded daughter, apple of her mother's eye, whose playground was wont to be the local, sweet and warming earth, to the lilting of the sea-salt swell, in the golden light of the sun and her mother's watchful gaze? There her days had been spent among familiar girlhood friends who assuredly shared every doubt and single fear, each secret of their girlhood years.

If her new home was to be a mere realm of shadows now, she too was formless for a while, cast from her glowing former self into a condition or a state of shadowy not-being for a fateful interlude. This concept of not-being, dreaded in Antiquity, may be a key to our approach to this baffling Underworld so familiar to the Greeks.

What is meant by this not-being is 'not, of course, PURE not-being, rather a sort of not-being from which the living shrink as from something with a NEGATIVE sign: a monstrosity that has usurped the place of the unimaginably beautiful . . .' (Jung, C.G., in Jung, C.G. and Kerenyi, C., 1949, p. 177). Does this then perhaps refer to a phenomenon which we would mistakenly label as a 'nervous breakdown', or state of 'depersonalization'? A kind of absence we perceive and may readily resent in what was an unquestioned presence, now suddenly revealed as an outrageous changeling, to our horror, grief and loss. Is it our hostility, our bewildered impatience that drives this state over the brink and saddles it with the crude, crass labels of our hand-to-mouth psychiatry? Is its true nature not instead a chaotic interlude, programmed for resolution; a deep and secret response to a prophecy of growth, a call to selfhood as the crown of life, always provided we can trust some inherent benevolence? Can we, today, gain insight into these states of psychic shock, which punctuate human life with its major transformations, that the female of the species is fated to undergo? What is more she has to bear the forces of the impact doubly, since the male, while he conforms to the bogus 'tough' image, to which we will be returning in the final chapters, projects *his* vulnerability, the fragile aspects of *his* nature, into the woman at his side, to add that burden to her own. This she can ill afford, who is already subjected by the very nature of her primal creativity to a series of shocks, of having to alternate through all the phases of her life between being and not-being; who is plunged time and again back into that Underworld to be engulfed by inner oceans, as each new tide comes running in, summoned by the ancient laws of her own biology, under the sign of the moon.

From the more dire aspects of this destiny the daughter is protected within the maternal circuit, though often impatient with certain jangling signs and signals of her mother's instability, as prey to this nemesis of bearing, giving birth and tending only to be sundered from her creation once again, throughout the summit-years of life.

A virgin is deemed innocent, and innocent means not yet hurt.

But here, as in the hour of birth, we find a hurt that afflicts both the maiden and her mother simultaneously. The Kore has been abducted. The red juice has been spilt; the seeds of the pomegranate eaten: an indissoluble union has been forged and finalized, but below the ground, in secret. The very being of the maiden has been undercut into shadowy not-being, to which we will return later, and something new is taking shape in the quiet, dark seclusion of the so-called Underworld. The former maiden will henceforth have divided loyalties. Her time will be divided up, and a portion will belong to a stranger, now her husband, as decreed by father Zeus. In the allegory of the Eleusinian Mysteries the plough has carved an open furrow, the seed been buried in the dark, or the corn dolly laid to rest in the omphalos. But meanwhile what of Demeter, the mother left all alone?

Unutterably empty now were the familiar four walls. Exuberant young life had flown in search of new nesting grounds in accordance with that Law of Life of successive generations, as opposed to the immortality claimed by brash Olympian gods whose time was drawing to an end. It is against this stormy background, in the sphere of that religion, that the myth elaborates its deepest conflict and meaning. For Demeter is caught up in several levels of the trauma. First, she knows the godlike wish, fuelled by omnipotence, to remain outside the stream of time and be creative for ever; but she also shares the human one to retain possession of her daughter to brighten her darker days and comfort her in her old age. Overwhelmed by both, she suffers a near disintegration which becomes manifest as a virtual extinction of her former will to live, as she falls ever deeper into destructive phantasies, dreadful anger and depression.

'Like the wild-bird' she sped, 'over the firm land and yielding sea, seeking her child' (Hall, N., 1980, p. 70). She does not eat, or drink, or wash. Bereft and grieving she wanders, alone and mindless, for nine days. Once, we are told, she comes to rest at an omphalos: that place of mythical connection between the Underworld and ours – a place or moment which affords an opportunity for insight, we could intuit today. She does not try to gain admission, nor, would it seem, does she expect to find her daughter at this stage. Psychologically, it is too soon. She, the mother, also has to undergo some transformation before the two can be reunited in any deep, creative sense that promises true benefit; which, if it fails to be accomplished, can lead only to protracted harm and the unresolved suffering of a chronic paranoia.

In the Eleusinian Mysteries when the initiates had fasted for, as we are told, nine days, and purified themselves in the sea, preparing to walk in procession to the temple where Persephone would appear to the crash of gongs and thunder, a great fire was seen, not only in the actual precincts but even in Athens, many miles away. In what light would we regard this purification by water, as by fire in the myth?

Utterly weary and depressed, the Goddess arrives at Eleusis. She sits

near the wayside by the Maiden Well, from which the women of the place were used to draw water . . . and she was like an ancient woman who is cut off from childbearing and the gifts of garland-loving Aphrodite, like the nurses of kings' children who deal justice, or like the housekeepers in their echoing halls. (Hall, N., 1980, p. 71)

Like that of an old, redundant woman is her experience of herself, whose life has slipped into the past, her former glory past recall.

In other words, the mother feels that she has come to the end of her creative life-resources, instead of seeing that she is actually at a crossroads. Blinded by omnipotence which traps her in the delusion of her immortality, she is really in a fearful rage, experienced as a depression as long as it is denied.

With these conflicts at their height she sits by the village well where mortal women come to draw the water of life from day to day: that water which purifies as a symbol of acceptance of our reality; the sanity which can acknowledge human mortality and hence the phases of our life. Viewed in such a light, this frame of the myth represents Demeter's earliest attempts to come to terms with her lot as an ordinary woman; for is it not on this foundation that our claims to achievement have finally to rest, lest we are all up in the air with the ever-present threat of madness: a flight from reality into grandiosity fuelled by omnipotence; the stuff of manic-depressive illness?

Deep in our best of hearts, we know that Aphrodite's garlands must, down the passing years, belong to younger women in the wings. But once this is recognized, the 'echoing halls' are at first perceived with a hollow sense of shock, not as a new lease or span but as the dreaded terminus of all true creative life. A moment of profound depression, which we today call menopausal, will darken a woman's life as long as she equates creativity with fertility, rather than envisaging her new spheres of influence. For these may well turn out to be quite as rich and rewarding provided that limits are accepted, and that which *is* is not attacked if it is not everything. 'Halls' imply ample space, meaning, of course, inner space. They 'echo' only where we doubt that ample inner resources are available to fill the void, and therefore fall into despair.

Meanwhile the daughters of King Celeus invite her to their father's house. 'Four were they and like goddesses in the flower of their girlhood' (Hall, N., 1980, p. 71, quoting Homer). Possibly to her surprise, these maidens are warm and friendly. In other words, for all her rage, all her destructive fury directed against her Persephone for having turned into a Kore and then gone off with a man, from which she fears retaliation, reality-testing now resumes and lessens her paranoia. A process of introjecting has been set going once again. The inner or unconscious darkness has located an 'omphalos' to the outer, conscious world. Transformation can commence, for now its ground has been prepared.

Furthermore, this recognition, this new sense of reality, can be observed in action now. For we are told that offered a place on the 'couch', a symbol in Antiquity for a marriage bed, she declines:

She would not sit upon the bright couch, but stayed silent with lovely eyes cast down until careful Iambe placed a jointed seat for her and threw over it a silvery fleece . . . A long time she sat upon the stool. (Hall, N., 1980, p. 73)

In this detail we can see the confirmation of a new and healthier attitude of mind, for the reference to her 'lovely eyes' suggests that she is looking inwards, to psychic reality, and thereby coming to terms with yielding her own place 'on the couch' to that younger generation which includes Persephone. They will now have the garlands, but are clearly none the less still concerned for her comfort, as Iambe's action shows. When red wine is offered her, she declines a beverage which might again go to her head, accepting in its place a drink of meal and soft mint, known to us as barley water, which initiates would later drink in the Eleusinian Mysteries.

Set on this course of improvement, to all appearances at least, Demeter is now engaged as nurse to the queen's baby son, by name of

Demophoön. But soon fresh troubles are in store. For finding herself, once again, with a baby in her care, when in reality she is past the age of childbearing, causes the old omnipotence to flare up once more into another phase of mania. As a nurse she is no one of great significance in her own book of words. She fears she will be overlooked, that her days as a great star and shining power have been lost, and, true to manic-depressive illness, denying depression and helplessness with omnipotence and control, she gets up to her old tricks again. This baby she will make immortal, deathless, even like the gods. Why should she, the mighty Goddess, be content with doing less? Accordingly Demeter lays the infant in the fire by night until he glows like a torch. But the horrified mother witnesses this scene by chance and puts an end to such methods. She wants an ordinary child. Never mind all this glory, this quest for immortality. The Goddess is furious. Her escape into omnipotence and consequent manic triumph have been blocked yet again. 'Witless are you mortals and dull to foresee your lot . . . be witness the oath of the gods, the relentless waters of Styx – I would have made your dear son deathless and unageing . . .' (Hall, N., p. 73, quoting Homer).

Demeter, having lost her Kore into whom she had projected her own creativity, as a mother often will, now past the age of childbearing, the glories of fertility, and facing old age and death, is still determined to uphold the myth of immortality by hook or by crook. She is so preoccupied with retrieving her former powers that she seems to have forgotten – in other words, to have denied – the loss of her missing child, and laid that urgent search aside.

This conflict was raging, as we should remind ourselves, at a moment when the Greeks were beginning to question the omnipotence of their gods. They were meeting with defeats on several battlefields and there was pestilence. Olympus was failing them. It is against this very background that Persephone's mother has to fight depression, to struggle for sanity, for good and loving solutions, even while destructive feelings are still in the ascendant. In other words, to use fire not for magic purposes but as a means for transformation, where the object is herself.

Depression was something new on the heights of Olympus. It had been a place for acting out, for satisfying all desires, gratifying every lust with infantile omnipotence, regardless of means or consequences. Concern was not in evidence. What ruled supreme on those heights were the earliest defences which, as we have seen, belong to the most primitive phases of development in the earliest months of life, which lead to madness and to death while they remain unmodified. Depression follows from the fear that there are no more loving feelings, that aggression may have damaged – even possibly destroyed – the very source of life and goodness.

When Persephone, the Kore, disappeared 'under ground', Demeter suffered more than grief, although grief was one component of very complicated feelings: she went into a fearful rage. Her daughter who belonged to her – a possessive Gorgon-Medusa – had dared to queer her pitch and have a mind of her own. The nice, obedient little daughter, of whom she was so proud for her flower-like beauty, had moved towards separation, the precincts of a separate life: had refused to be subdued and to stay at home with mother.

That she had not been carried off entirely against her will, as we, who like to see things black or white, are tempted to believe, is clear from the Homeric Hymn. For when she is parting from her husband to spend more time with her mother, back home, in her previous world, Hades encourages his wife:

'Go now, Persephone, to your dark-robed mother, go and feel kindly in your heart towards me: . . . and while you are here, you shall rule over all that lives and moves and shall have the greatest rights among the deathless gods'
. . . When he said this, wise Persephone was filled with joy and hastily sprang up for gladness. (Hall, N., p. 74, quoting Homer)

For her this act of separation had been accomplished with the spur of the hostility with which a daughter first turns from her mother to her father, filled with countless grievances; feelings that are reactivated with this second, later break, which in consequence is charged with painful ambiguity and terror of retaliation.

Do those lines not make it clear that Persephone has no desire to hand her new-won status in, to put the clock back to become the original daughter once again: sweet, compliant and submissive?

Certainly Hades was determined before he parted from his wife, who was to spend some time at home, that he was going to undercut those old, symbiotic bonds. The seeds of the pomegranate, once they were eaten, would ensure that their marriage was indissoluble, that the Gorgon mother's power would be rendered null and void. And his young wife was grateful.

If Persephone was still uncertain and anxious as to what the future held concerning her own status, her sense of identity at the deepest psychic level, at least she felt that her place as her husband's wife promised a new solution now. Everything else was still uncertain. What she did anticipate, partly by projection, was her mother's fearful rage: that knowing her Demeter would probably stop at nothing to seduce or rape her back to that earlier *status quo* she had so narrowly escaped, lately, with paternal help.

Here we can appreciate the myth's full ambivalence. The matriarchal world-order in which it has its roots was at the time hovering on the brink of dissolution into newer spheres of patriarchal influence with full father right. At a first reading we may well incline to the superficial view that the rape of the Kore, together with her mother's loss, was unrelieved tragedy. Mother should have her daughter back, at home with her, where she belongs. This feeling only underwrites how powerfully a part of us remains rooted in the past that each travelled through in infancy, where there was no room for father in that dyadic embrace: where the Elementary Feminine Character, holding and not letting go, maintained its unchallenged rule.

But as in a symphony a chord foreshadows the next movement, the opposite view is introduced with Helios's – the Sun's – remark – the masculine principle rising into ascendancy – that Hades is no unfitting husband for young Persephone, so what is all the fuss about? She wants a husband, does she not? is what he says, in effect, to the lamenting mother.

It is at this point in the myth that Demeter, fearing this masculine assertion, seeks the help of Hecate, cave-dwelling Goddess of the Moon, of the telluric principle, of the Elementary Feminine Character and mother–daughter symbiosis. As part of the tripartite goddess, Hecate clearly represents one aspect of Demeter, which is a regressive one harking back in time, back through the millennia, to that confusion of boundaries where only fusion exists, which we shall be looking at when we come to psychosis. A relationship which thrives in the telluric swamp, as in certain families which have been well documented and described in our own day (Laing, R.D. and Esterson, A., 1970).

Certainly, for Persephone this very first visit home must have seemed a daunting prospect, for all her wish to see her mother. Very probably she sensed that Demeter was depressed. Her deepest intuitions knew that she had become the object of her mother's envious attacks, for she was now the source of life, the very source of procreation against which her mother pitted, with virtual insanity, her own manic phantasies of omnipotent immortality.

Persephone anticipated a familiar recurrence from her earliest experience, a thread which ran all through her girlhood: that the 'good' mother, who had smiled so graciously on the obedient little girl, would on being thwarted turn all at once into a witch, a witch who emerged each time the child showed a mind of her own and refused to be subdued.

Furthermore, the young wife sensed that her mother's own marriage, to the womanizing Zeus, had not proved a happy one – this, Persephone might guess, would add fuel to those flames. True, in a sane interlude she had accepted the jointed stool. But as we know today, psychodynamic change does not happen overnight. To accept reality, the reality of our passing to make room for the young, rarely proves an easy lesson. 'Rage, rage against the dying of the light', the poet Dylan Thomas implores his father. But for womankind this death is died many times over, since her narcissism, her deepest feelings of esteem, may be so fatefully bound to drawing admiring glances; in other words, bound to her looks and her procreative function, which she has to yield long before the male will be stopped from vaunting his.

At this moment we are stuck, psychologically speaking. The daughter hesitates, fearful of this visit home with all these deeper implications. The mother is depressed and raging. As she pauses at the omphalos, the umbilical connection, the point at which the earth opened and swallowed up her child, prospects of communication still appear remote to her. For there is no going forward in such a state of mind of wild, unreasoning aggression: the death instinct turned loose, defused from the love of life.

With such dark feelings to the fore in an unstable mother, a married daughter's inclinations are naturally to stay away, fearing harm for herself and her procreativity – the child she may be carrying or has already borne. At such a moment she will turn for protection to her husband, as to a father formerly, if that relationship was true – or true enough to tide her over until a mother came to terms with the fact that her daughter has a separate destiny.

In the myth, how does Demeter suffer a change of heart? How does she, after bitter struggle, resolve her murderous rage and fury – her wish in phantasy to attack her daughter's fertility by destroying everything that grows in the precious fields? We are shown and told quite clearly as the story unfolds, if only we can pay attention to details which we tend to skip. But in psychotherapy we cannot skip any detail; we may not lose a single word, least of all the whispered one. We hear that, after the rumpus concerning Demophoön, Demeter stayed on for a while in the palace of King Celeus. True, she was waiting while they were building her a temple, but that was hardly the sole purpose; we can be sure of that. So for what reason did she linger, once she was fired as a nurse?

It was to teach the eldest son, Triptolemus, the arts which she had until that moment kept entirely for herself: to harness oxen to the plough and sow the waiting soil with grain from which fair harvests might spring. Neither does she stop at that, with her sudden change of heart, but gives her pupil a winged chariot with which to travel the wide world so he might spread the benefit of these agricultural skills far and wide among mankind (Larousse, 1959, p. 175).

Her total stay at Eleusis, to judge by these considerations, may well have been more prolonged than is generally acknowledged by the pace of the myth. If we pause to consider this extended sequence of events, it would seem that there was some delay after teaching mortal man, before that show of famous rage which eventually led to Zeus, her husband's, intervention. It seems as though she was still waiting, hoping that her transformation, this loving act of reparation, was going to be acknowledged: that she would now be rewarded by the return of her lost child. She may have felt so sure of this that she was prepared to wait while she was saying, in effect, 'Look, I have abdicated much of my omnipotence and mastered my destructive feelings. I have even handed over, so that you might see the proof, my precious know-how to these mortals and abrogated divine right. I have wrestled with myself to show love for mankind, even for the generations – and still my daughter stays away. What more am I supposed to do, lonely and superfluous, at the end of my tether?'

In the National Museum of Athens can be seen a bas-relief of Demeter and Persephone, standing face to face with Triptolemus between them. He is addressing the younger woman, towards whom he is turned, while the mother stands and listens as if waiting for the outcome. It is as though Demeter's pupil is persuading Persephone of her mother's change of heart, and that it is truly safe to return and to hope for a reconciliation, for a new relationship in which she need have no fear for her personal safety or that of her progeny.

Still the young wife hesitates in the Underworld, a realm which as we suggested represents a place of refuge for those who have lost the sense of their identity during times of transformation. Is this Underworld perhaps also allegorical for darker forces and tensions: an abyss of paranoia? It was located, as we know, at the ends of the earth, while the earth was deemed flat. Is that not where one would flee who feels persecuted by some great destructive force?

What confronts Persephone is that inner terror where a daughter lives in dread of maternal retaliation for attacks which she has made on her mother's inside babies in infantile phantasies: a common nightmare figure of a crazed woman with burning eyes. This can apply, as we know, with particular strength to a girl's first pregnancy. How many young women are compelled into precocious motherhood to test out these very fears as the only living proof that they are, in fact, not damaged, as they dread in phantasy?

How about Persephone? The Eleusinian Mysteries were celebrated in the third part of the moon-cycle, meaning the phase of the crone and of low expectations. They were also concerned with a return from the dead through the act of giving birth. Before, to the crash of thunder, the Queen of the Underworld appears, evoked by the hierophant, a mysterious ritual, focused on certain baffling objects, forms the centre of attention, on whose deeper meaning we can only speculate.

During the ceremony the initiates confessed: 'I have fasted; I have drunk the mixed drink: I have taken out of the cista, worked with it, and then laid it in the basket and out of the basket into the cista' (Kerenyi, C., in Jung, C.G. and Kerenyi, C., 1949, p. 191). Would the mystery clarify if this curious sentence is regarded as a dialogue, between Demeter and her daughter? Can the Eleusinian Mysteries be viewed as the total conflict, as seen by each participant? At first the initiates identify with Demeter. They fast and wander in her search, in her distraught state of mind, which in the agricultural cycle is symbolized by midwinter. They then purify themselves with water and proceed to the temple. There Demeter awaits them, seated on the Laughless Rock – the Agelastus petra – where she sat and grieved when her daughter disappeared. Beside her is a soft, empty seat which is held in readiness, but still unoccupied. In the background, in the shadows, barely seen, is the Kore, dressed in dark colours: a shadowy, troubled state of mind. A youth from a noble family, presumably Triptolemus, is waiting to participate, while the curious ritual with the cista is enacted.

This scenario constitutes the first part of the Mysteries and it was only to this part that a new initiate was granted admission. After that he had to pass a year in uncertainty regarding the final outcome. What did this, in fact, reveal?

Before we return to that, we have to ask ourselves the meaning of the second part of the sentence. There is certainly no easy answer. Enquiries of scholars and museums as to what the cista, or chest-like object, might symbolize drew a consistent blank. Clay figures of the Goddess with this object on her head were discovered throughout the later Greek colonies, frequently in tombs. Robert Graves (Graves, R., 1981, p. 326), however, seems to be in no uncertainty. According to him, the initiate says: 'I have fitted what was in the drum to what was in the liknos.' He then continues to explain:

We know what was in the liknos – a phallus – and on the analogy of the buskins ceremonially presented to the sacred king at his marriage, it may be concluded that the drum contained a buskin into which the phallus was inserted by the initiate as a symbol of coition.

The idea of the buskin Graves relates to the swaggering gait of sacred kings which implies a deliberate flaunting of sexual charms. But, he then explains, the king of the sacred marriage was originally killed after its consummation, but later only lamed by having his hip dislocated, so that he wears a buskin over his bull's foot. (A dislocated hip prevents the heel of the foot being placed on the ground.)

In other words, while Demeter was searching for her daughter, Persephone was consummating her marriage to Hades, as she now confirms to her mother. It has been thought by sources that the Eleusinian Mysteries were sometimes an occasion for sexual excesses in which the hierophant actively participated.

So what, in fact, was the outcome of the total Mysteries? What was their wider meaning? Cicero, after participating, said that he could now live in hope. In Athens they saw mighty flames. But to reveal the secret was punishable by death.

If the first part symbolized the hurt of mother and daughter, as symbiotic bonds are broken and the daughter's body is pierced by the allusion to a sacred marriage, the second part is of the essence of a holy revelation. To the crash of a great gong, representing Zeus's thunder, the Underworld – from whose domain none is known to have escaped, for even Orpheus failed to rescue Eurydice – grants its queen a safe return. Those who are assembled can now clearly see Persephone. Her appearance coincides with a mightly conflagration, with the presiding hierophant seated close to the fire, underneath a special roof, to shelter him from the flames: the fire of transformation. Out of the heat, smoke and thunder his high, chanting voice is heard: 'The Goddess has borne a holy boy: Brimos has sprung from Brimos', meaning a strong one to the strong one (Kerenyi, C., 1962, p. 99).

Birth in the flames: in the heart of the fire, in the transforming blaze!

At this moment the hierophant held up a single blade of corn to link these mightiest events to the agricultural cycle, which is now in human hands, as Triptolemus confirms by his very presence. Here was a re-birth from that dark domain and therefore hope of life eternal. Not Olympian immortality, reserved for the treacherous gods, but continuity of life born from the flame of suffering, from transformation, which means growth if love can win over hate, sanity over omnipotence.

What of the throne which stood prepared beside the Laughless Rock, to which the scholarly sources tend to make no further reference? Would we be wrong to believe that, at the ceremony's end, mother, daughter and child occupied this seat together? For when the Kore becomes a wife and bears a child of her own, and mother and daughter can emerge from their respective shadows – from their deep anxieties regarding their present status – do they not become mother and daughter once again? Are they now not empowered to embark, as a team, on the iconic purpose of preserving the next generation – in other words, the Holy Child?

Go to the Palazzo Bellomo; admire the memorials of Sicilian art since the Middle Ages. See that fifteenth-century Madonna with the son on her arm . . . ask that gentle priest what these symbols mean . . . and you recall the Lokrian Goddess with her child; . . . and Persephone with the babe in her arms, or again with Eros and holding apple and dove. And you think your own thoughts. (Zuntz, G., 1971, p. 178)

What a distance we have travelled from the Double Goddess to that marble stele of 'Demeter and Kore'. Neumann maintains that

where the two appear together one cannot make out at first which is the mother and which is the daughter – it is only their attributes that make the distinction possible – the maiden by the flowers she bears . . . the mature goddess by the fruit. (Neumann, E., 1974, p. 307)

The 'fruit' at times looks strangely phallic and the flower rather like a mushroom, perhaps the toadstool which was eaten at the Eleusinian Mysteries, where it induced transcendental visions (Graves, R., 1981, p. 334)? But this is not perhaps the place to entertain such speculations. What matters is this unity of Demeter and Kore as the central content of the Eleusinian Mysteries. The finding again of Kore by a reconciled Demeter, after both have been transformed. The essential reunion of mother and daughter: immortality of mortals while the generations thrive.

Here we need to ask again that central, unanswered question: why does the girl leave her mother? The most obvious reply within the present context is – so as to have a child which her mother cannot give her. But Lacan would also say: to enter the Law of the Father. Certainly Zeus had a hand in producing the narcissus. Just how irresistible the father's intervention is surely stands in this description of the fatal flower:

From its root grew a hundred blooms and it smelled most sweetly, so that all wide heavens above and the whole earth and the sea's salt swell laughed for joy. And the girl was amazed and reached out with both hands to take the lovely toy; but the wide-pathed earth yawned there in the plain of Nyasa, and the Lord, Host of Many, with his immortal horses sprang out upon her . . . (Hall, N., 1980, p. 70)

Once the two-headed goddess permits a separation into mother and Kore, the latter can be lured into the masculine orbit; not only sexually, not only for fecundation of earth by the sea's salt swell, but for a third principle: that of the wide heaven to make itself known and felt as her additional domain.

Every rape or male incursion is, in a sense, annulled by the finding again of the daughter by her mother, by 'the restoration after marriage of the matriarchal unity' (Neumann, E., 1974, p. 308) of the numinous dyad, to be threatened again by the next act of rape. A constant breaking and remaking of that relationship, adding greatly to the conflicts in every woman's life, every mother–daughter alliance.

Here we shall leave the three, mother, daughter and child, together on a single throne, as Leonardo would later immortalize that very theme: the Virgin with her mother, Anne, together with the holy child. We will leave this happy ending to focus on a darker outcome, still within the Ancient World. For before the God of Love, or rather his interpreters, doused murderous instincts with heavenly ideologies, this theme of sombre matricide throws an awesome clarity on modern case-histories, on our deeper human conflicts. Not until our recent era would testimonies of such depth begin to surface once again, many from the pens of women, to find fruition in the work of Freud.

5 WHO MOURNS CLYTAEMNESTRA?

Friends, women's love is for their lovers, not their children.
(EURIPIDES)

ELECTRA, of the House of Atreus, was an unhappy little girl. The poet's lines convey the doom of being a redundant child of a narcissistic mother, drunk on self-glorification and out to satisfy each spurious whim. As she grew older she became a menace, as such children often will.

When her mother killed her father she must have been an adolescent. We know that the great Agamemnon left his daughter for the war when her brother, Orestes, was a toddler, and stayed away for ten long years during which her mother took a lover. But the girl's grievances have an earlier beginning. Despite the pace of the events the three dramatists Aeschylus, Sophocles and Euripides, who between them provide us with three versions of this case-history, do not overlook the fact that her mother Clytaemnestra, for all her royal protestations, simply was not good enough, furthermore, that according to the Laws of Mother Right, of Demetrian concern, she deprived her daughter of her rightful inheritance, handing it over to her lover. But they also look deeper into that enigmatic cauldron we now associate with Freud.

We are told by the nurse, in the Aeschylus version, how little time Clytaemnestra, in truth, devoted to her infants; and it is this, as we shall see, that stirs Electra's deepest hatred when in those last, decisive moments she lashes her wavering brother into the act of matricide. It was the fury and despair of early infantile frustration, compounded by subsequent deprivation of a thwarted little girl, that finally drove the sword into the maternal breast.

— 73 —

When Agamemnon sailed for Troy to avenge the abduction of the much-sung, prized and lovely Helen, north winds kept the fleet at Aulis, putting Greek morale at risk, as the royal commander feared. This curse was attributed to the wrath of Artemis, protectress of all newborn life, one of whose sacred deer the king had killed in the hunt, prone as he was to acts of hubris by his flawed genealogy.

Under subterfuge of marriage he lured his daughter, Iphigenia, from home and her mother's side, to sacrifice her so the gods might relent and speed his sails. While he dallies at the wars, as these drag on for a decade, he takes Cassandra for his mistress, while Clytaemnestra settles down with her husband's enemy, Aegisthus, for her lover. Upon the king's triumphant homing from the Trojan war, with his mistress Cassandra, ostensibly to seek revenge for the killing of her daughter Clytaemnestra murders them with the help of her lover. Although she constantly claims law and justice on her side, for her younger daughter's death and her husband's adultery, her endless self-justification does not ring true in the event.

Years go by beyond the murder of King Agamemnon. As the saga unfolds it grows increasingly clear that Electra harbours hate and grievances against her mother. Although these appear to focus on the latter's murder of her father and loss of her inheritance, we recognize that they are rooted in her early infancy. We come to feel beyond all doubt that this forms the crucial issue of the dramatic theme.

While she thirsts for revenge her prayers are, in due course, answered. Orestes returns in disguise. He has, we hear, Apollo's blessing to revenge their father's death and kill the usurper to the throne. None the less, mother-killing, which was not on his agenda, poses daemonic conflicts once Aegisthus is slain as the god himself demanded. And it is at this point that the mother–daughter conflict seizes the story's reins and wrests them from the simpler hands of Olympian crime and punishment, as personality bursts through the classical design of fate. For even as we settle down as audience to some period piece, the timelessness of the unconscious reveals contemporary themes, preoccupations which we share with the dramatists of Argos.

The tale is set against a time when Mother versus Father Right was still hanging in the balance. The queen, to plead her innocence, staunchly upholds the former, when it suits her purposes, as does that brooding minx Electra when she whips up sympathy for her lost inheritance to build her case against her mother on more acceptable grounds than her infantile neurosis. The dramatists are not deceived.

Orestes, bolstered by Apollo, represents Father Right, which is concerned with revenging the usurper of the throne. The fact that the queen insists that her royal husband flouted all the Laws of Mother Right cuts no ice with her son. This Electra recognizes. In her state of regression she is desperately aware that to win her brother over to become her instrument she must open up his wounds inflicted on the common ground of infantile grievances. None the less, the tragic queen wields a powerful case in the light of the old Law and she argues it with passion to her final breath: 'When I married your father, I did not expect to die, or see my children killed' (Euripides, p. 140). This becomes her final cry before the thrust of the sword, which will silence her for ever, penetrates that flaunting breast. It rings for ever in our ears, since that ancient law still lives on in every woman's heart: that she has a right to find a protector in her husband, just as her father once shielded her as a daughter. In accordance with this lien Agamemnon's queen had expected conjugal right to confer on her a husband to protect her interests, father her children and stay at home to safeguard his progeny. Who else could fulfil this role, she pleads with poignancy. It is not as if this war she argues, poses moral issues; rather, it was fought over the 'much-manned' Helen, a hetaera still at heart. Why could Menelaus not 'handle his randy wife' himself, Clytaemnestra utters with feelings of profound contempt of the righteous matriarch as she compiles her case, awaiting the king's return once the beacon has been lit to announce the fall of Troy.

Indeed, lending her our sympathy, we find ourselves asking whether Clytaemnestra in that sense is not perhaps the 'sacred deer' whom Artemis is avenging in trying to keep the king at home: a trap which Agamemnon springs with a further act of hubris, the sacrifice of their own daughter.

Before the conqueror returns the Chorus side with Clytaemnestra in her war-widow's dilemma. These painful issues for the wife and mother of a family the seething daughter, taken up with her wrongs and deprivations, fails to comprehend, across the generation gap:

> . . . the heart within them [the armies] screamed for all-out
>   war!
> Like vultures robbed of their young,

The agony sends them frenzied . . .
soaring high from the nest, round and
round they wheel, they row their wings,
stroke upon churning thrashing stroke,
but all the labour, the bed of pain,
the young are lost for ever.
Yet someone hears on high . . . the piercing wail . . .
(Aeschylus [1977], 53–62)

This is a terrible compound image, where the 'rowing wings' become the oars, taking the men away to war, away from their true priorities, so that 'the young are lost for ever' to that domestic harmony which is their only hope for health, both in body and in mind, for generations still to come. And here we might remind ourselves that had the father stayed at home and not deserted his small daughter for the spoils of distant Troy, under the pretext of Helen, Electra and her little brother would in every probability have enjoyed happier prospects – as would all the children of this earth, if only peace were guaranteed.

The piercing wail finds its echo some seventy-five lines further on when the Chorus, still identified with the matriarchal queen, exclaim how

'The Kings of birds to kings of beaking prows . . .
. . . plunged their claws in a hare, a mother
bursting with unborn young – the babies spilling,
quick spurts of blood – cut off the race just dashing into life!'
(Aeschylus [1977], 118–24)

How the beak that ought to feed the young turned into that of a boat of war, to destroy the great bird's own progeny and subvert the mother's hope and capacity for trust and love! – the coherence of the family: the very ground of sanity. Was there ever set to words any more substantial plea against that crime of crimes of war? Can we leap the millennia to compare Clytaemnestra to the Mother Courage of Brecht and let imagination waive superficial difference?

Perhaps Clytaemnestra was just pregnant when her husband left for ten long years at the wars? Certainly, as a young wife she was still 'bursting with unborn young' which during the king's extended absence would never be born unless she took a new lover, by whom she had two more children, as the 'Earth Goddess' would wish in close allegiance with Artemis.

We are left in little doubt how much Clytaemnestra abhors war. She speaks of the 'mad desire that overwhelms armies with the lust to ravish what they must not touch'. Then she grieves most tellingly of the fate of every soldier's wife; and here, for once, the queen sounds true:

> '. . . *when a woman sits at home and the man is gone,*
> *the loneliness is terrible,*
> *unconscionable . . .*
> *and the rumours spread and fester,*
> *a runner comes with something dreadful,*
> *close on his heels the next and this news worse . . .*
>
> *. . . the rumours broke like fever,*
> *broke and then rose higher. There were times*
> *they cut me down and eased my throat from the noose.*
> *I wavered between the living and the dead.'*
> (Aeschylus [1977], 845–65)

Here rings the passion of a suffering that the child, Electra, never shared, and with which, for that very reason, she will lack all empathy.

Nor should she be asked to make this identification with a wronged and damaged mother in the interests of her healthy growth. This gulf between the generations, the essential hopefulness of childhood when it is juxtaposed to adult disillusionment, must of necessity be fostered, even at the painful price of a period of estrangement, until a daughter grown to mother may taste this cup in her own turn. Would Electra, long years after the telling of this woe is done, still reach her mother in the grave with new compassion and a surge of love, born of new adult understanding, as did Marie Cardinal (1984), whom we shall come to presently?

Agamemnon returns from the war. He stands proudly in his chariot, with Cassandra behind him when Clytaemnestra tells her husband why Orestes is not there to greet his victorious father. The recitation serves as pretext to air her grievances and fury, for she has but little time to rehearse her bitter case:

> '*That's why our child isn't here now in Argos,*
> *our child, our bed-bond's first bloodshoot,*
> *Our He-child, Orestes. No need for suspicion.*

He's in Phocis with Strophius, our ally and friend.
Strophius warned me of possible troubles,
the threat to your life in the perils of warfare,
the likelihood here of popular rising.
When people are down they get trampled further.'
(Aeschylus [1981], 81)

Here rings the voice of the Amazon who, left alone and defenceless, will stop at nothing to defend her all, embodied in her progeny. If we, the audience, soon doubt her complete sincerity, it only proves that matters are of infinite complexity. Yet how these words, on scrutiny, already make our blood run cold, as the queen now has her women lay the famous tapestries between the palace gates and chariot. 'Never set the foot that stamped out Troy on earth again, my great one' (Aeschylus [1977], 899–900) – she seduces Agamemnon into a further act of hubris, since these heirlooms are sacred. Such flattery, she knows so well, he is unable to resist. But behind this strategem lies the mother's true concern which is entirely for the earth, the life-generating mother, that she be not defiled by the trampling foot of war which abandons new generations and those who bear them in travail. Clytaemnestra knows full well that the great soldier's vanity will overlook this deeper meaning. And hardly is the king over the threshold of the family home, and divested of his bloodstained boots, when the mother of his children rails at him bitterly for having cut her daughter's throat, far from home, in distant Aulis: of having 'trampled the bitter virgin grapes for new wine' – his relationship with Cassandra.

These preambles are intended to try to pacify the Furies, the projection of her conscience. For soon she will confront them angrily with her repetitious theme: 'And he – name one charge you brought against him then', she hurls defiantly at the Chorus, when after the murder they turn around and cry out: 'you appal me.'

'He thought no more of it than killing a beast,
and his flocks were rich, teeming in their fleece,
but he sacrificed his own child, our daughter,
the agony I laboured into love
to charm away the savage winds of Thrace.'
(Aeschylus [1977], 1440–4)

Single-mindedly imbued with her age-old Mother Right, Clytaemnestra fastens on this sacrifice of one daughter to seek exemption from
the wrong she is doing to the surviving one. And she gets away with it,
to her son's bewilderment. For when in the final Act, hounded by his
mother's Furies, Orestes asks for all of us: 'she lived on. You never
drove her into exile – why?' (Aeschylus [1977], 610), the leader of the
Chorus counters: 'The blood of the man she killed was not her own'
(Aeschylus [1977], 611). In accordance with the ancient law, the
father is still the stranger: mere bed-bond in the place of blood-bond,
who has duties but no rights. By those time-honoured dictates of the
matriarchal era, where the mother–daughter couple still held a bond
of primacy over the parental one, the queen claims she is justified,
while she chooses to deny her grandiose double-dealing and lurid
inconsistency where her obligations to Electra are concerned.

Brooding on earlier grievances, Electra seizes on this pretext to
construct her official case with all the care of a great lawyer who
proceeds step by step to win the judge's sympathy for a rather dubious
client. Hear her turn to her father as she kneels grieving at his grave,
accomplished hysteric that she is:

> 'I need you too, my father.
> Help me kill her lover, then go free . . .
> . . . And I will pour my birthright out to you –
> the wine of my father's house, my bridal wine . . .'
> (Aeschylus [1977], 469–70, 473–4)

If she is to 'go free' after the slaying of Aegisthus, she knows that she
must base her case on her lost 'bridal wine', her rightful inheritance,
in order to convince the Furies. They, she knows, must be reminded
that as a girl without a dowry she will be driven to revert to a hetaera's
existence: one who has to sell her body, as in the bad old days of the
tellurian era.

That this is only window-dressing, that her fury and her rage, her
ever-simmering aggression, belong to her earliest childhood – the
'oral' phase, if you like – the dramatists know very well. For it is to
make this point that Aeschylus in his version chooses to bring on the
nurse. The children had been clearly left in her undivided care by a
mother who already even then had better things to do, even in those
distant years before her husband went to war:

> *'Red from your mother's womb I took you, and reared you . . .*
> *Nights, the endless nights I paced, your wailing*
> *kept me moving – led me a life of labour . . .*
> *Baby can't think for itself, poor creature.*
> *You have to nurse it, don't you? Read its mind,*
> *little devil's got no words . . .*
> *Maybe it wants a bite or a sip of something,*
> *Or its bladder pinches . . .'*
> (Aeschylus [1977], 736–44)

Aeschylus knew all about 'alpha function' and 'containers' and that this queen knew better than to give up a good night's sleep merely for a squalling baby. The nurse addresses Orestes in the presence of Electra, who knows that she is handing her the very toxin she will need in order to inflame her brother for the doing of the deed for the success of which she burns. And later, when he wavers, she reinforces this dose with this stirring reminder, once he had been sensitized by the words of his old nurse:

> *'So let her fawn. She can never soothe her young wolves –*
> *Mother dear, you bred our wolves' raw fury.'*
> (Aeschylus [1977], 411–12)

Here we must remind ourselves, in all fairness to Electra, that in early infancy she fared worse than her brother. For as the older child, adding insult to injury, her deprivation was compounded by the birth of a baby brother. Then later, when her hopes were raised of having mother to herself, when he was sent away for safety and her father went to war, they were dashed. For then her mother took Aegisthus in her place, to share the warm, cosy bed that the little girl coveted – craved with all the primitive passion that is bent on making good the fatally lost experience of primary symbiosis.

But it should not be forgotten that if the absence of the father was partly welcome to the small pre-oedipal girl, wanting to possess her mother and, still, her mother's breast, an oedipal part of her later hated Clytaemnestra for depriving her of him. For in every daughter's mind, if she loses a father, mother is to blame. She did not have sufficient charm to keep him here, at home, beside her, making mother doubly 'bad': a most deeply hated object, while father is idealized, leading to the denial that it was *he* who went away and thereby chose to leave his daughter, just as *he* sacrificed her sister. Terrible as this deed was, its implications for Electra could conceivably have been that Iphigenia enjoyed a special relationship to the absent royal father. When he found himself in trouble he sent for Iphigenia, and thereby 'rejected' Electra. In her unconscious mind the momentous deed at Aulis may have held a certain glamour. Father cutting daughter's throat has sexual connotations: Iphigenia was penetrated by the admired father and Electra was not. For this, again, she would blame her mother in her phantasy.

Without elaborating further we are left in little doubt that in Electra's inner world the stage was surely set for the most relentless hatred, which in these sombre circumstances would find an opportunity to be acted out to their terrible conclusion: even if not executed, still instigated by a daughter.

Aeschylus, in his version, portrays Electra as a victim, although he harbours no illusions as to her propensities. We meet her in the second Act, an innocent girl dressed in black, who has been sent by her mother, who has had an awful dream, to pour libations on her father's grave. Her attendant slaves, also in black, very clearly pity her for her loss and cruel fate. Raising the libation cup, Electra, for her part, turns to them humbly for advice. But if we listen closely we suspect a situation in which this thwarted girl is already, even now, testing her attendants' mood for her deeper aims and objects, of which she herself is only now becoming aware. She says:

> '*I'll need your help with this.*
> *What to say when I pour the cup of sorrow?*'
> (Aeschylus [1977], 85–6)

Suddenly this pliant pupil, as she had us believe, turns about and interjects, as an aside to her slaves: 'We nurse a common hatred in this house' (Aeschylus [1977], 101). I am no better than a slave under my mother's roof, is what she seems to say. But while we are still in doubt whether we have heard quite correctly from this daughter of a king, she returns to the part of the little innocent: 'I'm so unseasoned, teach me what to say' (Aeschylus [1977], 120).

Here the leader of the Chorus, who represents her wild aggression, still half-hidden from view, cuts across this show of meekness: 'Let some god or man come down upon them' (Aeschylus [1977], 121). 'Judge or avenger, which?' Electra leads the Chorus on. Blow for blow the leader prompts: 'Just say the one who murders in return!' (Aeschylus [1977], 123)

> *'How can I ask the gods for that*
> *And keep my conscience clear?'*
> (Aeschylus [1977], 124–5)

In what is in effect an internal dialogue, between her good and bad self, where 'conscience', we must be quite clear, is not identical with guilt, Electra continues probing, only dimly yet aware of the passion of her hatred, as it gradually breaks through and gathers black momentum in her own consciousness, with this soliloquy:

> *'I call out to my father. Pity me.*
> *Dear Orestes too.*
> *Rekindle the light that saves our house!*
> *We're auctioned off, drift like vagrants now.*
> *Mother has pawned us for a husband, Aegisthus,*
> *Her partner in her murdering. I go like a slave . . .'*
> (Aeschylus [1977], 135–40)

But it is not until this tragedienne recognizes Orestes, returned from exile in disguise, bearing Apollo's words: 'Gore them like a bull!' (Aeschylus [1977], 280) that the Chorus, representing the ascendancy of her bad self, now that she has an ally, whip up her paranoia until she finally regresses and is carried away in a veritable frenzy of murderous impulses:

> *'Both fists at once*
> *Come down, come down –*
> *Zeus, crush their skulls!'*
> (Aeschylus [1977], 388–90)

And it is at this fateful moment, when Orestes seems to waver, that she stings the young man's weakness to full intention with that goad: 'Mother dear, you bred our wolves' raw fury' (Aeschylus [1977], 412). Orestes is her instrument, perfected by the very gods. Here is her opportunity, nursed through the furious years, to realize her smouldering infantile phantasies which, since she has further regressed in the group situation, duly created by the Chorus, meet with no opposition, no inner obstacle belonging to maturity, no pause for pity or concern, in coming to their stark fruition. Unlike the run of other girls in the grip of these distortions, who may spend a lifetime brooding on identical wrongs, slights and seething phantasies, deep within their unconscious, Electra will act hers out.

We see her in her last appearance, in the *Oresteia*, leading the conspirators into the inner palace, which had been her childhood home where she knows every nook and cranny and where the deed shall be done within a matter of minutes. From a confused, uncertain girl, whose murderous feelings towards her mother finally clarify, we see her actualize their purpose until she serves as silent decoy when the trap is closing in on her mother – Clytaemnestra. For all her continuous bewailing of the death of her father – the father whom she idealizes, which is not the same as loves – we cannot credit these protestations with genuine sincerity. And we are right, for where a girl turns to her father in full flight from a frustrating mother, the feelings lack true loving depth, the grace of sincerity.

She wants her father, certainly. She also idealizes him in an attempt to build a refuge from the bad-mother image, in the hope thereby to lessen its persecutory quality. How much she idealizes him, with a total disregard for all reality, we can clearly recognize as she ignores every reference to the murder of her sister each time her mother raises it so as to justify the murder of her husband, Agamemnon. This act of hubris she ignores to suit her inner purposes, where the idealization serves as a primitive defence.

These neurotic pretensions Sophocles pinpoints clearly in his version of the case. Electra's sister, here named Chrysothemis, encourages her firmly to cease her noisy lamentations for her father's death, since otherwise Clytaemnestra will have no option but have her incarcerated. 'I'm sure/I feel our position as bitterly as you do', she addresses Electra as she tries to divert her (Sophocles, p. 78). Clytaemnestra, in this version, is initially portrayed as an exasperated mother nearing the end of her patience. All right, yes, she killed her husband, who was her daughter's father:

> *'It is true.*
> *I don't forget it;*
> *And I have no wish to deny it,*
> *Since it was not my doing alone;*
> *I had an ally – Justice.'*
> (Sophocles, p. 84)

'This father of yours,' she continues, 'whom you never stop weeping for, did a thing no other Greek had dared to do, when he so ruthlessly sacrificed your sister to the gods – the child whom he had begotten, at little cost of course compared to mine who bore her' (Sophocles, p. 84).

It almost seems that Electra has for once, on this occasion, very nearly heard her mother. We experience her wavering on the brink of better feelings and giving Clytaemnestra credit for her sorrows and her suffering on account of a lost child. She replies almost politely, for a welcome change; which we cannot fully credit: 'But with your leave, I would like to say what I think may be justly said for my dead father and for my sister', she begins (Sophocles, p. 85). 'Certainly you may', replies her mother with relief. 'If you always began in that tone, it would be a pleasure to listen to you' (Sophocles, p. 85).

Electra then proceeds again to exonerate her father in the shrill undertones of her usual idealization:

> 'So she was sacrificed; there was no other way
> To get the ships afloat, either for Troy
> Or homeward. This was the reason why he was forced
> Against his will, and after much resistance,
> To make the sacrifice.'
> (Sophocles, p. 85)

From there she plunges straight away into her chronic grievances, the very ones she dishes up at every opportunity:

> 'Explain, if you please, what justification you have
> For your present abominable way of life –
> Mistress of the murderer that helped you kill my father,
> Bearing his children to supplant the innocent
> Legitimate offspring whom you have driven away . . .
> . . . But I must not lecture you; you only retort
> Time and again, that I am insolent to my mother –
> Mother! – more like a jailer, with the slavery
> You put upon me . . .
> . . . Call me what you will –
> Vile, brutal, shameless – if I am all these,
> I am your true daughter.'
> (Sophocles, p. 86)

For all her earlier, good intentions, Electra is but a helpless victim in the grip of her deeper conflicts. Again, the girl is overwhelmed by her feelings of rejection; the fury that she has been displaced, from her mother's side and breast, by an 'abominable' lover, and new babies whose arrival stirred up earlier grievances at the birth of her brother.

In all three dramatic versions it is Electra alone who stands, at least to some extent, outside the prevailing laws of crime and punishment, in the hard, clear light of her neurosis. 'She burns with hatred against her mother' (Klein, M., 1963, p. 275). And at the end of the day, the gods and Furies pass her by as one too sick to trouble with, one might be inclined to say, and turn a blind eye on the grounds that her lost inheritance offers her sufficient case. We notice how in all three plays she conspicuously lacks that proud, creative stature of adult femininity where its hallmark includes a capacity for compassion like that which her mother is about to show.

We said that she had regressed. References are made to this in terms of her dirty clothes and dilapidated appearance: Euripides stresses how Aegisthus kept her at home, rather like a Cinderella, 'and would let no one marry her' (Euripides, p. 106). Later on, he paired her off with a peasant who did not feel entitled to take advantage of her and so never came near her bed. But none of this sounds quite convincing. The Electra who in the Sophocles version is prepared to commit matricide single-handed when she believes her brother dead would hardly forfeit a true marriage to kowtow to Aegisthus.

No. She comes across as frigid. It is surely her neurosis which locks her in such angry regression, that confiscates her access to vintage sexuality. Euripides, sensing this, at the end of his tale when brother and sister have to part once again on the paths of banishment from their cradle-ground of Argos, has Orestes, as he leaves to seek redemption in Athens, marry Electra off to his good friend Pylades, as if in the hope that now she will finally grow up.

Similarly, Sophocles refers to Electra's sadly 'lost inheritance' as a symbol for motherhood, certainly by implication, where she stirs her sister up to help with the matricide, clearly growing impatient at finding no response:

> *'Why woman,*
> *What are you waiting for? What hope is there*
> *To cling to still? A lifetime of regret*

> *For your lost inheritance, a dismal prospect*
> *Of ageing spinsterhood? You've little chance*
> *Of ever being bride or wife; Aegisthus*
> *Knows better than to let our tree bear fruit;*
> *Life born from you or me would mean his death.'*
> (Sophocles, p. 97)

Again, we are not quite convinced of this needling diatribe. For surely, in reality, Aegisthus has small cause to fear such an infant progeny for a prodigious length of time. Does he suggest a deeper meaning: that Electra is projecting her murderous propensities against the parental couple, out of envy of a sexual mother, into her future offspring?

When Clytaemnestra, as the sword of her son is at her throat, finally still calls out: 'Help! Death is upon us! Is there no one to help?' (Sophocles, p. 113) Electra, who is listening on the other side of the door, every inch eagerness to know her mother's bloody end beyond all residue of doubt, cries: 'There it is. Do you hear, do you hear?' She is practically ecstatic in her murderous lust. 'Strike her again, strike' (Sophocles, p. 113) she ejaculates, when Clytaemnestra still groans 'Ah' – showing residues of life, still wrestling grimly with extinction to the last and final breath.

Yes, that is how it was, says Sophocles with the shrug of the marketplace reporter, inured to the human cruelty which must be his bread and butter. Euripides, on the other hand, is more emotionally involved. He has a very tender ear for the ambivalence in all emotion. Here, brother and sister have easily decided jointly that Aegisthus shall be killed, in full public view, at his banquet for the nymphs, not far from the humble home where Electra is 'stabled . . . in a squalid shack'. But where shall they locate their mother so that she can be lured and slain in a secret, hidden spot, since Apollo's command did not include Clytaemnestra? Clearly by implication the proposed matricide is a different breed of crime – far from an everyday occurrence.

Electra finds a speedy answer of the utmost cynicism: 'Go and tell her I have borne a child, a son. When she hears of my confinement she will come' (Euripides, p. 127). 'Will she? You think, daughter, she cares for you at all?' (Euripides, p. 128) the old family retainer, devoted to his 'princess' since earliest childhood, asks. Here he personifies Electra's lifelong experience of being an unwanted child at

WHO MOURNS CLYTAEMNESTRA?

its most hurtful and raw. 'Yes; she will come and weep over my son's low birth' (Euripides, p. 128) comes the cynical reply, rooted in those painful feelings where the pain must be denied and converted into hatred, into burning paranoia. 'Once here, the rest is simple: she's as good as dead' (Euripides, p. 128).

Yet in her other heart, Electra surely must have known that the news of a grandchild would in her mother's passionate nature, that of a true matriarch, awaken such genuine fondness as would bridge the old estrangements. Yet how can this vindictive daughter, numbed and bruised with suffering, admit to such a positive in her mother's character, since at any thought of goodness her envy gets the upper hand, to strip her mother's personality of every asset once again?

When the queen, as predicted, soon appears in the distance, Orestes says touchingly, with a sudden change of heart: 'It is my mother' (Euripides, p. 138). One almost senses his relief that despite the phantasies and his sister's lust for murder she is, in fact, still alive, still a mother to turn to in a desperate situation; whereas Electra cries:

> *'Why, look!*
> *How fine she is – a carriage, slaves and her best gown!'*
> (Euripides, p. 138)

But what arouses only envy in his heated sister affects her brother differently: 'What shall we do, then? Are we going to kill our mother?'

'Have you grown soft,' slaps the response, 'as soon as you set eyes on her?'

'She brought me up, she bore me! How can I take her life? . . . It is wrong to kill my mother . . .' (Euripides, p. 138).

Feeling her brother weaken, Electra, never at a loss, threatens that his father's Furies will haunt him to his final day, if he fails his memory now. Did not the gods themselves decree it, she pursues her argument, twisting the precise instructions from 'the holy tripod's throne' to subvert his better feelings now that the trap is all but sprung.

On her arrival Clytaemnestra does not know that Aegisthus, in fact, already lies dead. She comes on to the scene in the full, glowing splendour of a great reigning queen. The Chorus welcome her as such and praise her 'great wealth and prosperity'. But Clytaemnestra shakes off the temptation of this proffered hubris in a deeply mournful mood, very possibly occasioned by the birth of a new life which she has come to celebrate. Humbly and sadly she replies: 'small compensation for the child I lost' (Euripides, p. 139). And then she asks her Trojan slaves to help her to the ground.

But here her daughter intervenes, some part of her still hoping for a sign of her mother's love, even if the tone is laced with her usual cynicism:

> *'Why should not I*
> *Be given the privilege, to hold your royal hand?'*
> (Euripides, p. 139)

Just as we find ourselves, despite the slightly mocking tone, hoping that a genuine wish for a reconciliation underlies her turn of phrase and hold our breath, she launches straight into a new attack, clearly fired by her current envy and hyped-up hostility, although it is attributed to other matters, rationally: 'I am a slave too, banished from my father's house to misery.'

On hearing the old accusations, Clytaemnestra, who was still evidently hesitating in the hope of better things, now replies with exasperation: 'I have my slaves here; pray don't trouble' (Euripides, p. 139). And following on this rejection Electra now, tit for tat, launches venomously into the full tirade again, while her mother, in her turn, goes over the well-trodden ground of her self-justification with these deeply stirring words:

> *'When I married your father, I did not expect*
> *To die, or see my children killed. He took my child*
> *To Aulis . . . held her high above*
> *The altar; then her father cut her soft white throat –*
> *My Iphigenia . . .'*
> (Euripides, p. 140)

She then elaborates how she would still not have killed him for that, but that he must add insult to injury and

> *'. . . bring home with him*
> *The mad prophetess; foist on me a second wife,*
> *A fellow-lodger – two kept women in one house.'*
> (Euripides, p. 140)

But Electra is relentless. Angrily the daughter counters that this is all doubtless very fine, but offers a distorted picture. For as she reminds her mother, were you not, as a wife, already 'before your mirror, smoothing out your hair' (Euripides, p. 142) with your Lord Agamemnon barely out of the house to command the fleet of Argos! And again, we find ourselves feeling for the little girl who had so anticipated this opportunity to have her mother to herself, seething with fury and dismay as she observed these preparations for an impending love-affair, not with herself but with a man who, to top everything, will be depriving her of her inheritance as well.

Summoning the patient wisdom of a maturer woman who has known great suffering, Clytaemnestra now bids for our sympathy in turn:

> 'My child, your nature
> Has always been to love your father.
> It is natural: some children love their father best,
> And some their mother, I'll forgive you.'
> (Euripides, p. 142)

She even ends by admitting how she regrets her grand revenge, suggesting that if time could heal the outrage of her earlier feelings, could it not heal their rift as well on such a hopeful occasion? We listen and we hold our breath as the old arguments fly to and fro, straining for a newer music until, still conciliatory in the interests of new life, Clytaemnestra says with kindness: 'Let's change the subject. Child, why did you send for me?' Is this, we almost pray, the moment for benign transformation? Are we standing on its brink? We know that the queen knows the reason, and for that reason hear her saying: 'It was surely not, Electra, to start fighting once again, but to make a new beginning'; or so we might interpret it.

At the same time we can see that she is clearly puzzled, with a first hint of suspicion as an old conspirator, about why the midwife or some neighbour could not, in her place, have offered the customary sacrifice for the birth of a son. None the less she goes indoors, to do her daughter this favour; to, we could say, 'find her again', as Demeter did Persephone, once the Kore phase was over.

With incomparable insight for such a distant age, Euripides shows us how unerringly he understands the deeper mother–daughter conflicts; that when the former's nature was, in her younger days, that of a sexual woman rather than a maternal one, this will stand unforgiven in the book of a daughter enmeshed in her early envy for such a 'wanton' display of dazzling creativity. For she, as a little girl, cannot yet produce a baby; she has no signs of owning breasts and despairs of possessing all this enviable equipment, the more so where she has attacked that of her mother and must live in fear of retaliation. Neither, stuck in her regression, can she hope to recognize that time, indeed, has wrought some change in the heart of her mother, if only she herself were able to make creative use of it. But this lies outside her scope.

Such a daughter was Electra – Euripides makes this very clear, even while he demonstrates how Clytaemnestra feeds those flames at every opportunity. For having only just agreed to meet her daughter's demands, unnecessary as they seem under the circumstances, she adds in the same breath:

> *'And then I must be off*
> *To where my husband's sacrificing to the nymphs*
> *Out in the pasture. [To her servants] – You there!*
> *Take the carriage away, and feed the horses.*
> *Give me such time as I need*
> *To make this offering to the gods; then come for me.*
> *[To Electra] I have my husband to think of.'*
> (Euripides, p. 144)

A moment for reconciliation, in which the she-generations might see themselves as bound together nurturing the tree of life, has briefly trembled in the balance, only to be lost for ever in time-old animosities. Built into the relationship, like some flawed foundation stone, these old resentments lie, ever ready to awake from a state of dormancy into full conflagration where infantile grievances have not been worked through and resolved on the part of the daughter, and modified too late in life, for such unruly natures, on the maternal side.

Despite his depth of understanding, Euripides has clearly lost patience with the hoity-toity House of Atreus. Bedraggled with their eternal feuds, its members cannot hold a candle to Electra's honest husband or, come to that, to the old man, the loyal family retainer, in the poet's eyes. As long as such as these grace Hellas, royalty and the gods may act out their elitist notions, but wine and cheese and yearling lambs, all maintained by honest toil, are what sustain a decent race of genuine nobility, he reminds us with a passion for common sense and sanity. It is the squalor of neurosis, with its ragtag pretensions and its infantile and boring gimmicks, which underlies the matricide; and it is certainly no higher justice that we are observing here, Euripides dares to say, if largely still by implication, from within that tradition of Zeus-given nemesis.

He gives the last lines to the Chorus:

> *'To be able to fare well,*
> *To avoid the frustration of misfortune:*
> *That, in this world, is happiness.'*
> (Euripides, p. 152)

The emphasis clearly falls on the handling of frustration, not, as the neurotic whines, on avoiding misfortune. Misfortune we cannot avoid. Being human means that we suffer deprivation, loss and pain. The decisive question, as every psychotherapist knows, is how we deal with frustration.

Every daughter will experience frustration at her mother's breast, and later at her mother's hands, just as every son will. The breast will not always be there. Mother and father need each other, in the closeness of their privacy, if the infant is to accomplish the fullness of maturity, regardless of initial tantrums and omnipotent possessiveness. Rival babies come along to become the 'top baby', or the baby at the breast. All these frustrations will give rise to murderous phantasies and, where they fail to be resolved, may accrete in a given phase, becoming the so-called fixation point for subsequent mental illness.

These breathtaking, deeper issues Antiquity had clearly grasped at a poetic level – our venue for time-honoured truth – to an extent scarcely bettered until our own, Freudian era. Did Freud not send us to the poets, if we were to understand female sexuality? Do we not confirm their findings in daily clinical experience? Every woman on the couch is to some degree a Clytaemnestra, or an Electra, or at a deeper level, both. How sadly we become mothers before time has offered us the playgrounds needed to grow up! How we are fated to be daughters of mothers who are still part child! – to be such mothers in our turn, where life may spin its web in circles.

On the Hellenic stage it was left to Athene to sort out the fearful legacy of the House of Atreus. It is, no doubt, significant that she herself had no mother, but sprang instead straight from Zeus. Free of these conflicts in herself, she alone could dispense fair judgement in this sombre case where phantasies were acted out with such tragic consequences.

— 91 —

With a sense of deep nostalgia, linked to one of foreboding, we leave the Ancient World behind. Whatever lies ahead we know, from flimsy school-year education, will scarcely equal this display of sheer virtuosity in depth as in detail, into our subject matter. Instead, as we now approach monotheistic law and order, to be embellished in its turn by notional purity and love, a heavy curtain plummets down on these deeper explorations, to be replaced by a crop of fanatical theologies which the pagan heart cannot digest, if its rhythm shall be popular in the best sense. Millennia, we know, will pass before mankind is ready to return to these excavations which the Hellenic world began with such unflinching fortitude, such a genius of virtually Kleinian depth for grasping human relatedness.

The mother–daughter constellation we will encounter in that phase, to hear what *she* may have to say with her own, hard-won voice, will be standing on the threshold of woman's autonomy as a full human being, even if that threshold straddles a handful or more of centuries. Patience will be required as we persevere and struggle through near eternities of relentless patriarchy until we strike that distant dawn.

If little that lies ahead for the next lap of our journey will match the grandeur of the grasp which has fired us so far, we have surely been nourished with sufficient inspiration to keep our hope and courage up as the gusts of.new religions, distilled in prophetic tantrums, seek to douse the deeper nature of the human psyche for all time.

PART II

1   AND THE ANGEL SAID

Five months after the angel had informed Zacharias, the husband of Elisabeth, that their span of childlessness would, so close on old age, flower into parenthood, he returned on yet another errand. To her young cousin, named Mary, he also promised a son. Both were virgins in the sense that their wombs were still unopened.

Only Luke sees fit to mention Elisabeth in the context of the Annunciation. Only he shows interest – a little – as to what passed in the hearts of these two women who very clearly knew the comfort of a close relationship. For hardly had Gabriel departed when Mary packed a modest bundle, to set off by herself, 'and went into the hill country with haste, into a city of Juda' (Luke 1:39). She knew the house of Zacharias, where Elisabeth had 'hid herself five months' (Luke 1:24). There the two remained together, Luke informs us, for three months. Mary then returned home, very roughly one month before her cousin was delivered.

The feeling which comes across is of two strong-minded women. Mary had, after all, questioned Gabriel pretty closely before she would approve this thing. And Elisabeth seemed in the habit of keeping herself to herself, like one who knows her own mind as she goes about her business, wrapped in her own inwardness. Was this not the sense in which she 'hid', for early in a pregnancy there is no other cause to hide, even if the circumstances prove unusual?

The poet Rilke is receptive to the way the women share, touchingly, their new condition as they seek each other out to achieve essential bearings on this new beingness:

> *At first it all went well with her,*
> *but oftentimes in climbing she already*
> *felt the wonder stirring in her body –*
> *and panting then she stood upon the lofty*
> *Judean hills . . .*
>
> *She had to lay her hand upon the other*
> *woman's body, still more ripe than hers.*
> *And they both tottered towards*
> *one another*
> *and touched each other's garments and hair.*
>
> *Each, with a sanctuary in her keeping,*
> *sought refuge with her closest woman kin . . .*
> (Hall, N., 1980, p.96, quoting Rilke)

What kind of women were they, then, whom we encounter like a dream? Before returning to that question, let us fill in the background to their stay beneath one roof, to their joint perambulation.

What is this distance we have travelled to hear the famous angel speak? What were the milestones of that journey where masculine supremacy, *logos* and conscious thinking, had sought to exile Mother Earth – and, as we shall be seeing, failed. For 'Mother Earth's warm, passive embrace had survived . . . and held the Middle Eastern cultures to its bosom' (de Riencourt, A., 1983, p.79).

The location, Bethlehem, is relatively near Argos; yet we find ourselves removed further from Zeus and Agamemnon than a mere twelve centuries compressed between the Trojan War and the Annunciation, which, come the winter solstice, still casts a holy spell over an unholy world.

Moses died approximately when the Greeks set sail for Troy. Under his leadership 'it was left to a small Semitic people to conceive of an uncompromising monotheism, which entailed the most brutal emancipation from the clutches of a mythological outlook' (de Riencourt, A., 1983, p.85). This coincided with a time when our Hellenistic sisters, walking in the golden era of the great philosophers, enjoyed ample new-found beauty, 'expressed in many ways, including painting, poetry and the emotions . . . ' (Swidler, L., 1976, p.1). Why then, must that desert God, under the most fearful threats ejaculated by his prophets, confiscate our rights to these? The answer is, in part, that

Yahweh was no longer in nature but beyond it, an unfathomable spiritual entity who led the Chosen People through the desert by virtue of a special compact between them. Thus, as fast as one mythology was destroyed, a far more abstract ideology expressed as parables took its place. The concept of the Chosen People fulfilling the Will of God. (de Riencourt, A., 1983, p.89)

This is all very well. But the compact was, of course, between Yahweh and the men: the male psyche, the animus. This God was not seen, but heard. He spoke to the human will through the power of the word. The numen of creation had mythically been transferred from the womb to the head. As far as we are concerned, this reversal would impose far-reaching consequences, for woman's image of herself underwent dramatic change. From a lusty pagan whole she would slowly be transformed into a cumbersome triptych, which is still waiting to be welded into a wholesome unity.

Yet she would not be subdued. Time and again she escaped from allocated submission to rise to visionary heights. We know that Miriam complained bitterly that the Lord spoke only through her famous brother. Why should her baby brother, Moses, be singled out for eminence? But lo, she was severely punished, summoned to the tent of meeting, read the riot act by God, and stricken white with leprosy, certainly for seven days, as a warning to keep her place (Numbers 12:10). Yet this was the same proud woman who went ahead of all her sisters to celebrate the Exodus, with a timbrel in her hand: 'Sing to the Lord, for he has triumphed gloriously; the horse and his rider he has thrown into the sea' (Exodus 15:21). Did she not, as a woman, owe him some allegiance for matrimonial regulations for which her abused pagan sisters might have envied her? In her we catch a fleeting glimpse, through the conspiracy of silence in which the Bible is steeped, of our own subject matter. For was this not the little girl who at her anxious mother's bidding 'watched and waited at a distance to know what would be done to him', when her baby brother Moses was hidden in the famous rushes; and then addressed the pharaoh's daughter, as she stood there amazed, beside the discovered child: 'Shall I go and call you a nurse from the Hebrew women to nurse the child for you?' (Exodus 2:7) – to hurry back and fetch her mother, as she had doubtless rehearsed for many anxious days on end, with such great presence of mind?

Be this but a fleeting glance, it opens some momentous vistas of the chain of captivities when the bond of mother and daughter was surely harnessed to the yoke which dragged the spirit of survival through those desert centuries as they comforted, sustained and also fought with one another. Did not 'the little minx Dinah', Leah's ill-fated daughter, cause her brothers to sack Sheshem, 'with their notions of honour and revenge' (Mann, T., 1984, p. 221), an event which contributed to Jacob's beloved Rachel dying while giving birth to Benjamin, far from the comforts of that town?

Paradox, ambivalence and ambiguity in Judaistic thought on women were, much as they still are today, surely excruciating:

He who has no wife dwells without good, without help, without joy, without blessing, and without atonement. (Genesis, Rabbah 18:2)

A woman is a pitcher of filth with its mouth full of blood, yet all run after her. (Talmud, b. Shabbath 152a [Swidler, L., 1976, p.10])

Such were the contradictions which would later pave the way for emerging Christian attitudes and for Mariology, intricately interwoven with the fate of the Great Mother through those millennia, in her unrelenting fight against a patriarchal culture as it threatens her survival from every side, at every step.

When we asked earlier what kind of women were they then, this Mary and Elisabeth, whom we encounter like a dream in the enchanted pages of that contemporary myth whose roots are the New Testament, the only answer which makes sense in terms of present-day thinking is – women who were unsubdued by that capricious thunder god. The 'meek handmaid' of the Lord, as in the entire legend of the Nativity, was a subsequent embroidery: a later addition to the Gospels, 'written more than eighty years after the events' (Warner, M., 1985, p.4) which are so hauntingly described and imprinted on the generations. In Luke's 'beautiful verses' Mary speaks only 'four times; in Matthew she is silent' (Warner, M., 1985, p.4). Any intuitive attempt to restore the two cousins sees them most convincingly as part of a women's group concerned with the preservation of the feminine principle, once we steel ourselves to lay later vested interests and their well-known fabrications firmly, if sadly, out of sight.

Such notions correspond with texts from the Gnostic Gospels discovered in Upper Egypt, in the strangest circumstances, in 1945. These Coptic translations from *c*.350–400 AD cast significant doubt on the all-male God who set his stamp on the Scriptures as we know them. 'Yet instead of describing a monistic and masculine God, many of these texts speak of God as a dyad who embraces both masculine and feminine elements' (Pagels, E., 1980, p.49). There are repeated references to a 'divine Mother'; '[she is] . . . the image of the invisible, virginal, perfect spirit . . . She became the Mother of everything, for she existed before them all . . . ' (quoted by Pagels, E., 1980, p.52).

This is in keeping with the thought that the term 'virgin had entirely different connotations two millennia ago from those it carries in our day:

The word virgin means 'belonging-to-no-man' . . . Virgin means one-in-herself; not maiden inviolate, but maiden alone, in herself. To be virginal does not mean to be chaste, but rather to be true to nature and instinct . . . The virgin forest is not barren or unfertilized but rather a place that is especially fruitful and has multiplied because it has taken life into itself and transformed it, giving birth naturally and taking dead things back to be recycled. It is virgin because it is unexploited, not in man's control. (Hall, N., 1980, p.11)

Certainly, to my mind, Mary was accustomed to taking responsibility for the decisions in her life: 'Then said Mary unto the angel, How shall this be, seeing I know not a man?' (Luke 1:34). Thereupon Gabriel had to make quite a speech until she finally agreed to this curious proposition. That she would later become a higher court of intercession on behalf of those who may travel for miles on their knees to beseech the Virgin of Guadaloupe, as in Mexico City, is a subsequent accretion and sorry testimony to the poverty which still prevails, for which there is no earthly comfort.

Leaving these matters to one side, the Goddess certainly survived in the heart of the masses. By constant change of location, as of embodiment, such as the Magna Mater who in 204 BC was carried aloft to Rome 'as the result of an oracle's prophecy that Hannibal could not be driven out of Italy without her intervention' (de Riencourt, A., 1983, p.128), her roots in the human mind held fast despite the raging prophets. Upon the Roman victory she was 'officially enthroned on the Palatine and her cult was adopted by the Roman State' (de Riencourt, A., 1983, p.128). She refused to be expunged.

If, when all is said and done, it is still impossible to 'get our teeth' into Mary, except in that cloud of incense which at this time enfolds 659 million Catholics, she remains a living myth which concerns us very deeply for our present purposes. For it imposed upon women the notion of purity. This was to set the seal of a catastrophic split between body and spirit, sexuality and mind, on the entire caste, which it has still not shaken off, while it afflicts the dyad with tempestuous dissensions.

There is in the New Testament quite 'a muddle of Marys' (Warner, M., 1985, p.344). We need not disentangle it except to point to the upshot which it carries for our theme: 'Our' Mary is a virgin, otherwise she is a whore, or a Mary Magdalen, failing which she is a Martha 'cumbered about much serving' (Luke 10:40), when she surely should be sitting at the feet of Our Lord, to be nourished by the Spirit. Three versions of Mary: three aspects of woman, crying out, still in our day, to become integrated into a true and living whole.

Daughters, we know, attack their mothers for their sexuality. Deep from the infant heart of their pre-oedipal yearnings they claim undisputed ownership of the beloved maternal body divided horizontally to exclude the lower half. But the split described above, now rooted in theology, has settled woman with a historic dilemma: a tax that she can never pay. Mothers remain exercised to represent virgins to their daughters, while the curse 'you little whore' is screamed at the hapless daughter, through many a summer dusk and dawn, to confirm that category of the disappointing daughter.

From the New Testament we seem to glean next to nothing of the nebulous Anne or Hanna. What went on between her and her famous daughter, Mary, whom the Council of Ephesus entitled Mary Theotakos, meaning Mother of God? Legends of purity would have it that Hanna took little Mary, just as soon as she could walk, to grow up in the Temple, in the paths of holiness. On this historians pour cold water: no Hebrew girl was ever reared in the precincts of that House. But where the written texts are silent, images help us out. St Anne, the virgin *and* her child – we find them as a single unit, embellishing the centuries. Mother and daughter clearly lack any separate, womanly existence, or signs of a relationship beyond the maternal one, which is wholly dedicated to nurturing new generations. This aspect of the partnership of time-honoured collaboration has survived technology and ever-changing social patterns. Regardless of new sophistication where both women may enjoy entirely different walks of life, professions or occupations, a baby draws them back together. It renews the flowering of a previous, early bond, may offer opportunities, sometimes, for its burgeoning where the first time round was missed; or, sadly, signals a return to the old power struggles and bitter animosities. But here is only one dimension. Here, in this relationship of the Holy Virgin to her mother, painful ambiguities, the torments of ambivalence, are ruled out and denied. Here all is love and adoration, as Leonardo portrays in his *Virgin and Child with St Anne and St John*; and he fixes that glowing trinity in our susceptible heart for impossible eternities: a lesson we should emulate. The Virgin's gaze rests on her child, as does St Anne's on her daughter: an idyll of maternity wrapped in holy mystery, shared with rapture by the three, with no cloud to darken it or threaten any sudden burst of the famous complications.

If the former goddesses of the classical pantheon assuredly knew jealousy and hatred as well as love, the mothers here are much too pure to be capable of sin, or any wicked emotions. The sinner was that other Mary who was safely split off and who never bore a child, at least as far as we are told. Motherhood is not for sinners, all these images confirm: only for the purest saint. Caravaggio, Georges de la Tour, countless masters great and small have in their thousands reinforced holy maternity in every struggling woman's heart.

In Brittany, as in Spain, during the early Renaissance, St Anne enjoyed a certain cult. St Anne as the grandmother is, in the event, exalted, as we see her portrayed towering over the Virgin, who is clasping her child: the powerful matriarch we still meet in Spain today as she rules over her daughters and their virginity, often with a rod of iron which nothing, it would seem, can bend, in the rural areas.

Such tenacious vigilance, such an ever-watchful presence – what a bone of contention: an entire skeleton on which hang the central issues of purity and separation. Hiding behind them both is the unspoken name of death. Only the older woman apprehends what lies ahead. The Gospels barely introduce us to the Mater Dolorosa. As we enter certain churches in South America we see the Mary dressed in white. Close to the gilded altar, in the warm light of the candles, she shines in her bridal joy as she dwells on the Annunciation and promise of maternity. It is not until we turn so as to leave the House of God that we see her, all alone, in the shadows by the door, dressed entirely in black. It is not without significance that the Gospels maintain virtual silence at this point, where woman knows what lies ahead with that archaic foreknowledge a mother senses every time a new life stirs within her womb already to threaten loss by the very act of stirring.

From the depths of her own sorrow, through the centuries to come, the Queen of Heaven would intercede for all her daughters upon earth who turn to her in their distress. Even so, her 'veneration invokes no corresponding rise in the status of women. On the contrary, the fertility ascribed to her reinforces the mythology that motherhood is the central point in a woman's life . . . ' (Warner, M., 1985, p.284).

We leave the New Testament with a mass of contradictions which remain unresolved. The feminine has been suppressed and yet remained resilient. The maternal world went underground at the same time as it was raised to the status of divinity, provided it was virginal. Woman was virgin or she was whore. Yet the Virgin has maintained her hold over her earthly daughters, regardless of this paradox, even to our present day. How is that to be explained?

When they asked Bernadette after her vision of the Virgin what her feelings might be now regarding the images so ubiquitous at Lourdes, she replied that these but slandered her beauty, which was beyond anything ever seen upon this earth.

We know with certainty today from experiences we have in deep psychotherapy that this inexpressible notion of radiant beauty springs from an enshrined imago of our earliest, own mother with that sense of perfect bliss granted us in infancy. It belongs to that preverbal place in which our senses rule supreme, when the mother is endowed with a horizontal split into a beloved upper feeding and a feared lower sexual part. Embedded in the unconscious, the former evokes a lifelong quest for rapture and for the divine. Nor can insight dismiss such a numinous imprint.

The contradictions above cannot, in my personal view, be resolved psychodynamically in psychological isolation. They rule the feminine psyche still where social conditions have remained static in the world today. They are active to some degree in the most emancipated woman, let us not deceive ourselves. How many of us still play at being a virgin to our daughters? How many of us suffer guilt if we exercise our right to a fuller life than the measured formula which exclusive motherhood provides? No, their resolution lies in the realm of wider change in the socioeconomic sphere. We shall see how avidly privileged groups of women seize every opportunity which the smallest chink provides, even if these are lost again, as is the sight of a lighthouse in the swell of heavy seas. The times ahead are turbulent as 'the first ghostly contours of the complete feudal system became visible, erected on the ruins of tribal law and tradition' (Power, E., 1975, p.9). Ahead of us lie the Dark Ages, as they have been aptly called.

2   LEARNED SAINTS AND BATTLING SINNERS

The position of women is often considered as a test by which civilization of a country or age may be judged. The test is extraordinarily difficult to apply, more particularly to the Middle Ages, because of determining what in any age constitutes the position of women. The position of women is one thing in theory, another in the law, yet another in everyday life. In the Middle Ages, as now, the various manifestations of women's position reacted on one another but did not exactly coincide; the true position of women was a blend of all three.
(EILEEN POWER, *Mediaeval Women*)

MARY, WE MUST NOT FORGET, was a daughter of the Tribes. Their stern traditions and taboos had certainly offered women a measure of security which through the centuries to come must have shone like a beacon over the unruly heads of invading barbarians, through the seething Dark Ages, during which the brightest fragments of earlier civilizations seemed scattered to the lumpen winds, while there was no one in a position to ascertain what had survived. When the sun came out again that beacon glowed by a new name: it was Christianity. The structure which now furthered it was the dawn of feudalism, whose 'outlook rested on one broad principle: only the "universals" are real; individual man is not as real as the estate to which he belongs' (de Riencourt, A., 1983, p. 230). Where there existed no concept, even for man himself, of a separate, autonomous entity, there could be no such hope for woman. 'Both were different types of organic cells, merged in a much vaster spiritual organism' (de Riencourt, A., 1983, p. 230). And yet, as in every age, women would achieve, regardless, influence and posts of power. Even if their numbers were inevitably very small it was enough to testify to a line of unbroken spirit which no age has ever quenched to the last and final spark.

The status of barbarian women had been relatively high, as Plutarch confirms:

If the Celtae have complaints against the Carthaginians, the Carthaginian Commander in Spain shall judge it. But if the Carthaginians have anything to lay to the charge of the Celtae, it shall be brought before the Celtic women. (Forrester-Brown, G., 1919, p. 11)

In the Teutonic tribes the chief deity was still a goddess, and we hear from Tacitus: 'They conceive that in women is a certain uncanny and prophetic sense: they neither scorn to consult them nor slight their answers' (Forrester-Brown, G., 1919, p. 11). Here was an effrontery which Christianity would seek to douse, and in no uncertain terms.

The Middle Ages were not dear to many a historian's heart, labelled as the period was as 'a vast insane asylum' (Forrester-Brown, G., 1919, p. 19). Before its Christian gates close in, let us hear this fond farewell to the world which it replaced, celebrated in the shape of a carefree enchantress, the figment of an illusion, dear to the human heart:

> *Aristion, so swift once to toss her tresses curling*
> *And her castanets that rattled in praise of Cybele,*
> *Lightly beneath the pine-boughs to the horned flute's music*
> *   whirling,*
> *She that would mix no water, as she quaffed her winecups*
> *   three,*
> *Rests here beneath the elm-tree shade; now no more lovers*
> *Gladden her heart, no vigils of maddened midnight hours.*
> *A long farewell, all revels, all follies! Now earth covers*
> *The sacred head that once went bright with wreathed flowers.*
> (Seltman, C., 1956, p. 183)

'And', added this nostalgic source, 'a long farewell to happiness for almost all girls and women was fated soon to come, for real hostility to women was on its way.' True. Yet on the other hand the exchange of women in marriage, often across great distances, even entire continents, lent to a minority both political and cultural power and significance:

a princess sent to a distant land for marital purposes became the head of a vast expedition . . . along with a great deal of authority over the expenditure of her often considerable financial resources. She could be expected to bring an alien influence with her which was often upsetting to local customs and traditions but was also a powerful agent in cross-cultural fertilization. (de Riencourt, A., 1983, p. 213)

Not that this meant 'happiness' as a foregone conclusion. It merely points to certain loopholes for certain individual women belonging to a noble class, who might wield far-reaching influence within two linked institutions: monarchy and the Church.

As to the majority, it surely oppresses us by a conspicuous, dumb silence, our perception of an absence: a lost and missing rank and file; for the run of 'common folk . . . rarely uttered a word above the whistle of a scythe or the hum of a loom' (Power, E., 1975, p. 11). Theirs was to serve and labour, to pray on Sundays and to die in the hope of better things in the world which was to come.

It was, we know, 'monasticism [which] dealt the final blow to the civilization of the ancient world' (Seltman, C., 1956, p. 183), and to it we are indebted for mother–daughter histories as they evolved within that orbit. Let us consider with amusement how alien its impact was and how insane the spectre seemed to observers at the time:

The whole island is filled, or rather defiled, by men who fly from the light. They call themselves Monks, or solitaries because they choose to live alone . . . They fear the gifts of fortune . . . they embrace a life of voluntary wretchedness . . . Either this melancholy madness is the effect of disease, or else the consciousness of guilt urges these unhappy men to exercise on their own bodies the tortures which are inflicted on fugitive slaves by the hand of justice. (Seltman, C., 1956, p. 111)

If here sounds paganism's horrified and disdainful judgement on the forces which would send it packing over centuries to come, the mothers and their daughters of the nobility saw the monasteries as a refuge from a profound misogyny. In them this elite – if they could afford this passport to a less odious way of life – sought shelter from a climate which was abhorrent to feminine sensibilities. In England between the years 1250 and 1540 there were between 126 and 136 nunneries. During this period there were no more than 3,500 nuns, decreasing to 1,900 in 1534. It was a life which offered them not only scope for education, which would not have been forthcoming inside bristling castle walls, but opportunities for power such as they would never find in the raucous world outside. In this respect these institutions functioned much like boarding schools for daughters of the nobility. They operated across enormous distances, including foreign frontiers, and often from a tender age such as we might think proper for a little nursery school.

Here we have to bear in mind that the mothers of that class often parted from their infants shortly after giving birth. Then a wet nurse was engaged; and barely could a daughter talk, when she might be sent away from home to the nuns for safe-keeping and for instructions fitted for the conduct of a virtuous life. In such a manner monasteries forged a close, enduring link, often over generations, between surrogate and natural mothers. The latter might take the veil either in widowhood, common as that status was, or even still during marriage with their husband's consent, often after his conversion to Christianity by a cajoling wife. Certainly the Middle Ages wove an ever wider fabric of feminine interrelatedness.

Inside the monastery walls, where surrogate and natural mothers, natural daughters and daughters in Christ shared high monastic office, which they often handed down as a precious privilege, we are vividly reminded that women's groups are nothing new. Given the brutal bond that earthly marriage at the time often proved to be, the wish to be a Bride of Christ in genteeler circumstances hardly comes as a surprise. And so within this social circuit we find that close identification between a mother and her daughters which we tend to see today in privileged professional circles – at least, where the relationship is a satisfactory one. Then, as now, where it is wanting – or where, merely for rebellious reasons in a headstrong adolescence, things take a different turn – we find St Trinian's-like proportions, as in this charming tale:

In the sixth century in Frankia, the princess Clothilde, daughter of King Charibert, became a nun at St Radegund in Poitiers. Clothilde soon grew dissatisfied with the life within those walls. She tried to enlist the help of her royal relatives to improve her conditions there, but to no avail . . .

So the princess took matters into her own hands and 'threatened to throw the Abbess over the precinct wall'. At this juncture many of her less belligerent sisters left the nunnery. Clothilde was excommunicated and expelled. But

she gathered around her a band of cut-throats, evil-doers, fornicators and fugitives from justice, and men guilty of every crime. Together they attacked the nunnery, planning to take the Abbess prisoner. The latter was suffering from an attack of gout, which made flight rather difficult, so she hid in the sanctuary of the Holy Cross in front of the reliquary. Here the cut-throats found her. They fell to squabbling among themselves over the prize, and in the confusion the prioress blew out the candles and tried to smuggle out the Abbess under the altar-cloth. The men, sensing what was happening, rushed forward, tore off the prioress's veil, and, taking her for the Abbess, carried her off by mistake. When they discovered their error, they rushed back, seized the Abbess and looted the nunnery. All this happened at the beginning of holy week. Rioting between Clothilde's gang and that of the Abbess continued all over Easter, and was only quelled when the King sent an army to Poitiers under the local count. Clothilde, always mistress of the dramatic gesture, went out to meet them carrying a cross before her and garbed as a nun, claiming the protection of her habit and her birth.

At the ensuing trial she threw every conceivable accusation at the Abbess:

keeping a man dressed as a woman in the nunnery for her own use; castrating the servants, playing backgammon; eating with lay visitors; holding engagement parties in the nunnery and making a necklace for her niece out of the gold from the altarcloths.

Nor had Clothilde found conditions at Poitiers up to her four-star standard tastes. The food was bad, service terrible, and she had to share a bathroom, while the morals of the nuns left much to be desired.

Several were pregnant at the time of the trial, though the judging bishops generously excused this as the result of their being left to their own devices, without an Abbess, and with the nunnery gates broken down. In spite of these accusations, the Abbess answered all and was acquitted; she had relations among the judges. Clothilde had gone too far, especially when, after attacking the nunnery, she had personally assaulted the bishop when he came to restrain her, treading him underfoot. She was returned to suffer the Abbess's vengeance.

'But', this most revealing vignette concludes, 'to have princesses in nunneries, in any numbers, was to invite such troubles, and one must wonder how happy an Abbess was when a royal lady arrived at the gates seeking the religious life' (Baker, D., 1924, p. 98).

Another mother and daughter struggled through to amity despite a phase of turbulence. Queen Margaret, born in Hungary, who became a Scottish queen, raised a family since labelled 'a Nursery of Saints'. St Margaret, as she became, had her daughter Edith sent to a nunnery at Wilton from a very early age, in the care of her aunt Christine, in 1086. 'Good Queen Maud' Edith might become, but clearly those years at Wilton were disturbed and unhappy ones, with little or no sign of her later piety:

I went in fear and trembling of my aunt Christine . . . and she would often make me smart with a good slapping and the most horrible scolding, as well as treating me as being in disgrace.

It was furthermore Christine who, to protect her niece, put a veil on her head:

I did indeed wear it in her presence, but as soon as I was able to escape out of sight, I tore it off and threw it on the ground and trampled on it and in that way I used to vent my rage and the hatred of it which boiled up in me. (Baker, D., 1924, p. 123)

'The incident,' we are told, 'in conjunction with others, led to Edith's departure from Wilton in the company of her father.' Had she persuaded her father, perhaps behind her mother's back, to let her out into the world on account of hateful restrictions? Were these the norm at the time or emergency measures imposed after the Norman Conquest, with its ensuing turbulence?

Very shortly afterwards both Edith's parents died. That 'The Life of St Margaret' was written barely a dozen years after her mother's death at Edith's instigation, as the new Queen of England and wife of Henry I, testifies to reparation, if not actual devotion. That earlier adolescent squalls ended in harmony is suggested when we read: 'Edith was very much her mother's daughter . . . a formidable personality and a restless piety . . . and devotion evocative of Margaret' (Power, E., 1975, p. 140).

Elfled, in her time, survived harsher circumstances and none the less still achieved, remarkable as this may seem, a deep identification with her mother, Queen Eanfled. Her father, King Oswy of Northumbria in the seventh century AD, vowed his daughter to God and to holy virginity if he defeated Penda of Mercia, which he subsequently did, near the river Winwaed. Barely one year old, the tiny princess was consigned to the cloister at Hartlepool and the care of her good aunt Hilda, with whom she later moved to Whitby, where she grew up.

Her early life hardly gave Edith an auspicious start, we would be inclined to think, towards favouring any close mother–daughter alliance. Such an early separation and a life of austerity would seem rather to provide ample ground for grievances and a sense of deprivation. But here, it seems, our preconception is faulty. For 'there was excellent wine, singing to the harp in entertainments at dinner and the nuns sewed stylish garments more fitting to brides of the world than to brides of Christ' (Power, E., 1975, p. 140). If the sisters were warned to keep well away from manicures and curling tongs, this merely suggests that there is no smoke without fire. Elfled would certainly have seen her mother from time to time, when she stopped off on her journeys which she made with the king, since monasteries served as inns for itinerant royalty as they crisscrossed feudal lands. And in due course she succeeded as Abbess of Whitby, jointly with her widowed mother, after Hilda died in 680.

But for all these illustrations, vivid as many are, histories such as these concerned important ladies and were surely few and far between in the total population. Saintliness and virginity make unlikely bedfellows with the daily wear and tear of that harsh reality based on tenure of the land, within a rigid hierarchy, riddled with misery, disease and cruel superstition, for the unsung majority. Just how thin on the ground and how patchy the impact of Christianity remained is still a chapter to be written.

With very little safety net, those ordinary women who stayed on the treadmill, each in her allotted place, must have held their act together under considerable duress. With continuous childbearing under wretched circumstances, thrown into a hard bargain, the hardships must have been excessive, all too often on the brink of ineluctable perdition – especially for youthful widows, not to mention unmarried mothers.

On one register is listed one Milicentia, who supported herself and her daughters born outside wedlock by brewing ale, while another,

Juliana Balle, supported her bastard daughter by pin-making (Shahar, S., 1983, p. 117). An 'incontinent' girl 'lost her inheritance'; widow's dower was guaranteed, under a charter of Henry I, as long as she did not commit the sins of fornication and adultery (Shahar, S., 1983, p. 118): it is not difficult to read a dark and struggling substratum of bedevilled womankind under the monastic elite – all eagerness to join those ranks. But the substantial dowries which were extorted by the system admitted *hoi polloi* only in the menial role of servant: for them no status of a nun!

Under these harsh circumstances we are not surprised to find references to infanticide

committed by women of the peasant class . . . in momentary madness and fear . . . A priest lived with a woman in his house for one and a half years, and only feared for his honour when he heard the cry of a newborn infant, and then dug a pit and forced the woman, who was half mad with grief and pain, to throw in the baby. (Shahar, S., 1983, p. 118)

Imagine the nine months of hell, of concealment and of terror, leading up to the event, while the gentleman in question read his sermons from the pulpit! 'If the infanticide came to light and the mother was found, she was sentenced to death by burning or by being buried alive' (Shahar, S., 1983, p. 118). Letters of remission might be granted for a first offence, but not for a second one. That women ran such awful risks under the circumstances suggests how harsh their outlook was, should they choose to rear the child: how cruel the ostracism in the case of a bastard.

But social change came to the rescue, even if for a minority. For once the towns began to grow, towards the end of the era, so trades came within the reach of women who were tough-minded enough to make the system work for them. It is here that we find the first abuse of child labour, several centuries before the Industrial Revolution.

Although loopholes now offered various possibilities for 'femmes soles' to survive, woman in practice was not 'a free and lawful person' (Power, E., 1975, p. 10). And so a girlhood as goods would habitually evolve into a wifehood as chattels to sustain that passivity which is the medieval mother's hallmark. In *Romeo and Juliet* we find the mother kowtowing to her Lord and Master's wishes regarding her daughter's hopes for marriage. It is the Nurse, as surrogate mother and closer to her charge's heart, who speeds the ill-fated romance as a much freer agent, since she is a single woman at this time in her life, while as member of a 'bawdy' class she is less tied to the upper crust's hypocrisy.

How little personality, as we see it in our day, was a concept at the time grows clearer when we consider that the bishops who were trying the rebellious Clothilde excused the pregnancy of nuns: 'as the result of their being left to their own devices, without an Abbess, and with the nunnery gates broken down' (see p. 108). That accounted for that. What more could you expect from children, with whom women were equated? The extent of true vocation among these noble-lady-nuns is difficult to assess. Probably these young 'princesses' and daughters of the elite had internalized a mother, natural or surrogate, who held a privileged position according to prevailing lights and so desired for themselves a comparable status. How far the Heavenly Father may have represented, as we shall soon see, a sanctuary from a 'bad' mother, who sided with her Lord and Master, or a tyrannical father who ruled with an iron fist, must remain an open question.

Yet we find an exception to this genteel passion play of somewhat sanctimonious puppets. *The Book of Margery Kempe* (1373–1483) is, as far as we know, the first autobiography composed in the English language. Daughter of a Norfolk mayor and mother of fourteen children, she embarked on this travail towards the end of her life, when it had to be dictated since the author could not write! Once we look carefully behind the unaccustomed style, with its self-denigration, we are alerted to a conflict, daring in its self-expression, which must have burst like a bombshell on current Christianity. The focus is, in fact, heroic, and it is a twofold one so wholly modern in its searching that it can take our breath away once we have achieved her wavelength. First is the question of our right to 'do penance' by ourselves, in the depths of our own soul, guided by privacy, without any higher promptings. Secondly, she agonizes, how shall we validate personal experience of our most complex feelings 'when she knew not how they should be understood: for dread that they are deceits and illusions . . .' (Goulianos, J., 1973, p. 32).

The premature and lonely burdens of such advanced self-scrutiny, of a mind in such precocious freedom and in total opposition to autocratic Christian doctrine, meant that Margery lived her life on the brink of psychosis, and in fact went over it after the birth of her first child. During that puerperium, overwhelmed with inner guilt, she was driven to recant, her startling audacity claiming that she had been 'ever hindered by her enemy, the devil, evermore saying to her that whilst she was in good health she need no confession, but to do penance by herself alone and all should be forgiven, for God is merciful enough' (Goulianos, J., 1973, p. 37).

She was rescued from her childbed madness by a vision of Christ offering loving forgiveness for having dared to presume entitlement to take charge of her own inner life. In gratitude she became a much-travelled, lifelong pilgrim, both by land and by sea, with all the attendant hazards for a woman at the time. We may regret that we hear no mention of her own mother or any daughters which she may have had, only one line about a son. None the less, Margery is a mother to us daughters where, in her utter loneliness, each forerunner will cast around for a spiritual mother, who has stood there before at that most solitary of places where we give birth to what is new.

We need, however, to move on from these religious enclaves to other mothers and daughters as they are represented in the literature of the day, even while we recognize that life and art may well diverge in significant respects. In the conspiracy of silence, references are scanty. Yet a source postulates: 'relationships between mothers and children, and between mothers and daughters in particular, must have existed . . . In what other way could generation after generation of girls have learned how to be women?' Should this degree of silence, as the author cogitates, be attributed less to misogyny than to sheer ignorance on the part of male authorship 'of the whole world within which women moved – that of the spinning room and the bedchamber – [which] lay outside the province of man's knowledge' (Stiller, N., 1980, p. 7)?

This is possibly quite true on the level of conventions. But there is a deeper factor, since this mysterious segregation continues largely to persist for all that unisex array of our consumer world today. There, its glossy surfaces merely serve to conceal that women have, in fact, remained a daunting mystery to men. Men 'know' but also do not know the woman's secret-garden hide-outs. The exclusion of man, scared away from those precincts by the oedipal taboo, exiled from the *jouissance* partaken of by the woman, tends to colour this core experience with lifelong withdrawal and suspicion.

We will return to *jouissance* in the life of the medieval woman after a more searching look at the mother of the day, whose hallmark was passivity in relationship to her daughter, as in other respects. We encounter her repeatedly in popular stories of the time, some based on actual events and composed in successive versions over several decades (Stiller, N., 1980, p. 17). They tell of young Christian virgins who chose imprisonment and death at the hands of a tyrant father rather than submit and marry a pagan suitor of his choice. The mother barely so much as figures in these horrific events, except for our understanding that her heart is with her daughter, while she must side with her husband since she knows no alternative. Accordingly we are told that in the case of Iuliene's mother: 'in the intent of her heart [she] abhorred the sacrilegious worship of Mars' (Stiller, N., 1980, p. 25), while the mother of Cristyne, with similar sentiments, falls at her daughter's feet and begs her to submit to her father's will, only to be rejected as her daughter 'storms out of the palace, forsaking her mother' (Stiller, N., 1980, p. 27).

As these several virgins turn from their cruel, earthly father, abetted by a two-faced mother, they address a heavenly one: 'You are the father; you foster helpless children . . . the maiden's prosperity.' Or: 'I am the Lord's lamb and he is my shepherd . . . that I may do according to his dear Will' (Stiller, N., 1980, p. 22). Where, we wonder, does an image of this God who loves and protects women then originate? Hardly from the Jehovah of the Old Testament. Neither, surely, from the Christ defaced by later Pauline teachings. To whom or what, we can but marvel, are they addressing themselves, in terms of primary experience in this hour of extremis? What knowledge of enduring love, for which they are prepared to die, are these girls projecting here into this loving protector.

Nikki Stiller argues that they are father-identified. Can we go along with that? Their earthly fathers hardly served as a model for love. Two authors of the time, (of the *Ancrene Riwle* and *Hali Meidenhead*) both hold out that a better life awaits woman as the spouse of Christ: 'Listen to me daughters and look and give me your attention; forget your people and your father's house. David, the psalmwriter, speaks in the Psalms to God's spouse . . . ' (Stiller, N., 1980, p. 31). If we find a source of *jouissance* anywhere in the Bible, it is surely in the Psalms. Might then, at an unconscious level, a reference at this point to David embody some esoteric meaning which we need to understand?

It would certainly appear that these maidens in their plight were prepared to die for – let us call it 'that Experience' which was surely rooted in a shining imago of Love. But with these vague, submissive mothers – and they certainly exist – where did this idea arise which informed their unconscious of an unconditional love offered by a 'heavenly' parent, regardless of the actual sex? The answer which presents itself is from an earliest 'instruction', or what Lacan called 'mirroring': as Klein, in her turn, would put it, from an 'internalized good object' during the first months of life, even if these two concepts differ quite considerably.

If we dismiss this idea, then we have to explain how generations of daughters, afflicted with tyrannical fathers and submissive, passive mothers, ever found the inner strength, the basic life-affirmation, to maintain their sanity and mother daughters in their turn, even if there could have been no shortage of psychosis then, as in our present day. But what interests us here is how there none the less thrived such vigour and vitality among the women of the time.

The explanation surely lies in early experience beyond cultural interdiction, to which we have just referred. It is amply confirmed in the course of psychotherapy, where woman patients may reach back to a 'good early mother' belonging to the dawn of life across traumatic interludes. For however nebulous this experience may be, as it surfaces in dreams or a dreamlike memory, the effect in therapy carries dramatic potency. As the patient reaches back to this maternal 'instruction', perhaps of the preverbal phase, that she is loved and beautiful as a future woman whatever that big world might say, her drab and colourless self-image undergoes a subtle change.

Denigratory life-experience often at maternal hands, like the mother's example where she is passive and cowed, may complicate the later picture of the girl's development as it becomes contaminated by cultural expectations. But by then, at deeper levels of the feminine unconscious, sufficient life-affirmation and *jouissance* have been sown to ensure its survival. Neither should it be forgotten that the realities which fostered the compliant mother of the day were largely species-orientated before a notion of selfhood was feasible for either sex. High infant mortality demanded large families. This made woman look to man as provider and protector with little energy to spare to reflect on her lot, let alone to instil rebellion in her daughter's heart.

Yet rebellion there was on the part of certain daughters. Once again it belonged to their phase as a maiden fighting for the next step forward to be mistress of her life in terms of inner convictions. The resulting conflicts are portrayed in stories of the time, like those of Osbern Bokenham. A Doctor of Divinity and a Suffolk man, born in 1392, he wrote *The Legendys of Hooly Wummen* at the request of assorted patrons, including nuns of a Cambridge convent, respectable families and various high-minded ladies; and Nikki Stiller suggests that 'his presentation must have expressed the interests or ideals or fantasies of this class' (Stiller, N., 1980, p. 24).

This was doubtless the case. None the less we find a hearing for both sides of the conflict, if we can tune into it. In these writings, Stiller says, it is by and large the fathers who direct their daughters' lives. And criticism of the fathers, however autocractic and cruel, is, she says, 'minimal'. But we must also bear in mind that the daughters of these *Legendys* are at their most turbulent – in that category of maiden, with all its subtle distinctions, which tend to be overlooked.

Before these maidens are put down, as the social group demands, the author makes quite a case for their independent stance, as when in 'The Lyf of St Cristyne' he initially asserts, with a hint of approval:

> *Her only purpose was to love and serve*
> *The omnipotent lord of heaven and earth,*
> *But in the meantime she kept secret*
> *Her holy intention from her parents.*
> (Stiller, N., 1980, p. 25)

Here she can queer her father's pitch – he wants to marry her off – for presumably her leanings are towards a monastic life. But then Cristyne goes too far when the dialectic swings into a more aggressive tack. So passionately does she insist on a mind of her own that she actually complains 'about her father's lack of intelligence' when he locks her up in a tower to worship his pagan idols:

> *'Now I perceive very well', said Cristyne,*
> *'That you want wit and understanding,*
> *And that you lack the influence of divine grace*
> *For understanding the mystery of these divine things.'*
> (Stiller, N., 1980, p. 26)

And shortly after this pronouncement she throws her father's hateful idols from the tower window. Hereupon her father has her maidens beheaded – as a warning, no doubt – and administers to her a sound medieval beating. At this juncture we hear:

> *When Cristyne's mother had plainly heard*
> *How she suffered such torments*
> *At the hands of her father, like a madwoman,*
> *Out of her wits with fear,*
> *She rent her clothes, strewed ashes*
> *On her head, and in that guise*
> *Went to the prison where Cristyne was.*
> *Falling to the ground and piteously weeping . . .*

She tells her daughter of her love for her, and pleads with her to give in (Stiller, N., 1980, p. 40). There is authentic passion here, carried to the very limits of what is culturally permissible. But her daughter rejects her and everything she represents in no uncertain terms. Now the wounded, frightened mother tells her husband 'everything that has transpired', which induces the enraged father to disown his stubborn daughter and apply to the law, which has the girl tortured.

What, we ought to ask ourselves, would have happened to the mother if she had sided with her daughter? Would she not share her fate and deprive her other children of their natural mother, meaning that such behaviour would not, under the circumstances, be species-orientated?

In the 'Lyf of St Lucye', also by Bokenham, Lucye's father had died, leaving Lucye and her mother Eutyce to their own devices in a loving, warm relationship where the two appear to relish an interlude of freedom from close masculine attention. But Eutyce catches dysentery and to save her life Lucye takes her to the tomb of St Agatha, who appears to Lucye in a dream where she states the terms for her mother's recovery. They are that Lucye shall not marry 'any mortal corruptor' but retain her virginity. (St Jerome would have been well pleased.) But the twosome's happy days together, following recovery, are cut short by the appearance on the scene of Lucye's suitor, who takes her to a Roman court which orders Lucye to the brothel and a continuous rape, to teach the stubborn girl a lesson: she has no business to have 'dreams'. Lucye's courage, when she insists that she would not be sinning since the inmates of a brothel are raped against their will, causes the nonplussed judge to accuse her of witchcraft (Stiller, N., 1980, p. 43).

The suitor, we might note in passing, intervened and conscripted the law only when he came to hear that mother and daughter were distributing their money far and wide as 'almes-dedes' – when it seemed, in other words, that the two might become both a social force and a liability. To a society which was focusing increasingly on individual wealth, this was an appalling prospect. The suitor also, very likely, had a beady eye on a nice, substantial dowry, which he saw going down the drain.

There was, of course, no Poor Law yet. That flimsiest of saftey nets was still lacking, at the time, to stand between an outcast woman and utter perdition should she choose to run the risk of such an abject fall from grace. The emphasis lay heavily on the virtues of self-maintenance within a submissive role once the drive for surplus capital had started getting under way. Even the monasteries, as we have already seen, stipulated a dowry for any seeking shelter in the status of a nun.

We find that Bokenham dangles a hint of free choice before his high-minded readership, only to snatch it away, as those who wish to exercise it come to a sorry end if they do not recant; if they do not submit to father's authority or, failing that, to the tears of mother, as his representative.

But if mothers withheld shows of affection from their daughters – or, as in *The Paston Letters* (quoted by Stiller, N., p. 51), subdued them as cruelly as any tyrannical patriarch – it seems that little girls and boys were very much in the same boat in this particular respect, for in the current literature 'tenderness to little children is never mentioned' (Stiller, N., 1980, p. 51), it would seem. Maternal affection, after all, if it is demonstrative, instils the germs of a sense of selfhood: of being wanted for one's self: on which experience medieval society placed a stern prohibition. For as we know from Margaret Mead, even if certain of her findings have recently come under fire, societies will rear their infants with a definite end-result in view, whether they are aware of it or not.

And so, within our present context,

mothers might teach their daughters to weep and serve and weep again; they might teach them, as does the Wife of Bath's 'dame', to snare a man; they might mix love drinks for them, to that end, as Iseult's mother does; they might bundle them off to convents or prepare them to lead an anchoress's life of comtemplation. What they do not seem able to do in the literature, generally speaking, is to give them respect and honour for full-blown biological womanhood . . . [thereby perpetuating that] . . . woman believed themselves to have been born inferior, and if they did not subscribe wholeheartedly to the idea, they seldom jeopardized their position by saying so. (Stiller, N., 1980, p. 57)

To say so is to stress the obvious. Let any one of us 'honour full-blown biological womanhood' in the Third World today and wait to see what would happen, if we are native to the place!

Where does all this leave us now? The minute we like to think that we have begun to see a definite picture taking shape – obedient daughters and passive mothers – an altogether different version is thrust into that very frame. Here is a woman writing in the twelfth century: a woman who is a wife and recent mother of a child. She is writing to her husband:

Consider [she said] the true conditions for a dignified way of life. What harmony can there be between pupils and nursemaids, desks and cradles, books or tablets and distaffs, pen or stylus and spindles? Who can concentrate on thoughts of scripture or philosophy and be able to endure babies, crying, nurses soothing them with lullabies, and all the noisy coming and going of men and women about the house? Will he put up with the constant muddle and squalor which small children bring into the home? (Abelard and Héloïse, 1974, p. 71)

These parents had but recently farmed their own infant out, to his family in Brittany, for they were married in secret.

She, Héloïse, the wife, had tasted the deepest joys of a mind which had been well and truly nourished, by her uncle, in her girlhood years. Not only that, but she had surrendered shamelessly, by her own admission, to extravagant sexual passion. Both partners had been guilty of taking an enormous leap beyond the confines of their time, towards a higher integration than their society allowed. That the uncle should burst in and castrate Abelard was, on a symbolic level, the only possible solution, as Héloïse herself insinuates in the passage we have quoted. However bitterly she chafed under her subsequent fate, a life of penance as a nun, she knew that she had placed herself in an impossible position within a polarity which was hysterically strung between sanctity-cum-learning, or the life of the body: 'that hidden gallery in a closed-off wing' (Stiller, N., 1980, p. 8). Not without reason were the Middle Ages known as a vast lunatic asylum.

One factor which helped to save the day for feminine sanity, precarious as it must have been under such circumstances, was that network of women, with its close fellowship, born of such deep inclination as is wont to germinate in the heart of the slave. Marriage, in the upper crust, tended to be patrilocal, so that a young wife would depend for sustenance on the women who accompanied her from home, as in the Old Testament. In this matter Brangain, Iseult's lady-in-waiting, stays loyally at her side through her trials and tribulations in her husband's distant country, as a loving surrogate, while 'several queens are depicted in the romance literature as fostering the young women who serve them' (Stiller, N., 1980, p. 100). And

whereas in Malory, Launcelot comes to the rescue . . . in the Old French La Mort du Roi Artu . . . even Guenevere, in some ways the loneliest heroine in English literature . . . depends upon another woman to save her from certain death at the most crucial moment of her crisis-ridden life . . . [For] she waked two of her damsels, the ones in whom she had the greatest confidence . . .

who assisted her escape to take refuge in a nearby forest, where there was an abbey of nuns who in the end took her in despite grave anxiety as to the various implications (Stiller, N., 1980, p. 108). The abbess, who was addressed 'My most dear Mother', as recounted by Bede, filled this part most loyally despite exceptions to the rule, but hagiographers tend to try to keep the natural mother in the family chronicles, to approve of their daughters' transference of loyalties.

How far into the later Middle Ages this motherly solicitude – known as the 'abbess-tradition' – offered a home from home is not altogether clear, but certainly this extended mother–daughter alliance permeated the era within a nurturing women's group. At its head we will find 'Oure blisful Lady, Cristes mooder deere . . . this welle of mercy, Cristes mooder sweete' (Stiller, N., 1980, p. 114, quoting Chaucer).

Salvation in the sense of rescue is the particular function of the Virgin Mother . . . all who call upon the Mother for help in their time of need receive it, and it seems her power is thus limited by her mercy and limitless compassion. (p. 115)

Moreover, the phantasy of rescue, as Helene Deutsch has pointed out, is a common one 'on the part of adoptive mothers and stepmothers' (Stiller, N., 1980, p. 240).

If the concept of the Virgin Mother has wrought much mischief among women by causing a tripartite split, medieval Mariology must have played a central part in helping them to maintain a degree of self-esteem through these adverse centuries. For the Hellenistic age bequeathed preposterous attacks on feminine procreativity which were soon seconded by Thomas Aquinas in more derogatory terms, where all the virtue of life is due to masculine substance and woman is designated as 'the inferior "workman"'. The Mother of God – for all her meekness, since she could officially only supplicate her son – had worked a crucial miracle in the hearts of her daughters by the fifteenth century, by a steadfast projection of an *active* loving stance.

Like some secret inland sea, for all its ambiguity, Mariology fostered a clear line of *jouissance*. Certainly it might float its impossible demands, imposing guilt and repression; it encouraged courtly love to serenade the non-sexual mother in her virginal purity with passionate, unfulfilled desire, but at the same time it furthered, as shrines and chapels multiplied with their tales of miracles, a new image of a mother in *loving activity*. And this was altogether different from the subjugated, passive version which, as Nikki Stiller found, pervades medieval literature.

In her *Revelations* we can find these trends confirmed by that great English mystic Julian of Norwich (1342–1413):

For we are doubly in God's making: that is to say, Substantial and Sensual. Our substance is the higher part, which we have in our Father, God Almighty; and the Second Person of the Trinity is our Mother in kind, in making of our Substance, in whom we are grounded and rooted. And he is our Mother in Mercy, in our Sensuality taking. And thus our parts are kept undisparted. (Stiller, N., 1980, p. 120)

Here, Jesus and his Mother begin to be equated, for she later refers to 'our precious Mother Jesus' (Stiller, N., 1980, p. 121). Body, substance and spirit begin to draw together here, as the curtain slowly falls on these Middle Ages.

No writer and no mystic can experience or express what is not afloat in the *Zeitgeist*, if only partly consciously. That integration of these aspects of feminine nature, after centuries of schism, was at last setting in would be difficult to doubt. For without it the great leap into the Renaissance, which offered privileged women virtually equal status, could surely not have been effected, since every new step forward implies the healing of an earlier split, if only to some extent.

Let us then say farewell to these hamstrung centuries, as far as women were concerned, by meeting one of those spirits, be they of either sex, who are timeless in the ease with which they salvage the best, everything that is most hopeful, from the maelstrom of their era for other members of their kind. A contemporary of Margery Kempe, Christine de Pizan, born in Venice (1364), was to spend her life in France, where her father was astrologer at the court of Charles VII. From a very early age Christine enjoyed full access to the well-stocked royal libraries with her father's proud encouragement, despite her mother's remonstrations, which reached crescendo height at times. The erudition she achieved was to stand her in good stead for, widowed at the age of twenty-five after an exceptionally happy marriage, with three young children to support, she turned to her pen for a living. In poetry, as in prose, she covered a great range of subjects, which include the only work, in French, in honour of Joan of Arc during her actual lifetime (*Le Ditié de Jeanne d'Arc*). But from this author – who was, furthermore, the king's official biographer – in all her *œuvre* we find only two fleeting references to her mother. The first of these briefly mentions 'the conventional objections of her mother' to her wide education, even though women's minds, she adds, are 'freer and sharper' than those of men (de Pizan, C., 1983, p. xiv). Then later on, from the heartland of her fully fledged career, we come across this haunting mention vibrant with evocation:

One day as I was sitting alone in my study surrounded by books on all kinds of subjects, devoting myself to literary studies, my usual habit, my mind dwelt at length on the weighty opinion of various authors whom I had studied for a long time . . . I had not been reading for very long when my good mother called me to refresh myself with some supper, for it was evening. (de Pizan, C., 1983, p. 3)

Here, like a bird on the wing, we catch a tantalizing glimpse of maternal forgiveness and a harmonious truce in which the two of them now lived, seemingly reconciled, as two widows together, since we know that her father was dead, in a relationship both warm and mutually supportive – indeed, we may perhaps surmise this mother's late appreciation of Christine's learned skills, which provide them with a living.

To Christine's own daughter we find no direct reference. Only from her poetical writings (*Le Livre du Dit de Poissey*) do we glean this charming memorandum:

In it she takes us, on a bright spring morning, with a joyous company, from Paris to the royal convent of Poissey, where her child is at school. She describes all the beauties of the country, the fields gay with flowers, the warbling of the birds, the shepherdesses with their flocks, the willow-shaded river bank along which they ride, the magic of the forest of St Germain, a little world apart of greenery and shade, filled with the song of nightingales . . . Then follows a description of the beautiful carved cloisters, the chapterhouse, the nuns' dress and their dormitory, the garden scented with lavender and roses, with one part, where small animals are allowed to run wild, left uncultivated, and the ponds well stocked with fish . . . They return to the inn where they are to spend the night, and after supper wander forth to listen to the nightingales, then dance a carole, and so to bed. (Kemp-Welch, A., 1913, p. 140)

No actual mention of her daughter. Yet she breathes in every word as we share the mother's joy and serene satisfaction that her daughter's environment is just as she would dearly wish it – in every virtuous respect and beauty of that tended setting. That she is brimful at peace, since these surrogate mothers are to each detail qualified to nurture her growing daughter while she herself provides the means, in those great libraries in the heart of the city. For it is, we understand, her inner happiness about her daughter, in the early springtime of her life, which causes her to rejoice in the springtime of the landscape, with its song of nightingales, while she dances before bedtime, still aglow from their reunion. What a taste of *jouissance* we imbibe from this passage! What stores she herself must have derived in her turn, from her own mother, despite any little tiffs, to have such vibrant perceptions to pass on to her own child – and to us, in such rich language as its joyous vehicle. How she rejoiced in her daughter is evident from her laments at 'the disappointment women of her day felt at the birth of daughters: she gives as its cause the need to provide young women with dowries' (Kemp-Welch, A., 1913, p. xiv).

From these evocative fragments, handed to us like a bouquet, we inhale the sweetness of a mother–daughter alliance sustained through three generations, as is so frequently the case where we find this achievement. At its centre glows this measured, richly endowed feminist, whose personality breaks through irrepressibly at times despite an austere convention which was one of self-effacement; for as this authority suggests: 'self-advertisement was not a medieval fashion ... this apparently humble attitude can be atrributed to the intense localization of life ... within which there is no need for self-advertisement' (Kemp-Welch, A., 1913, p. xiii). Besides, was this not 'a time when mankind still lay dreaming, or half awake beneath a common veil ...' (Fromm, E., 1984, p. 36, quoting Jacob Burkhardt).

But in most instances, and for the great majority, the dreams were closer to a nightmare for the wretched, battling sinners:

> *A poore widow somedeal steep in age ...*
> *... In patience ledde a full simple life,*
> *For little was her chattel or her rent.*
> *By husbandry, of such as God her sent*
> *She found herself and eke her daughters two ...*
> *Full sooty was her bower and eke her hall ...*
> *Her diet was according to her coat ...*

Nor was the father better off, lest we fall into that error:

> *... work in the fields ...*
> *He wading in mud, almost up to his ankles,*
> *And before him four oxen, so weary and feeble,*
> *One could reckon their ribs, so rueful were they.*
> *His wife walked beside him, with a long ox goad,*
> *In a clouted coat cut short to her knee,*
> *Wrapped in a winnowing sheet to keep out the weather ...*
> (Power, E., 1975, p. 74, quoting Chaucer from the
> *Nun's Priest's Tale*)

Little room for caroles and dancing here, except for rare festival occasions. How much did a Christine de Pizan know of this, her sisters' lot? How far could mothers such as these give their daughters 'respect and honour for full-blown biological womanhood', as Stiller pinpoints that failure? What could such fathers give their sons, it might be pertinent to ask, when there was too little 'Both in milk and in meal to make therewith papelots [porridge] to glut therewith their children that cry after food' (Power, E., 1975, p. 74).

The poor would remain the poor, with only, to our day and age, most pitiful alleviation. Nor were their like to know, as they stumbled behind the plough, little better than that wooden cross which blistered the hands of the slaves of Rome, that the age that gave us the printing press, Protestantism and gunpowder was already underway: an age which was to introduce genuine opportunities for virtual equality to a feminine elite, as a spin-off of that great European excitement known as the Renaissance. For had a time not dawned when woman, '. . . rid of her apotheosized figure, a true human being, [was] seeking, as man was also seeking, to become an emancipated individual' (de Riencourt, A., 1983, p. 231)? If not in northern climates, nor yet upon Atlantic shores, at least in the warmer regions of those eager, vying states known today as Italy.

3 LET HER HAVE A DICTIONARY

Let her have a dictionary, Latin and English, which she may often consult, and get to know what each word signifies . . . Let her get a somewhat large note-book (librum vacuum) in which she may jot down in her own hand, first words . . .
(JUAN VIVÈS [1492–1540]: 'A plan of studies for girls (for the Princess Mary)' [Susan Bell])

And truly if we would call the old world to remembrance, and rehearse their time, we shall find no learned woman that ever was ill: where I could bring forth an hundred good . . .
(JUAN VIVÈS: 'Instruction of a Christian woman' [Susan Bell])

We must keep before our minds the fact that women stood on a footing of perfect equality with men . . . There was no question of 'women's rights', or female emancipation, simply because the thing itself was a matter of course. The educated woman, no less than the man, strove naturally after a characteristic and complete individuality.
(AMAURY DE RIENCOURT, *Woman and Power in History*)

A RAY OF SUNSHINE and a beam of hope? A figment of reality with which to decorate the page, only to be lost again? For how many dozen women did this dream materialize?

It can be said with certainty that at the courts of Italy recent wealth and new-found power began to rattle at the bondage of the confines to a role. Here, at the heart of growing trade routes where weighty humanist ideas were carried side by side with goods in an exultant, ravenous commerce, appetites began to stir that life held more than peonage to the Fathers of the Church; while these continued to repeat: 'A woman must be a learner, listening quietly and with due submission. I do not permit a woman to domineer over a man: she should be quiet' (Timothy 2:11–13). Quiet together, we might add, with all the voiceless, meek and poor.

But if French ballads at the height of Mariology ended with the medieval refrain: 'En ciel un Dieu, en terre une Déesse', certainly the Renaissance saw, if not goddesses, some secular equivalents – high-spirited, unbending women, sometimes mother and daughter, in positions of inspired power. There was Isabella of Spain, with her four educated daughters; ill-fated Catherine at the hands of England's Henry VIII, and Eleonora, who would shine at the court of Ferrara and rig the sails of Columbus for horizons of the New World, with a passionate vision, while she founded seats of learning for great scholarship at home.

In France her contemporaries, the Regent Anne de Beaujeu and Queen Anne of Brittany, like Marguerite of Angoulême, who 'would have been a better king' than her brother, as the people said, were all substantial presences; while in the sixteenth century two powerful women held the stage: Elizabeth I of England and Catherine de Médicis had both been recipients of a formidable education.

As in the abbess-tradition, here we also find daughters who followed in their mother's shoes. Eleonora of Ferrara and her daugher Isabella both, in turn, married down and utilized this position to seize the reins of royal power from relatively passive husbands. But where queens and certain daughters might, in that glittering position, have the best of two worlds, others, lower than the throne, had to choose and agonize: 'Shall I marry or devote my life to study?' Alessandra Scala asked her friend Cassandra Fedele in the fifteenth century. 'Do that for which your nature has suited you', responded Fedele, not very helpfully (Labalme, P.H., 1972, p. 66). 'Both women understood that marriage and scholarship might be incompatible. Both understood that the pursuit of learning required deliberate choice, the repudiation of ordinary goals, and an extraordinary commitment of energies. Both married' (Labalme, P.H., 1972, p. 66).

These conflicts are still our own, even if the implications have grown in complexity with our deepening awareness of the part that mothering, or neglect of it, will play in the life of generations. It is of interest that these friends chose to turn to one another in their painful quandary, rather than to their mothers. The conflict would have been a new one to confront their generation and therefore unfamiliar to the women of the previous one. The maternal attitude, at an inspired guess, might well have resembled that of Christine de Pizan's mother – distinct disapproval. This may even put it mildly, to judge by the hysteria loosened on Florence Nightingale three centuries further on, with ample documentation (see Part III, Chapter 2).

Certainly we tend to find, in the consulting room today, that where a daughter is the first woman in her family to blaze a trail to new skills and higher learning her feelings of guilt at 'doing better than her mother did' may assume such dire proportions as to make the project founder at some stage along the line, time and time again in the most self-defeating manner. For primitive anxieties are mobilized in the unconscious against such forging ahead and seizing life with both hands – since according to the logic of archaic, concrete thinking, if there is 'more' life for daughter, then for mother there is 'less': mother's share has been 'stolen'. And however 'irrational' such a conviction, its deeper power is relentless. Second-generation daughters tend to find the going easier and are less hampered by their guilt, where mother's place was in the vanguard.

Such evidence as we glean from writers on the Renaissance suggests that learned daughters were, in fact, encouraged by their fathers to take the opportunities the era was offering them. This we find corroborated in the nineteenth century, when we are left in little doubt of the father's crucial role in encouraging his daughter, while supporting his wife in the turmoil of her feelings as daughters start to fly the nest, not into a husband's arms but into the rough-and-tumble of a stalwart career. Have we not seen how Zeus himself was our early prototype, even if this father's role was still a rather covert one? Yet for how many maidens must any chance for higher learning have 'wrapped them away' quite as irresistibly as that mystical narcissus led Persephone to wander in the Nyasan Fields?

The dilemma as expressed by Alessandra and Cassandra had existed previously. Then its true nature lay concealed in that the choice was presented as one between two institutions – marriage or monasticism. Projected into the outer world – in other words externalized into a mere choice of roles – its impact comes to us blunted. While here in Renaissance Italy, where it is conjured up in such startling, modern terms as intrapersonal, our being echoes painfully to this fated dialectic of two contradictory facets of woman's deepest nature, which confounds us throughout life, in all its stages, to this day.

Here our two protagonists belonged to prominent families: their aspirations furthered by powerful and ambitious fathers who did not feel threatened by feminine competition where their masculinity found full and meaningful expression. As far as women were concerned, these dazzling opportunities on the crest of new assumptions at the courts of Italy would shortly sink from sight again: 'it was to take far more sweeping changes in ideology and socioeconomic development to produce a major reassessment of the destiny of the "second sex" ' (Labalme, P.H., 1972, p. 57).

The very word Renaissance seduces us with potent glitter. But the shadows return as soon as we remind ourselves that as far as actual numbers of these highly learned women went, they were, in fact, negligible: 'there were perhaps a dozen who could easily be named; perhaps another twenty, less visible, could be identified; others perhaps existed whose identities will elude us; perhaps three in these centuries were famous' (Labalme, P.H, 1972, p. 67).

Fathers might like learned daughters and be very proud of them, provided they were potentates in an ebullient position. But this did not apply to husbands, as a general rule. Once the maiden was a wife, even if she was a prodigy, she should be seen but not heard as St Paul had decreed, since these issues run much deeper than swings of the social pendulum may readily mislead us. Widowhood might offer her a second opportunity to consult her dictionary and return to her books, if there were no schemes afoot to have her take fresh marriage vows in the interests of diplomacy. But marriage, as her mother knew, could certainly not be based on intellectual expectations: this message would be driven home with tears and repeated threats to subdue high-flying spirits.

Woe to the daughter who showed signs of a deeper thirst for learning or for creative self-expression, to those who reached 'Beyond their Sex' to threaten the deep alignments, the finely stitched otherness which is femininity. To the patriarchal eye such indulged in wild excesses and hateful rebelliousness, as Elena Cornaro (b.1646). Already as a little girl:

she was no sooner dressed in feminine garb and left free than – within a short time – all her quarters would be strewn with her garments . . . so that they seemed a battlefield on which lay the remnants of the massacre of luxury . . . Ribbons untied, hair-pieces unfastened, broken mirrors, . . . strewn pearls, torn veils, scattered ornaments, the whole arsenal of beauty sacked and destroyed. (Labalme, P.H., 1972, p. 140)

This obstinate child prodigy became the first woman to receive a doctorate at a university. Her subject was theology. But St Paul had decreed that a woman should not teach, although her status entitled Elena to do so now. The Bishop of Padua and Elena's ambitious father, a Venetian potentate, in due course fought the matter out, in what manner we can only guess, to a final compromise. The awarded distinction was in Philosophy! We can read between the lines that beneath the eulogies on feminine emancipation, exceptional as it was, the fundamental issue brimmed with uneasy implications. Although the details are elusive we remain with the impression that these facilitating fathers would withdraw their support somewhere along the early way. Did the displeasure of their wives add to other pressures from the wider social scene? It was all very well to conduct experiments in feminine education to produce an adolescent show-piece in that brief category of 'maiden', but with very few exceptions in the ranks of royalty this hybrid soon lacked scope and would gradually sink back into the maternal circuit to conform as wife and mother.

Where the daughters of an artist might, in certain instances, receive their training in their father's studio to ránk among the privileged – like Marietta Robusti and Lavinia Fontana – these escapists from the norm often tended to die young, doubtless partly undermined by inescapable conflicts in a precarious situation. Certainly success drew envy and dire hostility to engender self-doubt and despair to induce capitulation: 'withdrawal into marriage or into grief' (Labalme, P.H., 1972, p. 64), as one authority suggests.

Neither must we forget that the Renaissance, like previous forms of transient progress, for all the enduring seeds it sowed, rested realistically on widespread ignorance and squalor. If the gains of an elite stand inscribed in history, 'the women of the *popolo basso* remained in wretched poverty' (Bell, S., 1973, p. 206). If, like their medieval sisters, they toiled in harness with their daughters as water-carriers, washerwomen, keepers of brothels or of taverns, or hawkers who served the poor, these versions of Mother Courage certainly reaped few rewards from that glittering interlude where precious little help was offered by their more enlightened sisters, for two more centuries to come. Indeed, Elizabeth I, herself the beneficiary of an impressive education, had in her gracious time a Homily on Matrimony composed and often read in church on Sundays, quoting St Peter, who had preached: 'Ye wives, be in subjection to obey your own husbands' (Bell, S., 1973, p. 219). After a little chink of light and a rosy glow of promise, Protestantism soon arrived to echo those crushing edicts, and 'male authority was driven home with all the authority of the Church' (Bell, S., 1973, p. 219). 'Protestant women went back to the home and kitchen . . . [and] Luther blasted as a dangerous thinker the celebrated humanist and educator Juan Luis Vivès . . . Take women from their housewifery and they are good for nothing' (de Riencourt, A., 1983, p. 258). He sided with conformist mothers to prove their protestations right.

As far as women were concerned, any attempt to trace their story through the early modern centuries sweeps us into massive contradictions, a 'dizzying topsy-turviness' (Woodbridge, L., 1984, p. 74), unless we repeat, with the poet: 'Therefore when we take the side of the one to revile the other, we hurt the truth which comprehends them both' (Tagore, R., 1985, p. 44). But are we not, throughout this epic, struck with a sense of awe at how women, in their generations, utilized every windfall and each new crevice to obtain a firmer hold on the meshwork of the social order?

To the urban middle class, the poor in the cities and the peasant to the north of Italy, Lutheranism and Calvinism seemed to promise such a hold. For the Renaissance and Reformation were, in effect, two powerful arms, culturo-political and religious, of a sweeping forward flow: the age that brought the dictionary, provided us with gunpowder and, above all, the printing press. By the mid-sixteenth century the first authorized Bible was translated into English, so that all good wives should read the Gospel and Paul's Epistles. And despite a 75 per cent illiteracy, growing numbers of homes soon owned a copy together with Foxe's *Book of Martyrs* and Bunyan's *Pilgrim's Progress*.

Here we find that centuries before the Industrial Revolution brought her new opportunities in a humble economic sphere, this piecemeal process 'started woman . . . on that passionate journey, that vilified, misunderstood journey away from home' (de Riencourt, A., 1983, p. 285), in search of a new identity, however nebulous it remained through coming centuries.

If more women could read than were yet able to write, undeterred they began to set pen to paper in steadily growing numbers. From Margery Kempe's brave dictation less than three centuries would pass before 'The Female Wits', the women playwrights of the Restoration, earned their living by their pens; while scattered in their lonely outposts, in a thinly populated countryside, women took to diary-writing as though they had been born to it.

4 DAUGHTERS SET PEN TO PAPER

THE LADY ANNE CLIFFORD had barely reached the age of fourteen when she began her famous diary at the hour of the death of the Great Queen Elizabeth in 1603. Others followed in that habit, and we will stay for a while with these evocative details of the daily – almost hourly – lives of women as mothers and as daughters, as grandmothers and as wives, and in instances as sisters. These memoirs and diaries, which have come down to us – how many must have been destroyed – were written from that age-deep well of womanly loneliness, when woman herself has not yet grasped her mysterious potency and thus feels bleakly at odds with one and all surrounding her. They were confessor and companion, a source of solace and support. There were entries which were written to set some painful record straight, when there was strain among relations; others, when there were tears to shed over yet another infant's death, or anguish to be confronted in the aftermath of a drawn-out labour she had hardly thought she would survive. There were thanks to offer for survival when this had hung in endless doubt, or when an indifferent husband, or a cruel plotting one, offered an interlude of warmth, to raise her hopes of better times. Most certainly they were not penned with literary self-consciousness and a sharp eye on posterity. For sure, they were no Anaïs Nin, this early handful of women, whose joys and sorrows, for that very reason, etch themselves deeply in our minds.

Masterpieces would follow. But as Virginia Woolf remarked: 'Masterpieces are not a single, solitary birth, they are the outcome of many years of thinking in common, of thinking by the body of the people, so that the experience of the mass is behind the single voice ...' (Clifford, A., ed. Sackville-West, V., 1923, p. 39, quoting Virginia Woolf). Here, the author was writing of the indomitable Aphra Behn, for the quotation continues: ' ... all women together ought to let flowers fall upon the tomb of Aphra Behn, for it was she who earned them the right to speak their minds.' Yet surely, Lady Anne Clifford deserves a share of that bouquet. For all her undoubted genius, Mrs Woolf was, alas, a literary snob. So let us set the record straight by laying these flowers, in our turn, on the quiet resting place of Aphra Behn's predecessors, who in fact managed to combine prolific maternity with the ouput of their pens – the more remarkable for that, as more hopeful to ourselves, we who struggle on to integrate these two sides of our obdurate nature; something which neither Mrs Woolf nor yet her protégée above had attempted to do, for all their undoubted feats.

Anne Clifford, as we have just seen, began her diary with the death of Elizabeth I in 1603, when she herself was only fourteen, and continued it intermittently for a span of sixteen years. The marriage of her parents proved not to be a happy one and this example she would follow, as is so frequently the case: 'My mother was there, but not held as mistress of the house, by reason of the difference between my Lord and her, which was grown to great height', writes the fourteen-year-old (Clifford, A., 1923, p. 10).

She stood in awe of both her parents. Her father, George Clifford, the third Earl of Cumberland, was at sea when she was born, and almost ever afterwards. With all the impulse of a gambler he fitted out successive fleets to enrich his Queen Elizabeth, whose body came to London by water on the day the diary begins. In consequence, Anne's mother, Margaret, was left much to her own devices, often angry and bemused and even set aside for others, until in her own words she looked 'as a ghost that wanted the soul of comfort'. But Anne goes on to describe her as naturally 'of high spirits, never yielding to ill fortune or opposition' (Clifford, A., 1923, p. xxiii). These qualities would be passed on in ample measure to her daughter, who as the one surviving child, two little brothers having died, carried her mother's obsession that the estates in Cumberland should fall to mother–daughter lineage.

This object they both pursued unyieldingly over decades – in part, no doubt, as consolation for love each had felt cheated of by this courtier-absentee, for all that this suit cost Anne in terms of marital harmony. Even if she was to waver, in moments verging on despair, when her life seemed on the edge of ruin resulting from her stubbornness, at the deepest roots of her being her allegiance was to her mother. There it solidly remained, past that obdurate lady's death, albeit at the king's displeasure at such a wanton display of feminine strong-headedness. This mother–daughter alliance, dating from Anne's babyhood and the estrangement of her parents, had been forged to endure past whatever duress a world of men could apply, even at the sorest point of feminine sensibility: the Achilles heel of motherhood. How frequently we tend to find that disappointment in marriage forges mother–daughter bonds of this tenacious nature!

But well before these shadows – which form the main theme of the diary – fell, Lady Cumberland's own duties at the much-travelled court meant that Anne's childhood was, in effect, a roving one: a case of 'poor little rich girl'. For despite the devotion between mother and daughter, the demands which the court made on Lady Cumberland all too often cut across opportunities for closeness which they both so much desired.

In consequence we have a child who had to learn early to rely on herself and would go hungry for love, for all those royal connections; for all that little Lady Anne was a staunch favourite of the queen, arousing other children's envy, which isolated her still further. But the needs of the court all too clearly came first:

From Windsor the Court removed to Hampton Court, where my Mother and I lay at Hampton Court, in one of those round towers, round about which were tents where they died two or three in a day of the plague. There I fell extremely sick of a fever, so as my Mother was in some doubt it might turn to the plague, but within two or three days I grew reasonably well, and was sent away to my cousin Stiddolph's, for Mrs Taylor [her governess-companion of long standing] was newly put away from me, her husband dying of the plague shortly after.

And a few lines further on, on the move yet again . . .

my Mother being extreme angry with me for riding before with Mr Mene, where my Mother in her anger commanded that I should lie in a Chamber alone, which I could not endure, but my cousin Frances got the key to my

Chamber and lay with me which was the first time I loved her so well. (Clifford, A., 1923, p. 12)

Stern her mother must have been, whose own mother had died when she herself was rising two. And doubtless her own deprivation had, at least to some degree, subverted the more tender strands of simple, maternal love into that passion for property which, as we saw earlier, coloured this mother–daughter link to such a fateful degree. Speculation aside, once Anne Clifford became the wedded wife of Richard Sackville, third Earl of Dorset, she would shortly have to learn to lie in chambers all alone, for thwarting his lifelong intentions to dispose over Cumberland to satisfy his vanity as well as his extravagance.

This early marriage of two minors, on grounds of complex expediency, brought a far-reaching change in the life of mother and daughter:

The new Lady Dorset must go down into Kent to assume her duties as mistress of the great house of Knole, and her mother, lonely as she had never been before, must turn her face to the north and settle down in the old crumbling castle [Brougham] beside the Eamont, where she was still little more than a newcomer, some three hundred miles away. (Holmes, M., 1975, p. 19)

But after the brief happiness of her early married days, Anne's life would shortly, like her mother's, enter that domain of shadows – the sorrows of marital strife, for which her childhood experience and observation of her parents had prepared her so well. 'When my mother and he did meet their countenances did show the dislike they had of one another', her girlhood diary had read (Clifford, A., 1923, p. xxii). And although in her own marriage a certain fondness would survive the battle over her possessions, much suffering was to accrue once Anne herself became a mother to 'the child', Lady Margaret, at the age of twenty-four, only to discover her maternal vulnerability at her husband's constant machinations. 'Still further to annoy her, her husband decided that Lady Margaret, (then two) should be taken away from her . . . at once to London' (Williamson, G., 1922, p. 91). 'I wept bitterly over the whole circumstance . . . but to refuse permission would make my Lord more angry with me, and be worse for the child' (Clifford, A., 1923, pp. 25–6). The mother's only consolation was that little Lady Margaret had her nurse with her still and that these two would share a bed until the child was five years old. 'I wrote a very earnest letter to beseech my Lord . . . that I might go to Horseley and sojourn with my child . . . ' (Clifford, A., 1923, p. 70). But all she got by way of reply was her husband's request that she return his wedding ring.

For all these stark realities, Richard Sackville varied his tactics, tending to blow hot and cold. For some weeks later on we read: 'This night my Lord came to lie in my chamber.' Possibly as a consequence, by way of gratified reward, mother and daughter were reunited, in any case for a while. For in May of that same year:

Upon the 1st I cut the Child's strings off from her coats and made her use the togs alone, so as she had two or three falls at first but had no hurt with them. . . . The 2nd: the Child put on her first coat that was laced with lace, being of red baize.

But the child cannot hold her genuine interest for long once they are reunited: 'The 8th. I spent this day in working, the time being very tedious with me as having neither comfort nor company, only the Child' (Clifford, A., 1923, p. 66). She can clearly not sustain deeper contact with the Child once she grows weary of dressing her, like a little girl her doll. Perhaps there had never been any deep maternal bonding, for from the very start a wet nurse had been employed, who had evidently failed to prove satisfactory, as she writes to her mother: 'I have found your Ladyship's words true about the nurse had for her', who had taken with the ague . . .

so she had but little milk left and I was enforced to send for the next woman that was by to give my child suck, whom hath continued ever since, and I thank God the child agrees so well with her milk . . . It is a miracle to me the child should prosper so well, considering the change in her milk . . . If I durst be so bold, I would tell your ladyship that I take it somewhat unkindly that you have been so long without writing to me, for I never was so long without a letter from you . . . thus humbly desiring your blessing to me and to your God-daughter, I rest your ladyship's obedient loving daughter. (Williamson, G., 1922, p. 148)

A letter shortly afterwards gives thanks for a pair of gloves which her mother sent for baby Margaret, for whose birth she had travelled the long distance from the north, to become her godmother. The letter ends with these words, full of plangent appeal from the depths of loneliness and an ever-present fear of what must surely lie ahead: 'so long as you live and are there, there is still some hope for me' (Williamson, G., 1922, p. 152). Separated from her mother and exposed, all alone, to the tantrums of her husband, holding this lonely wicket for their joint purposes, seems, at times, beyond her strength. How, she pleads, is she to fare, once her mother is dead.

Nor was this blow far away. Lady Cumberland died shortly after little Margaret had been taken from her mother; as blow so often follows blow. But earlier still in that same spring, before these harrowing sorrows struck, Anne Clifford still spent some weeks, covering the Easter period, with her mother in the north. The actual journey took two weeks, through Derby, Lancaster and Kendal, 'where never coach went before mine' (Holmes, M., 1975, p. 42). It was to be their final meeting, and a halcyon time it was. Before their Easter Communion in the chapel at Brougham, in a burst of northern *jouissance*, the two of them 'made an expedition in a coach to Whinefell Park to see the woods which by this time would be coming out in their first spring green' (Holmes, M., 1975, p. 44). But hostile rumblings from Lord Dorset at this mother–daughter tryst reached them from the south, cutting their time together short. For the first part of the journey the mother accompanied her daughter, both riding in the dowager's coach, brief moments which would prove to be the last they were to have together.

Where the old Roman road plunges abruptly downwards and begins a series of hill-and-dale undulations that no cumbrous Jacobean coach could venture upon . . . when mother and daughter got to the brow of that hill they must have known, both of them, that this was the end. The coach was stopped, and by the roadside they had 'a grievous and heavy parting', and eventually Lady Anne rode on alone. . . . For Lady Cumberland, when once her daughter was out of sight, there was only a slow reversal of the coach and a lonely journey back to Brougham, now doubly desolate, for what was left of her life. (Holmes, M., 1975, pp. 46–7)

It was a matter of weeks. Within days of 'the Child' being taken from her mother, Anne, in her beloved Knole, from where she also could be banished, a rider from Cumberland brought the news that Anne had dreaded: Lady Cumberland was dead. Anne Clifford must fight on alone. At the age of twenty-six, with her own daughter, whose future now seemed so uncertain, barely two, her lifelong ally was no more.

Her daughter was, as we have seen, soon returned to her; then, hardly surprisingly, the child's health began to give cause for fresh anxieties. The 'miracle' referred to earlier showed every sign of wearing off around the little girl's fifth birthday:

All the winter my Lady Margaret's speech was very ill, so that strangers cannot understand her . . . and so out of temper that it grieved me to think of it . . . I verily believe all these inconveniences proceed from some Distemper in her head. (Clifford, A., 1923, p. 100)

The diary around this period also makes much reference to Lady Margaret's fits. Furthermore, around this time, as the diary records, she lost her nurse and bed-companion, and had to sleep all alone (Clifford, A., 1923, p. 104). On top of that, this was the winter of her mother's pregnancy. The baby's birth was overdue and the mother out of sorts. And when at last a boy was born, he died within several months. Certainly the little girl seemed to have suffered some regression, perhaps of an autistic nature, following this chain of blows. What strikes us as surprising is that its effects were not enduring, taking all things into account, all the disruptions she had endured in her brief life history. 'The child had her sixth fit of the ague . . . ' 'A fit lasting for 6 or 7 hours . . .' 'More fits . . . could hardly sleep.' On one occasion, we are told that 'the Doctor staid all afternoon' (Clifford, A., 1923, p. 54). But there were no psychologists to complicate this troubling scene; to put in their little spoke and stir the simmering pots of guilt, which would in time afflict subsequent generations, as we will see in due course.

Besides, all the Clifford women were made of the granite of their fells. After six years of widowhood, Anne Clifford was to thwart an obnoxious second husband regarding marriage schemes he had for her second daughter, Lady Isabella, born in 1622. Then, when she was widowed for the second time not long after her fiftieth birthday, a rapid succession of further Clifford deaths meant that she had finally come into her hard-earned own. In Cumberland she would enjoy thirty-three more years of life, almost a third of the whole, devoted to the restoration of the castles and the lands upheld by her roving father, and endured for by herself. She was, would we not say today, repairing the parental couple. Slowly, as she built and mended and refurbished those holds and piles of ancient masonry, so her own inner parents were able to desist from fighting and come at last to cohabit in some memorial harmony.

If in Cumberland she 'caused the bounders to be ridden' (Clifford, A., ed. Sackville-West, V., 1923, p. xxxii), according to that old tradition among owners of the land, these would in due course include seventeen grandchildren and nineteen great-grandchildren, from her two Sackville daughters. All of these would visit her and frequently stay on for months. As is so frequently the case,

she was not born to be a wife and a young mother; she was born to be a great-grandmother and a widow. The black serge and plain white wimple framing the hard old face became her more truly than the damask embroidered with gold that the tailor sent down to Knole from London . . . after the French fashion. (Clifford, A., ed. Sackville-West, V., 1923, p. xxxiii)

Whatever her earlier failings as a mother had been under such fraught circumstances, she had surely now won through to preserve the generations and thereby earn her *nunc dimittis*. Little could she have guessed that a later Sackville daughter, owning Knole in her turn and a true master of her craft, from that line of maternal pens dipped in the ink of centuries, would edit her diary to say in the Introduction:

Knole I have seen as Anne Clifford saw it, quietly magnificent, down there in Kent, with its great towers and wide lawns and glinting windows, and the flag floating high up in the cool empty blue. (Sackville-West, V., 1923, p. xiv)

Where such long records have survived do we not draw a deep, almost mystical conviction – far beyond the reach of words – of the mother–daughter link as an ontogenic epic to secure a cohesion between the generations, long after all the sound and fury of minor battles fade away?

A generation further on – for she was born in 1627 – we have Mrs Alice Thornton writing her autobiography. It takes us to her husband's death, when she herself was forty-three and the mother of nine children, born over the course of fifteen years. Hers was a close and happy childhood presided over by a mother who, although of noble birth, permitted little to distract her from her family life in Yorkshire:

Thrice in each day, at six, ten and nine in the evening, the family met together for devotion. The mother assembled her children every morning before breakfast, hearing them pray, and read or repeated Psalms and chapters from the Bible, and then they knelt for her blessing. (Thornton, A., 1875, p. vii)

No court or any other matters pertaining to a king or queen would come between her and her children, so that her daughter writes of her with the deepest tenderness. How refreshing are these pages, focusing as they do on this close-knit day-to-day, if we compare it, for instance, with Lady Fanshawe's contemporary writings, a memoir filled with social gossip from the courts of England and Spain (Fanshawe, Lady A., 1829).

Clearly, these differences partly point to class distinction, with their own priorities and different attitudes to children, between the aristocracy and citizens of worthy status, to which Mr Thornton belonged. But from now on we can trace, century by century, regardless of the changing surface of social mores and norms, the extent to which good mothering, or maternal ineptitude, leave their far-reaching impact, frequently on generations. Even so we still find, in Alice Thornton's life, those appallingly high infant mortality rates, which were doubtless partly due to the use of wet nurses, that aristocratic legacy soon to be decried by the courageous Countess Lincoln. Accordingly we read in the memoirs of Alice Thornton: 'About seven weeks after I married, it pleased God to give me the blessing of consseption. The first quarter I was exceedingly sickly in breeding, till I was quicke with child; after which I was very strong and healthy.' This first baby, a son, died half an hour after birth. The mother was very ill, 'but I confesse also that which moved me to use all means for my recovery, in regard to the great sorrow of my deare and aged mother and my deare husband took for me, farre exceeding my deserts ...' (Thornton, A., 1875, p. 84). Her second child, a daughter, born eighteen months later, was almost overlaid by a nurse, but that Mrs Thornton's mother, in the adjoining room, heard the distressing sounds of her tiny granddaughter choking and gasping in the night. Two more daughters followed quickly. The first of these, Elizabeth, died at the age of eighteen months:

It pleased God to take from me my deare childe, Betty, which had long been in the riketts and consumption, gotten at first by an ague, and much gone in the riketts, which I conceived was caused by ill milke of two nurses. And not withstanding all the means I used, and had her with Naly at St Mungo's well . . . for she grew weaker, and at last, in a most desperate cough that destroyed her lungs, she died. (Thornton, A., 1875, p. 94)

A little further on she returns to this loss again with that strength of personality which is so capable of grieving:

That deare, sweete angell grew worse, and indured it with infinitt patience . . . then she sweetly fell asleepe and went out of this miserable world like a lamb . . . Elizabeth Thornton, my third childe, died 5th September, 1656, betwixt the hours of five and six in the morning. Her age was one yeare six months and twenty one days. (Thornton, A., 1875, p. 94)

Her fifth child, a son, was born twelve months afterwards:

the childe staied in the birth, and came crosse with he feete first, and in this condition continued till Thursday morning between 2 and 3 a clocke, at which time I was upon the racke in bearing my childe with such exquisit torment, as if each line were divided from other . . . when att length, being speechlesse and breathlesse, I was, by the infinite providence of God, in great mercy delivered. (Thornton, A., 1875, p. 96)

The child lived for half an hour. So died her second son. 'This sweete goodly son' – she tries to account for her loss – 'was turned wrong by the fall I got in September before, nor had the midwife skill to turne him right.'

There follows a brief reference to the actual outer world:

About this time wee weare all in great confusion in this Kingdom, none knowing how the government of this land would fall, some desiring the contineuance of Oliver Cromwell's race to stand; others desired the return of the blessed King; and to establish theire arbetrary power againe . . . (Thornton, A., 1875, p. 98)

But her inclination is more for recording issues of concern to those who are dear and close to hand. With them she is constantly lovingly preoccupied, as only a recipient of deep maternal love could be:

To returne to my mother, who was bred up in her youth and infancy with much caire and sircumspect by the eyes of my grandmother, a discreete and wise woman, giveing her all the advantages of breeding and good education that the Court and those times could afford, which was indeed excelent for

— 141 —

gravity, modestie and pietie and other suitable qualities for her degree, as writing, singing, danceing, harpsichalls, lute and what was requisit to make her an accomplished lady. (Thornton, A., 1875, p. 101)

She continues to record how her mother was married at the age of twenty-one 'by the consent of her mother', and that it then pleased God to 'inrich' her parents 'with (the chiefe end for which marriage was ordained) the blessing of children, my mother bringing forth to him seaven, hopefully enough to live and to be comforts to theire parents' (Thornton, A., 1875, p. 102). She then returns, once again, to sing the praises of her mother as

liveing in much comfort and hapieness all my father's life, doeing much good to all people in each sphears wherein she actted . . . her children, freinds and servants found theire . . . a perpetual effluence of all graces and vertues flowing from so full a spring . . . (Thornton, A., 1875, p. 104)

Such a thanksgiving for a mother as the wellspring of life, common as it has remained in simple, everyday experience, has in recent times been swamped, even virtually silenced, by a flood of negatives running through our literature. Does this not possibly cast light on woman writers as a species? Might they be more driven by conflicts which originate in maternal deprivation? Could one urge for self-expression be rooted in psychic pain?

Alice Thornton's mother died, 'aged 67 years, 11 months and 6 days', in 1659, when her daughter was thirty-two and carrying her sixth child, William, who was to die within twelve days of his birth: 'my pretty babe was in good health, suckeing his poore mother, to whom my good God has given the blessing of the breast as well as the wombe . . .' (Thornton, A., 1875, p. 111). The wording of these lines suggests that Alice Thornton may by then have come under the influence of a pamphlet of the time, of some considerable importance, if for two quite different reasons. Let us examine it more closely.

5 MOTHER VENTURES INTO POLEMICS

THE PAMPHLET known as 'The Countess Lincoln's Nurseries', published in 1622 by John Lichfield and James Short, printers in their day to the University of Oxford, is undoubtedly a milestone of significance. It stands as an important landmark in the history of infant care and draws attention to the growth of a deepening awareness regarding the unique importance of maternal devotion as activity and deed rather than mere sentiment.

But beyond that it conveys a change in woman's self-image: her willingness to speak up, to promulgate what she believes in with a growing conviction that her views *can* make an impact. Soon, as we shall see, she will come to the hustings on issues of direct concern to herself and her children, as at the bidding of her conscience in her relationship to God. Not for some high-sounding cause based on masculine abstractions, but as a simple affirmation of the stakes she holds in life, she will make her appearance both in print and in person in the public domain.

This pamphlet is relatively little known, but its impassioned plea deserves to stand side by side with Rousseau's tracts on childcare which would be much debated just over a century later. It addresses itself, as was the custom, to a patron, in this case 'to the right honourable, and approved Lady Bridget, Countess of Lincoln', by then a mother of nine children, to continue in this vein:

For the better expressing and keeping in memory my love, and your wothiness

I do offer unto your Ladiship the first work of mine that ever came in print; because your rare example hath given an excellent approbation to the matter contained in this book: for you have passed by all excuses, and have ventured upon and do go on with that loving act of a loving mother, in giving the sweet milk of your own breasts, to your own child . . . your Ladiship's in the best and safest love, Elizabeth Lincoln. (Lincoln, E., 1809, p. 27)

The author was herself a mother of eighteen children and a relative by marriage.

The pamphlet then makes its appeal 'To the courteous, chiefly most Christian Reader' with a further preamble by Thomas Lodge, 'who being a physician as well as a poet had a professional title to preface the text "as her Ladyship's gentleman-usher".' He plunges in at the deep end of what was clearly at the time a fraught and controversial issue: 'The general consent of too many mothers in an unnatural practice (most Christian reader) hath caused one of the noblest and fairest hands in this land to set pen to paper: as ashamed to see her sex farther degenerate . . . ' (Lincoln, E., 1809, p. 28).

Now that we have been prepared, along with the most Christian reader, concerning what may be in store for us as a noble lady of the day, we quote from the actual text:

Because it hath pleased God to bless me with many children, and so caused me to observe many things falling out to mothers and to their children; I thought good to open my mind concerning a special matter . . . in sum, the matter I mean, is the duty of nursing, due by mothers to their own children. (p. 29)

She argues that to comply with what is natural is, in effect, God's ordinance. That Eve suckled her sons Cain, Abel and Seth, as did Sarah Isaac. That indeed the blessed Virgin, 'as her womb bare our blessed Saviour, so her paps gave him suck . . . '

'It is objected', she continues, 'that it is troublesome; that it is noisome to one's clothes; that it makes one look old, etc. All such reasons are uncomely and unchristian to be objected . . . ' (Lincoln, E., 1809, p. 29). Some, the author submits, may be excused from their duty on grounds of want, sickness or lunacy, but none who is in her right mind.

We shall say more presently of the wet-nurse industry and its multifarious evils for infant mortality, not to mention deeper issues of mother–child relationship. But from the memoirs of Alice Thornton, with the rich insights they provide into her maternity with its trials and tribulations, as with its countless joys, we derive evidence of the pamphlet's influence as far away as Yorkshire. For surely 'suckeing his poore mother, to whom my good God had given the blessing of the breast' suggests that source by its wording.

Elizabeth Lincoln was by no means the only woman who was venturing into print. Lucy Hutchinson, for instance, from a Puritan family, was a contemporary of Mrs Alice Thornton. This remarkable lady wrote *The Life of Colonel Hutchinson*, in other words of her husband. Appended to it we find a relatively modest fragment: 'The Life of Mrs Lucy Hutchinson by Herself'. Her mother was Lady Apsley, whose praises she amply sings in every detail and respect as a wonderful wife and woman and above all a mother in relation to herself:

After my mother had had three sons she was desirous of a daughter . . . My mother while she was with child with me dreamt that she was walking in the garden with my father, and that a starre came down into her hand . . . only my father told her, her dream signified she should have a daughter of some extraordinary eminency, which thing, like such vaine prophecies, wrought as farre as it could its own accomplishment; for my father and mother fancying me then beautiful . . . applied all their care and spar'd no cost to emprove me in my education . . . and being caress'd, the love and praise tickled me and made me attend more heedfully. When I was about seven years of age, I remember I had att one time eight tutors in several quallities. (Hutchinson, L., 1973, p. 287)

It was unusual for a mother not to oppose her husband's wish to educate a daughter, except in Puritan families, whose more serious view of life led to more thorough education. But we need to be quite clear that she would have envisaged any such 'improvement' purely as a benefit within the domestic sphere and not as a preparation for any independent life: a hard-fought battle which still lies an ample century away, with all its own sound and fury.

We need, however, to remember that in the seventeenth century growing numbers of women were venturing into print in areas which bear no connection with purely domestic matters. Some of these, as we shall see, had a more ambiguous relationship to their mothers, which can be traced in the writings of Margaret, Duchess of

Cavendish, born in 1623, and a generation later in those of the somewhat notorious Mary Manley. That they belonged to a wider group known as the Female Wits speaks for the deeper conflicts of admiration and denigration with which society responded to women entering polemics, publicly, with their pens. But others came to the hustings and into full public glare and resounding controversy which found its way into print more accidentally, more as a by-product of their deeply held convictions and the highly personal relationship they knew to God.

Anne Hutchinson's beginnings appear conventional enough, if we are deceived by a perfunctory glance which fails to take into account a streak her nature had derived from a passionate and headstrong father. In her remote home ground,

the example of Queen Elizabeth and some of her Court Ladies who studied Latin and Greek, meant nothing to the small gentry of Lincolnshire. From her mother, Anne learned to sew, to care for the sick, to prepare simples and preserves and to make home-brew. (King-Rugg, W., 1930, p. 10)

True enough. Yet none the less Anne had, before her life ended with a blow from a tomahawk in 1645, transferred her family and herself across the waters to the New World, as would others of her stamp, in obedience to God, whose other name is the freedom of the personality, regardless of mere circumstances.

How could it have come about that a young wife and mother of these outlying parts heard the preacher John Cotton in the distant church of old Boston, where she would ride every Sunday, with such hunger in her heart and mind? It was the man's experiential and deeply personal relationship to God, so refreshingly removed from institutionalized religion, which finally bade her follow him out to Boston in the New World, once she was certain in her heart that to be a Nonconformist was not to be a Separatist. If God spoke to her directly, so much the better, Anne believed.

What a long way we have come from passive medieval mothers! So profound was her conviction that her husband, sons and daughters, without exception, were infected and set sail for the unknown. Yet we have to bear in mind that Anne Hutchinson was first and foremost a loving wife and devoted mother. Hers was the kind of love which so readily spills over to seek more and still more channels out there, in the wider world, whatever the consequences.

New Boston was, at the time, little more than a village of fewer than a thousand inhabitants. Although she was mother of six daughters as well as of three sons, Anne Hutchinson lost little time and quickly plunged into the life of this small community. As only men could speak at various prayer-meetings, she held meetings in her home for the benefit of women. So came into life and being what may reasonably be seen as the first women's club in America. It was not born of abstractions. To Anne's maternal heart the predicament of the women, with its high mortality, was a cause of deep anxiety. Biennial, if not yearly babies, hard, often manual work, homesickness and a poor diet, lack of adequate, warm clothing, which was given to the men, cried out for remedy. Soon Anne started 'lecturing'. She gave the sermon at these meetings, originally for womenfolk unable to attend the church for various domestic reasons. The crowd packed in so they might hear: 'if you have the Grace of God in your souls you cannot displease Him.' This was Anne's experience, which she was setting out to share. But it proved anathema to the Fathers of the Church.

Anne was banished from Boston and shortly afterwards excommunicated. Her youngest daughter at the time was a mere four months old. Her grown daughters, Faith and Bridget, wept at the dreaded words: 'In the name of the Lord Jesus Christ and in the name of the church . . . I do cast you out; and in the name of Christ I do deliver you up to Satan . . .' (King-Rugg, W., 1930, p. 132). From then on Anne, newly widowed, was constantly on the move. Since her influence still grew, she was now accused of witchcraft by the Massachusetts court. She moved on into the wilds. There, soon afterwards, Anne's hospitality to indigenous Indians was to cost her her life. She and her daughter Zureyell met their death by a tomahawk. It was, ironically, the Indians who would suffer her to speak no more.

Facing the title page we can see a photograph of a statue of Anne Hutchinson. A well-built, middle-aged woman stands looking up to God, sheltering a little girl in the folds of her cloak. What must it have been like to be Anne Hutchinson's daughter, one who, like her mother, had a mind of her own? Gossip had it that when her youngest was recaptured from the Indians and restored to relatives, she protested vigorously. It is an interesting thought. Were this Hutchinson's high spirits, inherited from her mother, to take a very different turn? Did she perhaps feel suffocated by long prayer-house meetings and anxious high-mindedness, to opt instead for the wild in a different direction from the pioneering life, with its stringent difficulties and prescribed modes of thought?

That answer we may never know. But we can trace a line of women from the rebellious Clothilde, to the stalwart Margery Kempe, the mystic, Julian of Norwich, who saw Christ as a mother, and on to Anne Hutchinson, driving breach after breach into impersonal religion and thereby claiming the right to hold convictions of their own; convictions born of their own experience and for that reason deeply held, which in due course must surely lead to the self-created life. The precedents had been established, courageously here and there; and even if Massachusetts heaved a deep sigh of relief that divine intervention had, with a tomahawk, removed an obstreperous spirit from its worthy midst, this reprieve would provide but the merest breathing space until the advent of the Quakers ruffled smooth surfaces again.

Meanwhile these staunch echelons were gathering strength on their homeground of England, nurtured by their 'Mother', Margaret Fell, before they too would cross the sea, another unruly export which the New World must absorb. When Margaret Fell was born (1614), Anne Hutchinson was twenty-three. She was married to a local judge and life went quietly enough in their home, Swarthmoor Hall, further north, in Windermere. But when Margaret was thirty-eight and the mother of seven children – one son and six daughters, all of whom she nursed herself – a travelling preacher, one George Fox, with his fervent message of 'Christ within', preached in the vicinity. The year was 1652. His age was only twenty-eight.

Judge Fell was on his usual circuit. After his wife had heard the preacher, she cried in anguish out loud: 'We are all thieves: we are all thieves; we have taken the scriptures in words, and know nothing of them in ourselves' (Ross, I., 1949, p. 8). As her husband was riding home, gossip met him on the road. Neighbours told him that a 'travelling preacher had bewitched his wife and household' (Ross, I., 1949, p. 14). Margaret felt in a quandary. What would her husband say to her new relationship to Christ as the Living Word within, no longer to be purveyed by institutionalized religion in the person of Priest Lampitt, God's local overseer?

Margaret Fell's last and eighth child, 'little' Rachel, was born in the following year. From then on she lost little time in fostering the new movement which was known as 'The Friends', to earn the title of 'our nursing mother'. Had she not nursed all her own? Was her heart not large enough to overflow, as previously Anne Hutchinson's had been. Had mothers not begun to find new venues for their love, out in the wide world: society beyond their hearth?

Lampitt's response was less than charitable:

The plaiges of God shall fall upon thee and the seven viols shall bee powered upon thee and the milstone shall fall upon thee and crush thee as dust under the Lordes feete how can you escape the damnation of hell. (Ross, I., 1949, p. 27)

Priest Lampitt was but the spokesman for opinion far and wide. Fox and his followers would soon become familiar with the country's most derelict gaols. Margaret Fell wrote to Cromwell reminding him that he had promised religious toleration, but to little avail. By the time Rachel was seven, ministering to the prisoners, and to their wives and families, took Margaret away from home more and more frequently for ever longer intervals. She could draw some comfort from the knowledge that one or more grown daughters always held that essential fort and cared for the little ones, following her loving example. But being a devoted mother she fretted deeply, none the less: while none the less she had no choice. To be a mother to her own was no longer enough when others, in the wider world, needed devotion and care, as she painfully perceived.

Letters between the daughter in charge, back home in Swarthmoor Hall, and the mother on her travels, steadily flew back and forth:

From Swarthmoor, 22.7.1660. Dear Mother. My duty and dearest love is unto thee dearly remembered. By this thou may know of all the children's well being, and that Rachel is very well – and no way wants thee, but is well contented. . . . Thy dutiful daughter Bridgett Fell. (Ross, I., 1949, p. 132)

Back came the reply: 'My dear Lambs and Babes of God, the Father of you all, . . . Dear hearts, my way and time of return is not yet manifested to me . . . from your dear mother in the eternal life of Truth, Margaret Fell' (Ross, I., 1949, p. 133). Every letter of hers expressed this anxiety that she might return home, special concern for little Rachel and for Bridget's indifferent health.

Bridget married. And in 1661, although two hundred and seventy

Friends were imprisoned in Lancaster Castle under terrible conditions for refusing to take the Oath of Allegiance, Margaret Fell rode through the winter to be with her daughter for her first confinement.

Now Sarah was in charge at home, which was certainly as well, for Margaret herself would lie prisoner in Lancaster Castle from 1664 to 1668. She had suffered a sentence of praemunire passed against her, meaning that she was forthwith out of the king's protection: in other words, an outlaw, one whose home and estates could be seized and confiscated. Her greatest grief, however, was that she should be in prison when her daughter Isabel was married, at twenty-seven. She was furthermore distraught by news of Mary's serious illness, but had the comfort of knowing that she was lovingly tended by her own sister Margaret Rous with her husband, John.

In June 1668 Margaret was, at last, released. Back home, at Swarthmoor Hall, a spell of domesticity could briefly be enjoyed. There she found Sarah and Susannah, Margaret with her husband John together with their two babies, and Rachel, who was now fifteen. She would accompany her mother on a horseback tour through Kent, on to Sussex and Surrey. Visiting many Friends, after her long spell of absence, Margaret and her youngest daughter covered some four hundred miles, getting to know one another all over again.

Margaret had been eleven years a widow when she married George Fox in the following year. Although she owned house and land, George Fox determined not to meddle in the estate of his wife. This, we should remind ourselves, thinking back to Richard Sackville, was still exceptional at the time, as were the loving consultations between the couple and the children. The daughters all gave their blessing. 'Truly,' said daughter Mary, also married by then, 'I am very well satisfied with the thing and do believe the Lord requires it at your hands.' And 'little' Rachel, now sixteen, shared in these sentiments: 'I am of the same mind with my sisters and give my consent' (Ross, I., 1949, p. 216).

How close and loving were the ties between the women at Swarthmoor Hall, mother, daughters and sisters acting as surrogate mothers whenever the occasion called! Nor did Margaret Fox's work for the Society of Friends keep her from constant loving care for her nearest and dearest, for all the conflicts entailed then, as down the generations, in such a multifarious life as constitutes a monument to woman's life-affirmation.

Gradually the Women's Meetings, which she had initiated, took root and spread across the land. Women spoke and also preached. Margaret herself wrote a pamphlet on the right of women to exercise their spiritual gifts. These gifts would spread their influence in an ever-widening sphere, to attain to the status of social work in our day. Centuries before nursing, midwifery and social welfare were viewed as national services, we find these women pioneering such essential human measures as a natural extension of their maternal self, their deepest nature as women, to which sphere these institutions need urgently to be restored by free and generous endowment by maternal government.

It was Sarah Fell who kept the Minute Book for local meetings, but once again loving care within the closer family never faltered under stress of the wider obligations. For when Sarah's only child, Nathaniel, was born, Susannah was with her sister:

She hath been and is mighty careful and tender of me and my little boy (as I know she hath been of others of my sisters in the like condition) but I hope not to hurt herself; my husband and myself looks upon ourselves much engaged to her for her good company, love and cares, and to thee that thou art pleased to spare her; I hope it will not be to her hurt, being much to our comfort. (Ross, I., 1949, p. 335)

So Sarah wrote to her mother when the child was three weeks old.

Susannah herself married late, at the age of forty-two, when her only child was born. She nursed the baby herself, on her mother's advice, and could report in every letter that the baby was 'thriving'. Indeed, in this wider family, as in Anne Hutchinson's, infant and child mortality rates are conspicuously low, compared to poor Alice Thornton, Margaret Fell's contemporary, who had only learnt the hard way, as her Memoirs indicate. There is no doubt, in my mind, that the factor we referred to earlier as sanity, which is closely linked to common sense – the senses working in harmony, as it was defined by Bion – plays an important part in these wide differences. For must not each infant, first and foremost, survive in his mother's mind, meaning her acceptance of total responsibility? Before we take a closer look at the wet-nurse industry, let us say our farewell to Margaret Fox herself, who just before her eighty-eighth birthday died in her daughter Rachel's arms, saying: 'Take me in thy arms . . . I am at peace.'

We now return to the wet nurse, not in an emergency but as the cottage industry which it gradually became in parishes close to London, something far more organized in the interests of material gain than formerly, in the Middle Ages, when the nobility would employ a local woman, as part of her services. 'A sucking child makes a most dreadful spectacle', Sir John Acton remarked (Prior, M., 1985, p. 27), which only serves to illustrate the social pressures exerted on ladies of society to farm their own nurselings out. In other words, the practice was deemed unladylike. As we remarked earlier, it was 'noisome to one's clothes' and 'it makes one look old'. But what deeper motives lie behind these rationalizations?

The upper classes, then as now, were anxious to secure a succession, the more so with the prevalent high infant mortality. And although careful observers such as the Welsh physician John Jones, in 1579, remarked on 'the relatively robust condition of the infants of poorer mothers' who nursed their infants themselves, sometimes for up to three years, the conclusion was not drawn that a baby at the breast, and not a baby in the womb, was the best guarantee for survival and good health. Such is the power of rhyme over reason in matters of social predjudice. And so 'a Lady' would produce an infant almost annually, to lose them at the rate we have seen. Unlike their humble, working sisters, these noble ladies might give birth to fifteen, up to twenty children, even thirty in one case (Prior, M., 1985, p. 27), and still remain without an heir.

Since hardly all of them were fools, for all the undisputed power of social prejudice, what deeper 'reasons' are at play? We come closer to the crux when we look at the belief 'that sexual intercourse would corrupt the milk', meaning that 'conjugal debt had priority above the welfare of the infant' (Prior, M., 1985, p. 27). Yet, physicians of the time insisted that 'by experience we see that Mothers that live with their Husbands, and use congress, Nurse the Child without hurt' (Prior, M., 1985, p. 22). What we are seeing here is, in effect, the split between the sexual and the feeding mother, reflected in society, between the upper echelons and their working sisters of the day. 'As the Renaissance advanced, the image of the nursing Virgin waned in popularity' (Prior, M., 1985, p. 27). Poets and playwrights now began to eulogize fertility. Artists painted noble ladies caressing their big bellies. 'There was pressure to produce heirs because so many rich infants perished' (Prior, M., 1985, p. 27). Like so many other schisms nourished by a class system, this one prevails to this day with our 'classy' mothers vying for their Norland Nannies, while in our earlier epoch 'country glovers, hatters, tailors, shoemakers etc. took their wares to London and came back with nurse children for country wives to feed as a domestic industry' (Prior, M., 1985, p. 30). '"The nurse sayeth that her husband has a very easy-going horse . . . " Mary Verney was assured. But her infant son still died, transferred to a second nurse within a matter of weeks' (Prior, M., 1985, p. 32). Of this second nurse she wrote:

She lookes like a slatterne but she sayeth that if she takes the child she will have a mighty care of itt, and truly she hath toe as fine children of her owne as evor I sawe . . . poor child I pray God bless him and make him a hapy Man, for he hath had butt a troublesome beginning . . . (Prior, M., 1985, p. 26)

The attitude of the men often played a crucial part, as it still does today in so-called 'society'. Did Harrods not recently evict a nursing mother from one of their tea-rooms to the 'rest-room' for ladies, in other words the lavatory? The Countess Lincoln herself had once been 'over-ruled by others and misled by bad advice until it was too late' (Prior, M., 1985, p. 28). Her pamphlet was dedicated to her daughter-in-law, who with such staunch support breast-fed her own infants. Another mother rallying in support of her daughter's natural, maternal instincts took her son-in-law to task, successfully it seems, and against her own husband's wishes. Accordingly Anne Newdigate received this letter from her mother when her first child was born in 1598: 'I longe to heer how all thinges abowte your new Charge goeth, for I parswaed myself that my sonne Newdygat wyll not go backe with hys worde. I pray God send you well to doe with it' (Prior, M., 1985, p. 28).

The English sources convey a warmer relationship between nursing mothers and their daughters, such as Anne Hutchinson and Margaret Fell, than the more distant ones found among the 'upper crust'. There the mothers tended to regard their daughters as a distraction to be picked up from time to time when nothing much was happening on the wider social scene, to set them aside again as the first tally-ho sounded from more entertaining quarters.

Lady Mary Wortley Montagu (1689–1762) straddled several categories. Her own mother had died when she was barely three years old. When her father (Lord Kingston) remembered her existence, however, he seemed to have been proud of his eldest daughter's beauty and precocious intelligence. Hardly an auspicious start for the development of maternal qualities in a little girl. Yet she transformed herself, by virtue of an innate talent linked to headstrong determination, from an empty-headed socialite into a serious-minded author of considerable repute.

She eloped in her early twenties. Her father never forgave her and left his daughter a mere sum of £6,000 for her life, to revert to her own daughter. The early years of her marriage were lonely and unhappy. Her husband, Wortley, tended to leave his spirited young wife in remote country houses while he amused himself elsewhere:

When I gave myself to you, I gave up the very desire of pleasing the rest of the world, and am pretty indifferent about it . . . yet passing whole days alone as I do, I do not always find it possible, and my constitution will sometimes get the better of my reason. (Paston, G., 1907, p. 167)

And during her first pregnancy, another letter to her husband: 'I am in circumstances in which melancholy is apt to prevail even over all amusements, dispirited and lone' (Paston, G., 1907, p. 168). From these sorry epistles one would hardly conclude that their author was described as 'the wittiest as well as one of the most beautiful women of her day . . . ' (Paston, G., 1907, p. 201) or that she would soon rally to a life of intellect with conspicuous results, so that her daughter was born in more rewarding circumstances. Mary Wortley however was by way of becoming a well-known author by that time. Instead of fretting to no purpose in her rural solitude she had staunchly turned to writing and the resources of her mind, sublimating her frustrations with considerable success. In 1716 her *Eclogues* were published with support from Alexander Pope. Besides, the Wortleys were then living, on a diplomatic stint, in Adrianople, where the expatriate life suited Lady Mary better, as it would do throughout her life: 'Nobody keeps to their house a month for lying in, and I am not so fond of our customs as to retain them when they are not necessary' (Paston, G., 1907, p. 262). A second birth found this mother, clearly, in much higher spirits in this very different scene; and the letter continues: 'My grooms are Arabs, my footmen French, English and German; my nurse an Armenian; my housemaids Russians . . . ' She clearly relished this Tower-of-Babel, eclectic spirit that she owned and cultivated all her life with supreme disregard for contemporary opinion.

Yet, despite reading Homer, and busy with her own opus, Mary Wortley was described as 'a devoted, anxious mother despite her classical studies' (Paston, G., 1907, p. 174). But she was not a natural one, and once again her devotion was of that intermittent nature found so often in her class and position in society. Her self-image, none the less, was one of a devoted mother, as in this letter to her husband, when her daughter was eight: 'My daughter makes you her compliments. She is my constant companion, and I shall very soon have the reputation of the greatest prude and the best mother in all Paris, for I keep company with none but old women and little children' (Paston, G., 1907, p. 337).

Despite this picture of herself as a maternal idyll, Mary's intellectual passions lent it inconsistency, and troubled years lay ahead to throw some doubt on the concoction. Before she reached the age of twenty, Miss Wortley became Lady Bute. It proved a very happy marriage, even if at intervals a rather impecunious one, during which times these deprivations would evoke her earlier ones, to be expressed as grievances against this sanctimonious mother to her anger and disgust, as we can see from Mary's letter addressed to her estranged husband early in 1740:

I am sorry your daughter continues to trouble you concerning me. She cannot believe after her behaviour to me the last time she was in town, that it is possible to persuade me of any real affection, and all besides is an affectation that is better left off; now decency no longer exacts it. I am not only conscious of having in every point performed my duty by her, but with a tenderness and friendship that is not commonly found, and I must say this with truth, that even from her infancy I made her a companion and witness of my actions. She owes me not only the regard due to a parent, but the esteem that ought to be paid to a blameless conduct, and the gratitude that is shown by every honest mind to a valuable friend. (Paston, G., 1907, p. 374)

For all its self-righteousness the tone is a defensive one. But having lost her own mother at the early age of three, she may, for all her fine intentions, have lacked deeper maternal instincts, so that her daughter's remonstrations might well have been the symptom of this painful deficit.

Shortly after this was written Lady Montagu cast off her last maternal pretensions for her chosen lifestyle as an exile who would live in foreign parts until the last year of her life. Slowly from this safe distance a correspondence between the mother and daughter took on some regularity, although the tone was never warm or genuinely intimate, with its didactic overtones from the maternal end. Particularly did this mother display little patience for the repeated mention of financial embarrassment. Get off your backside and write, much as I had to do, one can almost hear her scold, when in effect she writes:

I will not trouble you with repetition of my concern for your uneasy situation, which does not touch me the less for having foreseen it many years ago; . . . God's will be done. You have the blessing of happiness in your own family, and I hope time will put your affairs in a better condition. The mortality of cattle was in this country [Italy] the last year, but as to milk and butter, I have long learned to live without them. (Paston, G., 1907, p. 345)

Motherless from a tender age, poor 'little' Lady Mary, even if she here speaks from an unconscious level, had learnt early in her life to turn maternal deprivation into a range of assets, if with chilly fortitude. This was as well with a husband who was pathologically mean, in money matters as with feelings. He was to leave a million pounds when he died in 1761, a few months before his wife. His income was, at the time, £800 a year, a tidy figure, certainly. But true to type, he prided himself on living on one-eighth of that, while the affairs of his wife were nebulous, to say the least. To this, life had accustomed her as one trained in the lifelong habit of denying her deepest emotional needs, as much as material ones; she had clearly built sound defences to make the best of a bad job. However, in the correspondence the deeper pain, which she denied, sometimes takes our breath away, like a fierce and icy shower, where we had bargained for warmth, as when those lines above swing, without the slightest warning, from maternal sympathy to querulous admonition. Ever resourceful, she herself had at the time, nearing sixty, bought 'an old shell of a palace' at Guttolengo, and was with great tenacity and the help of local people going from one 'horticultural triumph' to another, as her own major-domo in faraway Italy:

I generally rise at six and as soon as I have breakfasted, put myself at the head of my weeding women and work with them til nine. I then inspect my dairy, and my poultry . . . all things have hitherto prospered under my care;

my bees and silkworms are doubled . . . (Paston, G., 1907, p. 458)

The correspondence soon carried her decided views on the position of women and on how, as how not, to seek to educate a daughter:

Almost all girls of quality are educated as if they were to be great ladies, which is often as little to be expected as an immoderate heat of the sun in the north of Scotland. You should teach yours to confine their desires to probabilities, to be as useful as is possible to themselves and to think privacy (as it is) the happiest state of life. (Paston, G., 1907, p. 463)

Her granddaughter, Lady Jane, suffered some disfigurement on recovering from smallpox. Accordingly we come to hear:

28 January 1753. My dear child . . . I will therefore speak to you as supposing [Jane] not only capable, but desirous of learning: in that case by all means let her be indulged in it. You will tell me I did not make it a part of your education: your prospect was very different from hers. As you had no defect either in mind or person to hinder, and much in your circumstances to attract, the highest offers, it seemed your business to learn to live in the world, as it is hers to know how to be easy out of it. It is the common error of builders and parents to follow some plan they think beautiful (and perhaps it is so), without considering that nothing is beautiful that is displaced . . . thus every woman endeavours to breed her daughter a fine lady, qualifying her for a station in which she will never appear, and at the same time incapacitating her for that retirement to which she is destined. Learning, if she has a real taste for it, will not only make her contented, but happy in it. No entertainment is so cheap as reading, nor any pleasure so lasting. She will not want new fashions, nor regret the loss of expensive diversions, or variety of company, if she can be amused with an author in her closet. To render this amusement extensive, she should be permitted to learn the languages . . . [it] is no objection to a girl whose time is not so precious [as a boy's]: she cannot advance herself in any profession, and has therefore more hours to spare . . . There are two cautions to be given on this subject: first, not to think herself learned when she can read Latin, or even Greek . . . True knowledge consists in knowing things, not words . . .

The second caution to be given her (and which is absolutely necessary) is to conceal whatever learning she attains, with as much solicitude as she would hide crookedness or lameness – the parade of it can only serve to draw on her the envy, and consequently the most inveterate hatred, of all he and she fools, which will certainly be at least three parts in four of all her acquaintances. The use of knowledge in our sex, beside the amusement of solitude, is to moderate the passions, and learn to be contented with a small expense, which are the certain effects of a studious life – and it may be preferable even to that fame which men have engrossed to themselves and will not suffer us to share. You will tell me that I have not observed this rule myself – but you are mistaken: it is only inevitable accident that has given me any reputation that way . . .

The ultimate end of your education was to make you a good wife (and I have the comfort to hear that you are one): hers ought to be to make her happy in a virgin state. I will not say that it is happier – but it is undoubtedly safer than any marriage. In a lottery, where there are (at the lowest computation) ten thousand blanks to a prize, it is the most prudent choice not to venture . . .
(Payne, K., 1984, pp. 78–9)

This exegesis was followed by an apologia:

6 March 1753. I cannot help writing a sort of apology . . . foreseeing [that] Lord Bute will be extremely shocked at the proposal of a learned education for his daughters, which the generality of men believe as great a profanation as the clergy would do if the laity should presume to exercise the functions of the priesthood. I desire you would take notice, I would not have learning enjoined them as a task, but permitted as a pleasure, if their genius leads them naturally to it. I look upon my grand-daughters as a sort of lay nuns: destiny may have laid up other things for them, but they have no reason to expect to pass their time otherwise than their aunts do at present; and I know, by experience, it is in the power of study not only to make solitude tolerable, but agreeable. (Payne, K., 1984, p. 80)

So speaks personal experience. If these extracts are lengthy, and doubtless irritating to a daughter, they none the less offer us, and very straight from the shoulder of a tough, precocious spirit, insight into this prototype of a mother-author-wise-sibyl – one we will meet time and again, as in the person of George Sand. Often embattled in their earlier years, they glow in well-ripened achievement in the autumn of their life: a line of maternal beacons to which we may lift weary eyes in hours of disconsolation.

Shortly after her husband's death, and sick with cancer herself, Mary Wortley faced the end with realistic fortitude: 'I am dragging my ragged remnant of life to England . . . The wind and tide are against me; how far I have strength to struggle against both, I know not . . . ' (Paston, G., 1907, p. 463). She would die as she had lived, disdainful of material comfort.

As for that sparkling spirit, it survived in her daughter, as in her daughters in their turn. Fanny Burney met Lady Bute fifteen years after her mother's death, in 1787, and wrote in her famous diary, in her married name of Madame D'Arblay:

Lady Bute with an exterior the most forbidding to strangers, has powers of conversation the most entertaining and lively when she is intimate . . . Lady Louisa Stuart, her youngest daughter, has parts equal to those of her mother, with a deportment and appearance infinitely more pleasing; . . . they seem both to inherit an ample portion of the wit of their mother and grandmother, Lady Wortley Montagu, though I believe them both to have escaped her faults . . . (Burney, S., 1893, p. 201)

And on a subsequent occasion:

Lady Bute and Lady Louisa were both in such high spirits themselves, that they kept up all the conversation between them with such vivacity, an acuteness and an observation on men and manners so clear and so sagacious, that it would be difficult to pass an evening of greater entertainment. (Burney, S., 1893, p. 537)

The mantle had been handed down through mother–daughter generations again, in yet another instance.

If there was much speculation as to the nature of the complex personality of this progenitor – was she a woman of heartlessness, as described by Pope and Walpole, or a brilliant specimen of a great eighteenth-century lady, witty, charming and beautiful, an intelligent and thoughtful woman of high culture and blameless conduct? – this was not settled in her day.

Today we could safely say that she was probably all these: embodied all these qualities and quirks of personality, which could hardly have been integrated. Is that not asking too much of these precocious prototypes who so courageously pre-empted holdings which remain a challenge we are still struggling with in our own time?

6 RIGHTS OF WOMEN IN THE OPEN

DOUBTLESS the eighteenth century gave birth to a line of formidable forerunners in woman's slow, laborious quest for an integral identity. Step by step she advanced from that life of immanence, as de Beauvoir contrasts it, to 'man's freedom . . . and scope that marks the untrammelled existence' (de Beauvoir, S., 1977, p. 29). Almost furtively she moves from that first dictionary to her place in the libraries but, more important still, from abject submissiveness to a possession of her mind. True, here was, as in our day, a privileged minority: more of a prototype than a generality. But once we follow this thread, we will no longer be surprised to encounter a Fanny Burney, a George Sand or a Simone Weil, to mention mere illustrations.

The mothers and daughters we have met up to now provide us with a growing sense of how much a woman's life responds, in all its deepest processes, to the mothering she has received. This will become more explicit as we draw closer to our own time and start to reap the benefit of more detailed documentation. Meanwhile, on the frontierland between the eighteenth and nineteenth centuries we find a hard-won attempt at a new synthesis of two conflicted modes: namely of mother/wife and committed polemicist as a distinct mode of life in the person of Mary Wollstonecraft, to be the mother of Mary Shelley in the last hours of her life. The combination in itself, as we have seen, is nothing new. But the role of activist, in this latest example, had a wider grip on life and mounts a more substantial platform in the world of ideas than did Anne Hutchinson or Margaret Fox.

There is a further distinction which we have to bear in mind. All our forerunners to date, remarkable as they were in the context of their circumstances, arrived on their field of action by some accident of fortune. They had also, moreover, made a traditional break from home through the acceptable step of marriage. Christine de Pizan, for instance, was forced to live by her pen under duress of widowhood with its straitened circumstances. None of these had yet set out, as far as we can ascertain, to claim a life of independence from their earliest thinking years, as did the women we will now encounter – whereas Mary Wollstonecraft's (1759–97) dire childhood circumstances, as we are about to see, caused the girl to envisage such a departure for herself.

Mary was the second child of a family of five, and the eldest daughter. Her formative years were spent watching the grim decline of her father's inherited fortune in successive enterprises, most of them on the land. He knew nothing of farming, which simple reality did not serve as a deterrent as he dragged his wife and children from one failure to the next in a drunken, downhill life. But more significant where Mary was concerned was his abuse of her mother, who was readily reduced to 'tearful slavery' and to 'total submission' which, to the dismay of her eldest daughter, 'she accepted apathetically' (Nixon, E., 1971, p. 5).

By the time she was nine Mary had shouldered the role as her mother's deputy. She was blessed with an affectionate and idealistic temperament, and her resentment on that score was on behalf of her mother. Her own attitude to life was, as a consequence, determined, from an early age, by her mother's helplessness and state of abject degradation, so alien to her own strong nature – except, as will transpire, in her own relationships to men. Here, until she married Godwin, near the end of her days, Mary would throw her life, quite unheeding, at the feet of the most unworthy partners in the forlorn and stubborn hope that they might change their nature from callous indifference to one which was capable of love, of constancy and true concern. In this respect she was doubtless caught in a double trap: identification with her mother, as in the classical attempt to turn a 'bad inner' father into a better one in the person of a husband: the fate of so many women who time and time again marry violent or abusive men.

Where her mother was concerned, Mary, already as a child, took to sleeping on the floor outside her parents' bedroom door, where she 'heard the cries, the sound of descending blows, the tramp of feet, the utterances of an inflamed drunkard in the presence of his victim' (Nixon, E., 1971, p. 6). Unable to contain herself, she occasionally burst in to confront her raging father, who would shrink from her in fear. But as the family removed, in the wake of his failures, from Epping to Barking and from there on to Yorkshire, then close to London once again, while she nursed her youngest brother and grappled with her mother's fate, constantly before her eyes, Mary determined that she must win independence for herself as the only remedy to falling victim in her turn. Such a precocious feat of insight, one of the earliest on record, bears testimony how the powers of inborn constitution may help an individual to triumph over circumstances that would silence other lives, except perhaps for screams of madness ending in a padded cell. Never, never would she marry, she determined in her heart, 'for marriage meant servitude, unrelieved and hopeless. She must attain to independence and keep her freedom; this was her first goal in life' (Nixon, E., 1971, p. 7).

This resolve was made easier, we are entitled to suspect, in that she met with no response, no glimmer of appreciation, from the members of her family, for whom she might otherwise, by her generous and loving nature, have even sacrificed her life. Neither could she love her mother, who never showed her gratitude for such selfless devotion and reserved all her affection for her eldest son. Nor did Mrs Wollstonecraft have the slightest inkling of her daughter's burning needs for nourishment equally of mind as of spirit. None the less the family's wanderings in due course introduced an unexpected bonus into the life of this gifted child which brought Mary within orbit of caring surrogate parents and a friend of her own age, Fanny, who returned her love as no one ever had before.

It is of singular interest here that unlike many in her shoes, Mary did not identify with the sufferings of her mother to embark on a career of all-embracing masochism but utilized each new advantage to build her personality by spirited self-assertion instead of falling into ways of sullen rebelliousness or sterile attention-seeking. As early as the age of sixteen Mary threatened to leave home unless given her own room in which she might pursue her studies, once that flame had been kindled by intervention from outside. And when she reached the age of nineteen and had accepted finally that nothing at home would ever change, her personal road to salvation now became her sole concern and she made plans accordingly.

Her mother was, predictably, not remotely sympathetic. Mary had been her sole support for over a decade by then, but this had never been acknowledged. Was it not a daughter's duty to serve the family with no inkling of reward, or even of appreciation? Had the trap of such assumptions not swallowed helpless young women through untold centuries without so much as a trace? And would it not, we should add, continue to take this toll well beyond our day and age, even if more covertly? Even if the steel is sprung and baited with more subtlety, in psychological terms, than by Mrs Wollstonecraft.

Mary made her getaway with determined preparation, by the only route open to her at the time – that of an 'upper' servant – by accepting a post as companion to a rich and difficult widow who lived in Bath. 'To live with strangers who are so intolerably tyrannical that none of their relations can bear to live with them' – she later decried her lot in her first book, entitled *Thoughts on the Education of Daughters* published in 1787, only nine years afterwards, when she was twenty-eight (Nixon, E., 1971, p. 15).

Her situation with the widow was made harder still by letters from her younger sisters, Everina and Eliza, suggesting that she was shirking her responsibilities towards her own family. Mary hit back in reply: 'You don't do me justice in supposing I seldom think of you . . . for my anxiety preys on me . . . you don't say a word of my mother. I take it that she is well – tho of late she has not even desired to be remembered to me' (Nixon, E., 1971, p. 17). It is true that she had put some distance between herself and that hopeless situation, in the person of her mother, which she recognized as such. Yet that freedom she had won to surface appearances, was, as she discovered now, fraught with anxiety and with bouts of deep depression beneath that surface of bravado. Whether her comments here can be read as representing our first evidence of guilt as we will discuss it later must remain an open question.

Besides, her mother was dying. 'I think I love most people best when they are in adversity', Mary had written to a friend just before she hurried home to that unhappy woman's bedside through a long and trying illness. Again, as in her early years, she watched outside that bedroom door, ready to intervene when her father's quest for pleasure was more than the invalid could bear. 'A little patience and all will be over' were her mother's final words by way of late appreciation. They haunted Mary all her life and her life's work would be built as a bastion to redress those monstrous inequities which had marked her for life.

Indeed, if Mary had failed to rescue her defeated mother – to her anger, shame and grief – she was determined to succeed in a subsequent similar mission, although in reality it was less extreme than her phantasies coloured it. Her sister Eliza had, hardly surprisingly, made an unhappy marriage. She certainly seemed quite unhinged after the birth of her first baby. Having neither home nor means Mary, with Fanny's help, none the less abducted her to lodgings they secured in Hackney, a situation then as fraught as any serious crime. Even so they arranged for a legal separation; and when nothing would avail, her husband capitulated and eventually returned Eliza's baby to her mother. But how were the conspirators going to make a living? They determined to start a school and soon had twenty pupils as well as several lodgers so that they could keep afloat. By a succession of steps which would be rated heroic, in our present day and age, they were, at least for the time being, a proper going concern.

Mary Wollstonecraft was of course by no means the only woman who in 1784 had decided notions on the issue of Women's Rights. There were the so-called Bluestockings. There was Mrs Catherine Macaulay and Elizabeth Montagu, Fanny Burney and Hannah More, all of them outstanding women, who were pushing the lazy clock of social attitudes forward. However, all of these belonged to a higher social order linked to some financial means. Fanny Burney had received £2,000 in 1796 for her novel *Camilla*, and in 1814 the sum of £7,000 for *The Wanderer*: substantial riches in that day. But never once, throughout her life, did Mary let financial issues stand in her determined way. What she may have lacked in money she compensated for with passion and an unwavering belief in her inner resources. Besides, when money came her way, as she earned it by her pen, her first thoughts were for her sisters, who only grew to envy Mary her growing reputation in the literary world. Once her beloved childhood friend, Fanny, had died in Portugal, in Mary's and her husband's arms shortly after giving birth, Mary went desperately hungry for loving companionship. For all the worldly success which would come to her in time as a passionate polemicist, the emotional deprivation of her earliest years continued to eat away at her zest for love and life, to undermine her belief in herself at that elemental level where each of us must depend on that wellspring in our life. This erosion would result in two attempts at suicide, very nearly successful, and then her premature death at that moment in time when it seemed that she had at last dropped anchor in a sheltering harbour, too exhausted to survive. So subtle and profound, so far-reaching in the deepest crevice of the unconscious mind, can rage our earliest frustrations, where we went short of mothering, that some deep self-destructive drive, semi-quiescent through the years, finally triumphs to deal an ultimate, untimely blow, as fell in the present case.

By the time Mary's work *Vindication of the Rights of Woman* was published in 1792, when she was thirty-three, she had only five more years to live. It is not often called to mind that this milestone of a book, for which she is best remembered, followed on her *Vindication of the Rights of Men*, published two years previously. It is an interesting sequence. Mary Wollstonecraft was eager not to be written off as 'a Hyaena in Petticoats', as Walpole had labelled her, predictably, for her pains. Accordingly, in her dedication of the second work to the Late Bishop of Autun, the author of a recent pamphlet on the Rights of Women, she pleads that 'It is then affection for the whole human race that makes my pen dart rapidly along to support what I believe to be the cause of virtue; . . . ' (Wollstonecraft, M., 1792, p. 39).

Did Mary, at a deeper level, have first to pacify her father, before she came to the point: a passionate vindication of her poor mother, who was dead after a joyless life of continuous abuse? Her approach is somewhat circumspect when it comes to the rights of woman: 'in the present state of society it appears necessary to go back to first principles in search of the most simple truth, and to dispute, with some prevailing justice every inch of the ground' (Wollstonecraft, M., 1792, p. 39). This she then sets out to do, arguing passionately for educational and sexual equality in every aspect and detail, well aware that every sentence must inevitably arouse considerable opposition and personal hostility.

But knowing her story, as we do – and her readership at the time most probably had no inkling of it, nor would they have seen it as an excuse for these shocking propositions – we can see most vividly, before her grieving heart's eye, her focus on that wretched victim, none other than the author's mother. Particularly does this apply, with most painful clarity, in Chapter 4, which is entitled 'Observation on the State of Degradation to which Woman is Reduced by Various Causes'. Here the author claims, with a sombre indignation and fury rising from each word: 'Pleasure is the business of woman's life ...' (Wollstonecraft, M., 1792, p. 97).

Clearly as Mary had observed her poor mother's downfall at the hands of a man, who was in this case her father, she had been unable to learn at an unconscious level from this terrible example, with regard to her own lovelife. First she had lost her heart to a painter, Fuseli, a cold and egocentric man, married to another woman. Mary did not aspire to marriage, as we have seen before, and proposed in all naivety that she share Sophia's husband. Swept away by her passionate search for tenderness and warmth, she could see no wrong in this, and even wrote to its object: 'If I thought my passion criminal I would conquer it or die in the attempt' (Nixon, E., 1971, p. 78).

The prolonged unhappiness occasioned by this involvement was certainly not conducive to a wholesome state of mind. Nor did a visit to Paris in 1792 have a happier outcome since it was in that city, racked by the Revolution, that she soon met Imlay, an American and an apostle of Rousseau. Once again she lost her heart, and this time her body also, to an unstable partner, in every respect unworthy of her own passionate commitment. In 1794 she gave birth to his daughter, to whom she gave the name Fanny in memory of her much-loved friend. After an initial, tolerable, interlude the baby developed smallpox. Her mother nursed her devotedly and thereby saved her first-born's life, but meanwhile Imlay was clearly taking his affection elsewhere. Broken-hearted, Mary wrote: 'Will you not then be a good boy and come back quickly to play with your girls? ... My heart longs for your return, my love, and only looks for, and seeks happiness with you' (Nixon, E., 1971, p. 139). But Imlay was too weak to come out into the open with his own reality: that he no longer felt any interest or affection for the mother or his child:

A neglected cold, and continual inquietude . . . have reduced me to a state of weakness I never before experienced . . . God preserve this poor child, and render her happier than her mother . . . but for this little darling, I would cease to care about a life, which is now stripped of every charm. (Nixon, E., 1971, p. 141)

Imlay prevaricated and kept stringing her along in the manner the weak will always seek refuge in. Late in 1795 Mary could finally no longer deceive herself. She had in effect been playing hide-and-seek with reality very much longer than her inner strength could afford, undermined as it was by her early deprivations. Her last letter to Imlay ended:

... but I shall plunge into the Thames where there is the least chance of my being snatched from the death I seek. God bless you. May you never know by experience what you have made me endure. (Nixon, E., 1971, p. 192)

Mary had so far in her life, that of a single woman, been a total stranger to the harrowing vicissitudes every feminine psyche suddenly falls subject to once love and motherhood alter its fundamental texture in unpremeditated ways. Now she discovered, at those crossroads of utmost vulnerability, after giving birth once more – but this time to an actual living child – that she was no longer a match for those overwhelming sorrows, and doubtless rages, grown on the soil of old neglect and hitherto suppressed, which were now tearing her apart. On a dark and rainy night she climbed the railings of Putney Bridge and threw herself into the murky water. Already unconscious, she was pulled out of the running river and painfully nursed back to health.

For several months to come Mary hoped against hope to change Imlay's very nature and turn a bad, uncaring 'father' into a loving one: that familiar manoeuvre from whose lessons few have ever learnt! None the less, learn she did. And in 1796, a little restored in strength and relatively free of Imlay, she drew closer to Godwin, that profoundly kindred spirit, as she stealthily owned. Still terribly afraid of another injury, she now took the utmost care to check the ground of her new feelings. Whenever 'she was tempted to compare Godwin's unattractive physical appearance with more elegant forms she remembered how little happiness had come to her from this source' (Nixon, E., 1971, p. 203); while the relationship deepened, steadily, into a love which she had previously never known. Although they both recognized that their views against marriage would, if they were to succumb, expose them to ridicule, this was a price they had to pay. On 29 March 1797 they became man and wife, which paradoxical event met with a mixed response, as anyone could have predicted.

Little Fanny now belonged to a proper family after an abysmal start with a mother who had been deeply distracted and depressed. For many years she never doubted that she was Godwin's natural child, and Mary, pregnant for the second time, was brimful of optimism, on each and every one's account, that a lifetime of such sorrows had lifted its evil spell. Before the birth of the child she wrote to her husband: 'I must tell you that I love you better than I ever supposed I did when I promised to love you for ever' (Nixon, E., 1971, p. 240). But this delivery was not as easy as the first, owing to a retained placenta. Within a few days she was dead, and Godwin left all alone with two small daughters in his care, Fanny and Mary Godwin, both of whom would be marked for life by these exigencies.

Nine years after Mary's death, Godwin, a devoted father, married his next-door neighbour. Mrs Clairmont, who already had two children of her own, was not a bad woman in any obvious sense. But young Mary was a brilliant child with considerable charisma which mobilized her stepmother's exasperation and envy. Always an avid reader, she fell into the habit of retreating with her books to the grave of her mother in St Pancras cemetery. When, at the age of seventeen, she fell head over heels in love with the poet Shelley, a visitor to her father's house for a joint business venture in the realm of publishing, to elude her stepmother's unrelenting persecution she and her lover met at that comforting graveside which the romantic young woman seems to have visualized as her true maternal home. There Mary felt safe to pursue her own studies, as her mother had once done, and to seek fulfilment in love, safe from the frictions at home from which the unhappy Fanny, who lacked Mary's high spirits and intellectual brilliance, found no means of escape.

Shelley, however, was married to Harriet at the time. But to Mary Godwin's daughter this was hardly here or there once her passions were engaged, as they were to be with Shelley for the remainder of his life. This love was now to be her refuge, like her reading and her books, not only from the outer world in the person of her stepmother, who was always quarrelling with Fanny, but also, as we may assume in the light of developments, from an inner sense of deadness, of a black hole or depression, almost certainly related to earliest maternal loss. In this connection it is striking how throughout her life with Shelley, each time tragedy struck, with that unfailing tread with which it hounded their years, Mary would swiftly turn to her study of the classics as to any anodyne. Melancholy Mary was, quite obviously, at interludes, and also paranoid at times.

The death of Mary Shelley's mother had axed with a single blow a portion of her life-equipment, in a manner we deduce from successive tragedies, which amounted to a holocaust throughout her married life. In March 1815 Mary's first baby died. She had awakened to find her first-born dead beside her in the bed. Her diary entry of that day: 'Find my baby dead. Send for Hogg. Talk. A miserable day. In the evening read The Fall of the Jesuits . . . ' (Bigland, E., 1959, p. 66). Like her mother she believed that the mind's reason must prevail, regardless of the deeper cost. Two weeks later we read: 'Dream that my little baby came to life again; that it had only been cold, and that we rubbed it before the fire, and it lived. Awake to find no baby . . . Play chess with Hogg and then read Gibbon' (Bigland, E., 1959, p. 67).

Clearly, Mary could not mourn in the deepest, healing sense. Like those of us who suffer loss long before we know the word, who are ripped and torn from life in the person of our earliest mother, for whatever cruel reason, far too early to survive whole in body or in mind, she believed she could not risk facing that catastrophic experience of annihilation ever in her time again; so she resorted to denial and distractions from her mourning each time tragedy struck.

During her first five years with Shelley, Mary was to lose all three children she gave birth to. As though this was not enough, Harriet would drown herself as a final accusation against Shelley's faithlessness, and her half-sister, Fanny, take her life with laudanum when she was only twenty-two.

Fanny, having stayed behind to try to support Godwin, who had never recovered from the death of his first wife, had had a cruel time of it. She was devoted to the man she believed to be her father, and for that reason bore the brunt of her stepmother's antagonism and constant petty persecution. 'Write small, for Mama complains of the postage of a double letter . . . I am not well; my mind always keeps my body in a fever; but never mind me' (Bigland, E., 1959, p. 90), she wrote bravely to her absent sister. In a subsequent letter, Fanny blamed herself for all the troubles of her parents, financial and otherwise. Her next and final letter was written in Bristol, where she had fled all alone in final desperation. The last straw had been the news conveyed by an unknown source that Godwin was not her true father.

On receiving her last letter Shelley rushed off to Bristol and, full of premonition, followed flimsy clues on to Swansea. But he arrived too late. Fanny's body had been found in a room she had booked in the

Mackworth Arms Inn, the empty bottle beside her, with the following note:

I have long determined that the best thing I could do was to put an end to the existence of a being whose birth was unfortunate and whose life had only been a series of pains to those persons who have hurt their health in endeavouring to promote her welfare. Perhaps to hear of my death may give you pain, but you will soon have the blessing of forgetting that such a creature ever existed as . . . (Bigland, E., 1959, pp. 196–7)

We do not know whether Fanny 'knew' at a conscious level of her mother's fearful plight, or her suicide attempts, so early in her own, small life. We can only ask ourselves whether that 'unknown source' to 'volunteer' these tragic details had been her own unconscious mind. We know that her infant psyche would have tended to absorb the maternal preoccupation, in the dark night of despair, into its integral substance to be marked for a life where the outer miseries only served to confirm that her coming into being had been not joy but disaster to the one who gave her life.

This common existential guilt, one of those lifelong scars the best of psychotherapists will be hard put to lessen in its far-reaching consequences, would equally play havoc with her sister Mary's life. For had she not obviously 'caused the death' of her mother? The effect upon herself we will look at very shortly. With regard to the unhappy Fanny, she had clearly struggled on, for as long as her strength permitted, to repair the damage she had done – in her deeper phantasy – by being a support at home, where no support could avail for reasons quite beyond her scope. Godwin's wordly undertakings were as clumsy and inept as were previously those of her maternal grandfather. Both men were beyond any rescue operation in a realistic sense. But as we know, reality plays the most negligible role where the unconscious cries 'doom' and attributes it to the self. In this sense Fanny was doomed from the hour of her birth.

But Mary Shelley, as she had in the interim become, was at only twenty-five to face a final tragedy when a storm off Lerici, where they were staying at the time, sunk the *Don Juan* in which her husband was returning from one of his sailing trips. Shelleys phantasy life had clearly been preoccupied with death by drowning through the years. This Mary had intuited. On that occasion when he left the hated Casa Magni, on the shores of the lake – a house which had, from the start, filled her with dark premonitions – she had tried her very utmost to prevent him leaving her and Percy, her sole surviving child, who was barely three years old. But 'reason' once again prevailed and Mary had given in, to become Shelley's widow.

If we can arouse ourselves from such successive tragedies to take a closer look at them, we find at the deepest level a degree, if not more, of unconscious collusion. In the case of the death of her first son, pet-named Willmouse, a doctor whom Mary trusted had warned her explicitly that she must remove the sickly child from the heat of the Roman summer. That advice she had ignored, with the predicted consequences. Furthermore, she had 'known', if we may use that expression for the powers of intuition, that Shelley should not go sailing if he was to stay alive. I believe that we can fairly state that since she had lost her mother in her earliest infancy Mary did not believe, at an unconscious level, that she was able to keep anyone she loved alive. As a consequence lives slipped through her fingers that need not otherwise have done. With the death of her mother, with that earliest rupture of the postnatal womb, of her very earliest world, a gaping opening, or wound, never mended or healed, for all her own gifts and courage.

Like her famous mother, so she too was still to know the taste of being acknowledged as a literary celebrity – for her novel *Frankenstein*, and several other works. And later, when Percy married a girl who was to her liking, she drew great comfort from this event. She died in 1851, after a paralysis had left her virtually helpless but largely serene in mind, entirely preoccupied still with her beloved Shelley.

PART III

1 THE REVOLT OF THE DAUGHTERS

The revolt of the daughters is not, if I understand it, a revolt against mere surface conventionalities . . . but it is a revolt against a bondage that enslaves her whole life. In the past she has belonged to other people, now she demands to belong to herself.
(JILL LIDDINGTON, *Respectable Rebel*)

They must have been a nuisance; great girls wandering about in the night air looking at the stars instead of staying warm indoors and keeping things cheerful; writing diaries and wanting to read bits of them out aloud; lurking in their rooms; complaining of being bored; wanting intense conversations with their admirers; expecting their admirers to be interested in their views.

. . . a nature altogether ardent, theoretic, and intellectually consequent: and with such a nature, struggling in the bands of a narrow teaching . . . the outcome was sure to strike others as at once exaggeration and inconsistency. The thing which seemed to her best, she wanted to justify by the completest knowledge . . . 'I should learn everything then', she said to herself.
(SARAH A. ZEMAN, *Presumptuous Girls*)

ALL WAS LEADING up to this. We should have been prepared for it, but still it comes as a shock to hear the devil's advocate address us in the guise of woman. How have we come to such a pass?

For all the contradictory burdens which Christianity imposed on the nature of woman to confuse it utterly, it put the cat among the pigeons with a singular claim of far-reaching consequences: that the soul stands before the Trinity finally disencumbered of the accident of gender. For all the tantrums of misogyny, for all the patriarchal strictures, for all the fire and brimstone from the Fathers of the Church, this dictum remained undisputed; and thus the soul, if not its bearer, had the right to be improved by Divine Authority.

If, after the monastic era, this improvement was the plaything of a happy accident, dependent on the whim of fathers or some fortuitous constellation closer to a miracle, the pressure soon grew slowly from within the core of abeyant womankind to further their belated cause. At the time when Juan Vivès suggested that women should be provided with a dictionary, it took a masculine voice to pronounce such infamy; while even highly learned queens such as Catherine Parr (1513–48) and Elizabeth I (1533–1603) were wise enough to claim this particular distinction as a tribute owed to God in the interest of their subjects: '. . . and God that gave me here to sit, and placed me over you, knows that I never respected myself, but as your good was conserved in me' (Elizabeth I, in her speech to her last Parliament, 1601).

It all sounds very ladylike: even St Paul would have approved, so we are startled to read seven decades further on, in 1673:

Custom, when it is inveterate, hath a mighty influence: it hath the force of Nature itself. The barbarous custom to breed women low . . . hath prevailed so far that it is verily believed . . . that women are not endued with such reason as men, nor capable of improvement by education, as they are . . . (Mahl, M. and Koon, H., 1977, p. 51)

We have stumbled on the preamble to 'An Essay to Revive the Ancient Education of Gentlewomen', addressed 'to all ingenious and vertuous ladies, more especially to her Royal Highness the Lady Mary, eldest daughter to his Royal Highness the Duke of York'. The author is Bathsua Makin (1612–74), described by some as the most learned woman of her day, although there are no records of how she came by such a high-flying distinction. But it is known that she was employed by Charles I as a tutor for his children in mathematics, Greek, Latin, Hebrew, French, Italian and Spanish, all at a salary of £40 per year. This fell into sad arrears that were never made good despite repeated requests!

Here we have a forerunner, by virtually a century, of the future governess: that route by which 'gentle' daughters, like the Brontë sisters in their day, could make an often desperate bid for a modicum of independence, or to escape the dead-end blight of musty spinsterhood, at all of £16 per year with board, after laundry charges were deducted!

Half a century on we are bound to take notice of the first magazine produced by and for women. Its pages were written almost solely by one Eliza Haywood, whom Swift denigrated as a 'stupid, infamous, scribbling woman'. *The Female Spectator* (1722–46) was no idle collection of romantic little tales, but dealt with burning issues such as female education, literature, the arts and philosophy. The emphasis was still on souls: 'Why do they call us silly Women . . . There is undoubtedly no Sexes in Souls . . . Ladies, Your constant Reader and humble servant, Cleora' (Mahl, M., and Koon, H., 1977, p. 223).

None the less there came a moment, perhaps impossible to pinpoint, when the soul was shelved in favour of more robust aspirations. Change is defined in retrospect once an impassioned student joins forces with a field of study where both are worthy of respect. Perhaps the history of woman truly came of age only once her view of herself had begun to outgrow the limits of maternity, as we are about to see, in the context of the dyad. For decades before Jane Austen set that illustrious pen to paper, 'women had, in their hundreds, sat at home composing novels' (Spender, D., 1985, p. 5). In these works they explored aspects of woman's situation, to define 'the state of play' (Zeman, S.A., 1977, p. 2). This slowly introduced the notion that souls were all very well, but women also had a body which must be made allowance for.

Listen to this mother and daughter where Adeline maintains her right to disavow the bonds of marriage to enter a union of true hearts – and incidentally, bodies:

'To what Sir Patrick says of Mr Glenmurray I pay no attention,' answered Adeline; 'nor are you, my dear mother, capable, I am sure, of being influenced by the prejudices of the world. – But you are quite mistaken in supposing me so lost to consistency, and so regardless of your liberal opinions and the books which we have studied, as to think of MARRYING Mr Glenmurray.'

'Grant me patience!' cried Mrs Mowbray; 'why, to be sure you do not think of living with him WITHOUT being married?'

'Certainly, Madam; that you may have the pleasure of beholding one union founded on rational grounds and cemented by rational ties.' (Opie, A., 1986 [1804], p. 3)

It may come as a surprise that this novel was published in 1804 (Opie, A., 1986). The books referred to above, which the author must have read, included Mary Wollstonecraft's *A Vindication of the Rights of Woman*. Adeline based her views, with all their subsequent confusion, on that heroine's example. That young ladies in their thousands, lapping up this literature of conflicting messages, grew increasingly bewildered is not hard to believe. That their mothers had hysterics was no doubt inevitable.

'How!' cried Mrs Mowbray, turning pale. 'I! – I have pleasure in seeing my daughter a kept mistress! – You are mad, quite mad. – I approve such unhallowed connexions!'

'My dearest mother,' replied Adeline, 'your agitation terrifies me, – but indeed what I say is strictly true; and see here, in Mr Glenmurray's book, the very passage which I so often heard you admire.' As she said this, Adeline pointed to the passage, but in an instant Mrs Mowbray seized the book and threw it on the fire.

Before Adeline had recovered from her consternation Mrs Mowbray fell into a violent hysteric. (Opie, A., 1986, p. 4)

Adeline spends the night in a bed which she makes up on the floor of her mother's room, filled with 'tears of regret for the past and alarm for the future'. In the morning, her widowed mother pronounces in a faint voice:

'Adeline, my dear child, I hope you will no longer think of putting a design in execution so fraught with mischief to you, and horror to me. Little did I think that you were so romantic as to see no difference between amusing one's imagination with new theories and new systems, and acting upon them in defiance of common customs, and the received usages of society. I admire the convenient trousers and graceful dress of the Turkish women; but I would not wear them myself, lest it should expose me to derision.'

'Is there no difference,' thought Adeline, 'between the importance of a dress and an opinion! – Is the one to be taken up, and laid down again, with the same indifferences as the other!' . . . (Opie, A., 1986, pp. 41–2)

Doubtless scenes of this kind form a portion of the backcloth of the nineteenth century, as indeed of our own. What is important is the fact that they were painted by women who were, but without knowing it, part of a study group of their confounding situation, already laying the foundations of microhistory, as it would be pioneered thirteen decades further on in an ever-growing body. But it was only after Freud had given serious and substantial thought to the matter of lunatics that women and children were seen as subjects who were worthy of recorded history!

If, where women were concerned, '. . . their real business . . . was simply being available' (Zeman, S.A., 1977, p. 42), rude shocks were now in store, sometimes even in collusion with a mother, here and there. So in 1791 we hear the Marchioness of Boufflers apologize to her hostess, Mrs Montagu, for being late on the grounds that her daughter 'just as she was going to dress . . . was seized with a *dégoût momentance du monde* (a sudden distaste of society) and so could not wait on her' (Zeman, S.A., 1977, p. 265). Mrs Montagu's views on feeble follies of this kind we can very well imagine, having studied her letters to her daughter, Lady Bute. None the less this excuse hardly comes as a surprise, for we are growing more aware that during the last few decades daughters have begun to shock the world by proclaiming, certainly between the lines, that they are growing bent on steering their gentle, fluttering flotillas towards wild seas of subject status, whatever hurricanes arise.

This dreadfully alarming trend was clearly growing manifest in the English social scene from the later eighteenth century, when we find ample evidence in contemporary fiction. Take Fanny Burney's *Evelina*, published with great success in 1778. Innocent as this heroine was, she knew to each dot over the 'i' what her aims and objects were upon her entrance into the world. For she was determined to avoid the fate of her late shipwrecked mother, seduced into a foreign marriage whose flimsy evidence could be destroyed with a single little match, leaving her no alternative but a mute demise in childbed.

If young ladies now began to have their wits and act together in the vagaries of the marriage market, and shortly with regard to their wider destiny, then this tended to be viewed as a disfiguring disease that England had caught from France, which was by that time seething with revolutionary fervour, as a ghastly premonition of where such outrage was bound to lead, with 'such echo in England "as of a great storm in France with a dreadful sea rising" ' (Slater, M., 1983, p. 3). Doubtless the guillotine loomed as a terrible warning to the likes of Maria Edgeworth and Jane Austen at the time not to tamper with society, lest their own go up in smoke, but rather to confine themselves to such practical advice as:

not to preserve the delicacy and good sense of young girls in the name of God and Dear Mamma, but for their own sakes . . . to explain to them for their own good how much they should know and how much they should not know, and how to preserve their positions. (Zeman, S.A., 1977, p. 21)

But if we are sometimes startled as a female voice proclaims: 'I hate slavery! *Vive la Liberté!* . . . I'm a champion for the Rights of Woman' (Zeman, S.A., 1977, p. 15), the majority of wives were still manipulating husbands with time-old feminine strategy: the prime resource of the weak.

Here we have to bear in mind that where feasible dreams of independence were concerned, a yearly income of fifty pounds was the barest minimum on which to build its premises. And we are thinking of a time when the annual income of a woman spinner was £3. 11s. 7½d. (Pinchbeck, I., 1981, p. 145) or when a dairymaid who toiled an eighteen-hour day in the late eighteenth century would at the very most have earned the sum of £5 per year in addition to her board and keep. Women who worked down the mines, however, could on occasion rise to something like £12 per year, although it might be twice as much depending on the actual pit (Pinchbeck, I., 1981, p. 257). Only in 1886 did a bill pass through Parliament limiting the hours for women under the age of eighteen to seventy-five a week! Under these conditions, where sheer survival was at stake, such a workload surely left little surplus strength for dreams, except perhaps in hours of sleep.

We will find no bed of roses in this desperate understructure with its high morbidity in every aspect of life. It is painful to think of, or even try to imagine, the mothering which any daughter received in such dire circumstances. We will return to her kind, but meanwhile let us leave the nameless millions in those dark and tortuous tunnels and focus on the pyramid's apex of well-documented lives. Here woman's image of herself was evidently being forged into a distinct resource which would accrue and be ploughed back into that other inferno, to leaven it increasingly.

We start with Harriet Martineau (1802–76). Her autobiography, in three substantial volumes, represents such an advance in terms of self-scrutiny from the diary, say, of Alice Thornton that we may hardly think of change so much as inspired transformation. She herself has this to say in opening her Introduction:

and certain qualities of my own mind, – a strong consciousness and a clear memory in regard to my early feelings, – have seemed to indicate to me the duty of recording my own experience. When my life became evidently a somewhat remarkable one, the obligation presented itself more strongly to my conscience: and when I made up my mind to interdict the publication of my private letters, the duty became unquestionable. (Martineau, H., 1877, I, p. 1)

Meet the nineteenth century woman!

We stand humble and amazed before such authority, aware that we have scarcely traced its formidable evolution, except perhaps between the lines. Is that not, after all, the place where true learning has its ground: in some mysterious wellspring sunk by the grapevine of each age, rather than in increments of that dross we label facts?

My mother's account of things was that I was all but starved to death in the first weeks of my life, – the wetnurse being very poor . . . The discovery was made when I was three months old, and when I was fast sinking under diarrhoea . . . and never was poor mortal cursed with a more beggarly nervous system. (Martineau, H., 1877, I, p. 10)

She goes on to describe daunting early childhood terrors, both by day and by night; and we are left in little doubt that she manages to link a cruel legacy of neurotic difficulties, which she struggled to surmount but which also served as spur to her subsequent achievements, to this neglected start in life, including such an early brush with death. Certainly she forged these links between cause and effect with an intuitive clarity well ahead of its time, and anticipating Freud.

Her insight into these matters, those deep connections in the mind, are positively overwhelming:

My parents knew nothing of all this. It never occurred to me to speak of anything I felt most: and I doubt whether they ever had the slightest idea of my miseries. It seems to me now that a little closer observation would have shown them the causes of the bad health and fitful temper which gave them so much anxiety on my account; and I am sure that a little more of the cheerful tenderness which was in those days thought bad for children, would have saved me from my worst faults, and from a world of suffering. (Martineau, H., 1877, I, p. 11)

In other words, by the middle of the nineteenth century, when she was writing these lines, this daughter was in little doubt that insufficient mothering had laid such burdens on her life as often made her reel and stagger, while they also drove her on until, as we shall shortly see, her neurosis defeated her when she became an invalid – a case of hypochondria, in the last stages of her life.

By the time she was five the child was much preoccupied with ideas of suicide, so that she might escape to heaven from the injustices of which she felt herself a victim at home. She certainly describes her feelings of complex torment at the time as those belonging to a child which we would today consider quite seriously disturbed; the kind of little girl we meet in Mrs Klein's case-histories like, for instance, Little Erna: 'I had no self-respect, and an unbound need of approbation and affection. My capacity for jealousy was something frightful.' And she goes on to reflect, with her insightful regret: 'My temper might have been early made a thoroughly good one, by the slightest indulgence shown to my natural affections, and any rational dealing with my faults' (Martineau, H., 1877, I, p. 19).

At intervals her mother sent her to deliver harsh edicts to the servants in the kitchen, 'to bid them not to be so like cart-horses overhead', a task which would cause her torments. By the age of eight, she writes, all that she desired was some 'ease of conscience'. Feelings of perpetual guilt haunted her days and nights, as earlier the other terrors; the classical paranoia partly due to attacks she must have launched in phantasy against a mother who, she felt, was constantly denying her the loving response which she craved.

The birth of a little sister, whom she promised herself to shield from deprivations she had known, occasioned this keen interest from her spirit of enquiry, as she contemplates the prospect: 'that I should now see the growth of a human mind from the very beginning' (Martineau, H., 1877, I, p. 52). Here Harriet was pioneering baby-observation as it is practised nowadays by psychotherapists in training. She clearly longed to observe whether tender, loving care could in truth not obviate the torments which had dogged her childhood and showed no signs of abating by the time she was fifteen. How could Harriet have known, when she set out on this quest, that our rational intentions are readily swept away by stormy undercurrents? For despite her brave designs she grew ever more distracted when she saw that her mother much preferred the younger Rachel. Finally, one winter's evening, that particular abscess burst and she confronted her mother, beyond caring at the time, with all her anguish on that score:

'Harriet, I am more displeased with you tonight than I have ever been in your life.' Thought I, 'I don't care: I have got it out, and it's all true.' 'Go

and say your prayers', my mother continued; 'and ask God to forgive you for your conduct to-night; for I don't know that I can.' (Martineau, H., 1877, I, p. 87)

In fact this battle had been won, for 'henceforth a most scrupulous impartiality between Rachel and myself was shown'. But she goes on to mourn, with her constant refrain, that if only her mother had been more open to her pain, then 'I believe this would have wrought in a moment that cure which it took years to effect, amidst reserve and silence' (Martineau, H., 1877, I, p. 87).

Harriet never came to terms with the coldness of her mother, which others also confirmed. It rankled as a lifelong wound, to flare up at intervals and poison the entire system, for all its wider excellence and intermittent gifts for joy. Yet these very difficulties would prove in time to be a factor which drove her on relentlessly to seek complete independence at the first opportunity. Of the years from 1819 to 1832 she writes, with obvious satisfaction at this accomplishment: 'These thirteen years, extending from my entering upon womanhood to my complete establishment in an independent position, as to occupation and the management of my own life . . .' (Martineau, H., 1877, I, p. 97). Much like Mary Wollstonecraft, Harriet Martineau had aimed at complete autonomy; and this despite the gradual appearance of a major handicap. From around the age of twelve, it could no longer be denied that the child was growing deaf and would shortly be deprived of her hearing altogether. This deprivation brought one bonus by the time she was eighteen:

My mother, too, took me into her confidence more and more . . . as my deafness increased, and bespoke for me her motherly sympathy. For some years, indeed, there was a genuine and cordial friendship between my mother and me . . . and, from the time when I began to have literary enterprises . . . I was sustained by her trustful, generous, self-denying sympathy and maternal appreciation. After a time, when she was fretted by cares and infirmities, I became as nervous in regard to her as ever, (even to the entire breaking down of my health); but during the whole period of which I am now treating, – and it is a very large space in my life – there were no limitations to our mutual confidence. (Martineau, H., 1877, I, p. 99)

The eventual decline in the health of Harriet's mother would presumably have caused her earlier, latent paranoia to flare up once more, as is so frequently the case where infantile anxieties on the part of the daughter will link maternal deterioration, regardless of its actual cause, with attacks made on the mother in earlier phantasy. And since her thirst for studying still met with solid opposition within the wider family, this frustration only added fuel to the flames. Reiterating how Jane Austen, 'the Queen of novelists', was obliged to conceal her current manuscripts 'under a large piece of muslin' – if that story is true – Harriet draws this parallel in a cryptic understatement: 'thus my first studies in philosophy were carried on with great care and reserve' (Martineau, H., 1877, I, p. 101).

The threat to her avid learning came from the sewing circle, from which none of its women members thought to offer her exemption, hateful as it must have been with its superficial gossip; so that her self-chosen task of translating Tacitus, as well as her bible studies, had to be carried on during snatched and stolen hours, at either end of the day; with the fears of interruption always hanging over them.

Against such overwhelming odds her literary aspirations, and hunger after authorship, carried their first fragile fruit in 1821. Her first appearance in print, in a local periodical, *The Monthly Repository*, drew this sequence of events, a little like a fairy tale in her Cinderella life: her brother, newly married then, invited her over for tea and praised 'the fine sentences' of this 'new hand' on the paper, which was anonymous. When Harriet was thereupon stricken silent by terror, her brother spoke very gently:

'Harriet, what is the matter with you? I never knew you so slow to praise anything before.' I replied in utter confusion, – I never could baffle anybody. 'The truth is, that paper is mine.' He then laid his hand on my shoulder, and said very gravely (calling me 'dear' for the first time) 'Now dear, leave it to other women to make shirts and darn stockings; and do you devote yourself to this.' I went home in a sort of dream, so that the squares of the pavement seemed to float before my eyes. That evening made me an authoress. (Martineau, H., 1877, I, p. 120)

How many women whose natures are too highly strung by a creative incubus are lost for want of a supporting brother, nagged out of self-belief and talent by a mother's constant criticism and envious hostility? Had this sensitive child gone deaf to escape this persecution, where the outer only echoed a derisory inner-mother?

When Harriet was twenty-four her father fell ill and died. At the time her first, small book, *Addresses, Prayers and Hymns, for the use of families and schools*, 'was going through the press . . . and great was my father's satisfaction; and high were his hopes, I believe, of what I should one day do' (Martineau, H., 1877, I, p. 130). None the less she then tells us, almost overcome with grief:

The old habit of fear came upon me, more irresistibly than ever, on the assembling of the family; and I mourn to think how I kept out of the way, whenever it was possible, and how little I said to my father of what was in my heart about him and my feelings towards him. (Martineau, H., 1877, I, p. 130)

Here we have the classic terror generated in a daughter that mother will disapprove of her close relationship to a loving father; the more so when the daughter's talents, and/or her youthful beauty, are experienced by either party as an oedipal triumph which will eclipse the older woman.

Shortly after her father's death Harriet's brief engagement ended in her fiancé's insanity, and soon afterwards he died. Reflecting on her single state, which she then accepted thankfully as her true and natural lot, she analysed it in these terms:

The veneration in which I hold domestic life has always shown me that that life is not for those whose self-respect had been early broken down, or had never grown. Happily the majority are free from this disability. Those who suffer under it had better be as I . . . (Martineau, H., 1877, I, p. 132)

How acutely was she aware that her earliest deprivations meant that she would always suffer the most painful difficulties in an attempt to form that second of a human life's closest relationships, for which the first one may prepare us in that rich range of nuances, where we are fortunate enough; or leave us floundering, where it failed!

We cannot trace all the stages of her inspiring travail to overcome her difficulties and earn her living as a writer to build a life of her own, except for one or two landmarks. During a stay in London, with an uncle, she describes, in vivid self-analysis, a transformation for the better in her personality in these happier circumstances, which were further enriched by the warm encouragement lavished by Mr Fox, her editor and publisher:

The frown of those old days, the rigid face, the sulky mouth, the forbidding countenance, which looked as if it had never had a smile upon it . . . my

Sabbatarian strictness, and my prejudices on a hundred subjects must have been absurd and disagreeable enough to them: but their gentleness, respect and courtesy were such as I now remember with gratitude and pleasure. They saw that I was outgrowing my shell, and they had patience with me till I had rent it and cast it off . . . (Martineau, H., 1877, I, p. 148)

What a dazzling piece of insight!

But just when Harriet had high hopes that she might now remain in London, in this better frame of mind, and manage to maintain herself in her very frugal style:

to my disappointment, I might say, horror, – my mother sent me peremptory orders to go home, and fill the place which my poor young sister was to vacate. I rather wonder that, being seven and twenty years old, I did not assert my independence, and refuse to return, – so clear as was, in my eyes, the injustice of remanding me to a position of helplessness and dependence, when a career of action and independence was opening before me . . . The instinct and habit of old obedience prevailed, and I went home with some resentment, but far more grief and desolation in my heart. (Martineau, H., 1877, I, p. 149)

For all her intuition and remarkable insights, Harriet could not have known how rooted in the unconscious, how subversively ramified, were the components of this 'instinct', in every 'good' daughter's mind.

But Harriet was never one to take defeat easily. Within the space of two years she was back again in London to turn pedlar of her work:

Day after day, I came home weary with disappointment, and with trudging many miles through the clay of the streets, and the fog of the gloomiest December I ever saw . . . I set out to walk the four miles and a half to the Brewery. I could not afford to ride, more or less; but, weary already, I now felt almost too ill to walk at all. On the road, not far from Shoreditch, I became too giddy to stand without support; and I leaned over some dirty palings, pretending to look at a cabbage bed, but saying to myself, as I stood with closed eyes, 'My book will do yet.' (Martineau, H., 1877, I, p. 170)

So despite serious illness subsequent to such exhaustion, success at last came within reach: 'I think I may date my release from pecuniary care from that tenth of February, 1832' (Martineau, H., 1877, I, p. 178). She had reached the age of thirty.

But hardly had her feet touched on this hard-won *terra firma* when her mother, now a widow, staked the old traditional claims on a successful daughter as a haven of strength which was to have no bounds or limits. What was Harriet to do, child of her time that she was and of all time that went before, back to some atavistic dawn we still remain entangled in? By way of compromise she took a house in London where both of them might live together with an aunt and another. With this project in mind she wrote to Elizabeth, her mother, in 1833:

I see no other plan which promises equal comfort for all three parties concerned . . . and I have no doubt we shall make one another happy, if we at once begin with the change of habits which our change of positions renders necessary. I fully expect that both you and I shall occasionally feel as if I did not discharge a daughter's duty, but we shall both remind ourselves that I am now as much a citizen of the world as any professional SON of yours could be. (Payne, K., 1984, p. 90)

You shall be, she is saying, welcome to what is mine, but 'My hours of solitary work and visiting will leave you much to yourself . . . so now the whole case is before you, and you know exactly under what feelings I say, "come" ' (Payne, K., 1984, p. 90). It is a lengthy, detailed letter, strident with ambivalence and a foretaste of disaster, for Harriet must have 'known' that her ageing mother, deeply set in her ways, would surely never 'change her habits'. She still saw her eldest daughter as a fractious, trying child, in a delusional stance doubtless fortified by envy.

In her outer life and world Harriet now enjoyed access to whomsoever she might choose in the contemporary scene, and had a struggle on her hands against 'literary lionism' since her far-ranging work was making a major impact. But in her deepest, inner mind her earlier childhood neurosis, though modified, smouldered on, where the relentless ties binding her to her mother tugged at her, still unresolved. And so by 1839, after something like five years spent under a single roof, even though her travels often took her as far away as America, and then anywhere if it offered an escape, the strain of the anxieties bred by this relationship began to make itself felt:

I have mentioned before, in regard to my deafness, that I have no doubt of its having been seriously aggravated by nervous excitement . . . and thus in regard to the disease which at this time was laying me low for so many years.

It was unquestionably the result of excessive anxiety of mind, – of the extreme tension of nerves under which I had been living for some years, while the three anxious members of my family were, I may say, on my hands – not in regard to money, but to care of a more important kind ... My mother was old, and fast becoming blind; and the irritability caused in her first by my position in society, and next by the wearing trial of her own infirmity, told fearfully upon my already reduced health. (Martineau, H., 1877, II, p. 150)

Harriet – as she could see herself, and yet was helpless to avert – was eventually obliged to take refuge in illness, that classic feminine bolthole, as the trap was closing in and she could, for many reasons, see no other way out:

A tumour was forming of a kind which usually originates in mental suffering; and when at last I broke down completely, and settled myself in a lodging at Tynemouth, I long felt that the lying down in solitude and silence, free from responsibility and domestic care, was a blessed change from the life I had led since my return from America. My dear old aunt soon died; my mother was established at Liverpool, in the neighbourhood of three of her children; and the other claimant of my anxious care emigrated. It is impossible to deny that the illness under which I lay suffering for five years was induced by the flagrant violations of the laws of nature ... No doubt, if I had felt less respect and less affection for my mother, I might have taken the management of matters more into my own hands, and should have felt her discontent with me less than I did. (Martineau, H., 1877, II, p. 152)

How was Harriet to know, a century and a half ago, that this very discontent drove her on to accomplish what was quite beyond her powers, in a daughter's forlorn hope to change aversion to approval and the warmth for which she had longed since early infancy?

It is clear that Harriet failed, despite the reality of being the provider now, to claim her adult needs and rights against a controlling mother who continued to regard her as a tiresome little girl: as a disappointing daughter:

I was not allowed to have a maid, at my own expense, or even to employ a work-woman: and thus, many were the hours after midnight when I ought to have been asleep, when I was sitting up to mend my clothes. Far worse than this, my mother would not be taken care of. She was daily getting out into the crowded streets by herself, when she could not see a yard before her ... I rarely slept without starting from a dream that my mother had fallen from a precipice, or over the bannisters, or from a cathedral spire; and that it was my fault. (Martineau, H., 1877, II, p. 151)

Today we would recognize the death-wishes against her mother concealed in these anxious dreams. But insightful as Harriet was, painful secrets of this kind remained hidden in the dark until Freud had forged some access with his self-analysis. Even in his early work, *Studies on Hysteria* (1895), he had not yet recognized that Anna O's dreadful dreams that snakes were going to bite her father, when her arm was paralysed and could not fend the killers off, concealed her wish that he might die and she be set free from nursing to go dancing once again.

Harriet, as we would know today, for all her literary success and fame in the outer world, was still tied to her mother. Trapped by these inner circumstances, she could find the space which she needed for herself only in a five-year flight into illness. Plagued by her aggressive feelings and the old hostility, as well as by the unconscious guilt which these inevitably aroused, she did not have the inner freedom to suggest that her mother move to some of her other children. Indeed, Harriet had to spend these next five years on a sofa while an uncle saw to it that she had a personal maid. Quite unable to move, by all accounts paralysed, she could none the less still write a highly successful book, *Essays from a Sickroom*.

That disclosure of her suffering which led up to this illness, as this figured in that work, alienated her mother and sisters even further was no doubt predictable, as the author here confirms: 'and from that time forward they were never again to me what they had been' (Martineau, H., 1877, II, p. 172). We can hardly be surprised! There is no family of this kind – akin to a tribal tyranny – which cares to have its matrix of secretive abominations exposed to the light of day; even to helpful intervention by outside agencies, as any family therapist is bound to testify today.

After five years of illness Harriet's medical attendant suggested she try mesmerism, which wrought a rapid cure from what was almost certainly a serious case of hysteria. It set her free to enjoy ten peaceful and productive years, as the fruits of all her labours: 'But,' she writes of that reprieve, 'the spring, summer and autumn of my life were yet to come. I have had them now, – like the Swedish summer, which bursts out of a long winter with the briefest interval of spring. At past forty years of age, I began to relish life, without drawback . . .' (Martineau, H., 1877, II, p. 205). In this blissful interlude Harriet built herself a house on a lake in Cumberland. There she settled full of joy at the beauties of nature she had scarcely glanced at before, and a new-found peace of mind, presumably induced by her experience of hypnosis. Not even her mother's death in 1848 caused a relapse at the time: 'We did meet and part in comfort and satisfaction' for a last and final time.

The cure wrought by hypnosis, predictably, did not last. In 1854, when Harriet was fifty-two, she finally fell victim to a severe cardiac neurosis, with the most alarming symptoms, which were a classic of their kind. Medical opinion claimed that

the dilated heart is too feeble for its work . . . Before I left London, the sinking-fits which are characteristic of the disease began to occur; and it has been perfectly understood by us all that the alternative lies between death at any hour in one of these sinking fits, or by dropsy, if I live for the disease to run its course. (Martineau, H., 1877, II, p. 431)

Can we possibly detect a deeper sense of satisfaction in reflecting on these lines? Is Harriet here addressing a controlling inner mother, although the outer one is dead: 'Now you have it from the horse's mouth – you have to leave me in peace and permit me a servant.'

The autobiography ends when Harriet has made her will and returned to Ambleside, peacefully resigned to death, thoughts of which, she tells us, had preoccupied her all her life in a quite obsessional manner. She actually did not die for another twenty-three years, in 1877 at the age of seventy-five. Her mother had died at seventy-six, and she herself could not do better.

It can, of course, be argued that her heart complaint was 'genuine' or, as they like to say, 'organic'; that the 'sinking-fits' in truth belonged to a degenerative condition. But then we must remember that mind and body, throughout life, walk so closely hand in hand that we need not embark upon a lengthy argument to defend either view, but can leave Harriet Martineau in the care of devoted friends in the home she had built, and the life she had created even at so great a price.

We have scanned this life in some detail for its precocious insights into the lifelong consequences of an unhappy start due to maternal deprivation. Since the Ancient World closed down, the drama of these connections as far as records go, has been low-key and quiescent. It has passed, we could say, through a latency period in the course of centuries during which a daughter's life had little scope but to be a replica of her mother's. It is also growing clear, as we take a closer look at the relationship as the options for a daughter's autonomy begin to widen, how the strain accentuates infantile anxieties of a pending catastrophe at the heart of their connectedness in each of the protagonists. As Helene Deutsch has said: 'this spiral [of separation] laden as it is with ambivalence, leaves mother and daughter convinced that any separation between them will bring disaster to both' (Chodorow, N., 1978, p. 135).

This impasse could not have been resolved on purely psychodynamic merits. Only when the printing press began to facilitate a wider spread of ideas, and mushrooming urbanization, practically overnight, willy-nilly tore women out of some medieval dream to conscript them as a workforce, did reality provide the essential catalyst for change. Only once previously scattered women, sustained in cottage industries, were thrown into new intimacy of a harsh and common fate in the new industrial scene did these new conditions hold out, almost accidentally, a certain nebulous promise of unsuspected feminine worth, linked to an earning power, however cruel its exploitations.

These socioeconomic rapids carried everything before them. No relationship escaped. Each and all experienced the shattering of a well-set mould. But none were drawn into a more ferocious conflict, striving both to conserve and to revolt, than the mother and her daughter, whose nexus is the very heart of the fabric of tradition. From this time on they either fought, almost to the very death, in a blinding hysteria, to possess and to control, to maintain the *status quo*; or conversely to escape, to break the chains of centuries and begin to breathe the air of free choice and wider action which had previously remained the exclusive right of men.

2 A DAUGHTER
GOES TO WAR

NOWHERE does the sound and fury of such an all-out war come closer to a cataclysm than it does for Fanny and her daughter, Florence Nightingale; while her sister Parthenope, older by just one year, wildly seized the side of mother, to cleave this family in two.

Florence, born in 1820, did in fact not get away until she was thirty-three and had nearly lost her reason in the conflict which raged with such explosive altercations that her father, known as W.E.N., was virtually obliged to take refuge in his club (did such exist for that purpose?), the illustrious Athenaeum.

Finally he intervened, much as Zeus had once done. Instead of a narcissus the following has survived, written in his difficult hand on Athenaeum notepaper:

Memorandum April 20th 1853: 'I have this day reached the conclusion that Parthe can no more control or moderate the intensity of her interest in Flo's doings than she can change her physical form, and that her life will be sacrificed to the activity of her thoughts, unless she removes herself from the scene immediately – the only question being where to go . . . (Woodham-Smith, C., 1950, p. 111)

W.E.N. was clearly reluctant to confront his wife Fanny as the chief protagonist of the infighting at home. It must have been clear to him that Parthe, insane as she stood at the heart of this conflict, was no more than her mother's mouthpiece and *agent provocateur*. To wade into this gruesome snake pit was clearly more than he could bear, quietist that he was, given to escapism in a world of libraries. But now he cut the Gordian knot. At long last, and none too soon, he came to the rescue of his favourite daughter, Florence, by making her an allowance of £500 a year.

This might have resolved nothing except that Florence had by then succeeded in breaking through, by the most dazzling inner tactics under such fierce attack, to a sense of inner self and freedom: a vision of destiny. This heroic struggle had sapped all her energies and strength for the first third of her life. That she won against such odds surely testifies to more than feminine stubbornness: to an achievement of genius. Here we need to underwrite the case that feminine genius by the ton was expended on this struggle, and had to be doubly great by any unisex standards where a daughter still accomplished works of enduring value, as a surplus to the feat of wrenching herself to freedom. For had she not by that token been obliged to create a twofold masterpiece: first her self-image as a free, creative woman, and secondly an entire structure to underpin the enterprise in a reluctant outer world, one which until then had not existed for her wider purposes, her finicky demands for a new brand of excellence?

Fanny Nightingale herself had not been devoid of ambition. But as with all good Victorian wives, they were by proxy, for her husband. When her intended transformation of him from scholar recluse into public giant failed, as it was bound to do, 'she did not resign herself. She transferred her plans and ambitions to her daughters' (Woodham-Smith, C., 1950, p. 15). However, since her own vision was drearily conventional until much later when she basked in her daughter's reflected glory with as passionate a zeal as she had earlier opposed every step which led to it, she could only see in Florence an opponent to be thwarted to the very bitter end.

Florence certainly was different and unlikely to oblige Fanny's narcissistic daydreams. Thus we read in her diary: 'On February the 7th, 1837, God spoke to me and called me to His Service' (Woodham-Smith, C., 1950, p. 17). She was then seventeen and had to wait impatiently for another seven years until the details clarified in a second call: that she was to nurse the sick.

What was there in such a call for Mrs Nightingale to take such wild objection to? Certainly the conditions which prevailed in hospitals were distressing at the time. The sick were filthy on admission and filthy they remained. In 1854 Miss Nightingale wrote:

The nurses did not as a general rule wash patients, they would NEVER wash their feet – and it was with difficulty and only in great haste that they could have a drop of water, just to DAB their hands and face. The beds on which the patients lay were dirty. It was common practice to put a new patient in the same sheets used by the last occupant of the bed, and mattresses were generally of flock, sodden and seldom, if ever, cleaned. (Woodham-Smith, C., 1950, p. 58)

But Fanny's real objections lay in a different direction: 'the notorious immorality of hospital nurses. It was PREFERRED that the nurses should be women who had lost their characters, i.e. should have had one child,' wrote Florence Nightingale. 'The nurses are all drunkards, sisters and all,' lamented the physician of a large London hospital in 1851 (Woodham-Smith, C., 1950, p. 58). Some would alternate nursing with prostitution. But even these were not the roots of Mrs Nightingale's phobia. The truth was that by disposition she ran all too true to type – the helpless and frustrated woman whose personal growth could find no outlets and for that reason remained stunted, whose energies become subverted to such devastating ends where other lives are concerned and have to pay the final price.

Her husband had got away. Parthe had become psychotic during this dark interlude. Florence, near that fateful brink on repeated occasions, had always managed to pull back just in the nick of time, generally with the help of perceptive onlookers who recognized her qualities when she had virtually despaired. 'Dreaming', as she defined it to describe certain twilight states often prodromal to psychosis, became uncontrollable. She 'fell into trances in which hours were blotted out, she lost sense of time and place against her will . . . agonies of guilt and self-reproach were intensified by the conviction that her worst fears were being realized and that she was going insane' (Woodham-Smith, C., 1950, p. 76).

Parthe and her mother both continued to wield hysterics, screaming bouts and fainting fits. The latter accused her daughter of having 'an attachment of which she was ashamed with some low and vulgar surgeon'. She screamed and raved in public that Florence would 'disgrace herself' (Woodham-Smith, C., 1950, p. 56). Visitors would throw cold water and shake their heads in despair. These scenes became still more painful after Florence finally declined a proposal of marriage from Richard Monckton Milnes, a man whom 'she adored'.

She analysed this hard decision with admirable clarity and insight into her deepest self:

I have an intellectual nature which requires satisfaction and that would find it in him. I have a passionate nature which requires satisfaction and that would find it in him. I have a moral, an active nature which requires satisfaction and that would not find it in his life. (Woodham-Smith, C., 1950, p. 77)

This painful renunciation she had made with heroic courage and awesome integrity in 1849, anticipating some fulfilment for these clamouring qualities. But four years were still to pass in a constant inferno before her father's intervention.

By far the most significant aspect of this gruesome battle against a mother's stubborn will to keep absolute control of her daughter's destiny, and shape it in her style and image, lies in the inner struggle it took Florence to break free over those sixteen years by deep inner conviction that she was, in truth, a victim rather than a criminal. In 1851 she wrote – and here we recognize a landmark:

There are knots which are Gordian and can only be cut . . . I must expect no sympathy or help from them. I have so long craved for their sympathy that I can hardly reconcile myself to this. I have so long STRUGGLED to make myself understood – been sore, cast down, insupportably fretted, at not being understood . . . that I must not even try to be understood. I know that they CANNOT . . . I must TAKE some things, as few as I can, to enable me to live . . . I have long been treated as a child, and have so long allowed myself to be treated as a child. (Woodham-Smith, C., 1950, p. 88)

A fortnight after this catharsis she felt free enough to travel, at long last to Kaiserwerth for training in an institution of a kind which did not yet exist in England. She did so even at the risk that the heavens might fall, which predictably they did; for on her return from Germany Fanny and Parthe soon revived the familiar repertoire. Florence knew, beyond all doubt, that her former inner struggle must continue without rest. But her free and saner self had established some high ground which, inch by inch and year by year, would enlarge its hegemony, dragging the neurotic parts of her personality up towards that *terra firma* to maintain a breathing space and clear sufficient ground for action. 'I have come into possession of myself', she wrote in a private note in 1852. And to her father she wrote on her thirty-second birthday: 'I am glad that my youth is past and it never can return – that time of disappointed inexperience when a man possesses nothing, not even himself.' The gender is of interest!

As we might predict today, Parthe's response to this achievement was to become psychotic. There were delusions and delirium and a sensible physician told Florence that she should now, in everybody's interests, stop 'being devoured' and try to get away from home (Woodham-Smith, C., 1950, p. 103). Florence needed only minimal encouragement, for she herself had by now broken most of the inner chains. Aunt Mai, her most steady ally, reasoned with Parthe once again: 'My dearest Parthe, I feel for your anxieties and your dear mother's ... It seems to me we must let this ardent spirit pursue its way. To stop its course is quite beyond one ...' (Woodham-Smith, C., 1950, p. 126).

Others, too, could realize now that Florence had reached a point where none would be permitted to place any barrier in her way: 'beneath the fascination, the sense of fun, the gentle, hesitating manner, the demure wit, there was the hard coldness of steel' (Woodham-Smith, C., 1950, p. 128). And Mrs Gaskell continues, shrewd observer that she was: 'Her powers are astonishing ... She and I had a grand quarrel one day ... she said if she had influence enough not a mother should bring up a child herself; there should be crèches for the rich as well as poor ...' Then referring to her departure, which must have hit her family like a bolt from the blue: 'On Monday she said "I am going tomorrow" ... But it turned out she had written and made so many arrangements ... that they had nothing to do but yield' (Woodham-Smith, C., 1950, p. 129). Finally the opposition had admitted defeat. 'We are ducks who have hatched a wild swan', Fanny once told Mrs Gaskell. But 'in the famous phrase of Lytton Strachey's essay – it was an eagle' (Woodham-Smith, C., 1950, p. 129).

The year was 1854. England and France together had declared war on Russia, and with the approach of autumn the allied armies crossed the sea and landed in the Crimea. The stage had finally been set for the Lady with the Lamp when in October of that year, at the urging of Sidney Herbert, Secretary of War, the Cabinet formally appointed Miss Florence Nightingale as 'Superintendent of the Female Nursing Establishment of the English Military Hospitals in Turkey', which would later be extended to the Crimea as well.

Here was a sensation! 'It is a great and noble work', wrote Parthe to a favourite cousin. 'One cannot but believe she was intended for it' (Woodham-Smith, C., 1950, p. 141). And before the ink was dry, she and Fanny rushed to London to share in all the great excitement and bask in the reflected glory. Only Florence was 'as calm and composed as if she was going for a walk' (Woodham-Smith, C., 1950, p. 142). Her travail on arriving at the Barrack Hospital, a euphemism for a dump lacking all amenities to an extent that would have sent a lesser fighter and spirit screaming back home to England, cannot be enlarged on here. For virtually two years she had to fight tooth and nail to institute nursing comfort for the wounded, sick and dying of a valiant fighting force which had never previously tasted even the most sketchy, the most rudimentary care. Whatever diehard opposition queered her pitch and blocked her way her perseverance earned for Florence the undying gratitude of the ordinary soldier and his loved ones back at home. So high ran that tide of feeling for the 'Angel of Scutari' that a London meeting raised sufficient funds to enable Miss Nightingale on her return to 'establish and control an institute for the training, sustenance and protection of nurses paid and unpaid' (Woodham-Smith, C., 1950, p. 236).

Late that same night Fanny wrote:

This 29th of November. The most interesting day of thy mother's life. It is very late, my child, but I cannot go to bed without telling you that your meeting has been a glorious one ... the like of which has never happened before, but will, I trust, from your example gladden the hearts of many future mothers.

Florence duly replied: 'My reputation has not been a boon in my work; but if you have been pleased that is enough' (Woodham-Smith, C., 1950, p. 236).

But a leopard, as they say, does not change his spots. After Florence had returned, when the war was duly over, and settled at the Burlington to commence work on a Commission on Matters Affecting the Health, Efficiency and Hospital Administration of the British Army, Fanny and Parthe flapped and fluttered around her like demented moths. Florence had no option but, like Harriet Martineau, to resort to collapse and illness to fend off her persecutors. She accordingly set up a twofold barricade of sickness and excessive work as a legitimate excuse. How else could she send them packing to have occasional solitude and urgently needed respite; to re-establish, day by day, once she was back within their reach, the right to be her own person – not merely by appearances, by an outer façade which she had, of course, created, but by inmost conviction which always threatened to collapse?

How many daughters are still goaded, by the sheer, lifelong terror of somehow managing to lose their hardwon independence, into driving themselves to the verge of extinction? How else shall they escape that fate, experienced as worse than death, as more infernal than Scutari, of forfeiting their subject status to be an object once again of their mother's phantasies, manipulation and delusions? Florence's anxiety on this score was so acute that she certainly appeared to hover on the verge of death, at a time when no one yet knew about conversion symptoms. Her pulse raced, and she was given two cold-water packs a day to bring it down. In spite of her physical condition (which confined her to a sofa) she obstinately continued to work.

Fanny and Parthe, sobered by the frightening spectacle of her collapse in London, made only half-hearted attempts to join her. In June 1860 the Nightingale School for Nurses opened. Florence must, she felt, remain in the centre of London to be available at a moment's notice: she was indispensable! Only this could justify her phobic insistence to keep her family at bay. Besides, 'she had a morbid dread of being overlooked' (Woodham-Smith, C., 1950, p. 433) going back to her childhood when Parthe, not herself, had been her mother's favourite. The very possibility still carried associations too painful to contemplate. Clearly the early conflicts had, in truth, not been resolved in any enduring manner. On the brink of a relapse, she was but staving them off with their legacies of pain and sharp humiliation, where these dramatic ups and downs were but the tip of the iceberg.

When Fanny was seventy-eight Florence had not been home for virtually a decade. Now she felt she had no option but to keep her mother company during her father's absence on a visit to Derbyshire. She made stringent conditions in her opening campaign. Six rooms on two floors must be given up to her. She would work incessantly and never leave her room except to visit her mother; Fanny, frail and almost blind, was not to be indulged under any circumstances. Whatever the reality, in Florence's inner world her mother was still a threat and a menace to her autonomy.

Besides, as Florence raged, Fanny still continued to 'fritter her life away'. The conflict finds expression in her letter written at the time: 'I don't think my dear mother was ever more touching and interesting to me than she is now in her state of dilapidation. She is so much gentler, calmer, more thoughtful . . .' But then her hatred returns, as if by force of old habit, old memories she needs to nurse, and before the ink is dry she ends the letter with these words: 'I can't think Mama much altered except her memory . . . and her habits which have become worse, till now she is seldom up until 5 or 6 p.m. and then goes out in the carriage' (Woodham-Smith, C., 1950, p. 450). Does this not sound familiar? Are we not back with Electra in the famous carriage scene (see above, p. 87), just before the matricide? Had the great queen Clytaemnestra then not briefly seemed transformed, in her plotting daughter's eyes, into a gentler and more loving version, which would only reinforce the latter's ever-simmering envy, always stoked by a show of admirable qualities? Both Electra and Florence are briefly able to acknowledge this kindlier reality in one compartment of the mind. But split off from it, another, earlier, decisive one of rage against the sexual mother, queening it in a carriage, dominates the unconscious and ultimately wins the day for hatred rather than forgiveness.

To compound these difficulties, Parthe, who in recent years had been wrapped up in her own life and even published two novels, was now falling victim to a badly crippling arthritis. Florence felt the old, old trap closing in once more for a further period of eight months. It had 'taken more out of me than two years of real Crimean work', she wrote, fuelled by a fierce resentment that she had yet again fallen victim to her guilt – for having ever got away. To keep some grip on sanity she started work on a book: *Notes from Devotional Authors of the Middle Ages*. Does the process of writing not promise rescue from a world whose conflicts threaten to undo us? Florence needed, as she said, 'a taste of heaven in daily life' (Woodham-Smith, C., 1950, p. 526). For a while she freed herself in reality, as well. But hardly was she back in London when news reached her of her father's death. 'Once more there was no escape. Old, feeble and unwanted, Fanny had a claim which to Miss Nightingale was impossible to reject.'

'Oh God, let me not sink in these perplexities but give me a great cause to do and die for' (Woodham-Smith, C., 1950, p. 528). Such was her daily prayer during these endless years. Fanny was blind and senile. In lucid moments she would mutter, rambling back to the past: 'Where is Flo? Is she still in her Hospital? I suppose she will never marry now' (Woodham-Smith, C., 1950, p. 528). Neither of them could shake off the pall of earlier grievances which had marked them both for life. It was, wrote Florence, 'utter shipwreck' (Woodham-Smith, C., 1950, p. 528). 'Am I she,' she asked herself, in a private note, 'who once stood on that Crimean height? The Lady with the Lamp shall stand. The lamp shows me my utter shipwreck' (Woodham-Smith, C., 1950, p. 529). All her achievements swam before her as an utter failure now. Florence was evidently in a deep depression, knowing that her relationship to her primary object was in such serious disarray; reeling from a sense of guilt that she had failed her mother by being different and insisting on her right to live that difference to the full, even if she had to forfeit the reward and reassurance of the soothing certainty of having been a good daughter.

'Do you know what have been the hardest years of my life? Not the Crimean War. Not the five years with Sidney Herbert at the War Office when I sometimes worked 22 hours a day. But the last five years and three quarters since my father's death' (Woodham-Smith, C., 1950, p. 547). At last, on 2 February 1880, 'Fanny died peacefully at the age of ninety-two' (Woodham-Smith, C., 1950, p. 547). At sixty years of age, Florence at long last was free:

Not because Fanny was dead, but because she had become reconciled with Fanny and with Parthe as well. All her life resentment against Fanny and Parthe had been a poison working within her. During the last difficult years, before Fanny's childishness, helplessness and blindness, before Parthe's suffering, resentment had melted away

her biographer believes, on uncertain evidence (Woodham-Smith, C., 1950, p. 548). For a while she collapsed. As always, it was not for long. Soon Florence was once again embattled with India. India had not gone away; neither had other issues now awaiting her attention. Her health began to improve. She was no longer sofa-bound. Illness had lost its deeper purpose. The 'death-bed' could be thrown away.

Ten years after Fanny's death, Florence's sister Parthe also died. Florence worked on and on. Her many interests continued. But by 1906 the India Office, which Florence had served for so many years, had to be reminded of reality and asked to send no further papers on matters of sanitation to Florence Nightingale. The following year she was the first woman ever to receive the Order of Merit from the monarch. 'Too kind, too kind', the recipient murmured. Honours continued to pour in, but Florence was by now oblivious. On 13 August 1910 she died. A national funeral and place at Westminster Abbey were, at her request, declined. Her wish had been to lie at rest in the family grave at East Wellow, with two lines added to a single tombstone: 'F.N. Born 1820. Died 1910'. A deeper sense of belonging had finally won the day over lifelong paranoia.

This cataclysmic duet stands as a classic of its kind. Once a new age had tantalized generations of new daughters with sparkling opportunities, there are only variations to be added to the theme as each new place and time grow ripe with their own set of circumstances, however brilliant or obscure the details prove in every case. The pain and fury hardly vary. The means and methods barely change. On the therapeutic couch we have to work rites of passage through the identical mire, time and time again, to meet with failure or success and generally a bit of both. It is not easy to buy freedom to the extent that we would wish once earlier structures have been twisted, once the primary growth process has been somehow thrust off course. But once there is mobility between the generations, it is not only upward movement on the part of the daughter which may be seen to cause a rift. A mother's determination that her daughter return her own reflection in life's mirror, as though this were the only means to validate her self-image, may equally be frustrated where the latter declines to match maternal achievements. It seems that a daughter cannot win the moment she ceases to be a faithful replica.

This particular dilemma was very faintly foreshadowed by Clytaemnestra and Electra, where we half sense the great queen's hope that this rebellious little upstart would still relinquish her judgemental adolescence, stop her bloodthirsty plotting and grow into a woman who might do her royal mother credit. It rather lurks between the lines of the Sophocles version, where the mother agrees, even against her better judgement, to offer the ritual blessings for her daughter's 'child', as a final attempt at reconciliation. Did she hope that her compliance might yet rescue Electra from her entrenched position as an angry little girl, and thereby set them both free, to reign side by side together with some common understanding between two adult women in the place of former strife?

As we saw, it was too late. No maternal gesture could at this point have modified the daughter's fateful regression to an early paranoid position. This situation was repeated in the nineteenth century, between Aurore Dupin, later known as George Sand, and her daughter Solange. Aurore, as a little girl, had been a bone of contention between her wealthy grandmother and her mother, Sophie Delaborde, a seamstress in a Paris garret. After her father's death when Aurore was four, her grandmother insisted on a convent education, to salvage what could still be salvaged from her son's misalliance. Aurore took to books and new horizons of learning with a genuine zeal which became a lifelong passion although her mother remonstrated, deeply hurt, from afar that this bookishness was foolish, which dragged the unhappy child into a despairing conflict. Her own romantic way of life, Sophie felt, had served her well, with its ready access to the exuberance of the streets of Paris as a never-ending source of drama and companionship, even if this existence tended to be hand to mouth: why was it not good enough for her studious daughter now?

At the age of seventeen, just before she was married to the Baron Casimir Dudevant, Aurore, deeply pained by these ructions, wrote to her mother: '18th November, 1821. My dear Mother, . . . Why must a woman be ignorant? . . . Supposing I should one day have sons . . . don't you think the lessons of a mother are worth as much as those of a tutor? . . .' (Payne, K., 1984, p. 83). Within seven years of this letter she had borne a son, Maurice, and a daughter, Solange. When the latter was two Aurore moved with her to Paris, separating from her husband, whose passion for hunting and a dissolute life bored and disgusted her.

Although Sophie's tendency to blow hot and cold had earlier often caused her suffering, she now became her daughter's ally in this ardent bid for freedom. In this she recognized herself. Was Aurore, finally, not reverting, true to type, as a daughter of the streets of the enchanted capital? That their paths would shortly take such very different directions the mother, with her simple nature and romantic inclinations, could hardly have foreseen. To do so lay beyond her scope, despite all the warning signs of which she had been so critical. Accordingly, for the time being mother and daughter basked in a new comradeship doubtless rooted in their intense relationship during the earliest years, when the little girl would sit enchanted at her mother's feet, playing with that mere of colour, fabric remnants, bows and buttons in the cosy little garret to which songs from the pavement and the sound of life below rose to stir the imagination of the future writer.

Just before she made the move, at the age of twenty-seven, Aurore wrote to Sophie:

31 May 1831 . . . I really must venture to tell you, dear Maman, that you have very little idea what I am really like. It is a long time now since we lived together and you often forget that I am now twenty-seven years old and that my character was bound to undergo many changes since I was quite a girl . . . it is liberty that I long for. I want to be able to walk out quite alone . . . just as I like . . . You, dear Maman, have suffered much from the intolerance and false virtue, of high-principled people. How terribly at one time they blackened your beauty, your youth, your independence, your happy, facile character! What bitterness poisoned your brilliant destiny! If you had had a tender indulgent mother who opened her arms to you at each fresh sorrow and said to you, 'Men may condemn you, but I absolve you! Let them curse . . . for I bless you!', what a comfort it would have been to you in all the disgustingness and littleness of life! I need so little, nothing but the same comfort that you have. I should be satisfied with an allowance of three thousand francs a year, considering that I can already add to it with my pen . . .

She then returns once again to her need for total freedom, as her one priority:

Please judge anyone who criticizes me for it with the head and the heart of a mother, for both ought to be on my side. I shall go to Paris this summer. The more you show me that I am dear to you and that you are pleased to have me with you, the happier and the more grateful you will find me. But if I find bitter criticism and offensive suspicion in your orbit . . . I will enjoy the peace of my own conscience and my liberty. You really have too much mind and heart not to realize soon that I do not deserve all this hard treatment.

Good-bye dear little Maman. My children are well. Solange is lovely and naughty. Maurice is too thin really, but such a good boy. I am so pleased with his character and his mental development. I rather spoil my fat little girl. But the fact that Maurice has become so sweet now reassures me for their future. Write soon, dear Maman. Kisses with all my soul. (Payne, K., 1984, p. 86)

The last paragraph foreshadows, with ominous accuracy, the heart-aches that lie ahead in her relationship to her 'fat little girl', whom she describes as 'naughty'. Already the die was cast. Already she was projecting a trustworthy, substantial side of her personality into her 'good', 'sweet' son, and the more unruly aspects, her untrammelled need for freedom, of which she seemed to disapprove (at least at an unconscious level), into her daughter Solange, grieving for an absent father, as once her mother must have done. Thirty-six years further on she would write to Gustave Flaubert: 'Little Aurore [her granddaughter] is as pretty as anything and does a thousand gracious tricks. My daughter Lina [wife of Maurice] is always my real daughter. The OTHER is well and beautiful, that is all I ask of her' (Sand and Flaubert, 1979, p. 74). The chickens had come home to roost, for some of the reasons which we have given, rather than the stale assumption that 'mothers prefer a son'. But we are running on ahead. Aurore and Solange, who at the time was barely two, have only just arrived in Paris. Maurice stayed in the country with his father, Casimir, as a condition for making his headstrong wife an allowance and consenting to a separation after long months of wrangling.

Writing of that period in her autobiography, George Sand is full of her mother, basking in her support in this crisis of her life:

The first letter I wrote, on resolving to oppose my husband in court, was to her. The affection she returned to me was spontaneous, total, unwavering. Almost two years went by during which she became for me what she was in my childhood. (Payne, K., 1984, p. 84)

And it was Sophie, in fact,

who recommended to her daughter that she wear men's clothing: it was cheaper and more practical and would free her from the restrictions which both laws and customs imposed on her movements in Paris. Since Aurore's greatest desire at this point was to attend the theatre as often as possible (and to stand in the pit, which was cheaper than a seat but reserved only for men), she was delighted by her mother's ingenuity – and by the freedom she gained. (Payne, K., 1984, p. 84)

But the 'fat little girl' would, predictably perhaps, be destined to become an angry, envious young woman and a considerable thorn in her famous mother's side. She had lost her own father. As is so frequently the case she may well have blamed her mother, at an unconscious level, for this far-reaching blow, for Dudevant had been an affectionate father, whatever his failings from her mother's point of view. The succession of lovers – Jules Sandeau, Alfred de Musset and finally Chopin – would certainly have paid more court and conspicuous attention to their highflying mistress than to a little girl, although Chopin retained a genuine fondness for Solange which she, in turn, repaid, with attempts at seducing him in the grand oedipal manner.

None the less, if we reflect on these matters so far, we will observe a new strand in our unrolling tapestry. 'The more you show me that I am dear to you and that you are pleased to have me with you, the happier and the more grateful you will find me.' Here is this new woman of superb independence and a mind of her own, gained early in her life, who can yet openly acknowledge her deepest need for mothering. Having done so she is able to go on to proclaim that if she fails to receive it 'I will enjoy the peace of my own conscience and my liberty.' Because she has this inner freedom, precisely perhaps from knowing that she previously survived a bitter separation when her grandmother stepped in, she can openly acknowledge her dependency needs to their object in her mother. Herself already a mother and a woman who knows that she is able to rely on her creative resources without a shadow of doubt, even though she has as yet had little opportunity of putting them to that test, she can say to her own mother, 'I shall need your support and your loving concern every inch of the way.' She can say it in this manner, directly and unashamedly, precisely because she has her early good mother safely in her inner world for her lifelong purposes – but also because she has, for that very reason, achieved a degree of separation where she need no longer fear that dependency means merging, a blurring of the boundaries over which depersonalization always hovers as a threat. That she then comes unstuck in her relationship to her own and only daughter may well be the result of the split we have mentioned in her personality. For her maturing self-image, impressive as it was, George Sand had clearly retained all those parts of herself which were illustrious and substantial. This means that she had, however, been obliged to split off and project the wild-girl part of herself. The harum-scarum and untamed young creature, riding across open country all hours of the day and night and flouting every convention, was got rid of in due course and projected early on, as we have seen, into Solange, whose constitution made the worst of this tricky legacy.

There may have been a further factor. Since she had lost her own father at the critical age of four, George Sand's lovers must have represented a new-found father in her mind, with even greater urgency than is normally the case in a love-relationship. If this was so she would have tried to keep these lovers to herself and away from her daughter at an unconscious level. To this the child responded angrily and with envy since she was also fatherless, exacerbating rivalries which failed to be modified. So the stage was set for doom for both, in their relationship, where both were to cut their losses with no reference to the pain.

George Sand – as she had by then become by shortening the name of Sandeau, the lover with whose collaboration she wrote her first work of fiction – demanded two attributes from her children, proclaimed with stubborn persistence: one was total loyalty and beyond that, devotion, as she would receive from Maurice and later from his wife Lina; and secondly, that they pursue some solid and substantial passion of the creative intellect, as Maurice would with botany. This Solange failed to do, as she failed on the first score – held back, perhaps, by her neurosis, by her envy of her mother on so many accounts. George Sand was, after all, a difficult act to follow.

And so Solange was written off through all her developmental stages as a daughter unworthy of her mother's genuine affections. She eventually married a sculptor, Auguste Clesinger. Her mother, hoping she had got this difficult daughter off her hands, as no doubt for genuine motives and true generosity which belonged to her nature, gave her a substantial dowry. But the marriage broke up. Still in her early twenties, Solange took refuge from her husband's violent threats in a convent. He had squandered her dowry and she liked life's better things, though she showed no inclination to work for them herself, as was her mother's habit to the last day of her life. Now she hoped to extract new resources from the latter to feed her extravagant appetites, but also, as seems probable, her deeper sense of deprivation, displacing her emotional hunger on to the material plane. Accordingly she wrote to her from inside the hateful convent:

Having to live in isolation, with the sound and movement of life all around me – people laughing together, horses galloping, children playing in the sunshine, lovers being happy – it is not so much a matter of being bored as of being made to despair . . .

How minutely she depicts the sombre landscape of envy in these silent monochromes of a concentration camp! The same letter continues:

People wonder how it is that girls without minds of their own or any sort of education allow themselves to drift into a life of pleasure and vice! Can even a woman with judgement and warm affections be sure of being able to steer clear of all that? . . . (Payne, K., 1984, p. 87)

George Sand was furious. She herself was almost fifty. As mistress of Nohant upon her grandmother's death, the grand woman of letters basking in a reputation both substantial and unique, her ship of life at last was drawing from the swell of stormy seas into new and quiet harbours for the last third of its voyage. On no account would she permit that these earlier projections, with extra ballast of their own, be returned to her now to undermine the famous image. This she had surely earned, even if it proved somewhat different from that untarnished picture, as her unconscious must have known; and so she promptly flung back:

I spent many of the best years of my youth living in what you call 'isolation' working hard between four dirty walls, and let me tell you that, though I regret a great deal, I don't regret that . . . The only thing which will console you is money . . . and a great deal of it . . . I could only give you what you need by working twice as hard as I do now, and if I did I'd be dead within six months . . . besides . . . what is there to say that it is my duty to turn myself into a galley slave or a complete hack merely to supply you with money to burn? What I can give you, you shall have. You can treat this house as your home, on the sole condition that you don't upset everybody with your idiotic behaviour . . . So you find it difficult, do you, being lonely and poor, not to step into a life of vice? . . . All right then, just try a little vice . . . just try being a whore. I don't think you would make much success of it . . . a woman has got to be a great deal more beautiful and more intelligent than you are before she can hope to be pursued . . . men with money to spend want women who know how to earn it. (Payne, K., 1984, pp. 87–8)

It was doubtless just as well that Solange never took up her mother's cryptic offer. They must both have recognized that it was quite unrealistic. With such deep antagonisms reaching back into the past, they were hardly likely to hit it off beneath one roof. In this rich and golden autumn of her life, as she basked in the fruition of her work through the years, George Sand had learnt to cut her losses with a philosopher's gentle shrug, while Solange was not the daughter to come down from her envious high horse and strike a truce with her great mother. She had, perhaps, in a sense beyond her personal grievances, solidly founded as they were, unwittingly become a victim of blind and impersonal forces. A high tide was sweeping women in new and unforeseen directions, lifting some to breathless heights and dashing others out of sight. As in every time of change all of them were being lived by their cyclonic *Zeitgeist*, even if such a thought hardly entered their mind, to leave them doubly at the mercy of an unexamined force: Jung's collective unconscious.

What has emerged from this example is that the daughter's mobility, whether it be up or down, was experienced by her mother, in either event, as *away from*, as spelling out a shameful difference. This was seen as constituting a blind, preposterous threat, met with wild hostility and considerable furore rooted in an agony where identity itself, and all sense of personal value, both seemed equally at risk: where sanity and life itself were not uncommonly at stake.

There was a tearing and a rending that came so close to the core of some atavistic locus which had lain largely undisturbed through the millennia, as now appeared upon exposure to threaten every cohesion and future of the human race. For it owns a habitat in such dim preverbal depths and overgrown crevices, in such jungle reaches of some archaic unconscious, as no psychoanalyst and few anthropologists have ever quite set mind in yet.

Because they are the same gender as their daughters and have been girls, mothers of daughters tend not to experience these infant daughters as separate from them in the same way as do mothers of infant sons ... Primary identification and symbiosis with daughters tend to be stronger and cathexis of daughters is more likely to retain and emphasize narcissistic elements, that is to be based on experiencing a daughter as an extension or double of a mother herself ... (Chodorow, N., 1978, p. 109)

If such is the jargon that ensures a common language for sharing our thinking and making progress in this entangled field, it also devalues through its clichés the original mastery of Freud's splendid orchestrations. It does little to convey the grievous rawness of the wounding, the clinging, screeching and entangling, the disentangling and the mauling which constitute this massive crisis. For in its throes we are still trapped, even if aware in growing numbers of where we have remained ensteeped in the sea-witch's net.

3 IN AND OUT OF THE SYMBIOTIC NET

A N INTERESTING ILLUSTRATION of a daughter who appears to have separated out in so far as she became a literary phenomenon, financially viable, and yet remained deeply caught in the symbiotic trap of three successive generations, as is so commonly the case, was Louisa May Alcott (1832–88). Her mother, Abba – or Marmee, as she was immortalized in Louisa's *Little Women* – had come to marriage in her time expecting a continuation of the entanglement with the person of her mother – an intermittent invalid, half of whose twelve children died. None the less, Abba sang her praises as one who had 'loved the whole human family and gone about doing good . . .' (Saxton, M., 1928, p. 32).

This ominous portrait brings to mind Julia Woolf, Virginia's mother, painted unforgettably in the figure of Mrs Dalloway (*To The Lighthouse*), who devours everyone around her. Bronson Alcott, whom Abba married in her somewhat dreamlike state, was a remote, unfeeling man: 'We cannot', he at last responded to her long and arduous courtship, 'but feel an affection and esteem for this interesting female . . .' (Saxton, M., 1928, p. 37). Surely, Abba had been warned! Bronson Alcott would remain preoccupied with 'higher' things, as educator and reformer. This, in practice, implied continuous separation from his wife and family, who suffered great material hardship. Abba and her three daughters not infrequently went hungry and often bitterly cold. So it was little wonder that, predisposed as Abba was to a symbiotic tangle she turned her emotional hunger and longing for warmth and love on her only consolation in the persons of her daughters, as her everything and all. 'Her girls became her only resource. They received her tense surveillance. She followed their developments with breathless, unnatural anxiety' (Saxton, M., 1928, p. 80). The eldest daughter, Anna, formed a close attachment to her father. Louisa, the middle girl, resembled Abba physically as well as by temperament. As the perfect mirror-image she had every rhyme and reason for a close entanglement, which she never escaped, although her passionate nature and difficult behaviour in the course of early childhood drew her mother's disapproval in no uncertain terms. But the basic devotion, which ran deep between the two, only made the little girl always hate herself the more for causing the beloved mother hurt. And Abba's frequent bouts of illhealth, occasioned by miscarriages and sheer malnutrition, only served to compound Louisa's deep anxieties: a daughter's guilty feelings that she had damaged her mother. Her entire life became an endless act of reparation, a long-drawn-out sacrifice, whose instrument would be her pen. Later, when she reread her 1868 journal, written when she was thirty-six, Louisa noted in the margin: 'Too much work for one young woman; no wonder she broke down' (Payne, K., 1984, p. 113). Of the deeper nature of this 'work', as suggested above, she had little inkling.

Already by the age of ten Louisa showed signs of promise in the early poems she wrote. Abba was ecstatic. Since she clearly saw her daughter as an extension of herself, by that token Louisa's talent also belonged to her. She was the only brightness in her days filled with pregnancies and sorrow, neglect and indifferent health, necessitating rest in bed for days and weeks at a time.

When Louisa was ill, and highly susceptible to all her mother said and did,

Abba presented her with an engraving of a sick mother and a hard-working daughter, with the accompanying note: 'Dear Louisa, I enclose a picture for you which I have always admired very much – for in my imagination I thought you might be just such an industrious good daughter – and that I might be a sick but loving mother, looking to my daughter's labours for my daily bread. Mother.' (Payne, K., 1984, p. 112)

This, at an unconscious level, was in effect a maternal call for a reversal of their roles: Abba was to be the baby, to act out her phantasy of that symbiotic muddle which had never been resolved between her and her own mother, May. It was to seal Louisa's fate. From her early childhood she had already cast herself as her mother's rescuer. From now on she played the part with relentless compulsion by this verbalized command.

In Louisa's adolescence, her mother, running true to type, became increasingly intrusive. She would read Louisa's diary, even adding little notes: 'Hope and keep busy, dear daughter, and in all perplexity and trouble come freely to your mother.' Louisa wrote by reply that her mother was 'the best woman in the world' (Saxton, M., 1928, p. 162). This subversive correspondence grew ever more entangled roots in a soil of fierce ambivalence, whose clamouring negative components Louisa steadfastly denied. When, at the age of twenty-two, she set her sights on nearby Boston, this departure from the nest was certainly not accomplished in any deep sense of the word. No concept of separation clouded those symbiotic skies or that compliant mind. She was but taking the first step, not into her future life but to provide the wherewithal which her mother required, and her sisters back at home.

In due course *The Atlantic Monthly* began to publish her work. By 1860 Louisa May Alcott knew that her earnings had begun to ease her ailing mother's life. Long, intense bouts of writing alternated with periods during which she nursed her mother. In spring 1868, during such a spell at home in Concord, Massachusetts, Louisa agreed to write, at the prompting of her father, something like 'a plain story for boys and girls about childish victories over selfishness and anger' (Saxton, M., 1928, p. 3). What subject could be more up her street! The result was *Little Women*. Louisa Alcott's name was made and Marmee was at long last safe.

Awkwardly, the unconscious does not work in this way. Marmee's safety in Louisa's eyes had to be won day by day in endless, unremitting toil, for the remainder of her life. 'I hope success will sweeten me and make me what I long to become more than a great writer, a good daughter' (Saxton, M., 1928, p. 281), she wrote at the height of her success. Still she wrote and wrote and wrote. The money was coming in as a surplus by now and she was able to invest in up-and-coming railway bonds as long-term security. But even this could not secure Abba's survival for ever and in 1877 she died in Louisa's care. 'I shall be glad to follow her. I never wish her back, but a great warmth seems gone out of life, and there is no motive to go on now', her daughter noted at the time (Saxton, M., 1928, p. 344). She was, in fact, to survive for a further eleven years, sacrificing herself for her surviving sisters, even for Bronson at the end, by indomitable habit. Then, when her father died in March 1888, her own investment in life came to a sudden end and two days later Louisa followed her parents to the grave.

In the same century which witnessed Louisa's struggles we find other daughters, mostly from the middle class, making heroic strides as pioneers in the professions and in wider public life with considerably less trauma. Their mothers certainly shed tears and felt profoundly unsettled, as do many modern counterparts, during the various stages of this separating out; but they generally came to terms with the new *status quo* and later even basked in their new reflected glory through a contented old age. In these cases we will find that a good marriage of the parents stood firmly as the centrepiece. That the husband and father fulfilled both of these roles to offer generous support to either protagonist, as and when it was required, to soothe down troubled waters and thereby to facilitate a resolution of the conflicts, inevitable as these are. That they remain part and parcel of healthy development in every woman's life can no longer be in doubt, although individual cases passing through these 'growing pains' will always feel that they are unique.

The father's significance in resolving these tensions, built into the dyad's nature, grows clear as the first women doctors embarked on their tenacious struggle first to gain admission to the ranks of medical students and secondly to the profession. The Elizabeths Blackwell and, later, Garrett Anderson were both fortunate to stem from large, united families. Both had fathers who saw women as their human equals and worthy of an education:

Mr Garrett did not spare trouble or expense over the education of his children. He insisted that they should have the best he could obtain, boys and girls alike . . . To his daughters Mr Garrett opened the window of the world by sending them to boarding school . . . Mr Garrett stipulated that his daughters should have all extras at the school, including hot baths once a week. Such cleanliness made them marked girls. They were called 'the bathing Garretts' . . . In fairness to the school it must be remembered that in 1849 even in larger houses bathrooms were still unusual and the installation of one at Windsor Castle two years earlier was due to the reforming zeal of Prince Albert. (Garrett Anderson, L., 1939, p. 33)

However, the prince's reforming zeal sadly did not extend to his own daughters. For later, when Princess Louise visited, unannounced, Dr Garrett's consulting rooms for a little heart-to-heart, she asked on parting 'please not to tell her mother she had called, as she would not approve'. 'Queen Victoria learnt of the visit and was reported to be extremely annoyed' (Manton, J., 1965, p. 186).

While the Garretts were still bathing, Elizabeth Blackwell had graduated as a fully fledged doctor. Refused by countless medical schools, she persevered doggedly and was eventually admitted to one then scarcely known: Geneva, near New York, where her family had settled. Later she returned to England and became the first woman on the Medical Register, newly come into being.

With regard to Mrs Garrett's tremors at her daughter's aspirations, Elizabeth had this to say in one of the frequent letters sent to her sustaining spirit, Miss Emily Davis, who later founded Girton College as its first principal:

Aldeburgh, 26 June, 1860. I have had two hours talk with my mother, . . . and the result is, on the whole, sufficiently encouraging. They naturally feel very anxious about allowing me to enter upon such an untried life, and they are greatly puzzled as to the motive which can influence me . . . I believe they feel very nervous about either refusing or sanctioning it, but as long as I am very decided there is a good hope of their coming round. (Garrett Anderson, L., 1939, p. 47)

Here we can recognize the writer's buoyant optimism, doubtless partly rooted in her constant reference to 'they', a united parental couple, as much as in a temperament that brooked a minimum of doubts. But her daughter-biographer continues, with more tongue in cheek than her mother showed at the time:

Mrs Garrett did not accept new ideas readily. She was horrified at Elizabeth's suggestion and for some time her opposition increased. Thinking it a 'disgrace' that her daughter should leave home, she shut herself into her bedroom and made herself ill by crying. Elizabeth was much attached to her mother but clear-sighted about the maternal limitations. Also she could distinguish imaginary illness from real [a few decades before Freud, we might interpose], and imaginary grief from genuine. Mrs Garrett's attitude distressed her but she did not take it seriously. She was staying with Louie [her older sister who later died] in London when Mr Garrett wrote, 'you will

kill your mother if you go on'... Eventually a grudging assent was obtained.
(Garrett Anderson, L., 1939, p. 47)

For a while the father quailed in his role of referee, but he was a self-made man on a formidable scale. Unlike that dreamer of a father Mr Nightingale, driven frantic around this time, he was no heir to shilly-shallying. He also trusted that his wife had the strength to survive this squall with his loving encouragement, which conviction their daughter very probably shared since she believed in them both from substantial experience. And so this storm proved to be a minor stormlet in a teacup for all the ripples it produced, which we need not minimize just because they were resolved.

Unlike poor Florence Nightingale, Elizabeth's staunch support from her sisters and her mentor Emily Davis, who stood firmly at her side, enabled her to maintain a sane and serene stance even while her mother teetered on that maternal brink, as she calmly relays it to her steady friend: 'Bayswater, 17 Aug. 1860. I have been a good deal perplexed by receiving most melancholy letters from home, and about my mother' (Garrett Anderson, L., 1939, p. 61). Serener weathers soon returned to the relationship and helped Elizabeth to endure the long-drawn-out frustrations she was meeting on the road. It took years until she was formally admitted to full and proper student status, which meant that at intervals she had no choice but to carry out the obligatory dissecting under her sister's loving roof. And as the stream of life flowed on we find benign transformation in her ageing, widowed mother: 'Old Mrs Garrett wandered among the guests, welcoming the Doctors in radiant forgetfulness of her horror thirty years before when Elizabeth had become one of them' (Manton, J., 1965, p. 299).

The occasion was in May 1896 when Elizabeth had been elected as president to the East Anglian Branch of the British Medical Association. What a long way she had come; and she was acutely aware that her stamina was rooted in a sound relationship to a very loving mother, whatever limitations she had now and then, very understandably, displayed: 'To have had such a radiant centre in our family life is an immense blessing. It is not given to many people to get so near to their fellow creatures' hearts as my dear mother did' (Manton, J., 1965, p. 331).

Elizabeth Garrett Anderson, as she presently became, besides her public achievements, monumental as these were, pioneered a modern marriage quite unique for its day and still uncommon in our own. For she determined to combine marriage and motherhood with her other love in life. Soon after her engagement, when speculation was rife that she would now disappear in a sea of pans and ribbons, she wrote to a friend:

I do hope my dear you will not think I have meanly deserted my post. I think it need not prove to be so and I believe that he would regret it as much as I or you would. I am sure that the woman question will never be solved in any complete way so long as marriage is thought to be incompatible with freedom and with an independent career, and I think there is a very good chance that we may be able to do something to discourage this notion. (Manton, J., 1965, p. 213)

In James Skelton Anderson she had met a worthy partner who stood staunchly at her side to carry this proud project through. As a wedding gift he gave his wife a carriage and a sealskin jacket, so that she would be warm and comfortable on her daily rounds. On 9 February 1871 the two became man and wife at the 'very objectionable hour' of 8.30 in the morning, 'without millinery and almost without cookery', in order to avoid a crowd (Manton, J., 1965, p. 217). 'Are they not an original couple!' exclaimed an Anderson aunt who had travelled south for the occasion. She had hit the nail on the head with Scottish canniness more accurately than she knew.

After a week's honeymoon the new Mrs Anderson promptly resumed her old routine. Her walking boots were not unlaced until she dressed for dinner. At the age of thirty-seven she was expecting her first child. Although she engaged a wet nurse and a nanny after her, Louie was often seen with her mother in her carriage and even romping 'on the beds of a whole wardful of patients', to whom this was most probably quite a welcome distraction.

Louie left school at eighteen. 'She had decided to study medicine. Had she not inherited an interest in the subject? – besides a need to prove herself in the eyes of the mother whom, despite emotional friction, she so much admired' (Manton, J., 1965, p. 296). As a medical student in 1891, Miss Garrett Anderson found herself in a very different scene from the bleak hostility which had confronted her mother. Elizabeth was by then dean of the London Medical School for Women. She had nursed this project from 'a jumble of small shabby houses to a College of London University, and the Royal Free Hospital flourished in solid being' (Manton, J., 1965, p. 300).

Later, as an old woman, she travelled from Aldeburgh, once her childhood home, now harbour of retirement, to see her daughter leave London, shortly after war broke out, with the first unit of medical women for service in France:

The long train was being loaded with equipment, tons of lint and cotton wool, cases of instruments, crates of drugs and chloroform all marked Women's Hospital Corps ... Young women doctors in the uniform of the corps answered confidently to their roll call ... 'Aren't they splendid,' she said ... wistfully. 'If only I were a little younger, how I would love to be going with them.' (Manton, J., 1965, p. 348)

That their going was largely due to her own lifetime's work she could barely remember or take realistic credit for. 'So many helped me', she said by way of explanation.

How difficult women find it to take full credit for their genuine achievements outside the domestic sphere. They tend to feel that these were stolen. This we must in part attribute to the uncertain boundaries between their mothers and themselves, which will leave that legacy between themselves and most others throughout the phases of their life. The firmest ground for confidence in so many women's lives must therefore quake beneath their feet, as each fresh victory is snatched narrowly from the claws of madness, from sullen strictures and taboos: thou shalt not stir one iota from your life-giver's side. Yet such movement takes place even if the winds of change may blow from unexpected quarters.

And so during these same decades, when *The Englishwoman's Journal* was launched from Cavendish Square, when The Society for Promoting the Employment of Women was taking root in the same office and The Ladies' Institute, with luncheon and with reading rooms, made ladies clubbable; at a time when Josephine Butler was rescuing prostitutes and Octavia Hill was founding housing associations for the poor, when Harriet Beecher Stowe was setting more than America alight with her novel *Uncle Tom's Cabin*; when a holy indignation was firing genteel ladies of many a green and pleasant land, Britain's dark industrial hives, where employment meant survival for the unsung mass of women, were beginning to buzz with new-found, individual voices. A few of these are being rescued from the anonymity which shrouded their kind and class, so we may know them by name and glean a personal history.

In a great labour of love one such tale was given birth to only recently, in 1984 (Liddington, J.). Here is a world as far removed from the Garretts of Aldeburgh as are the gates of hell from heaven. One of Selina Coombe's very earliest memories is of her angry mother Jane in a worse than average rage, bundling her and her brother Alf into a donkey-drawn 'jingle', as the little Cornish carts were called, and driving to the navvies' camp where her father was at work, laying the new western railway. The purpose of the journey was to ensure that his wages did not go to his mistress, of whose ascendancy anonymous letters had lately warned his lawful wife. This humiliating mission, which marked Selina for life, was not some romantic drama but a matter of life and death for the family at home. Failure would have spelt starvation.

This soon threatened when Charles Coombe lay down and died in a typhus epidemic, whereupon Jane promptly moved her little family to the industrial North. There, the 'dark Satanic mills' held out a promise of survival at a time when the Cornish mines were in the grip of a depression and with them the whole area stripped of opportunity and prospects for any living wage. They settled in Barnoldwick, where girls of ten and over were expected to set to and work in one of the town's cotton mills, as what was known as 'half-timers'. This meant, in fact, a six-hour day, after which they went to school for what was called education. Jane, who worked so hard from home, at her sewing machine, could not have done without the three shillings a week which Selina brought in.

On the child's thirteenth birthday her formal schooling promptly ended. From now on she would work full-time, a fifty-six-and-a-half-hour week. Despite the savage conditions, the roar and pace of the machinery, she felt as proud as other children to 'tip-up' her first earnings into the weary hands of her mother, who had begun to suffer badly from crippling rheumatoid arthritis. She could still sew from bed by having her sewing machine placed near her on a wooden board, but she soon required nursing, so Selina left the mill. Then, from the age of seventeen until, when she was twenty-four, her mother finally died, toil as a part-time washerwoman had to be added to her burdens as home nurse and domestic skivvy, to compound a never-ending round.

Set free from these sombre years, as from some dark eternity, Selina Cooper set her sights on some self-education. If young middle-class ladies were obliged to confront the hysteria of their mothers on taking such a step, here, in the industrial North, once the women decided 'that a Women's Guild be formed for the benefit of the women co-operators, with similar educational advantages to those given to the men', the cry growled up loud and clear: 'Education for women! Let them stay at whoam! Who's to mind the chidder' (Liddington, J., 1984, p. 54).

So the struggle began.

Selina Coombe had meanwhile married and given birth to a son. John Ruskin, as his parents called him, was premature and frail. At only four months old he died from acute bronchitis, although Selina, at the time, stopped working in the mill to give her infant a chance. She kept her grief to herself. But Mary, her surviving daughter, describes how she had a scrapbook full of pictures of babies cut out of newspapers for some grieving time to come. All her spare energies were from that time on devoted to securing better conditions and education for women to avoid such tragedies. Never a masochist by nature, she was determined not to join the chorus that called mothers feckless in profound ignorance of the gruelling conditions.

Robert Cooper was already a dedicated worker-student at the time when they met, and he introduced his wife to a regular attendance at various evening classes. By the 1890s energetic articles entitled 'The Revolt of the Daughters' began to appear from the higher echelons: a pincer movement was thus growing, from above as from below; from the polished parquet floors as from the rough boards of the mills, so greasy that the women frequently chose to work barefoot.

Soon Selina's full involvement in the Women's Suffrage Movement found her dining with her titled sisters on a visit to the Houses of Parliament to taste a very different world: 'Yet here she was sitting down to share a "sole à la ravigote" and "pigeon en casserole" with Lady Frances Balfour . . . Mrs Fawcett and Isabella Ford' (Liddington, J., 1984, p. 107).

By the time their daughter Mary was one year old, Robert and Selina Cooper had at long last moved out of successive lodgings into their first rented house, as Mary vividly recalls it for the biographer in their close collaboration: 'very sparse . . . We had oilcloth [on the floor], and then a little rug – sometimes a pegged rug . . . Very sparse

... Very poor ...' (Liddington, J., 1984, p. 108). Mary's first memories extend to her mother working in this domestic scene, 'blackleading the stove, kneading the dough, washing the family clothes in a dolly tub and then hanging them up to dry in the steamy back kitchen' (Liddington, J., 1984, p. 109).

Already the little girl was acutely aware how her mother drove herself to rush through these heavy tasks and pour her strength and energies into the cauldron of politics, as a skilled public speaker who was always in demand. Was she not by this time the proud founder-president of the Briersfield Women's Co-operative Guild? 'My earliest memories, I'll tell you, are of meetings in this house. They stand out. And my grandmother's. Going to my grandmother's – she lived across the back-street. And I had an aunt lived over there. I was everybody's child' (Liddington, J., 1984, p. 109).

No notions in this clattering North of Divine Motherhood, that ambiguous concept born of an idle middle class once the home ceased to be the true hub and centre of a thriving cottage industry – of the economy of the nation. Yet with a haughty missionary zeal those who fostered this ideal sought to set its elitist stamp on the shoulders of the feckless poor with heartless high-mindedness. It was doomed to remain water off a duck's back among those who, then as now, have no opportunity to raise their hopes higher than survival from day to day.

Selina's growing reputation martyred her daughter at school. Mary's hard-pressed teachers, faced with unwieldy classes of hungry and sleepy 'half-timers', had, she found, scant sympathy for the 'suffragettes'. At the age of eleven, Mary sometimes found herself the youngest person present on a suffragette outing, wearing the sash of their colours, red, green and white, over her shoulder in her best Sunday clothes. She recalls how she was

teased when I was very little ... going to this school down here ... I used to have papers pinned on my back ... My Mother'd turn round and say, 'They've put another paper on you' ... 'Suffragette', 'Socialist' ... 'You're not upset?' I says, 'No'. She says, 'Well, you won't have to be.' She says, 'You can't be a suffragette and get upset.' And they gave over after a bit. (Liddington, J., 1984, p. 153)

She was every bit as proud of her mother's achievements as was Louie Anderson. Recalling a mine disaster when she was thirteen, and Selina's accounts of all those buried alive, she adds with quiet pride:

'And my mother's ambulance [training] came in handy' (Liddington, J., 1984, p. 243).

Mary left grammar school at the age of sixteen, 'armed with her commercial and shorthand certificates', and secured the coveted post of 'Lady Clerk' at sixteen shillings a week. It became her job for life. Her mother's valiant efforts to keep her daughter out of the mill and 'to benefit from the education neither of them [her parents] had been able to enjoy paid off' (Liddington, J., 1984, p. 268). It was, in effect, no less a triumph for Selina, than Louie's reading medicine had proved to be for her mother, Elizabeth.

Mary never forgot what she owed to her mother, whose image lit her own mind with that fierce, iconic glow of the common struggle. From November 1918, when her mother had become a parliamentary candidate – a project which remained still-born, due to controversies surrounding Selina's name, such as her pacifism and her fight for birth control as a state monopoly – 'Mary [was] fast becoming her mother's closest friend' (Liddington, J., 1984, p. 297). Indeed, when the Great Depression finally wrapped the North in that unforgotten pall and the Poor Law Officers were snooping into every home, Mary, as a wage-earner, chose none the less to stay at home, even if her parents were financially disadvantaged: 'because I was at home, he [father] couldn't get any outdoor relief. You had to leave home. Heaps of families were broken up ... Well, I stopped [at home]. And although I hadn't a big wage I WAS there, you see' (Liddington, J., 1984, p. 378).

During these desperate times,

Mary and her wage ... were the linchpin of the Cooper household. Selina was always bustling off to court, The Guardian's Committee, and the Labour Party Executive or the Education Committee meetings; but she never forgot that it was Mary's monthly wage that kept the St Mary Street household together. (Liddington, J., 1984, p. 379)

In 1946, when Selina lay dying of a long and painful illness, morphia clouding the mind of that fine fighter at last:

My mother lost me entirely until the last day. And then she said, 'Don't give me any of that morphia.' She was in the ambulance, so she knew what she was getting ... Anyhow, she says 'don't give me that stuff. I want to talk to you.' And she was as conscious and sane [as anyone]. And she says, 'I haven't a lot of breath to say a lot to you, but' she says, 'I never – I never got spoilt, you see.' And she says, 'I've said sharp things to you sometimes, but you know I've always loved you. Now give me the medicine,' she said. (Liddington, J., 1984, p. 447)

4 GENTEEL FURORE FOR THE VOTE

WHEN SHE wrote *North and South* in the 1850s, Mrs Gaskell created a new kind of heroine in the person of Margaret Hale. As the novel unfolds the girl is running on an impulse from the shelter of the house to shield the mill-owner, John Thornton, from a ferocious striking mob, wielding their heavy clogs for missiles. Mrs Gaskell knew very well that Margaret Hale would carry weight and conviction with contemporary readership. As a writer of her time – and it is interesting to note that she used the word 'unconscious' (Gaskell, E., 1973, p. 94) – she had reason to believe that a young woman of the day could well behave as Margaret did under such circumstances – that where events demanded it she would not falter, faint or blush, but stand resolutely in command of her own determination.

At the same time she describes a more 'old-fashioned' side to Margaret. In that context we can hear Margaret pleading with her mother that she might for the time being act as her faithful nurse, since the latter is suffering from a terminal illness. This matter having been agreed to their mutual satisfaction, we are somewhat flummoxed to overhear a debate which seems out of character and rather more suited to some earlier Jane Austen theme. Mrs Hale is here concerned about a certain white silk dress which Margaret plans to wear that night: ' "Then you think you shall wear your white silk. Are you sure it will fit? . . ." "Oh yes, mamma! Mrs Murray made it, and it is sure to be right; . . ." ' Margaret then quickly mentions several other dresses as possible alternatives: ' "Shall I go and put them on one after another, mamma . . . then you could see which you like best?" ' (Gaskell, E., 1973, p. 147).

But wait, we are not deceived. This is not the old submission of a daughter to mamma, but a loving pandering to a mother whom she truly loves and who she knows full well is dying, and so this remains a different scene, in its true and deeper meaning, from one of four decades ago in a Jane Austen setting. The 'Revolution of the Daughters' has had far-reaching consequences on woman's deepest self-image. Margaret Hale was, after all, very much her own person. She was free to come and go to a refreshing extent; in *North and South* we somehow sense that a thaw in the climate has got well under way, even if we cannot say with satisfactory certainty just when the wind changed direction.

We have used the term 'revolution' with its cataclysmic undertones which are one side of the picture when we confront important change. Yet change is always a spiral, as Mrs Gaskell conveys with towering conviction. It has one foot in the past, in the old, well-trodden ways, when one day, for a clutch of reasons, many obscure enough to appear mystical, it sets the other foot forward and firmly down in the unknown. Even the psychotherapist whose patient labours are sited at the most advantageous of observation posts will often shake a head in wonder at certain favourable upheavals, for all the conceptual 'explanations' which crowd a growing literature. Here too, in our present exploration, we are at intervals amazed as women wrest the very stuff of some immense, still unnamed struggle for human emancipation into soft hands and 'little' minds, as though they had masterminded change from its earliest inception.

But let us not lose our thread in abstract speculations. If Selina's daughter Mary has left us with the *cri de coeur*: 'I was everybody's child' (see p. 219), her words carry no bitterness: on the contrary, a burst of pride. Her mother, as she knew so well, was out there wheeling and dealing, committed to moving mountains, in the treacherous world, so that mothers and their daughters – and their menfolk in the end – might live to see a day of brighter opportunities.

If Mary could recall so clearly going to her grandmother's while her mother was away, now we hear another voice: 'My children now being old enough for me to leave them with competent nurses, I was free to join these ranks' (Pankhurst, E., 1914, p. 22). The speaker is Mrs

Pankhurst. The ranks in question are those of the Women's Franchise League, formed in 1891 in a fierce spirit of rebellion against the Household Franchise Bill, or Reform Act of 1866. This Act, the first popular extension of the ballot act in England since 1832, gave the vote to householders, but to male persons only.

All that we have hurried through has been leading step by step to this shocking confrontation between women and their men, between husbands and their wives, between daughters and their fathers in very many instances, as between the disenfranchised and outraged ministers of state, inevitably bolstered by the forces of law and order. At the head of this insurrection stood Mrs Emmeline Pankhurst and her daughters Christabel and Sylvia, even if the latter played a less conspicuous part. Emmeline Pankhurst's role, as is so frequently the case, had its own prehistory in maternal example:

I was fourteen years old when I went to my first suffrage meeting. Returning from school one day, I met my mother just setting out for the meeting, and I begged her to let me go along. She consented, and without stopping to lay my books down I scampered away in my mother's wake. The speeches interested and excited me. I left the meeting a conscious and confirmed Suffragist. (Pankhurst, E., 1914, p. 9)

In this way Emmeline Goulden, as the future Mrs Pankhurst, identified as a girl with her spirited mother, to become part of a tradition of growing social consciousness with its fast-extending vistas.

'Those men and women are fortunate who are born at a time when a great struggle for human freedom is in progress' (Pankhurst, E., 1914, p. 1), she writes with utmost satisfaction. She then recalls a bazaar whose object was to raise money to relieve the poverty of the newly emancipated Negro slaves in the United States. Her mother took an active part in this enterprise as well, and so the child, then barely five, knew the meaning of the words slavery and emancipation and would listen enthralled when her mother spoke to her of Eliza's race for freedom over the broken ice of the Ohio river, straight from *Uncle Tom's Cabin*.

If Elizabeth Garrett Anderson, a staunch supporter of the cause, had never doubted that she could combine family life with her other great passion, Emmeline Pankhurst's three daughters never felt that they went short of parental love and care. And after Dr Pankhurst's death, when the girls were in their early twenties, we are impressed to see how they related as full equals to their mother: essentially as fellow-fighters united by a single cause. When Mrs Pankhurst, newly widowed, wanted to run a business, Christabel, sounding more like an old friend, remonstrated: 'You are so clever . . . that it seems strange that there is not something more suited to you.' 'Mother had now', she continues to reflect, 'to fulfil a man's responsibilities in a world that wholly underrated the economic value of its political outlaws, women' (Pankhurst, C., 1959, p. 31).

As these young women were concerned for their bereaved mother's future, there was never any question in Mrs Pankhurst's mind that her daughters would achieve fulfilling, independent lives suited to their gifts and talents. And soon, when the Bar, in appreciation of Dr Pankhurst's life-work, made certain funds available, Sylvia, who showed a gift for painting, went to the Manchester School of Art, Adéla trained to be a teacher, while Christabel remained at home as her mother's right hand until she found her own vocation later, in the field of law. 'Those lectures were my gateway to a future so filled with inspiring thoughts and activity that I came to reckon myself the happiest person on earth. I found my aim in life', she wrote (Pankhurst, C., 1959, p. 40), thankful that her mother readily recognized that her youngest too must spread her wings beyond the role of her work as her mother's adjutant.

In Emmeline Pankhurst we find a woman who was satisfied with her involvement with life on many rewarding frontiers, and consequently would ensure such a future for her daughters. This concern did not extend to matters of their creature comforts, or which dress they ought to wear in order to catch a husband, but to the fullest growth of the personality so that each might truly thrive as a free individual. In this context Mrs Pankhurst saw it as quite natural that when the battle hotted up, with repeated prison terms and their torture of force-feeding, then these horrors would be faced by mothers and daughters side by side: ' "We shall sleep in prison tonight," I said to mother. Her face was drawn and cold when I said goodbye . . . It was for mother an hour of crisis. She stood utterly alone in the world, as far as this decision to militancy was concerned' (Pankhurst, C., 1959, p. 50).

Within hours of this exchange Christabel and her friend Annie were forcibly removed from a Liberal pre-election meeting in Manchester's crowded Free Trade Hall, for the crime of challenging none other than Sir Edward Grey with the offending words: 'Will the

Liberal Government give women the vote?' – words that had by now become like a red rag to the bull of masculine statesmanship. But removal was not enough for their political ends. Determined to be arrested to bring the issue to court, her hands held behind her back, Christabel's only option if she was to achieve her purpose, as she knew very well as a student of the law, was to stand her ground and, distasteful as it was, to commit a technical assault:

and so I found myself arrested and charged with 'spitting at a policeman'. It was not a real spit but only, shall we call it, a 'pout', a perfectly dry purse of the mouth. I could not REALLY have done it, even to get the vote, I think. Anyhow, there was no need, my technical assault was enough ... Mother came with us to the Police Court. We shivered rather on entering. Police Courts then were associated in my mind only with the sordid and discreditable. However, we were there. A benign magistrate, who had known Father, was not at all severe! But we gave him not the least chance to excuse or let us off. To prison we went. (Pankhurst, C., 1959, p. 52)

Almost four years further on: 'My release from Holloway was due on 22nd December, but Mother's rather longer sentence would keep her still in prison on Christmas Day. However, the Government relented, and Mother and Mrs Leigh were also released to the general joy' (Pankhurst, C., 1959, p. 118).

But the strain took its toll. The year is 1913:

Again Mother and Annie appeared on the platform. Mother was just released after a Hunger-and-thirst-strike and had to be wheeled to the platform in an invalid chair ... Pale and enfeebled, Mother said: 'I believe that the end of our struggle is in sight – but it is not yet here and we have to continue it to the end.' (Pankhurst, C., 1959, p. 257)

Shortly after this event, on returning to the United States for another speaking tour, when asked by immigration: had she ever been to prison, this dignified and lovely lady dismayed the officials on Ellis Island by replying: 'Yes, many times.' 'Held up at Ellis Island!' 'Indignation in the United States.' 'President intervenes.' 'Extraordinary welcome in New York', ran the newspaper headlines.

Whether she addressed a meeting, or was being marched to prison by sturdy officers, even in her prison clothes, Emmeline Pankhurst always looks the most gentle English lady, in keeping with her manner, which remained reasonable and calm under the utmost provocation and degrading circumstances. Nor was she the only one to maintain appearances of extraordinary composure, to the last feather on a hat. Her militancy had grown not from a soil of abstract theory but from a sense of grief and shock as she witnessed the conditions under which her poorer sisters had to struggle to survive, to give birth to their children, and keep some of them alive in the bleakest deprivation: 'These old folks I found sitting on backless forms, or benches. They had no privacy, no possessions, not even a locker. The old women were without pockets in their gowns, so that they were obliged to keep any poor little treasures they had in their bosoms' (Pankhurst, E., 1914, p. 24). Here we have an observation which no man would have made, for it belongs to the nature of women to be so preoccupied with questions of 'inner' storage, as of outer space, from the most ancient times.

Then, new skills in pottery, which was in the hands of women, were promptly utilized for the storage of grains – in other words for survival. So closely is woman's sense of her creativity bound up with her own inner space, as it serves the generations, that her genius finds fertile scope in that which is practical in its very widest sense. This is well illustrated in the case of Mrs Pankhurst when we read a few lines on in this chapter, which is headed 'The Making of a Militant':

But it does gratify me when I look back and remember what we were able to do for the children of the Manchester workhouse ... These little girls were clad, summer and winter, in thin cotton frocks ... At night they wore nothing at all, night dresses being considered too good for paupers. The fact that bronchitis was epidemic among them most of the time had not suggested to the guardians any change in the fashion of their clothes. (Pankhurst, E., 1914, p. 25)

She also concerned herself with saving scraps of bread from which to make nourishing milk puddings and other matters of this kind, natural to a mother's heart.

In other words this 'militancy', as it came to be known, and remains to this day under similar provocation, was rooted deeply in the nature of maternal preoccupation. Surely, once women had the vote, the suffragettes must have dreamt, their very nature would insist that such offensive omissions be swiftly remedied. That it has turned out otherwise, to women's deepest disappointment, at a time when they wield immense political power, only proves that the laws of progress are complex in the extreme and reach beyond those of gender.

Here we leave Mrs Pankhurst and the suffragettes. We still hear her steady voice in 1914 after war has been declared:

Our battles are practically over, we confidently believe. For the present at least our arms are grounded, for directly the threat of foreign war descended on our nation we declared a complete truce from militancy. What will come of this European war – so terrible in its effects on women who had no voice in averting it – so baneful in the suffering it must necessarily bring on innocent children – no human being can calculate. (Pankhurst, E., 1914, p. 363)

Again, in this impressive leader, who would now take her followers into Britain's war effort with the same brand of commitment with which they had fought for votes, it is the mother who is speaking; the same mother who wrangled with the prison governors that she be allowed to break their imposed rule of silence, 'to have the joy of seeing my daughter and the other brave comrades, and walking with them in the dismal courtyard of the prison' (Pankhurst, E., 1914, p. 132).

Already in medieval England, within the monastic system, we saw mothers and daughters, where opportunities raised them out of the domestic sphere, step together, side by side, into a new dignity which can belong to public office, where it is subject to true vision relating to the common good. In Emmeline Pankhurst and her daughters we observe this same process moving towards fruition in the spiral of progress. Despite setbacks and regressions, for outer as for inner reasons, there is no longer any doubt that this cultivar exists with a viability awaiting new development.

But before we take the progress of woman as an individual who can be both separate and also different from her mother – while she fulfils herself both in her private life and in the public domain – into the twentieth century, we should pause to examine certain *intrinsic* reasons for the common failure of this process to evolve. For in many respects, which demand investigation, these belong intrinsically to the nature of the dyad, to its *inmost* politics. In all the hue and cry of feminist preoccupation, these considerations have been thrust into the background.

It may not be without interest that in grappling with these issues for our present purposes, familiar as the subject seemed, I sustained a time of breakdown and had to lay the book aside for the best part of a summer. How far had I myself resolved the pitfalls of entanglements of the symbiotic trap? Here is a dark and fearful story, an underworld of lingering shadows, of the undoing of becoming, more sinister than that to which Hades brought Persephone, his bride. Yet once we face these trials squarely, how often we play Orpheus to our own Eurydice! The touching rescue operation with which the telling of this section ends carries us, I think, most truly into the essential core of the conflicts of our lifetime, of the present century, relating to our subject matter. It finally dispelled my doubts that I had reached *terra firma* well enough in that respect: that I had emerged from the cocoon sufficiently to keep on growing.

The illustrations I have chosen are clearly quite extreme, for which reason they belong to the dark end of the spectrum which I see as mental health. But their subtler manifestations, workaday as these are, still exert a stranglehold on the mother–daughter freedom to grow and reach towards the light; and these can be identified more readily with examples where the case *is* extreme.

The theme demands closer inspection, since its configurations account, in my considered view, for more sorrow and wastage, more frustration and backtracking in countless women's lives than any equivalent conundrum the hapless male can inflict. Whatever powers he may wield today in holding woman back from owning her rightful place as equal member at his side, it is largely in her collusion with the patriarchal edicts, with her own self-depreciation, with the raw material of her nature, that the deepest impasse hides in our present day and age, here, in the Western world. So confounding is its nature that it is tempting to regard this obscure phenomenon as a *folie à deux*, nesting at the very core of daughtership and motherhood, where no Columbus has yet gained firm and lasting foothold.

PART IV

1 WHEN THE WIND BLOWS THE CRADLE WILL ROCK*
Psychotic Interactions between Mother and Daughter

Maybe my mother cut the God out of me
when I was two in my playpen.
Is it too late, too late
to open the incision and plant Him there again?
All is wilderness.
All is hay that died from too much rain . . .
(ANNE SEXTON, *The Awful Rowing Towards God*)

Oh, Mary,
Gentle Mother,
open the door and let me in.
A bee had stung your belly with faith.
Let me float in it like a fish.
Let me in! Let me in!
I have been born many times, a false Messiah,
but let me be born again
into something true.
(ANNE SEXTON, *The Awful Rowing Towards God*)

'A RACE of free women would be the end of humanity, since freedom and childbearing are incompatible' (Jameson, S., 1984, p. 310). So wrote the mother of a son. She did not have a second child. Therefore she did not discover that to give birth to a

* An example of a nursery rhyme, where mothers can express their hate.

daughter, life to a future mother, will launch us, unsuspectingly, into a sea of turbulence of which we remain unforewarned even in this age of plenty where facile knowledge is concerned.

Beyond such privacy as shrouds begetting and the sequestered hour of birth, society, as High Priest of tradition, appropriates jurisdiction over a function which decrees the survival of the species, and willy-nilly confiscates epiphany and mystique. Sperm remains a simple matter, ephemeral in its swift flight. But mother giving form to mother knits and links the generations into a continuum which the neutral term 'a baby' buries surreptitiously even now. Yet the birth of a female child, the months of suckling and the years of rearing, will inevitably spell untold, secret differences from this process with a son, in joy, as much as serious trouble, beyond the small change of the obvious, from the moment that the cord is cut, from the first shadowy realization that a daughter has been born:

When I came round from the anaesthetic that late afternoon in January 1934, there was no nurse or doctor in the room. She and I were alone. I heard her before I saw her. She was making strong, broken noises of protest, sorrow, from some unidentifiable region near my bed.

'Yes, yes, I know,' I said. 'Never mind, I know.' Immediately she was silent, listening. In this soundless nought recognition started to vibrate like a fine filament between us; quickened, tautened. I swung in a living darkness, emptiness, in the beginning of the deepest listening of my life.

When, probably quite soon, Sister came in and said loudly, 'Here's your baby dear – a lovely daughter, don't you want to see her?' I started to sob. I suppose from happiness. (Lehmann, R., 1967, p. 98)

Do we cry from happiness if it is not also mingled with the most complicated sorrow? Sister's '*loudly* "here's your baby . . ." ' does its best to dispel the electrifying magic of 'never mind, yes, I know', with which this minutes-old mother here forewarns her daughter-child that by the act of drawing breath she is welded to an age-old bondage which the two of them now share and will carry to the grave: namely that any mother, invested in a replica, can never hope to revert to as inviolable a self as can the mother of a son. For has she not, by accident, beyond all realms of comprehension, in one stroke become the pawn in the mystery play of life? Must she not henceforth serve to the end of her days as a priestess-handmaiden of the biocreative principle to preserve the generations, as Leonardo understood when he returned to the theme of Mary and her mother Anne as they revert to unity in sustaining a new life?

Is it not the bride's mother who prepares the wedding feast as token that she is bound to nourish grandchildren to come; to return to the place beside the ever-rocking cradle in supporting her daughter through the travail to be renewed? Even if all younger women will be her daughter in one sense, even if as an ancient woman she will still feed the birds, the babies under the open sky, it is her flesh-and-blood daughter through whom she will be bound most deeply and irrevocably, most reluctantly or joyfully, with harrowing ambivalence, to that ever-turning wheel.

If, however, she refuses, or asks to be let off with less than a life sentence, then will madness, by default, be standing ready in the wings to mete out dire punishment for disrupting this holy line which, at an unconscious level, must insist on changelessness as we met it earlier in the Elementary Character of the brooding mother goddess.

Changelessness must be upheld. It must also be subverted: we have here an unholy dialectic from the outset in this making of new mothers. It is disruption and subversion which will be our present subject as we touch on several aspects of this unique totality. There is the crucial theme of boundaries. If you have a replica, how is difference instituted while sameness is maintained at either pole of the dyad? In the case of a male child difference tends to be clear, identification minimal, confusion more readily held at bay. Intrusion, predatory impulse, envy of all distinction are bound to play a greater part within the closed maternal circuit in which a daughter-child will spend a considerable part of her life-expectancy. That this part is growing longer in proportion to the whole is not insignificant in the totality of unrest.

Beyond boundaries and envy looms the third of the great issues: infanticide and matricide. Wherever there is no way forward for either partner of the pair, wherever there is stagnation, a strangulation of growth, for internal or external reasons, these rear their archaic head in the depths of the unconscious.

But it is the state of the boundaries between a mother and her daughter which must be our chief concern. It seems virtually certain that their substance will remain different and more permeable than those between her and her son – the one who is different, whose face is turned towards the world, whose destiny lies *out there*, far beyond the women's quarters, when these persist as a state of mind even in the nuclear age. Even in resolved cases, where a dyad has achieved the degree of separation which enables a daughter to build a singular life during early adult years, pregnancy, once it brings changes to her own mind and body, making them pervious to her infant, will of necessity restore a degree of perviousness to the original mother–daughter boundaries as part of that continuum: . . . 'the story is not at an end. Her life did not end then; it goes on echoing through mine, and will echo there until it and I are both silenced' (Jameson, S., 1984, p. 355). Author of forty-five novels, essayist and polemicist, according to all outward signs a truly 'liberated' woman, Storm Jameson knew very well that she must fight to the last ditch not to let the oldest strings of body, psyche – of her heart – entangle her out of her being. When her mother had begun her dying, three hundred miles to the north of the writer's hearth and domicile with her husband and her son:

'Don't go.'

For less than a moment I knew that I should hear that remote barely audible voice in the deepest recess of my brain, and those two words all the rest of my life. Then I closed my ears.

'I MUST go,' I said. 'But I'll come back – I'll come as soon as I can.'

She did not answer or lift her eyelids to look at me – as though she had lost interest. Or as though she had known all along that she could not count on me, had known I would fail her, and were turning away from me. (Jameson, S., 1984, p. 349)

Tell me, when you read these lines, what chance do you and I have? What deadly perils do we run in our separating out, even by the smallest chink, never mind the outer world of prohibitions laid by men?

The secondary perviousness which we introduced above almost certainly displays a qualitative difference from the primary osmosis which belongs to symbiosis and will spell the profoundest trouble, extended beyond its proper span, as when it comes to meet us here and already makes our blood run cold: 'Between Sylvia and myself there existed – as between my own mother and me – a sort of psychic osmosis, which at times was very wonderful and comforting; at other times an unwelcome intrusion of privacy' (Plath, A.S., 1976, p. 32). The osmosis in this case, to which we shall be returning, was in fact entanglement, handed down, as we are told, through entangled generations, as is so frequently the case. Here was a mother in the business – even if unknowingly – of appropriating her daughter's life to give her own a hungry meaning where it had eluded her. In this case it clearly serves as a defence against envy. As folk-language puts it well: 'Vor daughters ha' mornen when mothers ha night . . .' (Jameson, S., 1984, p. 48). And is this not accentuated in our present era of expanding opportunities in so many women's lives? In this tragic collusion the guilt at being better off leads in many instances to the scuttling of advantages: to young lives putting on the brakes at hard-won opportunities in tragic, self-defeating ways.

We will presently explore the madness of entanglement after a brief illustration of its very opposite, namely impermeability of maternal boundaries: the syndrome which Laing defined as the 'schizogenic' mother; the one who is incapable of maternal reverie, who simply cannot take on board signs of infantile distress and is compelled to reject all signals of the fear of dying and of falling to bits: the terror of annihilation which multiplies horrendously as a consequence of its rejection.

The dialogue which follows was taken from an interview between the mother and her daughter, Lucie, who was once again admitted to a mental hospital: a familiar routine in her young, disrupted life. In this material we encounter the classical 'double bind' where, first, containment is repelled only to be followed by denial of the existence of boundaries so that the daughter feels enmeshed:

Mother: *My time's taken up in trying to make life a bit easier. As for relationships and all that it just doesn't go into my line. Otherwise I'd forget somebody wanted that or somebody wanted the other. There's only a certain amount of time in a lifetime and if you're one of those unlucky persons who's got to accommodate people who can't do things for themselves, well there's not much time for analysis. As for relationships, I don't think of them. It's best not to.*

Lucie: *I still believe that quite unconsciously I miss my sister. I lost my sister about ten years ago and I think that subconsciously I must be grieving even now in a subconscious way which I'm not really conscious of. I must be feeling terribly lonely and not realizing why . . . At the time of her passing I was in hospital, you see, and I don't know much about it. You've really got to realize your loneliness instead of allowing yourself to be stunned by it . . . Don't you think when we were very young this sort of trouble was beginning and it showed and other people realized it and said so?*

Mother: *Oh I think there was a lot of ignorance. Don't forget you were born into an age of ignorance. (Laing, R.D. and Esterson, A., 1970, p. 61)*

It comes to us with some surprise that the patient here is Lucie, who was, we hear, in her late thirties when this interview took place. She had been in hospital, labelled as schizophrenic, for the past twelve years of her life.

Without going any further into Lucie's history, it strikes us very painfully how hard the girl is struggling against dangerous prohibition: to obtain some validation for her personal feelings. She knows her loneliness and grief, that she misses her sister, but this knowledge reaches us very heavily disguised. She does not really feel entitled to own or to express whatever might arouse anxiety, since she has learnt from hard experience that her mother cannot stand 'it', that she might in fact go mad if expected to contain it. For this is what her mother means by 'accommodating people'.

Having learnt that it is dangerous to come out into the open with her sorrows and her fears, her angry longing to assert her basic birthright for containment, Lucie resorts to strategy. She hurls, or projects as we say, the part of her personality which is in touch with her feelings and the feelings themselves into any willing listener: we are swamped with Lucie's grief as with the wider currents of her hatred of her mother. We want to get away from Lucie as fast as ever we can: to have the wretched girl locked up. But Lucie cannot handle it in any other way. She lacks the ego-strength needed to face the madness of her mother in its obscene violence, and remains fragmented.

Terrible is her awareness, reaching us in that grim code. She says 'we were very young' when 'this sort of trouble was beginning'. She knows she never had a chance, that there was no alternative if she wanted to protect her mother. She knew, almost from infancy, that she herself was called upon to be her mother's container, since mother cannot stand people 'who can't do things for themselves': contain their own anxieties, and her own into the bargain. Here, of course, she means infants during their infancy. Lucie, we can see, was doomed in this heroic bid to reverse the mother–infant status.

If we can stand our ground, and tolerate her projection, we can sympathize with Lucie. We were also daughters once. Our own anxieties were not always quite so perfectly contained. We too were anxious for our mother, bearing our anxieties when she was under stress or strain, afraid that we would drive her mad. 'Messy baby', mother scolded sometimes, driven to distraction. She was, we knew unconsciously, referring to anxieties we brought to her to contain, more than to the kitchen floor.

Lucie's wretched mother knows that she has made a mess of Lucie, behind her smoke screen of defences. 'Don't forget you were born into an age of ignorance.' She is referring to herself. In this distorted language she is skirting her own hopeless inability to contain her daughter's feelings. But to admit the truth would be far too persecuting. She simply could not stand the guilt. 'The defence against anxiety and guilt is paramount' (Segal, H., 1981, p. 147). Lucie's mother is crippled, but she cannot afford to let Lucie go free from the prison of their illness, since her envy of health and life outweighs her capacity for love. Nor could Lucie get away, short of a miracle. For she is tied to this sick-room which the two of them share at the symbiotic level. If someone took Lucie into psychoanalysis, the guilt that would be mobilized at 'leaving mother behind' would make it very heavy going, and, in any such instances, a self-defeating exercise, unless the mother, too, has treatment. A daughter's deepest impulse is to want 'to die' with her mother: not to have to live 'alone'. That she hates this stifling bondage is quite another matter.

Julie, another patient, was well aware of this. She *had* given up and 'died' by the age of twenty-six, when she told her psychiatrist that 'a child had been murdered' by herself or by her mother, and that she must tell the police (Laing, R.D., 1965, p. 147). The dead child was of course herself.

Mothers 'murder' their daughters to some degree every day. Where such a victim is able to drag herself to a psychotherapist, a drawn-out struggle will begin to discover ways and means to staunch the dreadful flow of blood, as in the last of these cases. For Marie Cardinal, whom we will come to presently, was literally bleeding, continuously and to death!

A third young woman in this series miraculously found a patron to sponsor her analysis. Her startling beauty won him over to this philanthropic act. From the moving account by her psychoanalyst (Milner, M., 1969) of this drawn-out marathon we obtain important insights into these hell fires burning in the mind of a daughter subsequent on total failure of maternal reverie. The degree of sadism which Susan's phantasies convey was very probably secondary to extremes of oral frustration and of inadequate containment, to which a psychotic mother had subjected her. But we must not forget that Susan's mother, when a baby, had one day been discovered in her dead mother's arms! There was no knowing for how long this catastrophe had endured. Susan's grandmother had, it was claimed, died of starvation. The daughter of a barrister she had been a victim too. No social class is immune from these experiences!

In the course of this minute account of the treatment situation we find a harrowing vignette of extreme maternal envy of Susan's youth and beauty. We see it clearly, for example, when Susan brought a boyfriend home. Her mother 'made open overtures to Angus. One day she came into her daughter's bedroom stroking her own breasts and muttering, "a new blooming, a new blooming" ' (Milner, M., 1969, p. 10). Here it is obvious that she dealt with her envious feelings by removing all boundaries and merging with her daughter in the confusion of total identification. If she *is* her daughter, Susan, there is no need to envy her. If she *is* her daughter, Susan, then *she* is young and beautiful, as we know that Susan was. Her appearance was like Garbo's, we are told by Mrs Milner, but she was not aware of this. She had got rid of her beauty, hoping thereby to be safe from maternal attacks: '. . . in her mother's mind her daughter never had any separate existence', Milner here confirms (1969, p. 41). Mother and daughter shared a bed until late into Susan's adolescence. Her mother once told her 'not to wriggle' when she developed appendicitis. How could Susan have a pain if her mother did not feel it?

Before we leave this tragic tale we will still take a look at the deeper connections between sadistic phantasies of attacks against a mother, as entertained by an infant, and the ensuing terror that these have certainly destroyed her – for ever, irrevocably. In someone as ill as Susan, these sadistic attacks remain active in the present, in response to all frustration which is inherent in the treatment, for which reason they emerge tellingly in the transference.

This is clearer when we reflect on two painful images which played an important part in Susan's analysis: '. . . staying with relatives, she remembers finding on the seashore a dead rat crawling with maggots and saying she would get a box and post it to her mother' (Milner, M.,

1969, p. 6). The second image which came up after some nine months of treatment was of a damaged milk-float. This belonged to a time when Susan worked on a farm. We really need to take it in the context of a certain session to connect deeper implications:

In a few months' time, on 14 July 1944, she was able to bring me her first conscious awareness of depression connected with an idea of an injured container of milk. She begins the session by asking where the bomb fell in the night, because she has seen debris all along my road. Then she tells me she realizes now that she was not happy at the farm; she liked the farm-work . . . but she was miserable out in the milk-float in the early morning, with its windows broken and the roof off, and all the house left in a mess. (Milner, M., 1969, p. 20)

After that Susan spoke of her fear of travelling on trains: that she would throw herself out.

Such material as this suggested [Mrs Milner then continues] that her depression was to do with a sense of hopelessness of ever feeling she could restore the injured milk-float mother, and that the only reparation would be to kill herself, throw herself out of the train, since . . . her mother used to say it was all her fault . . . (Milner, M., 1969, p. 20)

Linking these associations is, surely, Susan's fear of her own destructiveness with its sadistic overtones. A bomb has fallen in the night near her therapist's home. This causes her anxiety, for she asks where the bomb fell. She fears that out of her frustration at having spent the night alone, like many other grievances which will surface in due course as the analysis continues, she has made a bomb attack on her mother-therapist, as she did as an infant on her mother's milk-float breast, to leave little more than debris in her cowering phantasy.

The bomb attacks, we may suppose, would have been made with faeces. But mother's body and breast were also, it appears, attacked with sharp biting, tearing teeth. For the dead rat with the maggots represents a phantasy, which Susan has internalized, of a maternal breast which she has reduced to such a state. Since she often went hungry as a child, we are told, both for food and for understanding, her infant self would have experienced a biting and withholding breast. It would be biting because in a state of frustration, Susan would have projected her oral sadism into it: a sadism in part aroused

— 241 —

by excessive frustration in the absence of sustaining love.

The maggots are the other babies felt to live inside the breast, feeding to their hearts' content, since surely someone must be getting all that nourishing milk. Susan's envy and greed and destructive phantasies now turn her into a rat. She fears that she did not take in her mother's milk lovingly, or even gently for that matter, but tore into that withholding breast, as she fears that she tears into her mother-therapist, whom she will, for many years, experience as cruel and withholding.

Many years on from here Susan brought along a drawing. It was in pencil, of a tree standing in a total landscape, growing from a little hummock, shaped rather like a breast. Could this, Mrs Milner wonders, indicate the gradual growth of an environment which she feels in her unconscious is beginning to survive her sadistic attacks to offer her a ground for being; to permit the risk of sinking roots into this maternal soil without a new catastrophe overtaking the nursing couple?

We need to pause here, and consider that sons as well as daughters fall victim to schizophrenic illness. None the less, these phantasies of sadistic attacks on a mother's breasts and body, with their paranoid terror of maternal retaliation, mean different things to boys and girls, or men and women, later on. To a girl as sick as Susan, the onset of menstruation may be experienced as proof that her inside is destroyed, that she will never be a mother. That she might as well be dead and throw herself out of a train. In my own experience, the busiest preoccupation with thoughts of suicide belong to disturbed relationships with the parent of the same sex. A son requires his father's blessing, as a daughter does her mother's, to go forward into life with a sense of trust and optimism. But the girl is at a disadvantage.

Father and son, the clash of antlers, the masculine oedipal drama, its success or failure to evolve into scope for generous growth, has always been ritualized from tribal days to the present. Stone Age tribes still celebrate the girl's first menstruation in touching and thoughtful ways. Not so in our present day. Mother and daughter are abandoned shamelessly to their own devices, and left to fight or sort it out as best they can on their own.

Unlike those in the Ancient World we have singularly failed to create our healing myths. We need an updated version of Demeter and Persephone. We must today confront that saga and heroic epic of this separating out of a mother from her daughter, and the other way round. For it continues to loom as a paralysing threat over the life-land of the mother and the future of the daughter. If she leaves that body-home, which nurtured and instructed her for virtually two decades in the maternal circuit, will the mother not collapse, feeling empty and redundant, or perhaps retaliate by withdrawing her support for all eternity?

There are countless variations on this convulsive theme. They impinge on us continuously, if we are aware of it. Tales of failure and success crowd in on our imagination from a host of fairy tales of our earliest girlhood days. Maidens are locked up in towers, put to sleep for a hundred years, tied to their spinning wheels and kept at home, like Cinderella. Long before we go to school, we are already alerted to this ferocious tug of war as its cacophonies reverberate all around us, leaving few quiet moments. We may stand on the sidelines as two wrestlers fight it out: an older sister with our mother, or a cousin with an aunt, later on perhaps a schoolfriend, or the girl down the road. There may be screams in the night, sounds of a gruesome slapping: 'is she going to get away?' . . . our girlish heart within us trembles, sensing what may lie ahead.

This said, we must not forget that there are countless happy outcomes. Where a mother feels fulfilled and adequately satisfied with the achievements of her life, where she has no axe to grind and relatively few regrets of what has been left unaccomplished, of dreams that have eluded her to leave a gaping conviction that life has cheated her, there the outlook for the dyad will be a more auspicious one. Then there is little need for a frustrated mother to seize on her daughter's life, like a vulture on its prey, shamelessly laying claim to her daughter's achievements to steal them in the deepest sense; to initiate infanticide, a subtle drawn-out strategy in psychological machinations.

Let us look at two well-documented examples, one to illustrate each case: the first leads to suicide on the part of the daughter; the second leads to life, to a deep reconciliation, even if it took place after the mother's death, setting her daughter free at last into the fullness of her life as wife, mother and writer – a separate human entity, having narrowly escaped from the infanticide above with psychoanalytical help.

There is no shortage of material on the life of Sylvia Plath, including the relationship between herself and her mother: 'Between Sylvia and me there existed – as between my own mother and me – a sort of psychic osmosis' (Plath, A.S., 1976, p. 32). Already, a few pages back, we have met the mother of the poet in *Letters Home*. Aurelia Schober, later Plath, is not an insensitive woman. Her Introduction to *Letters Home* reads like an apologia. With this we can sympathize. Rarely has a mother's role come under greater scrutiny, much of it frankly hostile. We do not want to take sides and yet she tends to get our back up, long before we come to Sylvia: so much warmth, concern and caring, while we sense that she has not put all her cards on the table and is brimming with obscure resentment.

Much of this, we come to sense, is directed against *her* mother, who tends to come across as a bustling Austrian *hausfrau*, not entirely at ease in the onrush of the New World with its go-getting women. But the Frau Professor Plath, as Aurelia was at heart, idealized 'Grammy' Schober, as a good, kind daughter should; for everything about her person had to be exemplary.

It is difficult to trust her. Was she ever in touch with her own deepest feelings, with her own anxieties or the anxieties of others: of her daughter, for instance? Or did Aurelia Plath inhabit a shining, brittle bell jar too?

It takes two for a murder: the unanswered question is – how many for a suicide? How are we to account – assuming we are able to – for the fact that her daughter, then a mother of two children, aged only three and one, notwithstanding gassed herself, when she was only thirty, on an icy February morning, all alone in the house except for her two little ones?

'Her physical energies had been depleted by illness, anxiety and overwork, and although she had for so long managed to be gallant and equal to the life-experience, some darker day than usual had temporarily made it seem impossible to pursue . . .' (Plath, A.S., 1976, p. 500). These are the words with which her mother seeks to explain the tragedy. Yet if ever suicide was a foregone conclusion, since Sylvia's student years, then it was surely in this instance.

Of course people kill themselves when, as coroners like to say, the balance of their mind is temporarily disturbed. And if we read Sylvia's letters home, which cover those final months after her marriage broke down, when her husband, Ted Hughes, had found somebody else, a growing sense of desperation hits us with tremendous force. We can barely endure it. If ever death held the stage in a quaking human life, then we surely see him here, fat with the certainty that he has his victim nailed. But Sylvia, as we discover, will resort to denial quite as much as her mother. Both use primitive defences in a similar way.

She attributes her dire state to an inability to eat, with its attendant loss of weight and repeated bouts of influenza. All her energies focus on finding a good nanny instead of a 'bitch'. When she has a good nanny she is able to eat. Nobody would dispute that she needed good help, if only so that she could write to maintain her sanity. But there is more to it than that. This anorexia, as described, surely carries distinctive paranoid implications, rooted in the split between an idealized and a terrible 'bitch' mother who might seek to poison her in delusional phantasy. After all, we know quite well the details of that first suicide attempt, which very nearly succeeded. Neither had this earlier bid been on a sudden impulse. For weeks on end during that summer of 1953, after she received the news that she had not been accepted for a short-story writing class – experienced as a declaration that her talent was in question or, at a deeper level, being enviously attacked – she was totally obsessed with suicidal ruminations. Esther, in *The Bell Jar* (Plath, S., 1963, pp. 154, 166), ponders: should she maybe die at sea, cut her wrists in the bath, hang herself or, as Sylvia decided, take a massive overdose of the medication her psychiatrist had prescribed, hide away in the cellar and there die, undisturbed? Autobiography, blow by blow, *The Bell Jar*, ironically, had just begun to reach the bookshops in those first icy weeks of 1963 when Sylvia finally gassed herself. She published it under a pseudonym, and most probably Aurelia had not read the manuscript.

Sylvia's *Letters Home* begin in the autumn of 1950 when she went up to Smith, a prestigious women's college, where competitive fury between cliquish, chosen girls ran at blood-curdling heights. In order to make this dream come true, as much Aurelia's as Sylvia's in their conjoint drive for greatness, financial aid from various sources, including a scholarship, were duly obtained. But the need to prove herself, to be the golden girl of girls, to try to satisfy her mother, was only multiplied by these additional expectations which now rested on her: '. . . and [I] shall spend my life making you strong and proud of me!' (Payne, K., 1984, p. 177). These words, written in 1956 in a letter to her mother, had been Sylvia's signature tune from a very early age. After her father's death she drove her self-expectations with grisly omnipotence: 'I want, I think, to be omniscient . . . I think I would like to call myself "The girl who wanted to be God" . . . Never, never, never will I reach the perfection I long for with all my soul . . . my vanity desires luxuries which I can never have' (Plath, A.S., 1976, p. 40). Much of her lifetime Sylvia hovered on the brink of psychosis, since we know that omnipotence and death walk hand in hand.

The letters Sylvia wrote from Smith during the three college years which preceded her breakdown and attempted suicide were brimming with psychotic content: screaming with hypomanic and sometimes manic overtones. Brittle as overblown glass as the girl clearly was, quaking and boasting in turn, like a brass band which at times gives a perilous flute a split-second solo tune, only to drown it out again, a different mother might have seen the writing glaring on the wall. But that 'psychic osmosis' between this mother and daughter, whose common language excluded everything but superlatives, made Aurelia unreceptive to the terrible distress, the squealing of danger signals which Sylvia herself projected:

Dear Mother . . . I have been rather worried about a friend of mine . . . Her usual gaiety has been getting brighter and more artificial as the days go by . . . It seems that since Thanksgiving she hasn't been able to do her work, and now, having let it slide, she can only reiterate, 'I can never do it, never.' [Sylvia then continues] . . . but her parents were either deceiving her into thinking she was creative or really didn't know how incapable she was. The girl was in such a state of numbness that she didn't feel any emotion, I guess, except this panic. I got scared when she told me she had been saving sleeping pills and razor blades and could think of nothing better than to commit suicide. (Plath, A.S., 1976, p. 64)

Aurelia, the editor, some twenty years afterwards, adds the following footnote: 'Actually, the girl in question was not suicidal; perhaps Sylvia's earlier Thanksgiving depression was influencing her words here.' Does she, we would like to know, recognize in retrospect the gravity of these projections; that they are a death sentence passed by Sylvia on herself?

It would seem that at the time Aurelia let the whole thing 'slide' – this vital communication. Was Sylvia already then, at an unconscious level, not pleading with her mother to pick the dire signals up, and not, please not, to let them slide? But Aurelia's need for a successful daughter would remain so paramount that she could not entertain such dissonant anxieties. She also was a parent who continued to 'deceive' her child – not as to her actual talent, which was hardly in doubt, but by failing to recognize that her child lacked all foundation on which to base this superstructure, this dizzy and unwieldy burden that great talent has to be. I believe that she 'must have known', if only at an unconscious level.

By November 1952 Sylvia's letters home sounded just like the confessions of that 'suicidal' girl: 'I have wondered desperately, if I should go to the college psychiatrist and try to tell her how I feel about it . . . Life seems a mockery . . . Every day more and more piles up . . .' (Plath, A.S., 1976, p. 97). This long letter was signed 'Your hollow girl, Sivvy'. Aurelia's footnote to it reads: 'During the Thanksgiving recess, Sylvia caught up with her work and seemed to regain confidence and buoyancy' (Plath, A.S., 1976, p. 99).

In August of the following year, Sylvia was rescued from the cellar of her family home. She had been missing for three days when her brother, Warren, heard a faint moan from down there. The tablets she had taken in the bid to end her life proved to be the very ones which her psychiatrist prescribed. 'I kept them locked in a metal safety case', Sylvia's mother informs us (Plath, A.S., 1976, p. 28). During the next six months Sylvia was treated with electroconvulsive treatment and insulin coma 'therapy'. All concerned seem to agree that there was 'no fear the present neurosis will develop into a more serious mental condition . : .' (Plath, A.S., 1976, p. 128). And so, by February 1954, we have the golden 'Sivvy' back, writing home again from Smith: 'Needless to say, it is simply wonderful to be back here . . .' (Plath, A.S., 1976, p. 134). From 'here', nine more years would pass until the final suicide: Cambridge, marriage, two babies, separation and divorce: years during which a poet of acclaim would be born.

Already as a young woman Aurelia Schober had, it seems, been on that dangerous 'genius trail'. Since she had been in no position to take her life in her own hands, to pursue an education consonant with her own needs, it chanced as she was completing her pragmatic business studies, as her father had decreed, that she met her 'brilliant' future husband in her final year at college. Her senior by some twenty years, Otto Plath was her professor. The episode of their courtship, as of the entire marriage, sounds something of a period piece: 'Then I yielded to my husband's wish that I become a fulltime homemaker' (Plath, A.S., 1976, p. 39). What her husband said went, even to the nth degree. If he needed the dining table for some eighteen months to research his book on insect societies, each time guests were expected Aurelia first drew a map of each and every book's position, so that she could restore the volume and every single piece of paper to its right and proper place to avoid his displeasure!

Psychoanalysts today would possibly diagnose her as a precarious personality, often near the brink of complete disintegration, which keeps going with the crutch of primitive defences like omnipotence and denial. Sylvia's personality was possibly similar, except that her prodigious talent kept the wind in her sails, so that Aurelia was able to deceive herself that all was well with her daughter – as, of course, she needed to, to maintain her self-esteem at a tolerable level: to be able to survive.

So she maintained the self-image of a warm and caring mother, according to some studied text. 'My babies were', she soothes us, 'cuddled'. Yet we are bound to remark on her lack of understanding for the feelings of small children. Back home, after the birth of Warren, we hear her puzzled undertones: 'the one difficulty was when I nursed the baby: it was always then that Sylvia wanted to get onto my lap.' The books had clearly not forewarned her of *this* contingency. But a solution was at hand which would be fated to have far-reaching implication for her little daughter's life: 'Fortunately, around this time she discovered the alphabet . . . From then on, each time I nursed Warren, she would get a newspaper . . . to "read".' Sylvia was not yet three! The dreadful narcissistic wound of the birth of a brother was, from so early on, plugged and bandaged thoroughly with literary aspirations.

Of that catastrophe which broke her early world apart – never, it seems, to mend again – Sylvia had this to say:

Then one day the textures of the beach burned themselves on the lens of my eye for ever. Hot April . . . My mother was in hospital. She had been gone three weeks. I sulked. I would do nothing. Her desertion punched a smouldering hole in my sky. How could she, so loving and faithful, so easily leave me. (Newman, C., 1970, p. 268)

In due course her 'Viennese, Victorian' grandmother 'melted' a little:

I would have a surprise when mother came back. It would be something nice. It would be – a baby.
A baby.

I hated babies. I who for two and a half years had been the centre of a tender universe felt the axis wrench and a polar chill immobilize my bones. I would be a bystander, a museum mammoth. Babies! . . . Hugging my grudge, ugly and prickly, a sad sea-urchin, I trudged off on my own . . . As from a star I saw, coldly and soberly, the SEPARATENESS of everything. I felt the wall of skin: I am I. That stone is a stone. My beautiful fusion with the things of this world was over.

The tide ebbed, sucked back into itself. There I was, a reject, with the dried black seaweed whose hard beads I liked to pop, hollowed orange and grapefruit halves and a garbage of shells. All at once, old and lonely, I eyed these – razor clams, fairy boats . . . On this day, the awful birthday of otherness, my rival, somebody else. I flung the starfish against a stone. Let it perish. It had no wit. (Newman, C., 1970, pp. 268–9)

Never again will we hear a more truth-wrenching account of the feelings of a small child when the mother-as-part-of-me is ripped away prematurely for the needs of that child. From one minute to the next this small passenger of fairy boats, in which she sailed with her mother, had been designated 'garbage' in her own experience. The starfish here is herself: her good, trusting baby-self. Never again would she make her needs known to anyone at their very deepest level. To be dependent on another henceforth meant to 'have no wit'.

In the light of this catastrophe, the terrible events at Smiths' become more comprehensible. We can now understand why she had to hide her terror of 'not being up to it'. Why her feelings of despair, of being 'that suicidal girl', had all to be projected and got rid of, in that manner. Mother only existed while she was a part-of-me. Once the rupture had occurred, there were only razor clams: clamming up and self-destruction, unless she could reach out for help. But only a small part of her could contemplate such a thought, because it implied a need. When she was finally found dead, the phone number of her doctor was found close to where she lay – beyond all human help by then.

If that was Sylvia's predicament, her mother's inability to talk openly and freely about her own anxieties, her need to sweep them under the carpet, compounded the dreadful stalemate: 'Both Sylvia and I were more at ease in WRITING words of appreciation, admiration and love than in expressing these emotions verbally' (Plath, A.S., 1976, p. 32). Each was locked up in herself. Yet neither was to blame. Many children, after all, manage to recover from the birth of another baby, even if it is a shock. Many mothers may, perhaps, more instinctively pick up the catastrophic psychic pain and be more able to contain it, offering that 'garbage' child a gradual passage back to a capacity to trust that all, in fact, is not lost. That not being the only one is not the equivalent of being a total reject. But Sylvia would 'hug' her grudge. Never was truer word spoken. She would not forgive her mother, but instead would make her pay, at an unconscious level.

After this catastrophe of the birth of her brother Sylvia doubtless turned for comfort to her father. We hear her plangent expectations clearly in the 'ach Du' in the poem called 'Daddy' and then her plangent disappointment that this substitute could offer no warm body-language but only 'Luftwaffe Gobbledygoo' of a proper 'Panzerman' (Plath, S., 1965, p. 54).

This is not the place to dwell on her relationship to her father, although it also played a part in her self-destructive drives. What must concern us here is the vacuous relationship between the mother and her daughter. Sylvia needed urgently that Aurelia should understand:

'Don't talk to me about the world needing cheerful stuff! What the person out of Belsen – physical or psychological – wants is nobody saying the birdies still go tweet-tweet, but the full knowledge that somebody else has been there before and knows the WORST, just what it is like. (Plath, A.S., 1976, p. 473)

Sylvia is up in arms and lashes out at her mother. By the time she wrote these lines she had four more months to live. But she must have sensed unconsciously, since her student years at Smith, that her survival would depend on her mother's capacity to respond to her danger signals as they shriek between the lines of almost everything she wrote. Her writing *was* a plea for help: throw a lifeline around me, mother, tie it to your very being through the troubled years ahead. Who if not you will help me make an enduring bid for life, seeing that the urge to die is so hard on my trail? Talk to me about death, about a lifetime spent in Belsen, mother, as your garbage daughter, since you chose to have a son. At an unconscious level Sylvia Plath, the poet, sensed that no amount of acclaim from the wider world out there would make her feel that her mother really loved and valued her at the core of her naked being. That she would ever come to terms with that murderously angry and very frightened little girl whose only hope for survival was that she could start again. That she could become the baby whose growth and simple happiness was her mother's only wish. Then she could at last break free of those grandiose expectations which had thrust her life off course from its own joyful sense of being and trashed it into counterfeit.

Whether Aurelia Plath needed a genius of a daughter as urgently as that daughter intuited that she did, driven as she clearly was by her self-expectations and mountainous omnipotence, is not entirely certain. What is very much clearer is that she could not afford to contemplate the dereliction, the despair that constituted Sylvia's state of mind between her hypomanic phases, at any conscious level. Here the signals were denied and typically described as her 'natural buoyancy'.

For any mother to keep vigil with a daughter hovering in such outposts of extremis asks for more than fortitude of the will and intention, which Aurelia did not lack. It demands an inner security, its tolerance for anxiety and the ability to carry feelings of substantial guilt. These are the attributes which, through no fault of her own, Aurelia did not possess. And so this mother had no choice but to keep backing off from this life-and-death struggle with its reverberating signals, which disavowal Sylvia, who so urgently needed a good container, could simply not tolerate since in her perilous condition she read this incapacity as a brutal rejection.

Sylvia's deep anxieties that she had damaged her mother emerge in *Letters Home*. We notice them in her relief when her mother is 'fat' – in other words, well and healthy – or accomplishes new feats like passing her driving test. We hear them in the euphoric plans for her mother's visit to Cambridge, which, if we look between the lines of magical expectations, are an omnipotent attempt to put the pieces back together. For months before this event Sylvia reiterates, in the most terrifying detail, lists of treats she has in store, which are intended to accomplish this feat of manic reparation. To read them makes us sick and dizzy: not, seemingly, Aurelia. As far as we can assess, in the absence of her replies to this veritable deluge – several letters every week – Aurelia herself colluded in this frenetic make-believe. She proudly tells us that her famous daughter went through three typewriters!

Nevertheless, the bubble holds – holds until Aurelia's visit to the Hughes in Devon, in summer 1962. Then she recognizes that the marriage is in dire trouble, since Ted 'had been seeing someone else' (Plath, A.S., 1976, p. 457). Even the most golden daughter can have a marital crisis. Aurelia tells us that she herself moved in with the local midwife for the last part of her visit. Probably she needed to deny the whole catastrophe, even if the implication is a wish to be tactful. But we can see between the lines that in Sylvia's inner world the long-simmering paranoia, at the heart of which 'the terrible', the life-denying, death-dealing mother has her being, is coming into the ascendancy with a dreadful inevitability, just as the Archetype has often been described by Jung.

There had been previous glimpses during Sylvia's earlier breakdown in 1953, as recounted in *The Bell Jar*. Here is Esther coming round in the mental hospital, having been dragged from the cellar, by a hair's breadth still alive:

'Somebody to see you.' The nurse beamed and disappeared. My mother came smiling round the foot of the bed. She was wearing a dress with purple cartwheels on it and looked awful . . . Her face puckered up and quivered like pale jelly . . . (Plath, S., 1963, p. 182)

The mother here is clearly a very disappointed woman, who as far as Sylvia is concerned is still turning cartwheels of denial. In her drugged, befuddled state, Sylvia vividly perceives, purple with a dreadful rage, that this woman's main response is of a cheated mother. The golden genius of a daughter is seen to lie cracked and broken, like the mirror which the girl has just smashed, at her feet. The narcissistic investment, with its hollow, grandiose stakes, has all the gilt-edge rubbed off to reveal the bankruptcy of a darkening depression. Now, in the dynamics of this dangerous seesaw game of the symbiotic tangle, it is the mother who lies curled up, forsaken, in the cellar, a foetus fighting for her life, struggling to regain some shape from the quivering protoplasm to which she has been reduced by the golden daughter's breakdown, as Sylvia can recognize from personal experience, when she speaks of 'quivering jelly'.

The hatred which she feels for her mother, for always letting her down at the level of her infant needs for perfect, life-giving containment, erupts with startling ferocity in that story of the roses:

That afternoon my mother brought me the roses. 'Save them for my funeral', I'd said. My mother's face puckered, and she looked ready to cry. 'But Esther, don't you remember what day it is today?' 'No.' I thought it might be Saint Valentine's day. 'It's your birthday.' And that was when I dumped the roses in the waste-basket. 'That was a silly thing for her to do', I said to Dr Nolan ... 'I hate her', I said and waited for the blow to fall. But Dr Nolan only smiled at me as if something had pleased her very much and said, 'I suppose you do.' (Plath, S., 1963, p. 215)

Sylvia senses poignantly that this mother feels no cause to celebrate her daughter's birthday now, that in truth she feels bereaved of her glittering expectations: her narcissistic supplies. If it were St Valentine's Day she would be celebrating the rapturous festival that her child is still alive against such overwhelming odds. There would be a feast of love. The birth of a new beginning. All the rest is a façade which Sylvia knows will seal her fate. For she knows in her unconscious that in order to survive, there in the outer world, she has first to have a taste – which she lacked as a newborn infant – of surviving in her mother's mind, provided it could offer her some depth, the dimensions of a true container for her anxieties, instead of the narcissistic shallows which would burst into the rapids carrying her towards her death.

At this moment of crisis she is maddeningly aware that this reprieve will never happen if her mother fails to read the signals that death is hovering over her. 'Keep them for my funeral.' These words shake us to the core. We know that at this very moment a future bid for suicide has become reality. Aurelia has been informed. Coldly and sadistically the truth has been spelt out to her in symbiotic metalanguage.

Dr Nolan clearly saw that there might be some hope for Sylvia, if only she could keep in touch with the hatred for her mother which has briefly broken through when, under the stress of the visit, those feelings had for once escaped, like steam from a pressure cooker. Did she, we would like to know, suggest an analysis? For in the therapeutic setting such hatred could have been contained, slowly confronted and worked through. But it is highly doubtful that this symbiotic tangle was ripe, as yet, for the admission that any third and healing party needed to intervene as a life-saving measure, nor would it ever reach that stage before the gates of time slammed shut. For Mrs Plath such a course would have been too threatening: an admission of her 'failure' in her insecurity.

It is not irrelevant that in the United States, buzzing with talk of 'shrinks', of psychoanalysis, at both a flippant and a serious level, the very possibility of applying for such help is not pursued in this detailed commentary from its sunniest beginning to its bleak and darkest end. What an act of heroism is required from a mother to acknowledge that she is up against the frontiers of her own impotence and needs to go in search of help for her daughter from a stranger – who, she dreads in her heart of hearts, may steal and turn her child against her into one who is free to live her life as she will; in other words, to break free of the symbiotic trap.

As the brewing inner weathers of her paranoia deepened, Sylvia could still fool the world. Three weeks before she killed herself, she completely took in a family friend, Patty Goodall, who reported back to the States about 'the bright smile and eager American expression that greeted us as Sylvia opened the door', and how they 'NEVER STOPPED TALKING' (Plath, A.S., 1976, pp. 496–7). This good news was sent off on 19 January, to reassure Aurelia. On 4 February Sylvia sat down to write her last and final letter home:

Dear Mother, Thanks so much for your letters. I got a sweet letter from Dotty . . . I got a sweet letter from the Nortons and an absolutely wonderful, understanding one from Betty Aldrich . . . I have absolutely no desire ever to return to America . . . I have a beautiful country home, the car, and London is the only city of the world I'd like to live in with its fine doctors, nice neighbours, parks, theatres and the BBC . . . (Plath, A.S., 1976, p. 498)

Here we have hurled at us, in the Morse code of despair, in an avalanche of fury, the split between an idealized and a terrible mother. The latter comes under fierce attack, equated with America. London, Dotty and Betty are currently idealized: the other must be held at bay, far across the Atlantic.

Sylvia no longer needs a mother. She is saying, in effect, I have my own mother-land in my beautiful country home. I have my own drive, my car, and I have the BBC to spread my fame across the earth, where you can not appropriate it. But Sylvia was not psychotic, even if hovering on the brink of a lapse into mania or a total depression. Somewhere she was still in touch with her dependency needs, in which our sanity is rooted. For the last paragraph reads: 'I am going to start seeing a woman doctor, free on the National Health, to whom I've been referred by my very good local doctor, which should help me weather this difficult time' (Plath, A.S., 1976, p. 500).

A decade had elapsed since she mooted at Smith that it might be an idea to seek psychiatric help. At the time, her omnipotence and the omnipotence of her mother, had colluded to make that essential quest fruitless. For then they were still looking for quick and magical solutions, in keeping with their deeper needs: to produce a genius. ECT and insulin had been on offer on that trail. It is tragic to contemplate that when Sylvia Plath died, that trail had petered out on her. As a woman and a mother, she had now begun to come into open conflict with the acrobatics of the poet, and come close to the admission that she needed real help: that she must now invite another on the raft that was her life, if she was to make the shore because her babies needed her.

In that last letter home Sylvia coldly undercut, presumably, her mother's wishes to appear in a new role of a wonderful granny. It would seem that to those ends the three-year-old was to be shipped over to America:

I appreciate your desire to see Frieda, but if you can imagine the emotional upset she has been through in losing her father and moving, you will see what an incredible idea it is to take her away by jet to America. I am her one security and to uproot her would be thoughtless and cruel, however sweetly you treated her at the other end. (Plath, A.S., 1976, p. 498)

Sylvia, here, is much closer than ever before in her life to sorting out her priorities, and it is her motherhood that is springing into gear. 'No, you will not do to Frieda, mother, what you did to me', to satisfy your narcissism, to build up your self-esteem. 'Now,' she says, I have 'nice neighbours', who may take me as I am, rather desperate and confused, unlike yours, who want a show. The neighbours clearly represent not only the outer ones but also aspects of herself, parts of her personality which are beginning to accept that she does not have to be the world's greatest masterpiece: that she can feel small and frightened as a woman and as a mother.

But this heartening resolution of the relentless conflict between Sylvia Plath, the mother, who still put milk out for her children before she took her life, and Sivvy, mother's genius daughter, in favour of her maternal role and responsibilities, stepped into the arena just a little bit too late. On 11 February 1963, on a bitter icy morning, in the coldest of winters Londoners had known for years, almost within memory, Sylvia Plath was found dead in the kitchen of the house

— 255 —

Yeats had once occupied.

The conflict which we have witnessed here between the woman as a poet and that same woman as a mother is bound to be exacerbated by the interpersonal dynamics of the mother–daughter dyad for reasons we are coming to. At the intrapersonal level, where we had already met it earlier, in the Renaissance, it is illuminated by Plath's poem which appeared in the *Observer*, by some fateful irony, six days after her death, under the title 'The Fearful':

> *The thought of a baby*
> *Stealer of cells, stealer of beauty.*
> *She would rather be dead than fat . . .*
> (*Observer*, 17 February 1963)

Taken on its own merits, the intrapersonal conflict here focuses on a 'beauty' which is not physical. These cells that her babies steal with tragic inevitability are the units which build poems: the protoplasm of inspiration: a theft all too familiar to every creative woman who is 'fat' with actual babies as with those which are still unborn. But the destruction of beauty on that symbolic level reawakens painful echoes of a destruction in reality, heavily loaded in phantasy, of oedipal anxieties. Here every daughter is in fact – as in rivalrous intent – a stealer of her mother's beauty. And what is more, because the mother has herself been a daughter, she knows what it is all about: 'mirror, mirror on the wall' . . . which one shall be the sexual woman, which one shall reign as queen?

As long as Sylvia sees herself primarily as a poet, as long as she does not own her biological maternity at a fully conscious level, the rivalry can be denied; mother and daughter can each be 'queen' in an entirely different realm. But once the poet comes down to earth to take full responsibility for her actual motherhood, to 'queen it' in both destinies, in that case she has 'won', she has stolen the beauty which the mother once owned to leave her old and disempowered. She now bears anxieties of psychotic proportions which may well tip the balance in favour of suicide, as they ring loud and clear in an earlier poem:

What am I buying, wormy mahogany?
Is there any queen at all in it?

If there is, she is old,
Her wings torn shawls, her long body
Rubbed of its plush –

Poor and bare and unqueenly and even shameful.
I stand in a column

Of winged, unmiraculous women,
Honey-drudgers.
I am no drudge
Though for years I have eaten dust
And dried plates with my dense hair.
And seen my strangeness evaporate,
Blue dew from dangerous skin.
Will they hate me,
These women who only scurry . . .
(Plath, S., 1965, pp. 66–7)

If, at a phantastic level, the mother is experienced as ousted, in 'torn shawls', her body 'rubbed of its plush', then the mahogany is 'wormy' at a deeper level where inner reality is acknowledged. For a daughter needs to be on loving terms with her mother to build a true, creative life on a good, hard foundation: hard as sound mahogany.

But here the relationship, for all its surface gloss and glitter, was not a truly loving one. Oedipal anxieties that she had damaged her mother, who would retaliate and attack her creativity, had, as so often in these cases, caused Sylvia to flee to the other side of the Atlantic to establish her creative life at what she saw as a safe distance from the envious, 'bad' queen.

Bees are a link to the oedipal father. For an eternity of years, as an oedipal daughter, the girl 'dried plates', she was the skivvy, she was the honeydrudger who 'ate dust' in that hive where Aurelia, where her mother, was the queen. It was a hopeless situation. In fear she held her talent back and felt compelled to rein it in, in its freest expression. That would find its voice only once she had found a husband who would, in phantasy, protect her from an attacking, envious mother.

In writing on the basis of such wild anxieties she was using her gifts to secure a manic triumph that would cast the mother out. But the writing of her poetry kept Sylvia Plath in touch with inner reality. A part of her, a saner part, was able to recognize that the use of her great talent like 'a box of maniacs' to triumph over her mother, could lead only to doom: to psychosis in the end:

> *I have simply ordered a box of maniacs.*
> *They can be sent back.*
> *They can die, I need feed them nothing, I am the owner.*
> (Plath, S., 1965, p. 63)

In these lines we find the reason why so much creative talent in women is aborted. The terror is that it will be used to murderous advantage in the oedipal wars. Here, I believe, lies a deeper reason why women, since they are daughters, historically underachieve in comparison to men. Powerful as the boy's castration anxiety will be, it remains confined more closely to the purely sexual drive and therefore spills over less, in the realm of phantasy, into the wider creative sphere. What for him is but an act, at an instinctual level, represents for the girl an overture to motherhood – to procreativity which she cannot distinguish, at a symbolic level, from alternative forms of creative expression. These will for that reason fall under the inhibition of her castration anxieties to a more perilous extent.

In the case of Sylvia Plath her talent was too considerable to let itself be suppressed. Mother and poet in her were compelled to fight it out. Her life-task demanded this, and given help she might have won and integrated the two drives so that they could ultimately coexist in harmonious balance. But to win against her mother, against that cold perfectionist, as she had internalized her, was a very tall order:

> *Perfection is terrible, it cannot have children.*
> *Cold as snow breath, it tamps the womb . . .*
> (Plath, S., 1965, p. 74)

Between them mother and daughter had set up and pursued, each for reasons of her own, this quest for genius and perfection. It drove the mother in Plath, as she struggled to emerge with a saner set of values, back again and again into the arms of the poet and thus the wild manic triumph. Should she send 'the maniacs . . . back', or would they have to win the day, as it turned into the night of death on this terrible note in one of her final poems:

... but I
Have a self to recover, a queen.
Is she dead, is she sleeping?
Where has she been,
With her lion-red body, her wings of glass?

Now she is flying
More terrible than ever she was, red
Scar in the sky, red comet
Over the engine that killed her –
The mausoleum, the wax house.
(Plath, S., 1965, p. 67)

We shall presently see that this intrapersonal fight between two creative drives that inhabit every woman does not have to mobilize oedipal pathology – that the battle can rage *with* maternal support and loving understanding, which may prove to be the hallmark of that relationship in our present day and age, which we are now approaching. But before we come to that, a final case-history sets out the life-destroying conflict between mother and daughter, with its eventual resolution, so convincingly that it demands to be included. So let us now leave Sylvia Path for a cul-de-sac in Paris, for an epic of resolution, not so very long ago. 'Doctor, I have been ill for a long time. I ran away from a private sanatorium to come and see you. I can't go on living this way' (Cardinal, M., 1984, p. 10).

Already for several years, since the age of twenty-seven, the patient's menstrual blood has flowed almost continuously, draining her life away. Endless emergencies. But the symptom has defeated every gynaecologist. They have consistently advised: a hysterectomy, Madame. Her children are with her mother who is bitterly resentful. Her husband has accepted work, far away, in America. He visits only for short periods at lengthy intervals. 'The Thing' cannot be discussed. And yet Marie Cardinal's life revolves around her symptom, which has a life of its own. Days are spent on the bidet, or curled up on the bathroom floor.

The doctor listens carefully. He gives each word his full attention. The analysis shall start on the following day. Both are fully aware that the alternative is madness or suicide.

All night long the blood has flowed and dripped on to the floor, but her analyst insisted that she stop all medication as from this hour on.

At the appointed hour she arrives for her first session swaddled in cotton wool like a baby's diapers. 'Doctor, I am bled dry,' the patient opens her first session. She can hardly wait to get the five words out. 'Those are psychosomatic disorders. That doesn't interest me. Speak about something else' (Cardinal, M., 1984, p. 3).

With this slap in the face, with this assault on a myth – or rather on its dressings – the bleeding goes away and stops. 'The Thing' itself, the actual madness, has finally to be confronted. A woman who has so far lived as a stranger to herself, to the circumstances of her life, to the roots of her being, sets out on the long, hard journey to discover who she is, how she came to be that woman and how to face the light of day reassembled and intact, freed from insanity.

True, she has harboured inklings:

I knew I suffered from the divorce of my parents, who fought over me until my father's death. I knew that my mother unconsciously resented my birth. (I was born in the middle of their divorce proceedings.) . . . I thought I knew all about them . . . (Cardinal, M., 1984, p. 38)

She knew, yet she did not know. The pain, the humiliation, the concise manipulation by her insidious mother, with her beautiful green eyes, red-chestnut hair and tapering hands, who had subverted Marie's birthright, to grow up to be herself, throughout her childhood years – none of this had she yet suffered, in any detailed, conscious sense, when her analysis began. The agony, the deeper rages, of having been her mother's poodle, taught to jump through endless hoops in the hope of being loved: if not today, then tomorrow; if not this month, then the next; if not this year, then the next year; had all still to be unpicked, layer by layer, tuck by tuck, hem by hem, stitch by stich; all the delicate, fine sewing, a whole lifetime of defences, had now to be undone, first gingerly and gently, carefully, in mounting fear, hardly knowing what she did, and finally ripped apart in an orgy of excitement in which hope and terror mingled. Burning with hope to go free, there was the dread that she might fail and spend the rest of her sweet days in some pitch-black asylum.

The Algerian servants gazed upon her mother as a martyr. A delicate, refined lady whose own mother had come from the old country, to drain Algeria's salt marshes so that French wine might grow, be harvested and flow to riches, her days were spent among the poor, ministering like an angel. Her first-born daughter had died of tubercular meningitis. Her husband had tuberculosis, of which he later died when Marie was still a girl. Her next child, a son, was frail. His life was constantly threatened by the devouring malady. BCG immunization had been discovered just in time to ensure Marie's survival. Her mother was not interested in a lifeful, healthy child. Only when Marie was sick with one or other childish ailment could she all too briefly be the subject of those attentions for which she envied the poor, as a starving onlooker. Caught up in a cult of death, in ceremonial for the dying, in which the Catholic Church excelled, all her mother's emotions were, like a nest of vipers, entangled with that other daughter lost to her in infancy, a pure and innocent angel, white enough to idealize. Lost, she claimed, because her husband, when he returned from war to declare his love and sweep her off her feet, had not come clean, had not confessed that death lurked in every breath that the soldier exhaled. So she accused the death in him, in the ruffian, in the male, and turned her white back on Marie, the one who lived, who had survived.

Throughout Marie's childhood years she was the receptacle for her mother's lamentations for the child she had lost; these she poured over the longings of the daughter who survived: 'Ah! you don't have any idea, you didn't know her. She was an extraordinary child' (Cardinal, M., 1984, p. 93). 'Mama, you mustn't hurt yourself.' Marie's young years were devastated by a child's expenditure of everything she had to offer to 'take the weight off her' (Cardinal, M., 1984, p. 93).

How was this to be accomplished? At night she would steal out of bed and watch her mother, drinking wine, in her saintly solitude: 'I wanted to be the wine, to do her some good, to make her happy, to attract her attention. I promised myself that I would find her a treasure' (Cardinal, M., 1984, p. 55). To that end the little girl would scratch Algeria's red earth until her fingers bled for diamonds, emeralds or rubies. 'What a surprise she would have! Her face would relax, she would kiss me, she would love me' (Cardinal, M., 1984, p. 55).

How was that little girl possibly to discover that this day would never come? Obediently she would pay hated visits to her father to ask 'for the envelope', the weekly alimony that was such a drop in the ocean of all the expenditure for which she only was to blame. She was a drag on her mother. She was bleeding her dry. No opportunity was lost to make the small Marie aware of how, from the beginning, she incommoded her poor mother: that angel of righteousness, the saviour of Algeria's poor. Madame, who never spared herself, but delicate and beautiful, walked the pestilent streets of this abhorrent colony, which none the less was their home, which offered such rich recompense with its flowers and its sun, its beaches bathed by a warm sea, and its endowment of red virgin soil which yielded such ample harvests of all they planted there and sowed.

How that feverish Marie idealized that glowing icon. How she adored her mother. 'Look here, your daughter has grown some more. I can't buy her clothes on what you give me. She needs a coat, a skirt, two sweaters ...' (Cardinal, M., 1984, p. 92), so she heard the angel-mother on the weekly telephone wrangle with the consumptive father. 'At times like these in adolescence I began to think of suicide' (Cardinal, M., 1984, p. 93).

At night she would hear her mother lamenting her sister's loss: 'Ah, my God, my God'. She was so terribly devout. Then 'I knew she was on her bed, unwrapping the relics of my dead sister: slippers, locks of hair, and baby clothes. Nanny would then behave as though she were in church. She would cross herself, mumble prayers, her eyes suffused with tears' (Cardinal, M., 1984, p. 71).

Nanny's loyalties were split. Yes, she worshipped Madame. She thought that she was 'stern but just' even when she made the child eat her vomited soup, for she brooked no defiance. But she also loved the child with her whole Spanish passion. 'She covered me with kisses and cradled me, murmuring "*madre mia*" or "*probrecita*" and "*ay, que guapa!*" ' (Cardinal, M., 1984, p. 70). With this time-old adoration, a birthright due to every child, she instilled a buried core of self-belief in her heart. As luck had it, it sufficed to lay at least the rudiments of that essential foundation on which the analysis could build the slow ascent back to life, to the world of the living. So the simple Spanish nanny, under the Algerian sun, planted those seeds of hope which permitted the escape from the death-trap sanatorium to the cul-de-sac in Paris, many years afterwards; when Algeria was no longer 'home' for the fervent French who had insisted that she was the child of their procreation and therefore owed them gratitude, owed them childlike submission, however much she was exploited. Had not Marie herself been colonized in this manner? Did she not have to go to war, to mount an entire uprising, so she might finally go free?

But there is worse to come. As the patient grows stronger, as the analysand becomes conversant with psychic pain, to carry her memories like a precious burden which will one day set her free, we have to eavesdrop with her ears on this efflux from her mother:

'To find myself pregnant in the middle of the divorce! Do you realize what that means? I wanted to leave a man whose child I was going to bear! . . . There exist evil women and evil doctors who can do away with a baby in a woman's womb . . .'

But this, of course, the church forbade. This was a mortal sin!

'I went to find my bicycle . . . Nothing. I rode horseback for hours: jumping, trotting. Nothing happened. Believe me . . . I swallowed quinine and aspirin by the bottle. Nothing.' There on the street, in a few sentences, she put out my eyes, pierced my eardrums, scalped me, cut off my hands, shattered my kneecaps, tortured my stomach, and mutilated my genitals. *(Cardinal, M., 1984, p. 102)*

With a final thrust of the spade, the patient had disinterred the bid for her infanticide!

Marie Cardinal's mother was twenty-seven at the time when she toiled for that abortion. When Marie was twenty-seven, her symptom took hold. She would at last oblige her mother and do away with herself. She would finally submit and accomplish that abortion which she ought to have done, twenty-seven years ago, as a dutiful daughter: as one who really loved Mama.

Slowly, slowly, week by week, month by month and year by year, in the little cul-de-sac, the fragments are pieced together with the glue of psychic pain which was previously buried. The tormented little girl had been unable to endure it while she was at the mercy, as a helpless dependant, of the one who dealt her death in a thousand subtle ways. And there had been no appeal. To the Algerian entourage, the chauffeur, cook and to Nanny, to each and all who worked the land, to the poor and the beggars, as they showed their sores and stumps and chanted '*Ya Ma! Ya ratra moulana . . .*', this lady from the old country was their bread and butter, their veritable eucharist. They were her children, in that sense. Hysteric, sick as she was, she represented the adult in the colonial hierarchy, until the 'communists' arrived and she was driven out, back to France and to Paris, to be revealed as a fraud along with her entire class who had shared those pretensions.

In the crass reality of that northern land, the madness lost its hiding place both in mother and in daughter. Here, where she could tend no poor, not be worshipped as a martyr – where she could no longer bring flowers to her dead child's grave, while the other looked on and had to fetch and carry water until her arms and fingers ached, instead of her childish heart – her days would soon be numbered; cut off by the death which she had always harboured, like some secret poison; while her daughter's fight for air, for life and sanity, for her very *raison d'être*, was but newly joined at the gates of annihilation: the cards the child had been dealt from such a wicked pack.

As Marie grew stronger, she not only found peace of mind but discovered, very shyly, her endowment as a writer. Surprised, her husband recognized a healthy and courageous woman; one with whom he could rebuild an entirely new life, when he had almost lost hope. But once Marie would no longer be a vehicle for death, once she refused to carry her mother's insanity, when at last she developed a healthy egotism and determined to oppose her mother's regressive wishes to be taken in and nursed within her new-found family, the lifelong madness in the mother finally stood displayed: she had become an alcoholic.

She – who had always been the queen of a necropolis, whose taste for death and decay flourished in her love of tombs, her preference for the dead over those who were living, as she murmured to her dead child: 'I am going to make you a beautiful tomb, darling, it will be the most beautiful one of all . . . my little darling, my tiny girl, my love, my poor child', while the other went hungry – she was finally exposed in all her exquisite horror a few days before she died. (Cardinal, M., 1984, p. 143)

I always knew deep down that my mother was ill and, at the centre of the big ball of my love for her, there was a hard core made up of fear of her and of contempt tempered by pride. (p. 147)

But we are not quite at the end. The analysand recognizes that she still is not free. The stone, she knows, has been rolled from the mouth of her tomb, but a sense of nausea, of some distress, still 'unnerves' her. Marie reflects on a tree perceived in the shapes of bushes, found only in a dry and arid region of Brazil known as the Serato:

When one tries to uproot them, one discovers their roots . . . communicate with neighbouring bushes and that they converge in one thick stem that descends even farther while thickening, making its way finally as an enormous single trunk which bores into the earth like a sharp instrument. One understands that it is in fact an enormous tree which has buried itself twenty or thirty yards below the surface in order to find water. I was one of those bushes. But deprived of the trunk which drew the water from the depths, I was going to die. (Cardinal, M., 1984, p. 123)

Flawlessly she exposes every daughter's dilemma once she seeks to free herself from the tendrils of her mother. Could there be a solution? Not until this childhood phantom can be read as a person. Not until she has a name, beyond the epitaph of 'mother', which is hers and hers alone. As Marie had to listen to her mother's interview with the doctor now in charge of her case, this very revelation broke:

In this Parisian doctor's office, I met for the first time, Solange de Talbiac . . . called 'Soso' by her friends. 'Soso' in the sun, 'Soso' in the shade . . . 'Soso' in the garden of her parents . . . 'Soso' with unsuspected desire in her belly for the man coming towards her, the handsome Frenchman who smelled of adventure . . . The emotion was choking me. I found her so touching, so naive and so despondent: it was too late. (Cardinal, M., 1984, p. 207)

The doctor is reassuring. Matters can be set right. But Marie knows different. Her intuition had read this rambling confession as her mother's dying one. The next day finds Soso dead. But the hatred and disgust, the smell of death of a lifetime, still linger in her daughter's nostrils, still cloud her unconscious mind during the ensuing months, while the analysis continues.

Then, one day in early spring, Marie Cardinal is drawn, by some magnetic force, to her mother's cemetery, where her grandmother was buried not so very long ago. The gate squeaks on its hinges. She sits down on the greyish slab. She embarks on a soliloquy and finds that her finger is drawing s's in the sand. She can hear herself recall the gift of certain precious moments shared between the small Marie and her beautiful mother, brief and fleeting though they were, those audiences granted her by Soso. At last she lifts her inner eye, full of admiration:

Soso, how beautiful you were on the night of the ball, when you came into my room to show me your dress. I was already in bed. You dazzled me. I have never seen you more beautiful than on that night . . . you spun around to make the fullness of the skirt flare out. You laughed.

I love you. Yes, that's right, I love you. I came here to declare it to you, once and for all. I am not ashamed to speak of it. It does me good to say it to you and to repeat it! I love you. I love you. (Cardinal, M., 1984, p. 210)

We are nearing the end:

How good it was finally to love her in the light, in the springtime, in the open, after the terrible battle from which we were delivered. Two blind people armed to the teeth, claws exposed, in the arena of our class. What blows she had struck me, what venom I had distilled! What savagery, what butchery! (Cardinal, M., 1984, p. 211)

Did Marie Cardinal live happily ever after, we are entitled to ask? On the following day, and in the final chapter, the former patient comes to say goodbye to her analyst.

'Doctor, I am going to settle our accounts. I will not be coming here any more. I feel able to live alone now. I feel strong. My mother transmitted the Thing to me, you have transmitted the analysis, they are in perfect balance, I thank you for it . . .' The door closes behind me. In front of me, the cul-de-sac, the city, the country, and an appetite for life and for building as big as the earth itself. (Cardinal, M., 1984, p. 212)

In the Afterword Bruno Bettelheim reflects on 'the power . . . of a mother who harboured conscious and unconscious death-wishes against a child . . .' (Cardinal, M., 1984, p. 220). It is by no means uncommon, for a multitude of reasons. In the case of Soso it was a loathing of her husband; that this new life, which grew within her, renewed her ties to a man whom she wanted to be rid of. At other times the entire package of marriage and domesticity is experienced as a trap that closes when a child is born. There are, we find, as many reasons as there are mother–infant dyads. 'The mother, however, hates her infant from the word go.' Surprisingly, at first sight, this is Winnicott speaking; as he then goes on to say: 'Let me give some reasons why a mother hates her baby, even a boy' (Winnicott, D.W., 1975, p. 201). There follows a long list of reasons. Let me take a few examples:

The baby is a danger to her body in pregnancy and at birth.

The baby is not magically produced.

The baby hurts her nipples . . .

To a greater or lesser extent a mother feels that her own mother demands a baby, so that her baby is produced to placate her mother.

It is a formidable list, and then leads on to this comment: 'The most remarkable thing about a mother is her ability to be hurt so much by her baby and to hate so much *without paying the child out . . .*' (Winnicott, D.W., 1975, p. 202, my italics). The importance of this afterthought cannot be overestimated! For here is the dividing line between mental health and sickness: the frontier we must recognize and remain quite clear about.

The psychopathology at which we have looked in this part, has, of course, only illustrated certain universal issues. Variations on the themes of envy and symbiosis, of death-wishes and power-struggles, oedipal and pre-oedipal, in countless human circumstances, different epochs and cultures are as legion as grains of sand in the desert, on the beaches, but equally are components of much rich and fertile soil: is sand not used in potting compost? We paused to look at this wastage in mother–daughter life, because it had to be acknowledged, as a kingpin to our theme, that there are crucial *inner* stalemates, rooted in that relationship, which prevent our going forward, as we must and as we will!

It can, of course, be argued that the malaise which afflicts the dyad is, in truth, generated by male chauvinistic attitudes as they colour every aspect of human society. That if women could enjoy equal opportunities, in the very fullest meaning, psychopathology would abate. That favourable circumstances have a beneficial effect on human relationships, that generous provisions and wide social support prove facilitating factors in every single respect, is common knowledge in our time. That a good and warm rapport, esteem and mutuality across the difference of the sexes has become our end in view can no longer be in doubt. But that Winnicott's inventory of why mothers hate their babies will undergo intrinsic change is open to serious question. Do they hate their daughters more? is the question which concerns us. I find no evidence that they do, at the very deepest level. The contrary may be the case and does not lack confirmation in Karen Payne's anthology.

Paying a baby back, a daughter for our purposes, is a phenomenon of sickness. Had mothers paid their daughters back consistently, through the ages, for all the indignities which women have endured, all women might by now be mad. In so far as mental illness strikes more readily at women, as superficial telling goes, this can surely be ascribed to the specific nature of their vulnerability as being doomed to be conflicted to a perilous degree by the nature of their complex drives: their urge for multiple fulfilment given the implications of their biological destiny. But on the other hand the number of healthy, glowing women suggests that a deeper, healing factor to counteract the negatives that we have dwelt on so consistently must be quietly at work. The search for it will be the thesis in the last part of our book. With this chapter we will leave psychopathology which operates in pure culture.

We can assume that it colours the relationship of the dyad in the twentieth century, if to varying degree, much as it has always done. What we now need to examine are the new positives, the new-found strength and optimism, the mutual help and support which many mothers and daughters are discovering in our day, or maybe rediscovering within the technological age. For despite the fragmentation and the tragic heartlessness born of monetarist ideas, mutual help and support, a hopefulness and *jouissance*, always driven underground in epochs of our history, are showing signs of flowering into a belated spring.

Discontent and frustration, anger and injustice will fuel the drive for self-expression, the urge to be articulate, as signposts of growing strength. Self-love, we must not forget, is rooted in self-respect, where these two attributes in harness are the growing soil for wider love seeking new aims and objects, healthier alliances in all our relationships. Yet is it not from the nuances of the prevailing shifts within the mother–daughter dyad that in the last analysis these draw sickness or gain health?

PART V

1 TURBULENT TIMES
A Window on Ambivalence

*The feminist approach accepts, indeed anticipates, that the
mother–daughter relationship is bound to be ambivalent and
problematic and that its legacy is that the daughter (and indeed
the mother herself as a daughter) is unable to separate.*
(SHEILA ERNST AND MARIE MAGUIRE, *Living with the
Sphinx*)

IN 'A CENTURY ON THE COUCH' we saw that ambivalence, feelings
of love and hate directed against a single object, originally the
mother, makes its first appearance roughly in the second half of the
first year of life. This propensity becomes one of the most painful
aspects of our inner life. But in no relationship will it prove as
dominant, with such far-reaching consequences, as in the mother–
daughter dyad.

In their recent book, *Bittersweet*, Susie Orbach and Luise Eichenbaum (1987) set out to explore, on the basis of the ups and downs in
their close, long-lasting friendship, the specific difficulties which are
the universal lot between 'best' women friends:

*How can we understand these two phenomena: the easy, comfortable and cosy
feelings that women can create together and the difficult misunderstandings
which can shatter those feelings? How is it that women feel the preciousness
and importance of each other's support one moment and feel anger, envy and
betrayal at another? What motivates women's desperate need for each other
and their disbelief that they can have the acceptance they so want from one
another? How can we understand the closeness between best friends and the
bitter repudiation of that relationship when there is a falling out? (p. 43)*

In their lucid exposition they take these difficulties back to the girl's relationship, the first and formative one, namely that to her mother. Unlike that of the boy, the closeness of like to like, of replica to replica, will produce a 'merged attachment' between our two protagonists which, they argue, weaves a web of unremitting toil and trouble. Within its claustrum, as we have pointed out ₁at intervals, within the maternal circuit, the daughter learns by osmosis, by mirroring and by example, at the phase-appropriate stages, how to be what mother is and in no way something different. To be different spells dark travail: opposition, even hatred:

In absorbing the emotional imperatives that are to be women's way of being, we learn not only to be giving, intuitive, receptive, caring, empathetic, we learn too that it is ungrammatical to be separate, initiating, autonomous and self-defined. (Orbach, S. and Eichenbaum, L., 1987, p. 46)

The package clearly spells trouble. During interludes of merging both partners will experience a profound satisfaction, an ecstatic sense of love, which will in turn lead to terror of being caught in a trap and angry struggles to break free, on the part of both daughter and mother at times. In psychotherapy we find an overwhelming desire on the part of woman patients to throw themselves, as it were, into the mother-therapist (be it a man or a woman); this impulse will be shortly followed by severe anxiety and a hostile retreat.

Such a state of affairs reflected in the transference, with a faithful repetition of its original taboos on any real separation, must lead to ambivalence in the relationship, which even in the most favourable circumstances is never fully resolved. It flares up time and time again. No sooner have the manifold infantile grievances linked to all the frustrations which were inevitably experienced at the breast been partly modified then the resentments come up that here is a sexual mother whom the daughter has to share with father, as with other babies. When some of this has been worked through to achieve a time of calm during the so-called 'latency period', the turmoil will resume with the approach of adolescence, with its renewal of the struggle for a separate identity. For now the daughter must recognize that her mother will never give her the desired baby, meaning a life of fulfilment; that she must tear herself away from the beloved maternal body and start all over again to seek and find satisfaction out there, in the big, wide world – ultimately, moreover, beside a stranger: a man.

At every one of these stages which the daughter must endure, with hatred and hostility alternating with love, the mother suffers equally. For one thing she has to carry, as often as they will arise, her daughter's hateful projections of a bad and hostile mother – one who could, in phantasy, give her daughter everything from an ever-flowing breast: that missing penis, and a baby: every conceivable satisfaction, which she is felt to withhold. But where the mother operates at that same primitive level, namely of omnipotence, she insists that her daughter remains the 'baby inside' of the months of pregnancy, that thereby she dispels all feelings of the mother's emptiness; or failing that she should at least remain mother's 'little girl' who has no mind of her own, entertains no difference, and takes care of her mother to the latter's dying day without being so selfish as to want a life of her own. According to this deeper 'logic' the roles should become reversed, and the daughter turn mother into a cosseted baby in the days of her old age.

From what we have adumbrated it is very evident that the mother–daughter dyad must inevitably follow something of a stormy course, even if cultural factors will always vary its expression, as they will accentuate or diminish its full impact to a certain degree. If we now go on our way of a historical perspective, we see that where the angry feelings belonging to ambivalence have culturally to be repressed they may then be acted out, as in Clothilde's rebellion (see p. 107 above) or in Edith's wicked conduct when she tramples the veil (see p. 109 above). We know from our consulting rooms that such acting out tends to be resorted to by precarious individuals who split their hostile feelings off and/or deny their existence. Since they thus remain unconscious they can neither be experienced, nor can they be thought about and in that process modified to lead to more rational conduct, a less explosive response. An alternative solution is to turn the anger inwards, directing it against the self in self-destructive impulses. These may be somaticized, turned into 'conversion symptoms' or may, in other instances, lead to madness or to suicide. In the case of Florence Nightingale, as of Harriet Martineau, since the hatred of their mothers could find no open expression and so remained unmodified, both succumbed in the end. Both became paralysed, even if with different symptoms, for fear of acting out their feelings. In their case cultural norms, added to family constellations with an ineffectual father and an unstable mother, compounded a situation which was conducive to severe hypochondriasis as an instrument of self-destruction in two daughters who possessed outstanding talents and resolve.

We meet with ambivalence in the seventeenth century in the case of Margaret, Duchess of Cavendish, born in 1623. Her work as a writer belongs to an age

when children obeyed the command to honour their parents in their choice of epithets to describe them as well as in their deferential behaviour towards them [so that] her remarks necessarily conform to the pattern of conventional praise. (Grant, D., 1957, p. 35)

So Margaret sings her mother's praises: 'she treated her children with the greatest indulgence, denying them nothing that would make them happy . . .' (Grant, D., 1957, p. 36), while two pages earlier we have read of the mother's lamentable failings in the realm of education. Here 'an ancient decayed gentlewoman, kept for the purposes of instruction, could not teach, and her attainment stretched no further than elementary reading and writing' (Grant, D., 1957, p. 34). Notice that she puts the issue in strictly general terms to avoid hostile criticism of the person of her mother. Margaret would remain ashamed and painfully aware of her handicap due to such poor education. She put a brave face on it where her female character remarks: 'I do not repent that I spent not my time in learning, for I consider it better to write wittily than learnedly' (Grant, D., 1957, p. 37). None the less, a deeper truth of simmering humiliation and resentment surfaces in another character in one of her many plays: 'Let me tell you wife, that the reason all women are fools; for women breeding up women, one fool breeding up another . . . and ancient customs being a second nature, makes full hereditary in that sex' (Grant, D., 1957, p. 37).

Margaret struggled to conceal these bruises to her self-esteem with the primitive defences – denial and omnipotence – of manic-depressive illness, garish appearance and flamboyant retinue. It is not without interest that Virginia Woolf remarked:

What a vision of loneliness and riot the thought of Margaret Cavendish brings to mind: as if some giant cucumber had spread itself over all the roses and carnations in the garden and choked them to death . . . The Duchess became a bogey to frighten clever girls with. (quoted in Morgan, F., 1981, p. 66)

Never has manic illness been more brilliantly described than with these razor-sharp perceptions from an author who herself had felt neglected by her mother to a conspicuous degree, only to fall victim to psychotic illness in her turn, albeit of a different nature.

Later in the seventeenth century we meet another woman writer who expresses her ambivalence, largely with her pen. Here, as far as we can judge, the content of her protest is predominantly oedipal. Mary Manley's mother died when she was a little girl and left her daughter brimming with a whole range of resentments which find expression in her tales entitled *Secret Memoirs* (1709). On an island named Atlantis, the goddess Astrea meditates on the sad fate of ruined women, such as one Corinna here:

You will see there a young lady who has long suffered under the barbarous persecution of her mother . . . We find the lady born with an elevated genius . . . her father a chevalier . . . Her mother, a severe, parsimonious lady, allowed her no advantages from education at home . . . so that Corinna bred herself, and took a bent not easily to be straightened. (Goulianos, J., 1973, p. 103)

The oedipal phantasy then takes the following brash turn, as a classic of its kind, still in the same tale. She asks her 'dear Papa' for her fortune of 40,000 crowns, proposing this delightful plan:

'I'll take a little house, two maidservants, a woman, one footman and a coachman and you shall see how distinguishingly I shall live. Resolving never to marry, you will have my house to be easy in, when my mother makes you otherwise at home.' (Goulianos, J., 1973, pp. 104–5)

The tale is not dissimilar to Mary Manley's actual life, in which her relationship to mother-figures was so distorted that it caused her much unhappiness despite considerable success in her career as a writer.

A daughter's hostility directed against her mother and leading to ambivalence will often spring from her experience that maternal intervention, whether overt or covert, is thwarting her potential growth. But whether such intervention is seen as destructive interference which is bound to stunt the ego, or whether, on the contrary, it is ego-syntonic, furthering her life-purposes, as read in the daughter's book, will depend not only on the actual personalities but beyond that to a large degree on wider cultural norms. Let us take two illustrations a century and a half apart:

Suddenly Martha snapped, 'Oh, shut up and get out of here. I've had enough.'. . . Pity filled Martha. She at once remembered her mother's hard and disappointing life; she said to herself that, while she, Martha, was of a generation dedicated above all to self-knowledge, Mrs Quest knew no such obligations. She was appalled at her own cruelty. She said helplessly, 'Oh, damn it all, Mother!' She got up, sat on the arm of Mrs Quest's chair, and put her arm around the collapsed and shrinking shoulders. (Lessing, D., 1985, p. 288)

Before Elizabeth had time for any thing but a blush of surprise, Mrs Bennet instantly answered, 'Oh dear! – Yes – certainly. – I am sure Lizzy will be very happy – I am sure she can have no objection. – Come, Kitty, I want you upstairs . . . No, no nonsense, Lizzy. I desire you will stay where you are . . . Lizzy, I insist upon your staying and hearing Mr Collins.'

Elizabeth would not oppose such an injunction – and a moment's consideration making her also sensible that it would be wisest to get it over with as soon and as quietly as possible, she sat down again, and tried to conceal by incessant employment the feelings which were divided between distress and diversion. (Austen, J., 1986, p. 146)

At an initial reading the issue in both instances concerns maternal interference. Both mothers seek to act as subjects to their daughters as an object. Out in colonial Africa, Mrs Quest has descended, unannounced and uninvited, on her daughter Martha's household, to trample into every area of her life-relationships: her small daughter, her servants, her husband, Douglas Knowle, but above all, by time-old habit, into the sanctity of her relationship to herself. On this occasion too, we hear the mother typically proclaim: 'I want to tell you – it is my duty – I mean to say, everyone is saying you should have another baby' (Lessing, D., 1985, p. 289).

Let us look for a moment at the response of these two daughters, both on and in between the lines. Martha leaves her young husband. She refuses to breed, to produce another baby, in compliance with her mother or the dictates of her husband. Elizabeth, very firmly, turns Mr Collins down. She will, in time, marry Darcy, not because he is wealthy and therefore a better match, as her mother will rejoice, but because he is a man whom she feels 'comfortable' with after lengthy reflection and patient self-scrutiny.

Here we have two instances of a daughter's insubordination: twice the cat among the pigeons! But how differently these daughters respond to their respective mothers, whom they are going to oppose. Martha is frankly hostile and then overcome by guilt. Her hostility is an open secret. From the start her resentment at her mother's refusal to see her as an individual has coloured her entire childhood and will, as we anticipate, subvert her entire life. But unlike Martha Quest's running battles with her mother, which amount at times to full-scale war and bilateral defeat, Elizabeth does not engage in any head-on collisions. She never throws down the gauntlet and she steers clear of confrontation. It seems that ambivalence has not come on the horizon of the relationship in question for a variety of reasons beyond the purely personal, although this clearly plays a part.

'A mother' is certainly a very different entity as the centuries roll by. The Bennets and the Quests inhabit the most disparate of scenes. No century and a half to date has witnessed greater upheavals than the time which intervenes between Jane Austen and Doris Lessing: Elizabeth Bennet and Martha Quest. Industrial megalomania and two successive world wars have swept the stage like hurricanes to leave very little standing of that green and pleasant realm where ownership of the land still promised some divine exemption from a fall into the pit which was fast coming into being in the monstrous shadow of Europe's 'dark Satanic mills'.

Until the twentieth century, to draw a rough-and-ready frontier, the generations of that class conserve a continuum of seemingly delightful ease, even if we know quite well that it is behind the scenes already avidly eroded as money gains the stronger hand, a shrill and more insistent voice. So it was quite natural – inevitable, we might say – that mothers and their daughters would share the same preoccupations: how to keep a good table, purchase fine, becoming cloth, secure the ribbons to match – in other words, to preen and polish appearances in all respects in the interests of preserving a specific *status quo* which guaranteed their survival in a most comfortable manner: the only one they knew. In circumstances such as these, and we are at present concerned mainly with the *outer* ones, there is little case for crossing Mamma's well-meant aberrations. For we can certainly not doubt that Mrs Bennet, interfering as she is in the lives of her daughters, is basically well intentioned.

As long as that bubble held, daughters could remain compliant. They would not reveal resentment, openly and downstairs, in the face of episodes of maternal provocation, since none of these interventions queered their future and their growth as they themselves envisaged them.

But 'If for much recorded history . . . for innumerable generations, daughters have grown up to lead lives very similar to their mothers' (Payne, K., 1984, p. xiv), Martha Quest and her mother belong to two generations which have been flung so far apart in many basic assumptions as to be badly out of step. So great is the discrepancy between their respective ideals and feminine value judgements as to the nature and the goals of any woman's life that no attempts at bridge-building seem very likely to succeed. Already less than a third through Doris Lessing's epic, *Children of Violence* (1972–85), we anticipate a bilateral defeat for this mother–daughter dyad.

How fortunate in this respect are Mrs Bennet and her daughters, for reasons we have just seen. A little diplomacy on the part of Elizabeth will soothe any ruffled waters where disagreements may arise between her mother and herself. Besides, Elizabeth clearly knows all the rules of the game, since it is relatively stable in her own experience, so that mother and daughter are basically on the same side. In this charming small vignette we find that Jane, her favourite sister, has fallen ill at Netherfield, in consequence of Mrs Bennet's perennial machinations as a full-time matchmaker. A trifling consideration that horses were needed on the land would not detract Elizabeth, bent on visiting her sister and habitual confidante:

. . . walking was her only alternative. She declared her resolution. 'How can you be so silly,' cried her mother, 'as to think of such a thing in all this dirt! You will not be fit to be seen when you get there.'

'I shall be very fit to see Jane – which is all I want . . . The distance is only three miles. I shall be back by dinner.' (Austen, J., 1986, p. 78)

There is no reason here for hatred. No place for ambivalence. The disagreement focuses on matters of outer form. Mrs Bennet is not trying to restrict Elizabeth in any fundamental sense. In no way is she subverting such areas of autonomy as the social norms allow. She is not exerting a malevolent influence on her daughter's future life, her possibility for growth, but is merely set on ensuring that the conditions of that future life be as favourable as possible. Whatever little tiffs arise, whatever small cross-purposes briefly cross their common skies, mother and daughter are agreed on a single end in view: that a daughter become a wife, when each will have discharged her duty: the diplomatic ups and downs are mainly dyad-syntonic.

Martha Quest is by no means in such an enviable position. Like her entire era, she is thoroughly at sea. She has neither flares nor compass, and the aims which she senses that her mother has in view with regard to her future have not the slightest relevance to any which she blindly seeks. These are that she must get away to some patch to call her own, if only for a breathing space, if only just to take stock, for the first time in her life, while she senses quite correctly that her mother is intent on moving heaven and earth to subvert any such plan. Any state of affairs which is so thoroughly disjointed, so perversely out of kilter, must evoke hostility in both protagonists – life-thwarting as it is. Here, with the unhappy Quests, we are a million miles removed from that benevolent stasis which the Bennets inhabit. Furthermore, this scene is set against a fragmenting background of Hitler's machinations marching, of an entire era trembling and stricken with uncertainty, sending waves of utter panic quite as far as Africa.

Another safeguard is missing, has been lost by default where the dyad is concerned, since the Bennets held the stage. There is no wider family to shore up the generations. All those maternal sisters, known to a daughter as her aunts, who people the world of Jane Austen, as of George Eliot still, who always tended to contain any element of fracas in the mother–daughter field, as indeed in any other, have simply gone down the drain in that unsettled interim. In such a bleak scenario, mother as much as daughter, Mrs Quest as well as Martha, must each stand her ground alone within a sense of desperation of being lost to one another, where neither is in a position remotely to satisfy the other's inbuilt expectations for mutual comfort and support. Such a state of affairs, in the wider social context, is bound to accentuate grievances and hostilities already rampant in this case.

At the point where we came in, where Martha snapped at her mother, she had at the age of twenty-two finally aroused herself and made an unexpected stand against constant maternal carping on the theme of Caroline, Martha's little girl. 'Well, my dear, I mean to say,' Mrs Quest had commented, 'she's so small for her age, and you let her go into the sun without a hat, and she's always with those black things . . . they're so dirty' (Lessing, D., 1985, p. 288).

Even now, Martha still tries her hand half-heartedly at a little diplomacy, despite its provocative undertones: 'She looks remarkably well on it . . .' But Mrs Quest is relentless in her persecuting style: 'She's very pale and exhausted', strikes the maternal reply. It is precisely at this point that Martha snaps 'I've had enough'. Her mother, who has always subverted her daughter's growth with a strident attack on her capacities, is now also undermining this very sensitive point of Martha's need to believe in her new maternal functions. This is finally the straw that will break the camel's back.

We are in the early 1930s. Even if in Southern Africa the white man's clock is standing still, Martha Quest has picked up signals from the wider world out there that a blueprint now exists for a life of her own: a format which will offer her possibilities for growth, for fulfilling her potential, which she senses must exist once circumstances help her to find it, once she can remove herself from the belittlement which her mother dishes out at every opportunity. And again, we have a father who hangs back on the sidelines and does not take his daughter's side, offers her no encouragement in her fight to achieve a more positive self-image, a real belief in herself. But Martha Quest has, suddenly, put one foot in step with time, an age which pays lip service to a daughter's separate life; and her mother now senses that the worm has turned: her hold on her only daughter's life is evidently slipping. For Martha has at last shown signs of frank hostility: has brought it out into the open, even if the show is followed by instant signs of remorse. Her ambivalence is now more than a subtle innuendo, a strategy of loaded hints.

Likewise in the consulting room we find that our sweet, compliant daughters, who cannot when they come to us say boo to the smallest goose, as they gradually grow stronger, as split-off parts come together where the ego integrates, will start to show their anger, even frank hostility, more openly and directly, over many months and years. We know that this begins to happen once each experiences herself as a whole and stronger woman; as one who is self-reliant as she grows to believe in her inner resources; that she can stand on her own two feet and need no longer live in terror of dire consequences if she is critical of mother, if she feels angry or even murderous at times. Once such feelings are acknowledged, once they can be expressed, they are gradually divested of their omnipotence; of terrifying phantasies that their object will drop dead: the whole world go up in smoke; that, like the blind Samson, they can bring the temple down by laying hands on its pillars.

How far it is possible to resolve these fateful issues – as we all become students of depth psychology – finds a delightful illustration in a contemporary scene of mother–daughter attitudes when faced with ambivalence:

I have had a bad day, but am too impressed by the badness of my day to notice that yours has been bad too . . . In the kitchen we stand and look at each other, pale with exhaustion . . . I know I am not being a good mother. I drive you to your music lesson and promise you a hot drink at the end of your wet walk back. When you return I am on the telephone yet again to a publisher with whom I am discussing the prospect of this book . . . You write me a cryptic note: 'I like that. I thought you were going to make me a hot drink.' I respond by crumpling it up and throwing it in the wastepaper basket. Later . . . you explain that you don't mind not getting a hot drink, what you mind is a promise that is not fulfilled. I feel humbled by this logic and your charity.
(Oakley, A., 1985, p. 81)

To childhood memories of my own generation, two previous to this, it sounds like utopia. Until after the Second World War only the exceptional girl would have in this manner confronted an exceptional mother. The rest of us went in terror of that spectre who contained the projections of our anger, which could turn into the 'murderous mother' of anxious phantasies that may or may not have corresponded to the reality. Also, until Freudian thinking gradually permeated a resistant society, more and more effectively, mothers tended to deny that they were 'murderous mothers', sometimes under provocation, or at moments when their life had plunged into disarray. 'I could murder this child', given expression to, will generally clear the air to 'but I love her, all the same'. Once this ragbag of feelings is at last out in the open, a genuine relationship rich with honest give-and-take becomes a possibility.

Mothers, quite as much as daughters, have to carry a burden of painful ambivalence, as we saw earlier itemized by Winnicott, even if Mrs Bennet succeeds in living out her days in beatific quiescence. Supported by her family and the values of a steadfast era, she bows out on this hopeful note: 'Happy for all her maternal feelings was the day on which Mrs Bennet got rid of her two most deserving daughters. With what delight and pride she afterwards visited Mrs Bingley and talked of Mrs Darcy may be guessed' (Austen, J., 1986, p. 393). It is interesting to see how, on the other hand, she deals with her angry feelings when one of her other daughters, Lydia, elopes with Mr Wickham, threatening her family with unspeakable disgrace. When this crisis was at its height, we have the following scene:

Mrs Bennet, to whose apartment they all repaired, after a few minutes' conversation together, received them exactly as might be expected; with tears and lamentations of regret, invectives against the villainous conduct of Wickham, and complaints of her own sufferings and ill usage; blaming every body but the person to whose ill judging indulgence the errors of her daughter must be principally owing. (Austen, J., 1986, p. 303)

Mrs Bennet continues to blame one and all concerned except for 'the "poor dear child!" ' (Austen, J., 1986, p. 304). We must also remember that if the daughter were to blame, that blame would attach remorselessly to the person of her mother, seeing that the latter is responsible to society for unfailingly producing an immaculate product.

Once Lydia returns home, as an honest married woman, 'smiles decked the face of Mrs Bennet, as the carriage drove up to the door' (Austen, J., 1986, p. 328). Not a word of reproach crosses the maternal lips. It is left to Elizabeth to convey to her sister at least a hint of the outrage and distress they had all felt. For when Lydia, triumphant, comes out with 'Lizzy, I never gave you an account of my wedding, I believe . . .'

'No really' comes the tart reply; 'I think there cannot be too little said on the subject' (Austen, J., 1986, p. 331).

How does Doris Lessing see the issue in our present day? In the first place she tells us that Mrs Quest herself had suffered deprivation, orphaned at an early age on the death of her mother: 'It was all her own fault, they said, because she had insisted on dancing all night when she was five months pregnant' (Lessing, D., 1978, p. 170). The resentment of the child at this cruel abandonment by a thoughtless, flighty mother still adheres to Mrs Quest like unpleasant sticking plaster. But in the Freudian era it will go a certain way to explaining the nature of her maternal shortcomings: that, a victim herself, she takes it out on her daughter, by the now familiar laws of cause and effect.

In her deeper phantasies, we can understand today, even if Lessing does not make this crystal clear, that a resentful little orphan at the core of Mrs Quest feels that she has failed her mother. At that unconscious level of infantile omnipotence, she should have kept her alive. Had she been a lovely baby, her mother would have stayed at home. There would have been no need for dancing. So runs that recent metalanguage to whose logic we are subject whether we like it or not. She nurses to make up for it – to try to make her mother better, which project is, in manic style, displaced on to other patients. As a grim part and parcel of this manic reparation, her true anguish is denied. Her deeper anxieties that she caused her mother's death are buried in her inner world, to which she has no access. All her bad-daughter feelings get projected into little Martha from the very word go. Unlike Mrs Bennet, who clearly wishes that her daughters have a better deal than she, we do not feel that Mrs Quest genuinely wants her Martha truly to have a better life than her own blitzed existence. Mrs Bennet's childhood was one of straitened circumstances. Soon her dreams came true, when her daughters were maried into greater affluence.

Not so with Mrs Quest: 'Her powerful unused energies surged through her, and soon she was again lying wakeful, thinking in hatred of her daughter' (Lessing, D., 1972, p. 85). Mrs Quest was unfulfilled. But, even more important, Mrs Quest was full of envy. She envied Martha her youthful body. She had attacked it since she first noticed her daughter's growing breasts. Angry that Martha's childhood smocks had, one day, to be replaced by dresses with a waist, she grumbled, calling her a 'pouter pigeon' (Lessing, D., 1972, pp. 23–4). Already we can see the omens for this mother–daughter dyad written darkly in the sky.

Martha Quest escapes to London. But as she struggles with self-knowledge, with that new commodity to which her generation, as we heard, is dedicated (see above, p. 276), she knows there is no escape from an inner, envious mother who has always hated her. She knows she cannot escape from this lifelong incubus. Accordingly the sense of freedom which she briefly enjoys after her escape to England tarnishes all too soon, as the new sky presses down to become a dirty lid. Martha Quest is caught, and she knows it.

Martha Quest is teetering on the brink of destitution. Lydia, in her day, was saved; not because she deserved it on the grounds of personal merit but because the society of which she was still a member, even if her membership had to be paid up by others, could not permit or afford such a serious default.

No such society, no such organic coherence, cradles the wretched Quests a hundred and fifty years later. Once she is widowed, Mrs Quest seeks refuge on the farm of her son Jonathan. But the young couple kick her out. If that was certainly the truth, truth is no commodity for the likes of Mrs Quest. Their naivety, if we can call it that, belongs to earlier centuries. Man is the animal that speaks. The same, of course, applies to woman. Subject status is attained on paths of meaningful discourse. But in her swamp of metalanguage, punctuated with veiled threats and murderous innuendoes, Mrs Quest remains barbarian; she belongs to the tribe which at least has its ritual to sustain relationships on which human life depends: the survival of the group.

Martha, meanwhile, has gone to ground in a most unlikely hide-out, the house of Mark Coldridge, where she has begun to learn, if in a haphazard fashion, the ABC of human discourse. But she remains unsure how to apply it to her mother. She has not yet understood that both need to speak that language directly and fearlessly to enter into dialogue where feelings are the subject matter.

Under the roof of Mark Coldridge, where Martha has some kind of job as a live-in factotum, all the languages known to man from the year dot are spoken. There is Mark's mother, Margaret Patten, some kind of timeless matriarch who holds the power and the purse strings; his son Francis and his wife, Linda, when she is at home. We also find the boy, Paul, whose mother, Sally, gassed herself in the family's flat in Cambridge. Since his father, Mark's brother, has rather better things to do than to care for the child, he is always on the heels of Linda, who, whenever she takes leave from her mental hospital, inhabits the Coldridge basement. Linda Coldridge may be mad, but she speaks an honest language. When the desperate little Paul, who runs from pillar to post, asks Linda finally, at the end of his tether: 'Linda, are you my mother now?' 'No. You have no mother.' 'Are you Francis's mother?' He really has to get this straight. 'Yes. No. I suppose so. Not really. I'm not much good at being that kind of person. Some people aren't' (Lessing, D., 1978, p. 187). After well over a thousand pages, maybe a thousand and a half, we have got to it at last, from the mouth of a mad woman. There are mothers, Paul is told, who are not that kind of person. There are mothers who just aren't.

Martha, in this unwieldy background, tunes into all these languages. She wants to make some sense of life. But now, before she is ready to deal with it on her own terms, horror of horrors, Mrs Quest, now a woman in her seventies, who has never been a mother – at any rate that kind of person, even if she was a nurse – is planning to descend on her. For Martha, it is much too soon: 'she was not cured of anger, of hatred', however much she wants to be.

Martha's anger belongs essentially to an era when a daughter can tell how matters stand with her own life. She can measure it by others who have made a go of theirs, who have taken up the options which are on offer in her time. It is, she knows, bad enough if a daughter has a mother who is not that kind of person. But it is, she has discovered, still a thousand times worse if, unlike Linda Coldridge, who is crazy at times, such a mother fails to spell it out; if she continues to deny it; if she pretends it never happened – because she cannot face the guilt so that it can all be out in the open: the guilt, the anger, the despair. For a daughter needs a mother who is built to be a mother so much more than any son. She needs that model and that teacher to imbibe a host of skills. These skills of woman must be learnt from the first hour at the breast. Failing that, as with Mrs Plath, they must be swotted up from books, those dreadful bibles which have millions of lost daughters on their conscience whose mothers longed to do their best but themselves had never known a mother, in the best and truest sense, when they were little storm-tossed girls.

In the story of the Quests the drama draws to a close in true twentieth-century manner – or rather, to be more precise, postwar twentieth-century style. Faced with her mother's visit, Martha now begins to feel that she is surely breaking down: she might become another Linda. She lies in bed, in the dark, quite unable to get up, in a terrifying state on the brink of dissolution. In her room is a suitcase full of her mother's letters. They begin 'My Darling Girl' and they end 'your loving mother'. This is what we might expect at this dangerously late hour of Mrs Quest's nemesis. It tends to be the fate of mothers who are not that kind of person but seize a mask and play the role.

Martha trundles to the basement to ask Linda for advice. You'd better keep away from shrinks, comes the cynical reply. Linda is speaking from experience. She had herself, in fact, not managed to keep out of their hands. There is, we find, this Dr Lamb, well ensconced on the sidelines of the foundering Coldridge clan. Determined to steer clear of him, terrified of the clamour of her need for attention, of drawing close to anyone, Martha sets her reeling mind on a kill-or-cure course of DIY salvation. She starts reading Freud and Jung, feverishly, by the basketful, while she denigrates their insights.

It was painful and exhausting: 'Martha heard herself crying. She wept, while a small girl wept with her, mamma, mamma, why are you so cold, so unkind, why did you never love me?' (Lessing, D., 1978, p. 234). Martha is now in touch with a baby-part of her which went short of mothering from the moment she was born. The pain is excruciating. Did Mary Wollstonecraft, her daughters Fanny or Mary Shelley, weep aloud at night like this? Mary Shelley read her classics, Fanny took an overdose, Mary Wollstonecraft came close to some sort of diagnosis of her needs for warmth and love in her letters to Imlay, heart-rending as they are with their unassuaged hunger for human, for maternal warmth; but the hour for full appraisal of the universal aspect of this predicament at the core of woman's life was still a long way off.

With Martha Quest we have arrived in the present: in our lifetime. We are also witnessing in this daughter's dilemma the fascination and the dread commonly experienced at the thought of psychotherapy. Once or twice Martha weakens. She lays the clever books aside and, driven by her pain and emotional hunger, she goes to see Dr Lamb. 'What Dr Lamb must do for her was to give her back her pity . . . She must be able, when her mother came, to pity her, to love her, to cherish her, and not be destroyed' (Lessing, D., 1978, p. 244). A tall order in the few hours which are available before Mrs Quest arrives.

Mother and daughter try their best. In some recess of the mind each is bound to be aware just how much is at stake for their health and well-being: their inner equilibrium. But horrid words keep slipping out of the prisons of their mouth. 'You know, we don't all have the same ideas about life, do we?' (Lessing, D., 1978, p. 285) – that most fateful of thoughts escapes from under Martha's tongue. She could have bitten it off. And, 'Wouldn't it be better if you tried to – accept me as I was?' All Martha's life, past and present, trembles in that ambiguous tense.

Mrs Quest now seeks refuge in obsessional cleanliness. She cleans the house. She cleans and cleans in an angry, hopeless bid to be wanted, to be of use, and clean the nasty, hostile feelings, spilling everywhere like dung, until Martha, who is now at the end of her tether, spells out very loud and clear: 'Mother, look, Mark can perfectly well afford a charwoman, you know' (Lessing, D., 1978, p. 294). In other words: 'Look. It's too late. Surely you know as well as I that we hate the guts of one another.' Three thousand years have passed since Electra could not say it to that great queen Clytaemnestra and had to murder her instead. Murder was the only language in the absence of true discourse. Martha feels she needs to say it, that she ought to come clean, if she is to find her pity, any love for her mother; but she is too afraid at this late hour in the day.

Martha, now *in extremis*, since matricide is no solution except, of course, in phantasy, resorts again to Dr Lamb, against her previous better judgement. Martha, after all, inhabits, with a part of herself, the Freudian twentieth century. She has left the tribe behind more effectively than has her mother.

'You know that you have to tell her to go.'

    'Yes.'

    'Well then?'

    'I can't. I can't . . . if I kick her out I sign her death warrant. I know that.'

    'So you feel guilty that you are murdering your mother.' (Lessing, D., 1978, p. 295)

This conversation could never have taken place in the day of Mrs Bennet and her daughter Elizabeth. It denotes momentous changes. Stupendous conflicts are irrupting into human consciousness after millennia of a life as archetypes in the depths of the unconscious.

Dr Lamb is not, of course, Martha's analyst. Martha is not contained in that ongoing process and so he cannot say to her, 'nevertheless, you would like to.' Because Martha Quest is set on DIY treatment, this confession to another cannot possibly be made within a healing dialogue which might, as she so badly wants, restore her pity and her love, at any rate sufficiently to modify the awful hate; to start to make it bearable.

At this moment of stalemate Mrs Quest seizes on the last and only way out. She sits for hours in her room muttering to herself: 'Filthy pigs. I'm expected to clean up after their mess, pigs. I'm nothing but a servant and she's a whore' (Lessing, D., 1978, p. 297). A motherless, frightened child, Mrs Quest flees into madness while little Martha takes refuge: 'Mark and Martha lay in each other's arms, in a cave of soft, protective dark' (Lessing, D., 1978, p. 296). In Mark she finds a 'good mother', for the moment anyway, while Mrs Quest exudes poison. In the morning: 'Whore', she said. 'A decent woman shouldn't be under the same roof . . .' 'Mother, the taxi will be here soon' (Lessing, D., 1978, p. 297). Martha has finally decided to take the bull by the horns, with the support of Dr Lamb.

Dr Lamb sits and listens patiently to Mrs Quest . . . 'her years and years of resentment focused on Martha' (Lessing, D., 1978, p. 298). Then the useless Dr Lamb, as he has been designated by the women of the Coldridge clan, quietly, respectfully, poses a dynamic question: 'If you two don't get on, perhaps it would be better if you weren't in the same house?' When Mrs Quest returns to Martha she says, 'in a normal, almost jolly voice: "I've changed my ticket. I'm flying tomorrow." ' She never mentions Dr Lamb, for Mrs Quest cannot think. She is unable to make links. Her states of mind are archaic; even if she is a nurse her mental processes belong essentially to the Dark Ages. She has remained in their thrall, as countless millions still do today.

We are nearly at the end. Mother and daughter

went to the air-terminal in a taxi . . . They chatted about small topics till the flight was called, then as she vanished from her daughter's life for ever, Mrs Quest gave a small tight smile, and said: 'Well, I wonder what all that was about really?'

'Yes,' said Martha, 'so do I.'

They kissed politely, exchanged looks of ironic desperation, smiled and parted. (Lessing, D., 1978, p. 299)

We assume it was for ever.

Is it a coincidence that hints of an apocalypse now make their entry in the saga? '1956, as everyone knows, was a climatic year . . . The only safe subject was the bomb' (Lessing, D., 1978, p. 378). Three hundred pages further on we find ourselves in the midst of the prophesied apocalypse (Lessing, D., 1978, p. 666). There is no need to dwell on it, for it is all projected 'out there', into the outer world. But within the inner world of Mrs Quest and her daughter, at the heart of the dyad, we can, I think, take it that inner turmoil without end followed on this final parting at the air-terminal when, as the flight was called, she, Mrs Quest, vanished from her daughter's life for ever.

We have a later rendezvous with the unhappy Martha Quest. We will need to focus on certain hidden positives in that enigmatic basement in the rambling Coldridge house. Doris Lessing is too great a writer not to balance plus and minus, even if the various fragments of this subtle exercise have to be excavated before we can make further sense of the patterns of the whole, of their meanings for our subject. But first we must consider guilt, this new, this stupendous issue, as it now stands revealed at the heart and core of the mother–daughter dyad.

2 THE EMERGENCE OF GUILT

We all know that if we detect in ourselves impulses of hate
towards a person we love, we feel concerned or guilty. As
Coleridge puts it:
>*to be wroth with one we love,*
>*Doth work like madness in the brain.*

(MELANIE KLEIN, 'Love, guilt and reparation')

THESE ARE KLEIN'S opening words on our *unconscious sense of guilt*. Those of us, she continues, who are oversensitive to the opinions of others, who tend to be constantly dissatisfied with themselves and have what is commonly called an 'inferiority complex', are at a deeper level suffering from unconscious feelings of guilt. These arise from a fear – she elaborates the point – that they are incapable of loving others well enough or of mastering their aggressive impulses, so that they dread that they are a danger to those they love.

In our sojourn on the couch we saw how individual infants arrive at this painful point around the second half of their first year when aggression and love are both experienced together and against the same object which is no longer a breast, a breast seen as-a-part-of-me, but can be appreciated as mother, as a whole person, even if that transition is naturally a gradual one. From that starting point 'these feelings of guilt and distress now enter as a new element into the emotion of love. They become an inherent part of love, and influence it profoundly both in quality and quantity' (Klein, M., 1937, p. 311).

Half a century on feminist psychotherapists are seeking pathways forward from what they decry as a patriarchal legacy in the concepts and practice of psychoanalysis, seeing that at its inception woman's experience of herself was that of a subordinate, a second-class citizen and member of society. They agree that there are depths of suffering that continue to elude therapeutic endeavour, seen as the 'serious consequences of patriarchy' (Ernst, S. and Maguire, M., 1987, p. 50).

At its roots, they believe, lies the inability of the daughter to separate from a merged relationship consequent on a mothering which conveys to the girl from her earliest infancy that, unlike the boy, 'she should develop a facility to contain her own neediness' (Ernst, S. and Maguire, M., 1987, p. 59). The lack of a sense of identity, as of authentic life-purpose, which this inculcates inevitably gives rise to a daughter's rage against her mother: a rage which may surface only in the course of psychotherapy, by which time it has already coloured all the relationships and undertakings in her life through its manifestations at an unconscious level. At the same time this hankering for the merged relationship, while its remains unstilled, prevents a successful separation, for it increases her aggression and multiplies the cause for guilt.

According to a less sectarian analysis of Dinnerstein's (Dinnerstein, D., 1987), human beings of *either sex* suffer 'primordial rage and grief against the mother for loss of oneness' (Ernst, S. and Maguire, M., 1987, p. 219). But women have, by collusion between the sexes, until now borne the brunt of these emotions which men have tended to evade for biotechnological reasons through escaping into activism out in the wider world, where they play the part of rulers.

With this viewpoint I agree. It may in psychotherapy often only take longer until a man will admit to feelings of emptiness, low self-esteem, to that lack of personhood habitual to the woman, for all the power he may wield, all the success he enjoys in his brittle world 'out there'. But the experience of outrage at having been short-changed by 'mother', leading to attacks of guilt, while a universal one, will have different repercussions in the case of the girl. She will subsequently live in dread of retaliation from her maternal object; but rather than focus on this catastrophic phantasy – the female castration complex – will deny it to live in a more free-floating guilt and generalized anxiety with degrees of depression, whose dynamics remain unconscious without psychotherapy.

If we take the point of view that both women *and* men, sons as much as daughters, are existentially in the same boat in this respect: that

human development is prompted through loss, and that life hereafter will always be a deeply ambivalent experience . . . that satisfaction can only be temporary – [since] if it were permanent human beings would have no mental life. (Ernst, S. and Maguire, M., 1987, p. 230) that basic uniformity will none the less not rule out certain clear-cut distinctions in dyadic experience for the boy and the girl. The causes of both aggression on the part of the infant, the child and later adult against the maternal object, and subsequently of guilt, will be gender-specific in a great complexity, even if they also share a certain homogeneity.

For our present purposes let us take a closer look at burdens which guilt imposes on the mother–daughter dyad. Here the initial sense of oneness is qualitatively different from the case of the boy since the primal experience of replica to replica induces an extended merging. If Orbach is correct that its fulcrum at one level is the issue of unresolved neediness, it is precisely the merging which will open in this case the floodgates of a massive projective identification as a lifelong vicious circle. This process will shunt to and fro all the wrongs and grievances experienced by woman as an individual, as a member of her sex, as mother and as daughter, and is therefore gender-specific. In the case of the boy this mechanism is cut short by biological difference and by the advent of the father, which will normally prohibit the boy's longing to merge with the maternal object. For the mother–daughter dyad the paternal intervention is, where mental health prevails, also an essential bonus. It will transform this sticky claustrum, with its fierce restrictiveness and indistinct bound-aries, into the relative reprieve of the triangular relationship, despite a primitive resentment which this curtailment of symbiosis will on the other hand evoke. Where this expansion fails, where it is not facilitated by the mother's attitude or where the male fails to impose his role as husband and father, a claustrophobic stagnation which belongs to the 'Elementary Feminine Principle' will take over and impinge on prospects of healthy growth by undermining separation (see 'The Great Goddess Creatrix'). In such a situation the daughter enters adolescence and biological womanhood seeing it as her life's task, at an unconscious level, to assuage her mother's neediness to a far greater extent than is normally the case. It is a question of degree, since by that process of projective identification which was mentioned previously, this particular compulsion will colour every daughter's life, where it is experienced as a constant demand over and above all others which reality will impose, to a certain extent. This means that at a level of everyday experience mother's happiness and well-being will invariably be one of her main preoccupations, however much she may resent it because it makes separation still more unattainable at an unconscious level and unthinkable at a conscious one:

I went around the house to the back door, thinking, I have been to a dance and a boy has walked me home and kissed me. It was all true. My life was possible. I went past the kitchen window and I saw my mother. She was sitting with her feet on the open oven door, drinking tea out of a cup without a saucer. She was just sitting and waiting for me to come home . . . (Olsen, T., 1985, p. 52, quoting Alice Munro)

My life was possible, she says. Because a boy had kissed her and might lead her by the hand away from mother and her kitchen, from mother in 'her faded, fuzzy Paisley kimono, with her sleepy but doggedly expectant face', casements had briefly opened on a separate future. My life, she says, was possible. But at that moment guilt came in, sneaked in on her like some avenger, and in the moment it arose stole all the possibilities of such a miracle for ever.

How well this image of the mother, sitting with her poor old feet on the open oven door, implies a state of neediness which the daughter must assuage, since at the same time it implies the chronic absence of the male, the essential husband and father, precisely when life holds out the prospects of a happy parting. How well the image of the faded, fuzzy kimono conveys fuzzy, faded boundaries.

There is, we find, a great confusion in the minds of our patients, once they start growing stronger, between self-assertion and aggression, as I am certain there must be in the mind of the infant. Is it not when self-assertion as a simple drive for growth – indeed, as its prerequisite – comes up against a counterforce of opposition in the mother that, repeatedly frustrated, it is churned into aggression, which spills over into hate, which in turn fuels guilt? And will this very counterforce not be very much stronger in the mother–daughter dyad than in the case of a son, since the mother equated any differentiation with a loss of life itself, while on the other hand the daughter will resist this maternal opposition with angry vehemence: the more so once the outer world offers ever-widening options for a separate life. If Simone de Beauvoir says: 'I have the body of a woman – but clearly I have been very lucky. I have escaped many of the things that enslave a woman, such as motherhood and the duties of a housewife' (Schwarzer, A., 1985, p. 36), such a statement belongs unequivocally to the present, to the twentieth century, with all its opportunities for a liberated life for a minority of women.

In fact, it is of interest that in all the ground we have covered, no single mention of guilt, expressed at a conscious level in the actual context of the dyad's interactions, was encountered until we heard that Martha Quest was appalled at her own cruelty – in other words, experienced guilt – when she had attacked her mother, even if that attack was made under utmost provocation (see p. 276 above).

We need to differentiate between the guilt of a mother and that which afflicts a daughter within their relationship. The latter has clear origins in infantile development of the depressive position, in the wake of earliest attacks that are made in phantasy against the primal care-taker. It is object-specific from the start, we could say; while that on the mother's part does not seem to belong to primary experience. Only deeper reflection on maternal envy – as also on aggression, for all the reasons we have listed – will persuade us that these feelings, experienced in adult life, will trigger the remorse and guilt belonging to their primitive, primary manifestations.

Certainly it would seem that until widespread contraception made motherhood an act of choice, a contract freely entered into (theoretically, at least) instead of woman's destiny, mothers left an impression of having been immune to guilt. Had they squared their guilt with God, on the weekly Sunday visit, as belonging to some breach of the wider Ten Commandments? There is no eleventh which says 'you must always love your children'! Besides, until the Freudian era with its laws of cause and effect gave women this latest stick for their already aching backs, only an exceptional woman like Harriet Martineau would make a fruitful connection between the quality of mothering and that of a daughter's life as she enters womanhood.

But in our day the worm has turned. The very opposite applies as we observe how the mothers of a cultural elite, whose awareness of these matters is rapidly filtering through into the universal culture, scrutinize their performance with a stark relentlessness, which amounts to persecution, for the most minimal default. Today every hint of failure induces painful pangs and maternal heart-searching, reaching epidemic heights that show no sign of abating:

6 Nov '54

My darling, I have been doing a lot of hard thinking since I saw you off on the bus at noon today. I have concluded that a Friends school was a mistake for a girl like you . . . I feel very bad about this. I mean about my judgement in this respect . . . And I have become convinced that your acne is a psychosomatic reaction to all this. I feel certain that if I had you here with me for a month it would clear up completely . . . We all love you terribly. Mother. (Payne, K., 1984, p. 285)

If, from such anxiety on the contemporary scene, we let our thinking return to the Diary of Mrs Thornton, whose poor infants passed away in the most dismal succession with a mere line or two of maternal resignation, since motherhood was destiny, the increase in maternal guilt resounds in our inner ear as plangently as the Chorus in Greek tragedy. But nowhere has it found expression more poignantly and raw than from the pen of Tillie Olsen, in a classic of our day. A mother stands ironing, tormented that her daughter's teacher has recently made this request:

I wish you would manage the time to come in and talk with me about your daughter. I'm sure you can help me understand her. She's a youngster who needs help and whom I'm deeply interested in helping. (Olsen, T., 1980, p. 11)

So the story begins, with words as unforgettable as any hand ever set down on paper: 'I stand here ironing, and what you asked me moves tormented back and forth with the iron.' As she stands ironing, as she has done all her life, far too often, for too long, with the same exhausted motion, her mind cuts paths back through the years with the heart's unerring instinct, aiming for a lifelong abscess, like a scalpel in the surgeon's hands, but without an anaesthetic:

She was a beautiful baby. The first and only one of our five that was beautiful at birth . . . I nursed her . . . but with her, with all the fierce rigidity of first motherhood, I did like the books then said. Though her cries battered me to trembling and my breasts ached with swollenness. I waited till the clock decreed . . . She was a miracle to me, but when she was eight months old I had to leave her daytimes with the woman downstairs to whom she was no miracle at all, for I worked or looked for work and for Emily's father, who 'could no longer endure' (he wrote in his good-bye note) 'sharing want with us.'

I was nineteen. It was the pre-relief, preWPA world of the depression. I would start running as soon as I got off the streetcar, running up the stairs, the place smelling sour . . . when she saw me she would break into a clogged weeping, that could not be comforted, a weeping I can hear yet. (Olsen, T., 1980, pp. 12–13)

This is only the beginning. The pain continues in that vein, reaching a crescendo and a partial resolution to which we will be returning.

If guilt was not out in the open before the present century, that is not to say that women did not sense in their hearts that the quality of mothering is a genius handed down the line of female replica. Here is an archaic task force which shares the unitary knowledge that if she is to hold together in the concertina nature of her cyclical existence, a she-child needs a special building, but at the same time also knows that for a multitude of reasons, inner as much as outer, partial or total failure is the order of the norm. For woman remains subjected to her ancient maternal function. Subjected is the crucial word. 'Subjected' to within the best and deepest meaning of the word, a creative submission as was Mary's when the angel spoke. Such creative submission to the creative principle falls in the category of the divine, while at the same time it demands a supreme elimination of any other fulfilment of the personality, almost like a higher law. Yet a mother *is* a person by unalienable right, since she is a human being. Here is flaw and rub in a never-ceasing conflict.

Aware of its heavy toll, some mothers will restrain the infant daughter in their arms from extravagant and dangerous dreams, only to feel guilt for exercising such restraint. Where, on the other hand, a mother offers her encouragement, aids and abets her daughter's future on life's widest playing fields of equal opportunities, she dreads that she is raising hopes which are doomed to be dashed on surviving archaism. Here a mother, Helen Claes, defines this conflict very clearly in the 1970s. In a letter to her daughter she admits how she 'floundered in a sea of guilt, torn between repressing your individual personality' and the ever-nagging fear of supporting her bid for a free, creative life.

Gradually Helen Claes overcomes her diffidence:

We (your father and I) agree that life should be as adventure-filled as you can make it. We have always hoped that you would surge ahead and do some of the really interesting things that most people only dream of . . . much love and a long, exciting life of adventure, Helen. (Payne, K., 1984, p. 5)

Her daughter dropped out of college and finally became a painter. During this 'messy' phase, despite her anxieties concerning the eventual outcome, Helen wrote . . .

but you are you and no matter where you go I'll never lose you (dead or alive). I'll fear for your welfare at the same time envying your strength of purpose to endeavour to do what you must . . . with love and happy hope, Mom. (Payne, K., 1984, pp. 5–6)

How many conflicting roles a mother has to reconcile in our present day and age. What changes she must undergo, what inner upheavals she must suffer in being mother to a daughter, even more than to a son. How her being has to swing from the symbiotic matrix of 'The Elementary', step by step through the phases of 'The Transformative' (Neumann; see 'The Great Goddess Creatrix'), separating, letting go, protecting and defining, stepping back and letting be, steadily disentangling every inclination which screams out to possess; fighting back a thousand fears of personal insecurities, anguish for her own survival, furthering and encouraging to the last bated breath, while others stand and disapprove by archaic tradition, until each runner in her turn stuns these dubious onlookers as she notches up another gain at the finishing line.

Where the stakes are so enormous, how can failure be ruled out and the chorus of Cassandras not sometimes triumph in the bitter end? But guilt as it afflicts a mother if she commits herself fully to her daughter's unrestricted growth will afflict a daughter too, in that very same arena, even if the psychodynamics differ greatly in her case. For precisely where she perseveres, where she climbs her tree of growth, towards the self-created life, following the inmost urgings of inbuilt authenticity, this is experienced on her part as an archaic violation. For here she is the instrument that must cut the holding cordage of those very bonds and chains that promised lifelong anchorage in a sweet, familiar harbour, to head for open, unknown seas and nebulous affrays beyond.

Born of this, fierce convictions grow on that devastating threshold that the one who is left behind, the faithful mentor of her growth, may perish as a consequence. For now in anxious phantasies, underpinned by concrete thinking and by a process of projection of her helpless baby-parts, which must initially be shed on that first journey – out, into the unknown – it is the abandoned mother who now becomes the helpless baby, cast away and left behind, even if her circumstances in actual reality are relatively safe and sound. The pain of what this means to mother, the guilt of causing her this pain, prove almost unsupportable. The terror is that both must perish, since at some deeply buried level, deeper than any separation which the naked eye can judge, the two assuredly are one; and pain and perishing and loss are forever on the cards:

24 February 1909

My Angel Mother,
Don't be startled or afraid. I have something to tell you which – with the help of recent presentiments – you, I know, are half expecting to hear. If you ever see this letter it will mean that after joining the deputation I have been arrested and shall not see you again until I have been to Holloway Prison . . . My darling Muddy, you will never know, I trust, the pain it is to do this thing without your sympathy and help – with, on the contrary, the certainty that it shocks and hurts you and makes you suffer in numberless ways . . . You will be angry. If it could be only that. But you will be hurt through and through. (Payne, K., 1984, p. 199 [Constance Lytton (1867–1923) to her mother Edith, wife of the Second Earl Lytton, Viceroy of India])

If this is at the gates of prison, the next is at the gates of death. Executed by the Nazis for membership of the Resistance, when her son was only eight months old, Hilde Coppi wrote to her mother on the last day of her life:

My Mother, my dearly beloved Mama,
Now the time has almost come when we must say farewell for ever. The hardest part, the separation from my little Hans, is behind me. How happy he made me! I know that he will be well taken care of in your loyal, dear maternal hands, and for my sake, Mama – promise me – remain brave. I know you feel as though your heart must break; but take yourself firmly in hand, very firmly. You will succeed, as you always have . . . the thought that I must leave you alone at that time of life when you need me most! Will you ever be able to forgive me? (Payne, K., 1984, p. 204)

In these two examples we have mothers who were strong, who by nature or through circumstances were privileged in that respect. But where a mother is precarious, her life already beaten down, the valiant flame of her struggle flickering into dying embers; then the guilt a daughter knows if she fights on to go forward, determined at whatever cost in terms of personal sacrifice to make more of her own life than could the one who gave it her – the guilt at not turning back to stay behind, beside her mother, in the place that may become, she knows, a deathbed for them both – can become a life sentence:

My God! She's dying. Mother is dying! I tried to think, to make myself realize that Mother, with all this dumb sorrow gazing at me, was passing, passing away for ever.

. . . She had seized me by the hand. She had begged me to come and see her. And I had answered her, 'I can come to see you later, but I can't go to college later . . .' (Yezierska, A., 1984, p. 251)

To add to her remorse and guilt, when the coffin lid was closed others turned on Anzia, the bad girl who had left her mother to go to college to become no less than a 'teacherin', after she had slaved for months to buy the essential clothes in which to scale these dizzy heights:

The undertaker, with knife in his hand, cut into Father's coat and he rent his garments according to the Biblical law and ages of tradition. Then he slit my sisters' waists, and they too did as Father had done. Then the man turned to me with the knife in his hand. 'No,' I cried. 'I feel terrible enough without tearing my clothes.'

'It has to be done.'

'I don't believe in this. It's my only suit, and I need it for work. Tearing it wouldn't bring Mother back to life again.'

A hundred eyes burned on me their condemnation.

'Look at her, the Americanerin!' (Yezierska, A., 1984, p. 255)

How Anzia – now a teacher – must have remembered in this bitter hour her previous meeting with her mother, several years before. She had then finally made that desperate break from home, ruled by an archaic father straight from the Old Testament. With iron determination – had her father not called this headstrong daughter *Blut und Eisen* (blood and iron) – Anzia had gone to ground in a bleak and icy cell, at six dollars a month – that dream, a room of her own, in which she studied by night to catch up on the education that might carry her to college. Here it is, in her own words:

So cold it was, even the gas froze. I stuck a candle into a bottle, took up my grammar . . . My feet were lumps of ice. How could I study? But I would. I must . . .

A rap came to the door . . .

— 299 —

'Mother!' I cried. Yes, there stood my mother, a shawl over her head and a big bundle on her back. She threw her arms around me and kissed me hungrily. 'In a night like this, I thought you'd need a feather bed', she said, throwing the bundle on my cot . . .

'All the way from Elizabeth [Street] for you to carry it,' I cried. In the sputtering light of the candle, her sunken eyes gleamed out of their black sockets with a dumb, pleading love that made me hate myself for my selfishness . . . Hours she travelled, only to see me for a few minutes. God! How much bigger was Mother's goodness than my burning ambition to rise in the world!

'Mother! You're so good to me. What can I do back for you?' I said, feeling small under her feet with unworthiness.

'Only come to see me soon.'

'I'd do anything for you. I'd give away my life. But I can't take time to go way out to Elizabeth. Every little minute must go to my studies.'

'I tore myself away from all my work to come and see you.'

'But you're not studying for college.'

'Is college more important than to see your old mother?'

'I could see you later. But I can't go to college later.' (Yezierska, A., 1984, pp. 170–1)

Let us return to Tillie Olsen, that mother who stands ironing, in a deluge of guilt of how she failed Emily, who had none the less developed a vivid gift for mimicry:

One morning she phones me at work, hardly understandable through the weeping: 'Mother, I did it. I won; they gave me the first prize; they clapped and clapped and wouldn't let me go.'

Now suddenly she was Somebody, and as imprisoned in her difference as she had been in her anonymity.

She began to be asked to perform at other high schools, even in colleges, then at city and state-wide affairs. The first one we went to, I only recognized her that first moment when thin, shy, she almost drowned herself into the curtains. Then: was this Emily? The control, the command, the convulsing and deadly clowning, the spell, then the roaring, stamping audience, unwilling to let this rare and precious laughter out of their lives . . .

She is coming. She runs up the stairs two at a time with her light, graceful step, and I know she is happy tonight. Whatever it was that occasioned your call did not happen today.

'Aren't you ever going to finish the ironing, Mother? Whistler painted his

*mother in a rocker. I'd have to paint mine standing over an ironing board
. . .' She is so lovely. Why did you want me to come in at all? Why were you
so concerned? She will find her way . . .*

*. . . let her be. So all that is in her will not bloom – but in how many does
it? There is still enough left to live by. Only help her to know – help make it
so there is cause for her to know – that she is more than this dress on the
ironing board, helpless before the iron. (Olsen, T., 1980, p. 23)*

We know, as Winnicott has taught us, that this 'rare and precious
laughter' is often born in a child the burden of whose life has been to
inspirit seeds of laughter into the dark and chilly soul of a depressed,
despairing mother. We know that Emily may grow, as her mother
senses in her pain, into a precarious being who may always 'drown into
the curtains', to emerge into the limelight of a cruelly curtailed instant,
as did that waif Norma Jean who bloomed as Marilyn Monroe out of a
void of inner darkness. But we also know of hope, and of mutual
sustenance, provided that the dyad holds with sufficient love and trust.
When despite all inbuilt difficulties, it does not yield to despair, to its
own annihilation, as in the case of the Quests.

Reflecting on these illustrations it is easy to forget how recent in the
dyad's history is the growing consciousness of guilt to be confronted
squarely, lifted out of the precincts of institutionalized religion. How
very recently George Eliot, who became an atheist in the years of her
youth, was still struggling to establish

*that morality did not depend on religion: a woman need not lose her sense of
duty, her obligations, when she lost her faith; atheism was not a licence to
behave badly but a freedom to behave a good deal better than the lazy and
hypocritical Church demanded. She saw that loss of faith was coming and
that it could be a yawning and terrifying gap. She filled it in with the
affirmation of the importance of goodness. Without religion society was still to
be knit together with rules. (Zeman, S.A., 1977, p. 100)*

Doubtless guilt, in bygone ages, where it must have existed in the
manner Klein pronounced, was more of an amorphous, woolly-
headed affair, a vague, uncertain *mea culpa* whose precise origins did
not need to be located. It is certainly the case in our consulting rooms
that many a woman patient, when she first comes to us, feels guilty
about everything that is troubling in her own as much as in the wider
world. Only when she grows stronger may she place her sense of guilt

where it actually belongs, with failures in her personal life, including those towards her daughter.

To be able to feel guilt in its unalterable context requires ego-strength in an individuated being who has forged a self-created life, whose consciousness has broken free from the collective unconscious, with which it was largely merged until recent centuries. Accordingly did we not hear that in the monastic era certain nuns became pregnant for no better reason than that the gates had been left open; as the downfall of Lydia Bennet lay with that scoundrel Wickham, certainly not with herself.

In this, the twentieth century, psychodynamic understanding has imposed new discipline on such unlikely postulations. We find this reflected in the neglected work of Otto Rank, psychoanalyst of Anaïs Nin, one-time member of the inner circle of Freud and founder of 'Will Therapy'. Due for rehabilitation, Rank conceptualized 'the will', bearing no connection to that of the philosophers, as the original creative core of every personality. A 'force . . . which acts, not merely reacts, upon the environment . . . in itself a first cause [which] produces something new' (Lieberman, E.J., 1985, p. 357). His aim in psychotherapy centred on the patient's need to recover this will and so break free of neurosis, which Rank envisaged as a state where the will was stifled and negated. In this context he would see the mother–daughter constellation in its archaic negatives essentially as a neurosis which would be lifted only when the function of willing had at last been restored to both protagonists, despite the guilt which is implict in this freeing operation. It is, according to Rank, the most gifted individuals who relinquish the struggle for this central task of life: the quest for its unique meaning.

A mother's growing awareness that she has many gifts and talents, besides her maternal ones, which cry out for fulfilment, even at the cost of stealing a share of her life-energies from her actual babies, must be faced unflinchingly and implemented in our day in full knowledge that the conflict between the call of the spirit and the cry of her child will multiply her guilt and anguish. For once a mother, she is torn between creative undertakings and the drive to exercise full maternal reverie for one child after another through her years of childbearing as of rearing those young lives which must initially depend on her for everything. Certainly in the past only few confronted this relentless tug of war. The rule was to escape into a life of childlessness. In our next illustration we see the conflict in the raw. Although the children here are sons, the guilt is near-identical and has rarely been conveyed with graver immediacy:

Entry from my journal November 1960

My children cause me the most exquisite suffering of which I have any experience. It is the suffering of ambivalence: the murderous alternation between bitter resentment and raw-edged nerves, and blissful gratification and tenderness . . .

March 1966

Perhaps one is a monster – an anti-woman – something driven and without recourse to the normal and appealing consolations of love, motherhood, joy in others . . . but as soon as he felt me gliding into a world which did not include him, he would come to pull at my hand, ask for help, punch at the typewriter keys. And I would feel his wants at such a moment as fraudulent, as an attempt moreover to defraud me of living even for fifteen minutes as myself . . . A few minutes! But it was as if an invisible thread would pull taut between us and break, to the child's sense of inconsolable abandonment, if I moved – not even physically, but in spirit – into the realm beyond our tightly circumscribed life together. (Rich, A., 1977, pp. 21, 23, 29)

How clearly we can visualize that while this poet gave life to creatures of flesh and blood and knew the life-shaking rewards of bodily dedication, she went in terror of her life – her other life, that of the spirit: 'For it is really death that I have been fearing – the crumbling to death of that scarcely born physiognomy which my whole life has been a battle to give birth to – a recognizable, autonomous self, a creation in poetry and life' (Rich, A., 1977, p. 29).

But now we take it one step further. As though the conflict of the artist-mother is not grave enough, within its own specific coils, there is beyond it the concern of its impact on her mother lest she be burdened by this vast travail. Will poems or works of art prove to be a substitute for a living infant in the eager grandmaternal arms? Must the ageing mother not be rescued from barrenness in the autumn of her life? Is a grandchild not the gift a daughter owes to her mother, for the gift of her own life? How inexorable are these laws which stand intrinsic to the dyad.

Paula Modersohn-Becker was a contemporary of Rilke's. She ranks among the great painters and died at the age of thirty, within eighteen days of giving birth to her first child, a daughter. Leading up to that event, to that fatality in giving life, had been years of bitter struggle between her two conflicted natures, whose destiny it seems to be to turn their back on one another, to coexist in enmity.

Barely conscious of these issues which were inscribed in her young life, she marries at twenty-five, a fellow-artist, Otto Modersohn. She has been drawing and painting since the age of sixteen, when she has her first lessons during a stay in England, away from her family. Frau Becker writes to her daughter: 'Dear heart, how happy I am that you are having such sound lessons in drawing. It is my greatest wish that you can focus all your energies on this field and I am so very grateful to Uncle Charles that he can facilitate this great good fortune ...' (Modersohn-Becker, P., 1979, p. 47). Although she is happy in her marriage, in a home of her own which is also their joint workshop above everything else, although close to her mother in that near-sisterly fashion to which the dyad can attain in fortunate circumstances, she is drawn away from her, and repeatedly to Paris by her relentless urge and daemon, to follow the artist's life and abjure that other call of her nature as a woman. Time and again it draws her back to home and husband, to the hearth she has endowed with so much love and love's generosity. Yet at heart – not of the daughter, woman, wife or future mother, but at that other core of her discipleship to art – it had already been decided by her 'will', or incubus, that by the time that she was thirty, the break with home must be accomplished to follow her true destiny. Accordingly, in her thirtieth year, the day after her husband's birthday and her mother's long-planned departure for Italy, an eagerly awaited treat which was not to be disturbed by such sorrowful events, Paula left, this time for good, whatever the consequences and the cost of that fateful step might be.

That her husband's persistence in a deeper collusion with her nature as a mother would defeat her in the end, that the defeat would cost her life, no doubt because she was already, somewhere, depleted by the conflict, she was not as yet to know. Not yet, as this time, finally, as she certainly believed, she set up her modest studio under the beloved eaves of the French capital, where she had begun to meet with the first sweet taste of recognition. 'Dedication to Art has also something selfless. Some give it to people, others to an idea'

(Modersohn-Becker, P., 1979, p. 389), she had written to her parents at the age of twenty-three while her father was still alive. Already then, before she had even met her future husband, she felt a need to justify, to the two whom she loved best, that hard life-course ahead of her, before its details could be known, its tragic outcome be defined. But the painter's greatest fear at this moment in her life, this breach with every human tie and link that had brought sustenance, was that she might have to forfeit the most precious bond of all, beside the one to her art: her mother's love and understanding. Seven years previously, writing in 1899 of her struggles with her work: 'I write this especially for mother. I think she feels that my life is one long continuous egoistic drunken joyousness' (Rich, A., 1977, p. 229).

And now that she had made the break from everything she held dear – what would her mother say when she returned from Italy and had to face the dreadful news that her daughter's marriage-nest in the peace of Worpswede, that workshop of two kindred spirits, in which she must have invested all her grandmaternal longing, lay stripped and plundered of her hopes – that these had now been transposed from the cradle to the easel, and such a distant one at that? Only a cousin took her side during those weeks of anxious waiting: 'Must all of us who love Paula, and have until now always known her as a fine, upright, good person, not take the leap to believe in her still, across all that has happened?' (Modersohn-Becker, P., 1979, p. 399).

But when Frau Becker did return, after a detour to Rome, she sent to her distant daughter these unforgettable lines on 8 May 1906:

My beloved child, could you not have turned to your mother in such a hard time? How often I have looked for you, called to you, and then thought I must desist, and give you space within your silence. I had no idea how heavy your heart was, or I would have let Rome be Rome a thousand times to come to you. Otto's letter, which I enclose, justifies your going so touchingly, that I have no word to add and thought: when the two of them are so inwardly agreed, it must be right. That your relationship one to another might have sustained a real break never entered my mind. . . . And there, you poor child, assembled in silence so much hurt, so many disappointments, until that pyre caught aflame! How heavily we all share the pain which has overtaken you both, I can hardly say. When I looked forward so passionately to my homecoming . . . it was to Worpswede. It was your house, your garden in blossom, your welcome in that white dress, your beloved, shining eyes, that can pour out such blessing, such sunshine. In all of my life I have known no other, who has the strength to warm her house, her table, her guests, with such lifefulness as it is granted you. And yet, all of a sudden, has your fire and your light been extinguished in you so you have no more to give away. Oh Paula, why could you not have come to one of us, to myself, to Kurt, to Milly – to have yourself loved and taken care of until it went better with you. Even the richest natures must, after all, fall on times of inner poverty and great neediness . . . How you must have suffered so terribly during these months, my Paula, body and soul, you must be sick. May I come to you? Only say the word and I am with you in two days . . . your devoted mother.

And two days later the reply from Paris: 10 May 1906:

My dear mother, that you are not angry with me! I had such fear that you would be angry. That would have made me sad and hard. And now you are so good to me. Yes, mother, I could no longer endure it, and will probably never be able to endure it again. It was all too confined, and not that, and ever less that which I needed.

I am starting a new life. Do not distract me, let me be. It is so beautiful. The last week I have lived as in ecstasy. I believe that I have accomplished something which is good.

Do not grieve for me. If my life should not lead me back to Worpswede, none the less, the eight years I spent there were very lovely.

I also find Otto touching. That and my thoughts of you make this step especially hard.

Let us await developments peacefully. Time will bring what is right and good . . . You, dear mother, always stay close and give your blessing to my doing. I am your child. (Modersohn-Becker, P.,1979, pp. 445–7)

From what depths of compassion, from what heights of concern, do these two communiqués, that bring tears to our eyes, travel to the written page. And what a distance from the turmoil of Demeter and Persephone. How urgently our present day requires rewriting of the myth, where loss of maiden to mother is, for all its timeless content, crossing such a lofty pass where the atmospheric oxygen ever threatens to give out: where so few have stood before in such purity of purpose to be shared between the two, far from any wayside inn.

Within a mere eighteen months Frau Becker was a grandmother, and her Paula-child was dead. 'What a pity', were her final words in their ultimate enigma as she lost consciousness when the embolus struck. It seems that the two women, of spirit and of flesh and blood, could be reconciled only in the final arms of death. But through all the difficulties, decision-making and breaking and remaking yet again, mother and daughter walked together to those dark and final gates.

Concern such as we have witnessed here can override ambivalence and calm the strident tones of guilt. Yet as far as we can see, it is a generosity which has arrived recently, born of an expansiveness, as possibilities for women to achieve a rich, rewarding life – not as a rare exception, but more and more as a rule – were found on offer here and there as their locations multiply. Very clearly here the outer, as it grew more benevolent, triggered a benevolence in the dynamics of the dyad.

Until then the exception was all but crucified by an *unconscious* guilt for raising herself beyond the reach of her mother and her sisters, in the narrow as in the widest sense. We recall how Mary Wollstonecraft, after her wretched mother's death, experienced such guilt towards her sisters whom she struggled to support, despite their ingratitude and envy. Florence Nightingale and Harriet Martineau both fell ill prematurely and had to pay that heavy price for having bulldozed their passage to such premature success, without true separation at a deeper psychic level, for all its persuasive show.

All these forerunners certainly had cause to fear general social disapproval. But this, I believe, was secondary to the inner dynamics, where guilt plays such a leading part. This is amply confirmed in clinical work today. Few cases tend, in my experience, to prove more intractable than those of a gifted woman whose mother suffers from serious mental disturbance which has evidently laid most of her life to waste. For such a daughter to consent, with the ill part of herself, to let her therapist lead her out of the shadows of her illness and her incapacities into a full, creative life, presents a drawn-out, bloody struggle with the dragon-beast of guilt long after it is dragged into the patient's consciousness.

To add to the difficulties, it is not uncommon to find an entire family which is stricken in such cases and forms a tightly ravelled tribe, where any member who defaults to stake a claim for health and life is persecuted by a sense of dire disloyalty, both by the others and from within. In this respect the women's movement, with its growing support groups, is playing an important part. In my clinical struggles I heave a sigh of relief when I hear that such a patient has taken her first

halting steps away from such a stricken mother and a haunted family –
from that incestuous isolation in its very widest sense – towards others
who are struggling, as a group, to free themselves. To free themselves
from the belief that they are being self-indulgent; to recognize a
rightful duty which each owes to herself, to prevent her own resources
from also going down the drain out of false loyalty, which in truth is an
allegiance to self-destructiveness and the secretive toiling of an
ensconced death instinct. To be clear on this issue will require careful
work in any psychotherapy.

Guilt, of course, we must acknowledge, is not the only factor here.
Envy and the fear of envy from those who are 'left behind' requires
patient, close attention, often over many years. While we pay due
regard to the more malignant Kleinian concepts which underlie a
daughter's guilt, such as the phantasies of having in her infant greed
sucked the maternal breast dry to her exclusive advantage, to kick the
empty husk aside; of having scooped the very life out of the maternal
body, to put it to selfish use and self-aggrandizement at the expense of
a mother who is left damaged, far behind, we must never underesti-
mate forces for health and life which will in many instances, with the
least encouragement, begin to burgeon like the desert after but a little
rain.

A daughter's guilt, as we have seen, reaches back to an early phase
of the dyad's evolution, when it is intimately linked to fears of
retaliation. It was clearly operative when Persephone absconded in the
Nyasan Fields to put herself within the orbit of 'The Law of the
Father' in the language of Lacan. This essential move in the interests
of her growth and separation from her mother will evoke, a daughter
fears, a hostile/envious attack from the person of her mother. Small
wonder that Persephone was reluctant to return to the raging Demeter
from her hide-out in the Underworld and her husband's protection.
No doubt the Eleusinian Mysteries celebrate at one level the dawning
recognition that the Law of the Father does not intrinsically negate the
basic continuity, the essential flow of life, within the woman
generations.

The daughter fears retaliation for an additional reason to the fact of
separation. There are certainly theories, derived from the consulting
room by following the transference, that in the woman's unconscious
her (pro)creative achievement is symbolically equated with possession
of the penis, meaning that she has stolen it from the phallic mother.

There is confusion at this point between the actual penis and the symbolic phallus, to induce substantial guilt on account of the theft, vivid in her phantasy (Chasseguet-Smirgel, J., 1970, p. 106).

This is a sensitive time in a woman's therapy. When she begins to manifest and own her creativity in one or more spheres of life, she will often grow anxious and show many signs of guilt. Unravelling of the material slowly points to a terror that the mother-therapist – for these anxieties belong to the mother-transference, regardless of the therapist's sex – is in a bad way: on the point of death or of collapse. At a phantasy level this mother has been maintained, or literally propped up, by an indwelling penis, which the creative daughter feels she must have appropriated, for how else could her endeavours have met with any success?

This specific phantasy of stealing mother's penis compounds anxieties of incest of the later oedipal phase. Interpretations along these lines produce little inner light and accentuate the guilt. They will make it difficult for the woman on the couch to achieve a meaningful, namely numinous, connection to the father of her childhood: her inner father here and now. But is it not possible that the oedipal daughter *is* fertilized by her father in a consecratory but not a biological sense; that once this has been accomplished she returns in this manner – of bearing the creative seed – to the maternal circuit? There she learns to be a woman who harbours the paternal blessing which will help to actualize her creative potential once the time for this is ripe in her overall development.

In *her* case, in other words, this *symbolic incest* will assume a higher order, whereas that between *son* and mother is of a regressive kind, for which reason it will come under that stern Taboo whose dawn is in the Totem days. ("There are grounds for thinking that totem prohibitions were principally directed against the incestuous desires of the son' [Freud, S., 1913, p. 5].) Only now are we approaching insights from which to evaluate what portion of a daughter's guilt in truth fallaciously belongs to a symbolic order, to the spiritual domain, which is not its proper locus, and how far it is enravelled in infantile sexuality and culpable in phantasy.

Certainly this last dilemma, which belongs to concrete thinking and earliest anxieties, must first be worked through and resolved on its primitive merits which belong to the oral phase before spiritual components make their inner presence known. But once that task has been accomplished, 'incest' as patrimony can subsequently be taken up, when it appears in the material, through which work the inner father achieves a numinous aspect of great spiritual importance. Here, it would seem that Jungian thinking offers Kleinian emphasis a creative path forward.

While the psychotherapeutic task must direct its first attention to those primitive aspects of infantile development, as conceptualized by Klein, Mahler and other workers, it may not then neglect those components of the mind which are often labelled 'higher' or spiritual faculties. Yet even these have their roots in earliest development since they must surely grow from the soil of our love in its struggle against hatred, in a sublimated form.

Here we might now return to take a more detailed view of the subject of maternal hatred. As we saw earlier, Winnicott (Winnicott, D.W., 1975, pp. 200–1) has given us eighteen reasons why every mother hates her baby, even when he is a boy. What he however does not mention, while mothers sense it vividly, is that this maternal hate, and in consequence her guilt, must be greater in degree towards the child who is a daughter: who is her mother's replica. Let us mention just a few of the more obvious reasons. There is, first of all, the fight for narcissistic supplies in terms of love and admiration on which women depend to such a clamorous extent for a favourable self-image. Where this pernicious issue is insufficiently resolved, the skies of the relationship will certainly be less than sunny. As in the tale of Snow White, the beauty of a daughter may arouse murderous feelings in an envious, ageing queen.

A mother is held responsible for the end-product in a daughter whom she is duty-bound to socialize, so that she may be desirable, in keeping with current trends. Again, her own self-image is relentlessly at stake. Here she is in a double-bind; for in obedience to those dictates she knows that she may have to damage her daughter's natural talents: her inborn nature and directions; to incur her hostility, while she herself must suffer guilt, albeit at an unconscious level.

Her daughter will in time displace her, in a way her son will not.

Her daughter comes on the stage of greater permissiveness and wider opportunities than applied to her own time.

She is increasingly absolved from dutiful obligations towards the old and infirm, namely herself, in her old age; and set free to go her way.

These are only the more obvious reasons why a mother will experience hatred towards a daughter and for that reason suffer guilt to a greater extent than in the case of a son.

If I am here contradicting statements which were made before that there is no evidence that mothers hate their daughters more than they may hate their sons, it is finally a question of a total balance sheet. For the mother–daughter dyad carries specific benefits of support and *jouissance*, companionship and consolation which may amply recompense these listed negatives.

Lastly, an observation which is old as the hills but has to my own knowledge not surfaced in the literature – that girls appear more vulnerable to maternal deprivation and carry their resentfulness to greater lengths than their brothers, who can later make it up in mothering from their wives. Antiquity was certainly well aware of the fact. Orestes was much more willing than the murderous Electra to forgive maternal failings, as we saw earlier.

A later interesting example are the Dickinson siblings. Emily and her sister Vinnie could not conceive of being mothers and retired into spinsterhood, whereas their brother Austin married. Oral preoccupations which amount to obsessions irrupt like an eerie chorus into the poet's work. They draw attention vividly to early maternal deprivation; for Mrs Dickinson, as this Freudian author claims, was often seriously depressed:

> *It would have starved a Gnat –*
> *to live so small as I –*
> *And yet it was a living child –*
> *With food's necessity . . .*
> (Cody, J., 1971, p. 44)

We can, of course, not rule out that this starvation may have been classically self-imposed in the anorectic pattern; but we find the same connection in the unequal fate of marriage versus spinsterhood in the brother–sister case of Harriet Martineau.

Now it could well be claimed that, as Susie Orbach argues throughout her recent work, daughters always go short of essential mothering in the merged relationship which is specific to the dyad (Orbach, S. and Eichenbaum, L., 1987, pp. 43–50). But within that Orbach-given, persuasive as her findings are in our state of piecemeal knowledge, we still have massive variations we can liken to a spectrum in this particular aftermath. There is, we find, a close connection between the mothering received and the deeper wish to bear a child: 'As a result of good-enough early mothering there develops a capacity to create a live child in fantasy' (Steedman, C., 1986, p. 91, quoting Winnicott). Girls do not play with dolls, as is often claimed today, because they are given them but because they identify with a good and loving mother whom they wish to emulate. In other words, for a woman to be able to believe at a deep unconscious level that she could conceive a baby, and rear her child successfully, the experience of being loved and nourished to her satisfaction in her own infancy is a firm prerequisite.

This is certainly confirmed in clinical experience. In the first place women have more problems with orality, with over- and with undereating, than seems to be the case with men. Secondly, many women enter psychotherapy filled with a great despair that they do not want a child at some deep, instinctive level, while they long to want a baby. Then, as psychotherapy grows into a deep experience of being wanted, known and loved, where sessions are in time equated with a satisfying feed, the wish for motherhood develops, rooted in her new conviction that she now has the resources to be a mother to her child.

I have very little doubt that mothers like their daughters, know – as they have always known at a deep unconscious level, long before the time of Freud – that a woman's happiness, her entire self-fulfilment, is built at her mother's breast. Although it is true to say that a mother may feel pangs that she has been displaced when her daughter has a baby, the deeper, overwhelming feeling is of immense relief that she has not failed her daughter, once the latter has become a new mother in her turn. A childless daughter, read as failure, is yet another cause for maternal guilt.

If women know in their guts that this is how the matter stands, every time I raise the issue of excessive guilt between mother and daughter with a male psychotherapist he demands that I 'prove it'. Why is he so insensitive? I find myself pondering. Why does neither clinical work nor day-to-day observation of a wife or woman friends serve as useful evidence? Or is this something which emerges with greater clarity, with deeper persuasiveness, in the mother-transference, in relationships between women?

I believe that the actual sex of the psychotherapist can play a decisive part in biasing which material enters the transference. The issue remains controversial, nor is this the place to argue such a case in any detail. Freud himself was aware, as were others subsequently, that the gender of the analyst plays a certain part in the vicissitudes and unfolding of the transference. Papers to this effect appear at intervals in the profession's leading journals. Certainly woman therapists find repeated evidence of how deeply guilt colours many of the deeper aspects of the mother–daughter dyad, to a greater extent than that of mother and son, as we have adumbrated.

It is also fascinating that men, in my own experience, do not like to hear of mother–daughter altercations. For them a heated reference to aspects of a 'bad' mother must of necessity be unacceptably disturbing, since the subject reinforces sexual anxieties.

So dominant, in my view, is the part played by guilt in blocking creativity and an easy, joyful give-and-take within the mother–daughter dyad, that I see its modification as one of the important aims in psychotherapy with a woman. Only the other day, while I was struggling with this chapter, in light-hearted conversation with a Kleinian friend and colleague, I asked him: 'Look, what would you say to one of your woman patients once she starts to talk about her excitement at discovering that her creative potency, much of which she has denied, now seems boundless suddenly?'

He said, without much hesitation: 'I would interpret such remarks as serious self-idealization.'

'Oh dear,' I countered with a sigh, 'I would experience such relief in recognizing just how far guilt must have been modified.'

3　A SALUTE TO MARTHA QUEST

It is the challenge to have the courage to look and listen to her
own depth, regardless of whether what she may discover accords
with what she has been in the habit of considering right.
(EDWARD E. C. WHITMONT, *The Return of the Goddess*)

Woman's sacrifice occurs on the animus level when she gives up
being the beloved one at any price, as the patriarchal culture has
taught her to be. The price for her transformed rebirth is to accept
her own reality and to commit herself to what she discovers
herself to be, even though by prevailing standards this may be
regarded as ugly and repulsive.
(EDWARD E. C. WHITMONT, *The Return of the Goddess*)

MARTHA QUEST had, as we know, struggled blindly since her teens to achieve some remedy for a growing sense of adriftness, for some abeyance of herself, a total lack of inner locus from which she might put down roots into the process of her life. We were worried about Martha. We had sensed that her autonomy, her claim to authenticity, her struggle for subject status – which she took up from time to time, only to lose her grip again – had been subverted and disrupted. From the earliest beginning, doubtless from her infancy, her integral life-space had been hijacked to serve as a container for her mother's psychic pain; had been invaded and attacked, infiltrated and poisoned by the one who should be trusted to have stood guardian over its sanctity and growth. Instead it had been vilified by her mother's projections of all she hated in herself, above all the overwhelming sense of being an unwanted child which grows from the soil of that deprivation where earliest needs have not been met. Mrs Quest had lost her mother, who was in any case inept, at a very early age. Martha has been deeply wounded by this projected legacy.

The fact that we can make this statement places us fair and square in the twentieth century during which we have become aware, in considerable detail, of the nature of the wound, as of its genesis in the earliest transactions of the mother–daughter dyad. So, in a sense, were the Greek poets when we heard Electra cry: 'Mother dear, you bred our young wolves' fury.' But here maternal default is considerably less specific. Nor is it the poet's task to draw or to apply conclusions from his dreamlike utterance. That he will leave to others, while the seed may lie dormant with a medley of its kind, in the soil of the unconscious for countless centuries, even for millennia.

Today we can be more precise:

The discovery of woundedness, particularly of childhood trauma (trauma means wound), as an almost universal factor of human motivation and behaviour, is one of the most important discoveries of modern depth psychology ... But the wound underlies and motivates the search. The wound is part of that identification of consciousness which, if it is to know the good, must also incur the pain of the bad. (Whitmont, E.C., 1983, p. 195)

We can now postulate that it is the actual search, directed by consciousness and therefore consciousness itself, which appears to have changed rather than the nature of actual unconscious content: more of this in the next chapter.

This becomes evident the moment we envisage Demeter and Persephone, or Electra and Clytaemnestra, entering the consulting rooms of any psychotherapist at work in the post-Freudian era. He or she would certainly see their troubles as familiar, as accessible to consciousness, in almost every respect. Demeter might be diagnosed as a menopausal depression. She is suffering from the sense of ultimate redundancy, of having nothing more to offer, since she equates fertility with the sum total of a woman's creativity, her rhyme and reason for existence: a murderous envy of the young, who have taken the stage and displaced her utterly: a dreadful narcissistic wound exacerbating previous ones. The psychotherapist might think in terms of an underlying manic-depressive illness, looked at from the angle of her enormous omnipotence, and then perhaps rule this out as she seems very open to trial interpretations, such as that she might see herself as an ordinary person and that her angry feelings are perhaps neither as powerful, nor as enduringly destructive, as she evidently fears. For the goddess, we recall, managed to come to terms with her new situation quite remarkably well, even if the process proved to be a very painful one, as will always be the case. Insights along these lines will ease her suffering, which becomes something she can think about instead of acting it out.

The anxieties and turmoil of young Persephone would also prove familiar in our present day and age. At the dark end of the spectrum, she could very well present as a puerperal psychosis. She might possibly fear, in one of its many versions, that her (internal) mother would want to attack her infant. If psychotherapy was, in this young mother's case, brought to a healing conclusion, her unconscious would stage an 'Eleusinian Mystery'. She would rise out of 'the underworld' of deep depersonalization, where she dwelt among 'the shadows', as will often be the case in a major transformation, and together with her infant be reunited with her (inner) mother, to stand as joint guardians over that holy task – to preserve the generations.

Again, Electra and her mother would present few surprises. The daughter might be obsessed with matricidal phantasies. She might well have regressed to murderous, dirty states of mind to explain her dilapidated person, to which the poet draws attention. It is quite a common story. She suffered infantile frustration. A little brother was born to compound her misery, her sense of rejection and exclusion. Her mother was, we rather feel, a cold and narcissistic woman. She attacked the girl's father and he found himself a mistress. Perhaps he died or disappeared, but the girl was deprived of her essential father and blamed her mother for the fact.

During her early therapy she might idealize the absent father and rage by the month and year against her cruel, unloving mother. Then, in the course of time, there might be a turnabout. There might be dreams leading back to early dyadic bliss. With this in the transference she might become one of those patients, quite familiar enough, who would want to act this out in the most concrete terms:

She was pulled by yearnings to suck on my breasts, or crawl into my vagina; she needed to hold my card inside her brassiere between sessions. Such symptoms revealed her severe difficulties with separation, object constancy, and early trauma. The idealized transference expressed her yearnings for a wished-for mother ... Her own mother was a beautiful, extremely narcissistic and ungiving woman. (Mann Kulish, N., 1986, p. 399)

Such a patient might Electra very possibly have been, until she slowly came to terms, given a favourable outcome, with her psychic pain and deprivation.

Her mother, on the other hand, a very different woman from the more loving Demeter, would in all likelihood never be in a position to admit a need for help. Like the ageing Mrs Quest, isolated more and more by her narcissistic rage, Clytaemnestra might well lose all genuine contact with her children, with the up-and-coming generation who are 'pushing her out', to drift ominously into senile psychosis, and sit muttering invectives in a corner all alone until she peters out and dies, unnoticed and unsung: an unattended funeral, rather like this vignette from the life of Martha Quest, here in dialogue with Dr Lamb:

'And how is your mother?'
'She's dead. She died less than a year after she went back.'
He said humorously: 'And that was your fault?'
'When you say it I can't help feeling it might be – but not when I think it over.' (Lessing, D., 1978, pp. 338–9)

Such is the end of Mrs Quest. But Martha can by now, we notice, *'think about'* these painful issues, unlike a year or two ago when she first consulted him in that state of mute distress which belongs to symbiosis, to the phase which Neumann called the Elementary Feminine, while its hold remains unchallenged.

This exchange with Dr Lamb transpires during a visit which Martha pays him quite some time after her mother's abrupt departure, not to talk about herself but to obtain his view on the prospects for Linda at this stage of her illness after yet one more relapse. As far as Martha is concerned, a very serious search is on for the following reasons: first that, as we have heard, Martha was of a generation dedicated to self-knowledge: to think about her inner world; and secondly this consideration – that consciousness itself has changed.

Through eight millennia this faculty has passed, as in the development of the human individual, from the omnipotent-magical, through the mythical and on to the mental phase. In other words, from symbiosis as absolute and unquestioned, with its pressure 'to belong' rather than 'to be' or 'do' (Stelzer, J., 1986), on towards the dawn of myth where the resounding words 'I am' are uttered first by mortal man (Whitmont, E.C., 1983, p. 50). How far Odysseus had to travel, cut off from woman, from his faithful wife, to find that moment in language; while matriarchy as it was originally instituted had to draw to an end for the reason that it 'gave woman a false, because magical prestige' (Whitmont, E.C., 1983, p. 122). What is more, subjected to the cycles of procreation with their flux and instability, their primitive anxieties rooted in the preverbal, may she not have maintained one foot in the magical order of the Great Goddess so that her moment in language may well be of a different order, the subtle realm of intuition: the utterance of the Sphinx, rather than the realm of *logos* valued so highly by the male?

In some part of her being woman still remains 'unspoken'. If Odysseus spoke 'I am', Demeter and Persephone could not utter such a meaning. They lacked access to discourse and had to act their drama out like the women in the Coldridge basement when we first encounter them. What is happening down there? Are these mute entanglements meaningless and haphazard; are they in some way related to that phenomenon, the idealization of a madness – meaning feminine madness – which sprang up in the sixties, with its strong inclination towards anti-psychiatry; or are they looking for a language intrinsic to a new status which we have called womanness, to stake their own, true right to be?

Martha's first undertaking, once Mrs Quest was safely airborne, was to go and visit Linda, who is back in hospital. She finds her sitting on her bed in 'a greyish dressing gown, which was rather grubby. And her beautiful hands had blood-stains around her finger tips' (Lessing, D., 1978, p. 329). Her former flatmate, Dorothy, has also slashed her wrists again, for lack of the appropriate words. She will shortly kill herself with a large overdose. Martha asks quietly: 'Linda, why don't you just come home . . . You could come home and try to be part of everything' (Lessing, D., 1978, p. 331). Linda does come home to try.

What has just taken place in this important exchange, which could easily be overlooked? Martha has in effect decided to take responsibility for a 'mad part' of herself, for that part which is unspoken, for the first time in her life; for that part of herself which has consistently evaded any getting to grips with taking charge of her life, in the same respect as Linda.

Initially there is confusion, since projective identification takes over in the classic manner: 'Good Lord, am I in love with Linda? . . . Silence . . . Then as the muscles of her mind relaxed, and an accepting darkness came back' . . . there dawned a possibility to 'think about' the situation. Martha, as we will recall, had lately done a lot of homework, which is now to bear fruit!:

If she was in love with Linda, then it was with a part of herself she had never been introduced to – even caught a glimpse of. This was the language of a schoolgirl crush! This unknown person in Martha adored Linda, worshipped her, wished to wrap her long soft hair around her hands, said, poor little child, poor little girl, why don't you let me look after you? (Lessing, D., 1978, p. 383)

Here Martha starts to integrate a needy part of herself; for that language, if 'mad', paradoxically belongs to a stringent discipline of our Freudian here and now. She had formerly attacked 'it', hating and resenting 'it', in episodes blackened by a venomous self-hatred because she felt as a child that her mother could not stand 'it', this needy part of herself, since she had not met her needs. Subject to her mother's projections, helpless at their receiving end, she had only seen herself as a ghostly negative, namely with her mother's eyes. Now she starts to use her own, even if initially she rather swings the other way: she is enamoured by her needs, by her vulnerability. Having parted from her mother – literally, as we know, but also metaphorically by sending the projections back – Martha is now in a position, for the first time in her life, to accept that her wretched mother will never meet her baby-needs because she is not 'that kind of person'. Having taken this step, Martha is able, finally, to raise the possibility of meeting certain needs herself from her inner resources, which she can now begin to own. Here the basic ABC of her own maternal instinct for her needy 'baby-self', but also in its wider sense, can begin to germinate. Here Lessing has conducted us, seemingly unaware of these deeper implications, to a crucial watershed: a missed opportunity in terms of this important work (*The Children of Violence*) for a profounder resolution than she will later offer us, as we will shortly see.

It is generally the case in the mending of the psyche that as we grow to be aware of areas of fragmentation and of splits inside ourself, the process of healing is already under way. Here, in this unsavoury basement, a split imposed upon woman since the advent of the Holy Virgin, between intactness demanded of a simple Jewish girl by a god of the patriarchs, and the Mater Dolorosa who must bear and lose a child, is, in this dreamlike scene between Martha and Linda, beginning to come together. Beneath the appearance of dissolution which can mislead us easily into wholesale disavowal of this 'feminine madness' lies hidden an important task, which has lain unattended for all of two millennia.

Are we back with the Virgin? Not this time with the obvious split between the body and the spirit to which we pointed before ('And the angel said') but with an important variation: a dissociation between the divine commission of invulnerability and woman's vulnerability in secular human terms.

'In the androlatric system "virgo" came to mean "virgo intacta": a chaste or celibate woman. Intacta means "untouched by anything that harms or defiles, uninjured, unimpaired" ' (Whitmont, E.C., 1983, p. 136). And where, through Christian centuries, woman failed to conform to this iconic vision, in its impossibility, then she became unholy, then she was a harridan to be burnt as a witch, or otherwise excommunicated as one who was in serious trouble: outside the Law of the Lord. Here we meet with the confusion that a woman 'in trouble' must inevitably spell sexual incontinence, an assumption which would never be applied to a man!

But why, we have to ask ourselves, must the woman preserve this quality of intacta, why must she be chaste and humble? Whitmont gives us one reply: 'Lest the abysmal power of the feminine dissolve his [man's] firm will and render him over helplessly into the maelstrom of transformation' (Whitmont, E.C., 1983, p. 136) – man's transformation from intacta, the magic of omnipotence, the phallus as sole signifier, into the common human lot: of vulnerability.

Here, the elementary aspects of the old Great Goddess would have colluded with the male. Let everything remain unchanged in the virtue of the archaic. For did not her ancient power, eight millennia BC, rest on the Great Round, where all things ever shall remain entirely within her grasp: holding and never letting go: resting on her static laurels: not entering the stream of time, the truth-land of mortality?

That is all very well. But here we must remind ourselves of a second reply to the question we have put: that there are no attributes which can exclusively be imposed on the psyche from without. Let us not forget that woman carries a fair share of blame for this particular quandary, this notion of virgo intacta. For did she not in her infancy, like the little boy, also split the early mother in two horizontally and do her best to demolish the lower, 'wounded', sexual half to preserve the iconic image of the ever-flowing breast, the pure, unsullied feeding mother? Is she not also guilty of wanting time to stand still?

None the less, transformation, the transformative character of the Elementary Feminine, has been quietly active through the millennia, and is certainly at work in this curious involvement between Martha and Linda, where its object is to reinstate feminine vulnerability, injury and impairment so that their specific nature may begin to filter through into woman's consciousness along the high road of experience which is lived and not denied. For it is only through this process, at whose heart lies our acceptance of all the conflict, come what may, that a complementary range of strength and resiliency, tough-mindedness and endurance, which belong to womanness, can gradually be acknowledged so that all these attributes, wrongly labelled 'opposites', may work towards integration. Only when this is under way can the immensity of the maternal project enter the field of scrutiny to be seriously assented to by genuine personality, in the place of blind instinct groping along time-old paths in archaic isolation. Failing that, some deep unease, which may amount to revulsion, gnaws at the centre of the dyad and will generally lead to some far-reaching subversion at the heart of propagation, however silent and unseen.

Martha and Linda had both, albeit in their different ways, been unable to assume maternal responsibility. Along with millions of women, still encumbered by the split, by the above dualism, they had sensed unconsciously that motherhood presented them, as matters stood, with yet another obstacle to the integrity of subject status. That the package of marriage, entered into as a bolt hole in the hope of achieving wholeness, of eluding the split, and closely bound to motherhood, threatened to perpetuate or even deepen the fragmentation they sensed themselves entangled in.

Martha had, as we know, abandoned her daughter, Caroline, when she left her first husband, and except for occasional pangs of guilt given her but little thought; while Linda Coldridge, wife of Mark and mother of their son, Francis, had escaped into psychosis: 'I am not that sort of person', she told the unhappy Paul when he came down to the basement like an abandoned puppy, yelping for maternal warmth, after his mother's suicide.

Martha, Linda and Sally are not by any means unique. No longer able to conform, due to some deep, unconscious protest, to that obscene iconic image, to the model of 'intacta'; resolutely disinclined to serve as handmaid of the Lord, to sacrifice a range of options on the altar of maternity, while she is overwhelmed with guilt at such a 'selfish' refusal, how is woman to resolve the conflicting imagos imposed on her by motherhood? Either she abandons the project on those impossible terms in steadily growing numbers in our Western world today, or she rejects the child, particularly if it is a daughter with one part of her personality – her split-off vulnerability, her unresolved baby-needs – which her infant now expresses and owns so vociferously, when she was taught she must disown hers by generations of mothers who were taught to in their turn. Did we ever, let us think back, hear our stoic Mrs Thornton murmur a word regarding needs beyond, perhaps, a little ration from the good Lord above, doled out on Sundays in the church?

Far from being uninjured, unharmed and unimpaired, undefiled and all the rest, these mothers of our day and age sense a cruel paradox at the heart of their existence which offers two alternatives: childlessness by rebellion, yet fearful of profound regrets once it is perhaps too late, or submission in the confines of a masochistic stance: a sacrifice of their own needs while they minister to those of their children and their husbands in a never-ending round, with little thanks from the angel who set the whole thing in motion!

It is a double sacrifice, and Lessing poses it like this:

> . . . to herself she [Martha] was able to say precisely what she feared. It was the rebirth of the woman in love. If one is with a man, 'in love', or in the condition of loving, then there comes to life that hungry, never-to-be-fed, never-at peace woman who needs and wants and must have . . . For the unappeasable hungers and cravings are part, not of the casual affair, or of friendly sex, but of marriage and the 'serious' love. God forbid. (Lessing, D., 1978, p. 313)

Nor are matters improved by Winnicott's ideal of the 'good-enough mother', a carbon copy of the Virgin, even if in modern dress. It comes to us as a relief that Freud and Lacan recognize that every mother must, in truth, sooner or later in each case but invariably too soon, frustrate the illusion of symbiosis while furtively maintaining it. If, regardless, the intact and the wounded state of woman continue to be kept apart, the split is brought into the open – moreover, by the man, struggling side by side with woman in her quest for a solution.

But before maternity, as we have just indicated, marriage as we play it out poses the same dilemma. As Freud himself knew very well:

'Even marriage is not made secure until the wife has succeeded in making her husband her child as well as in acting as a mother to him' (Freud, S., 1933, pp. 133–4). Making this statement he was not to know that half a century on 50 per cent of marriages would be ending in divorce, of which 50 per cent was at the demand of women. Yet, as we are well aware, it is only on these terms, on this humiliating ground, that men will consent to play the protector and provider for this all-demanding nest. But let us not deceive ourselves: woman colludes in this arrangement. If marriage resurrects his symbiotic yearnings, in ministering to them she feeds her own vicariously, although there are hopeful signs that this game is now played out at an increasingly conscious level.

Certainly until these pitfalls at the core of woman's life can become part and parcel of our growing consciousness, Marthas and Lindas will remain enmured in their thousands in such 'basements' in perplexed bewilderment, devoured by a dreadful guilt as to 'what is wrong with them'.

Further, in this blind submission to her provider, to the male, into which she is drawn, because heterosexual love already sets into motion her maternal reverie long before the milk comes in for the first infant at her breast, she risks a further mutilation. For the feminine psyche, by its nature, enshrines an urge towards the secret of unitary reality, for our present purposes of vulnerability *and* strength, of human weakness *and* resiliency, and the need to uphold it for harmonious functioning. Where this quest is opposed by an overruling husband who mocks his wife's natural bent as madness and the woman, in her turn, collapses into subservience, in keeping with archaic dictates, she will suffer impositions which are alien to her truth. Under androlatric rule, with its tendency 'toward awareness by means of splitting' (Whitmont, E.C., 1983, p. 60), a chronic sense of mutilation so subverts her core-being that it threatens to extinguish her belief in herself, her fountainhead of *jouissance*, to leave a sense of worthlessness and depths of chronic depression: a deeply masochistic trance.

Exposed to those uneven odds she is left, as matters stand, with only two alternatives: flight into the single state or, failing that, flight into madness, since it conserves her inmost truth in that painful disguise. Was not the threefold split of Mary into spirit, mind and flesh the origin of this malaise, unknown to the Ancient World? Was Eve cast out of Paradise for offering to the male the fruit of a forbidden tree, where opposites – good and evil – grew side by side, capable of digestion into unitary experience? This the Godhead would not have. For the God of Genesis had only recently set foot in the domain of the Goddess to curb her magical disorder with the omnipotence of the word. 'Let there be light', said He, in this preverbal symbiosis where mother and infant dwell formless, an interflowing entity. 'The earth was without form, and void . . .' (Genesis 1: 2, 3) when He came on to the scene. And was his creature, woman, Eve, now that he had ordained, had with a word created order, by cleaving awkward opposites, to restore chaos and confusion, to reinstate the primal dark?

Why has the Feminine, as a psychic principle, rebelled against this 'law and order' as it was dictated by the faceless God of the Tribes? It was generated by the *omnipotence* of the word, the word which denied the wound of terminating symbiosis; a word which stood unsubdued by the symbolic order which is born of the wound. It was the word in concrete tantrum against creation by gestation, inherent in the Feminine, which led human consciousness into the present cul-de-sac of 'the extroverted rational and material orientation of the mental epoch of contemporary modern man' (Whitmont, E.C., 1983, p. 74) and has for blood-soaked centuries obfuscated our way forward to a new phase of consciousness: 'a realm culturally and collectively uncharted as yet, TERRA INCOGNITA' (Whitmont, E.C., 1983, p. 75). For all the chaos and confusion in that basement habitat, below the surface of the earth, paved and asphalted over, where these mothers can no longer comply with demands of the 'intacta' aspect of their maternal role, this realm is blindly being sought in a reconstitution of that breathless beginning where a second Genesis takes cognizance of the wound – the cut from the maternal body, and whatsoever springs from it.

And it is down here that woman, for all that she appears more whole in the outer world of many choices, which tries to sell her the illusion of being empowered and unhurt, is at last refusing to be fooled, in the person of Martha Quest. As the mother of a daughter whom she had no choice but to disown in her search for subject status, but on terms of her own truth, she senses from before the word, from some dim, preverbal region that motherhood in its truest sense is still awaiting new signals. That as a conscious undertaking, sacred in a modern sense, beyond biology and instinct as much as social fabrications, it will start to be achieved only when woman within her inner world can begin to integrate what has been split off and denied; for 'the dignity of a daimonium, even a satanic one, sexuality, neediness and aggressive violence cannot be controlled by rationality and good will alone' (Whitmont, E.C., 1983, p. 9). The three, of course, belong together as long as they remain repressed. For instinct demands mastery and mastery spells violence if it is inhibited in its original meaning, which is 'to do', to 'make work'.

With these women in the basement we are back with surrogate mothers, as we saw them in the Middle Ages, dearly sustaining one another, and as they have regrouped again within the present women's movement – not just its intellectual factions with their impetuous debates primed by sophisticated reading, but growing from a grass-roots level where neighbours seek each other out to clarify and to accomplish the ancient theme of harmony against such overwhelming odds: those of a pseudo-rationalism which refuses to mourn the wound, the implications of our severance from mother-as-a-part-of-me.

The blood which is on Linda's fingers and runs from Dorothy's slashed wrists is the symptom of a protest by women who are tantalized and driven near or into madness by that illusion on offer in the outer world today, sold by the name of 'equal status'. A spurious and transparent bribe, it offends against her deepest nature to struggle towards a realm of unitary experience which is advertised today as a tawdry unisex. Yet psychoanalysis itself has only just begun to grapple with this enigmatic issue of authentic womanness. As a status it is still unspoken, still in search of its words and authenticity as much in the Freudian ranks as in the language of the streets.

If the women in the Coldridge basement were addressing this conundrum, in tens and hundreds and in thousands, that vanguard then was premature. To shake at emotional habits which remain a sedative for our human distress, as we confront its components in our unresolved infantile omnipotence in all its ramifications, requires collective resolution. It is gathering momentum and we must thank the Martha Quests, lonely, isolated victims, in the dawn of a new age whose sun is long-delayed in rising. No Martha Quest can on her own rescue an androlatric era hurtling towards the extinction of every single living thing.

Certainly, as the victim of the projections of a mother whose experience of herself is, like Mrs Quest's, of a helpless, angry victim, a seething non-entity, Martha was bound to be defeated at that moment in time. Neither did Doris Lessing then envisage an inner resolution by which these women could emerge from the impasse of their lives, and she solves the dilemma in a stultifying cop-out by staging a 'catastrophe' in the outer world instead. Whether by leak of poisonous gas or by radioactivity – the details remain obscure – the British Isles become 'Destroyed Area 11'. Even Lessing, who has her finger so closely on the era's pulse as it affects the life and very substance of her woman characters, could create no alternative in her visionary imagination.

Here we are bound to say that no solution can be achieved on the part of a daughter by packing her mother off in a jumbo-jet in the fervent hope that this is the last of her. Any tactics of this kind seen in terms of 'getting rid of' belong to the old vicious circle of splitting off and projecting the helpless non-entity back and forth *ad infinitum* without the courage to acknowledge this nebulum each in ourself. This, in turn, requires help to confront the psychic pain which will have to be released in a gradual acceptance of such a hideous legacy. Yet how, under her circumstances of early inner violation, could Martha possibly conceive of any relationship, including a therapeutic one, in which she will not be exploited and/or intruded into according to the noxious pattern of her primary one? If a patient like Martha eventually takes the risk of entering psychotherapy, it may take years of work until she can begin to trust that the intentions of the other are possibly benevolent.

But if she does not find her way into a healing one-to-one – and there are grounds to believe that Doris Lessing lost belief in psychotherapy – we can see that Martha Quest, like her author, does not lack courage. She is struggling in her millions in the basements of this world, in isolated, hidden places, to which she has dragged herself like a wounded animal. She has taken refuge there in the pretence of being 'mad', or to play 'the little woman', or the receptacle of man's sexual phantasies, or the world's greatest mother, or forever-caring daughter, until she finds a way forward, through the risky paths of trust, into true relatedness. Then she will come into contact with men and women of her kind who are ready to confront as those who will resist that chaos and woundedness that must become part and parcel of unitary experience – those who are ready to admit into a growing consciousness those splits of a fragmented psyche which withdraws into make-believe rather than face the pain of a sentient being which can confront the fate of a separate entity cognizant of mortality.

This requires a diagnosis which rests on an open ground where sociology, depth psychology, biology and ethology can shed their assumed omniscience, to meet and show a willingness to learn one another's secret language. It requires furthermore a classless, multiracial taskforce which is not afraid to scrutinize 'the delicate manner in which human beings stifle one another at the point of reproduction' (Ernst, S., and Maguire, M., 1987, p. 72); or to seek to understand how the sexes collude in perpetuating this malaise.

From such a conference, from such an ongoing workshop and the feedback it provides for the cultural ecosphere, woman could gradually emerge with a more holistic self-image – one in which the polarities of daughterhood and mothership can begin to integrate into a life-experience woven of a span of projects and succession of phases which refuse to be locked into one or other role, but are lived as certain aspects of an ongoing process of remaking herself.

4   WE ARE WARY OF
THE GODDESS

You can be healthy without knowing you are healthy, handsome
without knowing you are handsome . . .
   Our minds grow, in one way or another: and sometimes in
ways that our senses are unable to register.
(ERIC RHODE, 'Life before words')

. . . behaviour can be changed by changing the conditions of
which it is a function.
(MELVIN KONNER, *The Tangled Wing*)

And if the assumption of responsibility for one's discourse leads to
the conclusion that all conclusions are genuinely provisional and
therefore inconclusive, that all origins are similarly unoriginal,
that responsibility itself must cohabit with frivolity, this need not
be cause for gloom.
(JACQUES DERRIDA, *Of Grammatology*)

WE HAVE TRAVELLED a great distance, and done so inconclus-
ively. Such formal thought as was conscripted rested entirely on
the merits of a deeper resonance; a meaningful connection with
memory traces and convictions already sitting in my mind. To learn to
trust experience and to eschew the clever word where it fails to strike a
chord, to be like a little child in this singular respect, is highly suspect
in this day and age of what Dinnerstein calls pseudomastery. But if I
now set about tidying up certain loose ends, it is for my own benefit
and not to satisfy the susceptibilities of scholars.
   Throughout this exploration of the mother–daughter dyad, two
threads have run consistently and are readily discernible. One is the
theme of separation, the other of authenticity of woman as a sentient
being. Both issues lie at the heart of transactions which emanate from
the core of the dyad and are gender-specific in various crucial
respects. Some of these appear to rest on the classical foundations of
Freud's Oedipus Complex for the boy and the girl, while others have
more recently been put forward and described. The issue of their

connection is an important one since inconclusive separation would appear to encourage inauthenticity. We saw how the package afflicted Martha Quest as the daughter of her mother and also that this recognition belongs to our present century but went into no further details, an omission we will now make good to obtain certain bearings as we approach our journey's end.

Feminist psychotherapists, for the present, take the view that woman's psychic pain, which is rooted in the wound of inadequate separation of the mother–daughter dyad, can be attributed to a state of *merged attachment* that they regard as unique to that relationship in a patriarchal society. This is how it is defined, like some incestuous tug of war:

At times, each mother can respond selflessly to the needs and initiative of this little girl ... But, oftentimes, mother has difficulty with her daughter's expression of need and this easy relating is disrupted. The mother who continually restrains both her own needs for emotional nourishment and her own initiatives is unable to respond to her daughter in an open and generous way. Her responses to the child are characterized by annoyance and withdrawal ... The emotional ambience of the merged attachment, then, contains these contradictory aspects. The relationship is at once the soothing, safe protective environment and the utterly disappointing, frightening, painful place where all can be lost. (Orbach, S. and Eichenbaum, L., 1987, pp. 49–50)

The story rings entirely true. The question is, is it specific to the mother–daughter dyad? Did Adrienne Rich not rage and mourn that she treated her small boys according to this formula? That she resented bitterly, with the part of her that was a poet which was fighting tooth and nail for the poet's physiognomy, the way the little boys' needs would come between her and her work with its imperious demands which gave her life its other meaning? I cannot, for the life of me – meaning my life in the kitchen as in the consulting room, in the library and the supermarket, at my desk and in the nursery – feel persuaded that the problem lies where Orbach delimits it on the symbiotic map, as the exclusive plight of the mother–daughter dyad.

What, as far as I can see from my own observation, *is* gender-specific is the range and extent, the content and velocity of projective identification which is found to operate in that relationship: in the connectedness between replica and replica. To modify its effects can prove the main undertaking in psychotherapy where the patient is a woman, which is to say where she is a daughter.

That a mother will at times withdraw the flow of her attention from the infant in her care, because she is a human being with her own preoccupations, her own needs and desires, is a simple fact of life which our patients who are male rage against as painfully. That the man can compensate for this trauma later on in the context of his marriage or similar relationship, where he demands mothering and is likely to receive it, is surely a separate issue. Why a woman, as a wife, is reluctantly compelled to turn herself inside out to cater for her partner's yearnings, why she seeks to staunch his wound, and deny her neediness, has been set out well and clearly by Dorothy Dinnerstein.

She deserves our close attention as she strives to understand 'the ways in which mental life pushes women in the direction of fulfilling the demands of the social environment, such as taking on the tasks and responsibilities of mothering' (Dinnerstein, D., 1987, p. ix). Once again the trouble lies with earliest symbiosis which, since it is unresolved throughout later adult life, drives women to seek a *vicarious* satisfaction for their infantile yearnings by offering to the male the fulfilment of his with constant reverie and attention. In this manner neither sex must come to terms with the sad fact that mother-as-a-part-of-me declines to be a fact of life in a painful reality. The price of this general denial is levied mainly from the woman as she panders to her man from her own necessity at the vast expense of her authenticity: an incessant haemorrhage of life's precious energies, a flow, a flood which she resents but lacks all remedy to staunch.

Dinnerstein blames our 'sexual arrangements' in the sphere of parenting. She argues that in consequence of the child's exposure to the all-powerful mother in tyrannical authority, woman 'bears the brunt of the initial experience of loss of the infant's oneness with the world' (Dinnerstein, D., 1987, p. viii). This in turn will induce a deep misogyny in men who, in their determination never to fall again into those cruel, powerful hands which dealt their earliest frustrations, do their utmost to restrain woman from having access to any part of worldly power. Indeed, if she as much as ventures any view or opinion relating to the wider world she will be ridiculed and/or put down, or failing that quite simply ignored. Petticoat rule shall not prevail. There is no need to enlarge. It tallies accurately with every woman's experience, and sadly still on the couch in too many instances. 'All you want is a penis' – well, you cannot have it: there! Here, indeed, lies the fulcrum of patriarchal leverage.

Having made her diagnosis, Dinnerstein then prescribes that we do away with this age-old division of responsibility for basic human concerns which makes *each* sex subhuman. Then only will our enterprises in the social and political sphere gradually become infused with a benevolence which, lacking today, carries the ever-present threat of catastrophic consequences. It all sounds plausible enough. What she does not reckon with, as I see the situation, are the inborn symbiotic needs of every living neonate. Even baby ducklings will, as ethologists have shown us, if deprived of their own mother, attach themselves to a substituted cardboard box, or a mere human male with relentless determination. Can we not conclude from this, as from other evidence of our daily observations, that the human neonate, which is born prematurely in the neuromuscular as in the mental sense, will rely on omnipotence to maintain a state of fusion with *any* primary care-taker by operating to the full those early, primitive defences which have already been described? None the less, shared parenting is appearing on the scene of evolution in our time as part and parcel of our culture as the sexual arrangements with regard to parenting reflect changing attitudes.

Change takes place on many levels. Some we monitor with hindsight while we still lack the key to the mystery of others, particularly in the field of neurochemistry. This only underlines the need for the different disciplines concerned with human behaviour to each come off their high horse and work towards a consensus in trust and in humility. That we have witnessed change in the mother–daughter dyad, from a primitive connectedness which is entirely unspoken into a relationship where a vanguard is struggling for the most sophisticated truths of the human heart and mind, is hardly open to dispute. While many shadowy imagos of an archaic nature live on, unaltered in the depths of the unconscious mind, there is also transformation both of a successive and of a mutative kind.

This needs to be explained by the relationship between the conscious and unconscious, even if the connections between the two hemispheres and that forecourt, the preconscious, are far from fully charted yet. But what is clear is that we have something of a two-way traffic:

It is wrong to suppose that communication between the two systems is confined to the act of repression, with the Pcs. casting everything that seems disturbing to it into the abyss of the Ucs. On the contrary, the Ucs. is alive and capable of development and maintains a number of other relations with the Pcs., among them that of co-operation. In brief, it must be said that the Ucs. is continued into what is known as its derivatives, that it is accessible to the impressions of life, that it constantly influences the Pcs., and is even, for its part, subjected to influence from the Pcs. (Freud, S., 1915a, p. 190)

Freud presently goes on to say: 'But the Ucs. is also affected by experiences originating from external perception. Normally all the paths from perception to the Ucs. remain open and only those leading from the Ucs. are subject to blocking by repression' (p. 194). In other words there is no reason why certain layers of the Ucs. cannot be modified, even if deeper ones of that vast geology may slumber inaccessible to what transpires in the outer world through the millennia. Do we not, after all, in our foetal development, still briefly carry gills and other atavistic remnants, as though the computers of genetic intelligence will require an urgent nudge towards accepting that changes have been undergone since they were first programmed?

Once we think along these lines we are able to confirm that all human relatedness has undergone degrees of change and will in every likelihood continue in that direction, since external perception doubtlessly includes ideas, even if we make allowance for their massive rejection just because they threaten change. Does not the brief history of the psychoanalytic movement testify to this truth with considerable *éclat*?

Certainly separation between the two protagonists of the mother–daughter dyad has moved in hopeful directions during recent centuries, while we continue to locate the archaic stranglehold of the Elementary Feminine Principle of the ancient Great Goddess at work in our unconscious mind.

Here it might be of help if we draw up a list, even a partial one, of some of the deeper reasons why separation poses a specific impasse to the mother–daughter dyad. Unresolved grievances provide a most potent glue, as we discover to our cost in the course of psychotherapy.

The mother has withheld from the girl sufficient milk to build her up for her own maternal task.

The mother has kept father possessively for herself. She has not facilitated a share and share alike: a closer father–daughter bond.

The mother has withheld a penis, meaning the daughter's share of power and authenticity in the wider world.

She has withheld all manner of sexual satisfaction and a baby, so that the girl 'has to leave her' – to find fulfilment in the wider world among 'strangers'.

The mother is envious and attacks the daughter's beauty, her sexuality and babies, and other good qualities and wider aspects of her daughter's growth.

She wants to keep the girl at home to help her with her own children and to take care of her in her old age.

The mother has deprived the girl of her own childhood playtime to varying degrees: first by demanding help with the housewifely chores and secondly, more ominously, by projecting her own neediness and feminine dissatisfactions into her. In cases which border on severe psychopathology this conveys to a daughter that she is responsible for keeping mother together so that she does not 'fall to bits': in other words a reversal of the mother–baby tie, of maternal reverie.

If we now look at this from the mother's point of view:

The daughter reminds her, more acutely than any infant son, of her own neediness and unfulfilled emotional hungers, and her general lack of prospects out in the wider world.

She possesses youthful beauty and sexual prospects and will soon displace her in the sexual arena.

She will one day become a mother and (despite satisfactions which a grandchild will bring) will enrol her yet again in the nurturing of infants when she has deserved some rest.

The daughter may have brighter prospects and richer opportunities in the promise of autonomy in wider creative fields.

She clearly wants to separate, ungrateful hussy that she is, and thereby makes her mother feel that what she had to offer her was patently not good enough.

In separating she will leave her old mother unsupported, with a deep sense of rejection.

These conundrums are unique to the mother–daughter dyad over and above the list which Winnicott gave us earlier, where he states why every mother must have hatred for her infant, side by side with her love. Throughout the pages of this book we have borne witness to these age-old issues at work while noticing a tendency to their resolution as we draw closer to our time, which is not to overlook the fact that the archaic quagmire still threatens each and every dyad.

Can we point to any factors which have led towards the light, to these signs that sanity is in the ascendancy? It seems to me that there are two of outstanding significance: first the role of the father and secondly growing prospects for women in the wider world, which offer them creative roles beyond the domestic sphere, beyond the confines of wife and mother.

It transpired here and there that an actively present male, both as husband and as father, facilitated separation of the mother–daughter dyad. Zeus, that old philanderer, plays an important part, already in the ancient myth. In the first place it was he who made that narcissus grow in the Nyasan Fields, as a fragrant phallic symbol which proved irresistible to his maiden daughter, the youthful Persephone. Secondly he stepped in, when nothing else would avail, to soothe the raging Demeter by proposing the famous pact that her daughter would divide her time between her mother and her husband: that all was certainly not lost. He distinctly took his time in stepping into the arena, much as 'Wen' Nightingale took refuge in his club and libraries until he finally intervened to give Florence her allowance, her basic economic freedom that she might remove herself, in the very nick of time before succumbing to madness, from the maternal roof quaking at its every seam. We saw how, on the other hand, Mr Garrett stood staunchly at Elizabeth's side in furthering her education, supporting his wife when she quailed at the thought of her daughter embarking on a medical career.

These are clear illustrations of how the father facilitates the separation of the dyad. Psychoanalytic thinking takes the issue further back, to earliest infancy where the breast is already seen as a 'combined' object of male and female attributes: hard nipple, soft breast envisaged as a cavity flowing with tantalizing juices. Certainly infants who are 'allergic' to the mother's milk present as difficult cases in later psychotherapy. In my experience they are 'allergic' to the thought of father in the most resistant manner, which of course is not to say that the allergy may not have biochemical causes, operating side by side with psychodynamic ones. In other words the infant brings constitutional inclinations which will further or inhibit healthy triangulation to bear on this specific scene, while the mother's capacity to make room for the father, from the earliest months, by permitting play at the breast to introduce the space required for the father 'to appear' as a welcome third party is a firm prerequisite.

It is very possible that the mother may have greater difficulties in this task where the infant is a daughter; that there is more mutual clinging, a stickier, more resistant bonding in the mother–daughter dyad; that the boundaries in this case will remain more permeable to all manner of osmosis as for projective identification. I have very little doubt that these propositions hold, even if I cannot 'prove' them. But it also seems likely that the father's active stance, masculine determination to disentangle his wife from her proclivities and to lead his daughter out to acquire a growing taste for everything that is on offer in the wider world of *logos*, can counteract the tendencies for enwrapment natural to this dyad.

Here we run up against an interesting complication. Let us return to Emily (see above, p. 19), the little girl, you will recall, who insisted at twenty months that 'Daddy has something funny in his vulva.' We meet a psychoanalyst, herself a woman, listening to her woman patients with a new, refreshing ear:

A number of female patients have reiterated to me a view of men in which certain stereotypic features recur: men, these women assert, are emotionally closed, unable to be receptive or empathetic, and without access to inner feelings or inner sensations . . . In brief: these women are determined to believe that men are lacking something crucial . . . they [the women] ultimately report versions of a fantasy that the capacity to be genitally open is a capacity that can be endangered, can be lost, and indeed has been quite literally lost by the male sex . . . that men have actually been closed over genitally, and that men therefore represent the frightening possibility that such a thing could really happen to a woman . . . I suggest that castration anxiety, in men or in women, is anxiety over losing that genital which is actually possessed. (Lloyd Mayer, E., p. 331)

What this woman analyst is drawing our attention to – apart from a new version of castration anxiety, where the girl's interest focuses on 'a something, rather than a lack of something' (see above, p. 19), is a familiar theme and a day-to-day complaint on the lips of many women. Men, they say, *are* closed over, emotionally unavailable in the way that women are. They never listen, never share deep experience and feelings with feminine eagerness. Women are more and more aware of the pain this causes them, the intense sense of frustration:

'Whatever would I do', they mourn, 'without my close women friends?' That this grievance has become an almost universal one is at last out in the open.

Doubtless the nuclear family has accentuated it. It has cut women off from the intricate support – and, of course, the enmity – within that wider world of women which was taken for granted until recent decades. But for our present purposes it opens up the question whether the little girl turns back from the father to a liaison with her mother not because, as is claimed, he does not give her a baby, but because he disappoints her in precisely those ways these patients have reiterated and women generally grieve? Worse than that, because he mocks, even if unconsciously, every part of her equipment which bears proud testimony to her primary femininity. Since she senses that her life can run its own, true course only where she is on track for this, she returns to the maternal circuit for confirmation of it there. She may or may not find it within that sequestered place. It may be lacking in the mother, in which case she is twice in trouble.

But we also find the opposite: that where a father is open and not emotionally 'closed over', where his feminine self is well and truly integrated, so that he can be responsive to his daughter's 'openness' and her vulnerability, she may in certain instances be so entranced with this companion, this masculine partner to her primary femininity, that she remains disinclined to leave and seek any further. There are many kinds of nun. Some have a heavenly and others an earthly father in a state of congruence with her interiority.

But why do fathers mock their daughters in so many instances: Why do they shrug the advances, the bid for close companionship of the little female off? Is it simply fear of erotic arousal? Is it the father's knowledge that one day he will give her away to another man, a stranger, and so lose out in any case? Does he sense a prohibition coming from an envious wife? Does he see her as 'stupid', unworthy of his interest, in so far as he projects a 'stupid' part of himself, since he is not omniscient? There is no simple, easy answer to this paternal distancing, even if in other instances we find a close relationship between a daughter and her father where it is not in evidence.

Perhaps this frequent hurt to a girl's self-esteem, this blow to her healthy narcissism, is her early introduction to this 'lack of something' in the man, to his state of 'being closed over' which we specified above. How do we account for that? Is it due to the boy's sudden, anxious expulsion from his first love, from his mother and her sensuous domain? His sudden loss of that region where 'there is no need to name functions, or to label creatures with attributes: everything just is. Flowers blossom without some divine edict which insists that they should blossom. There is no fall from grace if they fail' (Rhode, E., 1987, p. 47). Does every approach to woman threaten to stir memories of a sweet Aeolian note that breezes carried long ago, whispering absolute belonging, only to be shattered by the word employed in chilly reasoning? Is *logos* now his exiled state? Has the door to Paradise closed behind him for all time until woman finds the key for him in a second round which may, alas, fail to revive the original ecstasy?

Psychoanalytic thinking is at present inching forward into this realm of the preverbal, the body-Braille of the dyadic, those dumb two-way communiqués redolent of the greatest passions and their far-reaching consequences for every child's future being that we receive and convey in the span of any lifetime. Compared to this, adult passion may dwindle into shadowlands. Is this intoxication to be encouraged or forsworn? Is the aim of psychotherapy to restore us to those regions, to that wild, elusive frontier where the symbol is born out of 'intrapsychic conflict between the "repressing tendencies and the repressed" ' (Segal, H., 1981, p. 51)? Or shall it be the straight and narrow of a respectable science?

Certainly the adult mind fears a return to those regions of early merging and fusion, the very basis of bonding, that which has been most repressed and so evokes the uncanny. For the longing to return is confused with regression: with the closing of the trap which, provided it is conscious, does not constitute this risk. The boy, as we have often seen, has clear-cut cause to fear it, as has the girl for different reasons: the threat to her authenticity: the life which she shall call her own. But I have in my work with women on occasion unearthed a further anxiety missing from the literature. Let me give an illustration. An imaginative, gifted woman of great sensuality which was viciously repressed, and yet kept breaking through in dreams and in her free associations, would sometimes fear that I was mad. This fear came up conspicuously on those occasions when we pushed the boat of our work together far from shore into the deep. As we started to share a sense of utter, joyful freedom in following our perceptions from every point of anchorage in the approved conceptual field, this patient would begin to panic. She would sooner or later pull us up sternly on our tracks by producing a reference to the well-established work of a male analyst. When she did this I experienced a certain sense of relief, of having been pulled to order, as well as one of keen resentment. She had, it seemed to me, cut short the promise of some unique experience. In due course it came to me, as these events were repeated over months, at intervals, that we shared in equal parts a common anxiety: mother and daughter left alone to their own devices – in other words where they could give their feminine imagination and creativity full, untrammelled, conjoined rein – would end up in unrestrained sheer bacchanalia. Does Lacan not remind us that *jouissance* is a something where 'the drive touches on an area of excess'? That it expresses 'something more than pleasure which can easily tip into its opposite' (Mitchell, J. and Rose, J., 1982, p. 34).

Energy is pure delight, as William Blake shared the experience. Did Freud not send us to the poets, who have never found woman a puzzle? *Jouissance* is energy manifested in pure being, where we can experience it and remain unafraid. It threatens to escape from a benevolent state of balance only where it cannot be suspended between two equal signifiers in creative intercourse: the masculine and feminine components of the human psyche in an integrated state of bisexuality. Here we recognize the concept of psychoanalytic thinking that we heal neurosis only once we are able to accept, to give our ready consent to the parental intercourse of our outer as of our inner parents. Only this acknowledgement in its fullest implications, physical and procreative as much as the spiritual, can give the mother–daughter couple permission to flower safely, in its own unique sphere, within a structure where each process is the container of the other. The patient mentioned above was still unable to accept her parents as a sexual couple; to permit me as a mother a separate, full creative life.

If we have earlier seen a list of negatives which obfuscate separation of the mother–daughter dyad, we have now to bear in mind the many-fold positives, the joys and even ecstasies which are inherent in this contact between replica and replica where only tenuous boundaries constrain the magical illusion of union as lifelong bliss.

Here is a state of shared experience which does not require words. Here are soft, familiar bodies replete with all that sustains them and cushions symbiotic yearnings when they need replenishing. Here are minds which are at home in familiar subject matters that will not drag the feminine psyche into painful abstractions, lines of thought which must leave physical comforts far behind to total discomfiture. Here are perfumed silences of a homoerotic nature in which she is able to feel safe. There is no end, once we begin, to counting the blessings of a union which makes the thought of separation into a sentence of exile, most dreaded by the feminine soul. Who, if we are to consent to such a hateful mutilation, will in that big, wide world out there replace this wellspring of being, this underpinning of the strains and stresses of our fraught daily life? Can woman, yet, entrust the man to partner these intricate expectations? Did she receive encouragement from the father of her childhood to this finicky end?

If such intense hobnobbing by a process of osmosis still seems questionable to my readers, let me once again quote Freud: 'It is a very remarkable thing that the Ucs. of one human being can react upon that of another, without passing through the Cs.' (Freud, S., 1915a, p. 194). It is my personal conviction that this particular process is a specific function of maternal reverie and that even if it can and will affect the male, woman's susceptibilities to this phenomenon are considerably greater – a positive liability – and operate to a degree where it can deal life or death to so forceful an extent that it belongs to the uncanny, as in this illustration:

By the time Ms M was referred for psychiatric treatment, Eleanor, her only child, was two years old and had been diagnosed with a non-organic failure-to-thrive syndrome . . . She had refused almost all food since the age of five months, although her parents had coaxed her to eat in every way they could devise. (Lloyd Mayer, E., 1985, p. 487)

To cut a long story short, her mother viewed the child's conception, and her existence, as a crime, subsequent to sexual play with her own father when a child. She was, she felt, undeserving of the joys of motherhood. Any child in phantasy was a product of her incest.

These matters came to light in her fourth interview with a psychoanalyst. Their content had 'previously been if not entirely unconscious, profoundly disavowed by her'. The vignette now continues:

This material was of course very interesting. However, I was unprepared for what followed its emergence. After the session described above, Ms M went home, made her usual cajoling offer of food to Eleanor and Eleanor surprised her mother by taking it. Indeed, she remarked that she was hungry, went on to eat her dinner that evening, and began to become the essentially normal eater which she has remained to the present five years later. Ms M, to the best of her knowledge, had altered nothing in her approach to Eleanor. (Lloyd Mayer, E., 1985, p. 487)

Many-fold and highly complex are these issues which are specific to the mother–daughter dyad, in essence as in degree, and which will further enwrapment. When we mentioned factors which facilitate separation, we spoke of woman's growing prospects which offer her creative roles beyond the domestic sphere. The evidence for this remark requires no substantiation. But we had also seen that the guilt of a daughter can play an important part in denying her access to these advantages, certainly to the full, in a realistic keeping with her innate capacities. The same applies to a mother. Writing of men and women writers, a friend of mine, Adele Wiseman, has the following to say:

Indeed, it is considered somewhat heroic and even a sign of genius in a man if he behaves with irresponsible selfishness in his personal life. He is considered redeemed by his utter devotion to his art. The exact reverse is usually true for a woman artist . . . [who] is faced with largely artificial choices and has her guilts set out for her. (Wiseman, A., 1987, p. 54)

As a mother and as a daughter she faces archaic conflicts if she seizes her life with its many-fold choices and widening opportunities courageously with both hands. Indeed, last night, as we sat talking, Adele spoke of the recent deaths of half a dozen friends of hers: well-known Canadian women writers. Their average age at their death was in the early fifties, two decades earlier than the present average for her countrywomen. A shiver ran down my back. I hardly dared let myself think, even now at sixty-three, of my struggles and my guilt, for fear that I would turn to stone: be stricken with paralysis of my creative faculties. Few will know what it cost me to publish my first book: an autobiography (Herman, 1985). In it I had set out, as truthfully as I knew, how certain personal difficulties had sprung from early years dominated by a mother whose ideas on child-raising were, to say the very least, at cross-purposes with mine. For my mother, in her eighties, it proved an anxious testing-out, while I quaked in my shoes. The upset I might cause my colleagues by taking the unusual step of coming clean before my patients over details of my private life was nothing in comparison. It does credit to us both, tough-spirited that we are beneath our respective failings, that we both lived to tell the tale and drew closer in respect, in mutual trust and in fondness, than at any previous time.

However great their difficulties in this area of new projects, in engaging one another truthfully, come what may, daughters and mothers are overcoming them heroically. Dinnerstein sets out the issue in her own forthright way:

Like the male, she is equipped with a large brain, competent hands, and upright posture. She belongs to an intelligent, playful, exploratory species, inhabiting an expanding environment which it makes for itself and then adapts to. She is the only female, so far as we know, capable of thinking up and bringing about a world wider than the one she sees around her . . . She thus seems, of all females, the one least fitted to live in a world narrower than the one she sees around her. And yet, for reasons inherent in her evolutionary history, she has been, of all females, the one most fated to do so. (Dinnerstein, D., 1987, p. 20)

Dinnerstein sees the reason for this discrepancy in the fact that women 'have been obliged to invest major energy in the biological task of perpetuating the species' (p. 20). While this is doubtless true, we have begun to understand how the tug of war within the dyad produces other inhibitions not directly related to obvious biology, although chicken and egg are difficult to disentangle.

Biologists are certainly providing ample food for thought relevant to our subject matter. If our present approach has been largely psychodynamic this, of course, cannot discount the significance of findings of women scientists who are studying the brain, hormones or behaviour, human and animal. The awkward thousand-dollar question 'whether the sex differences in behaviour each has observed – in the field, in the clinic, and in the laboratory – have a basis that is in part biological' (Konner, M., 1984, p. 106), they have without exception answered in the affirmative. 'These women', the author pays his dues, 'are doing a balancing act of formidable proportions. They continue to struggle in private and public, for equal rights and equal treatment for people of both sexes; at the same time they uncover and report evidence that the sexes are irremediably different' (Konner, M., 1984, p. 107), and that this difference is grounded in biology.

Indeed, 'in 1973 it was shown for the first time that male and female brains differ structurally' (Konner, M., 1984, p. 121). At the same time we are told that nerve cells in the brains of rats undergo major change where the rat pups are deprived of sufficient stimulation or are, on the other hand, exposed to an environment which is rich in this respect. This improvement also applies in the case of older rats, if not to the same extent. Which is the cart and which the horse in relating structure to function, in equal opportunity?

I have a niggling intuition that psychotherapy, by substantially enriching the emotional environment which was previously bleak in terms of genuine intimacy with its wide range of feelings, has a similar bearing on neurochemistry as on neuroanatomy, closely linked to the changes it effects on the mind, however mind is constituted.

Here are breathtaking vistas which we are unable to pursue beyond merely raising their tantalizing horizons. But we can state with certainty that where a woman overcomes her guilt and her diffidence, her constant autosubversion largely rooted in the dyad, and lives her projects to the full in each and in whatever sphere of her natural inclinations, in growing authenticity, so her capacities will grow in that very direction, like the athlete's in training, as she embraces the world with all the vigour of her nature.

Such an uphill struggle is of course a piecemeal one with its vanguard as its rearguard; as in every campaign:

... the populations consist of different historical layers. There are people who, psychologically, might just as well have lived in the year 5000 BC i.e. who can still successfully solve their conflicts as people did 7,000 years ago ... On the other hand, there are relatively few who have reached the degree of consciousness which is possible in our time. We must also reckon with the fact that a few of us belong to the third or fourth millennium AD and are consequently anachronistic. (Jung, C.G., 1952, p. xxv)

Freud belonged to this small number – except where his thinking about woman was concerned. Here the patriarch's obsessions obstinately won the day and painfully cramped the style of the scrupulous explorer: 'It is true that the influence [of the sexual function] extends very far; but we do not overlook the fact that an individual woman may be a human being in other respects as well' (Freud, S., 1933, p. 135). In my experience this 'may be' still threatens every woman who enters psychotherapy. Unless she gives careful thought to her choice of therapist she may still be suspect goods, still burdened with a legacy she is unlikely to shake off conclusively on the couch.

Having said this, I agree entirely with Dinnerstein when in her preface she admits that although she is disturbed 'by the sexual bigotry that is built into the Freudian perspective', she does not share 'feminist preoccupation . . . with his failure to jump with alacrity right out of his male Victorian skin, [which] seems to me wildly ungrateful' (Dinnerstein, D., 1987, p. xxiii). Indeed, as Norman Brown reminds us: 'In the hands of Freud, psychoanalysis was a living organism in constant evolution. Since Freud's death orthodox psychoanalysis has become a closed, almost scholastic system, itself no exception to the general cultural trend towards stereotype and sterility' (Brown, N., 1959, p. x). I hope that with these comments I have paid my debt to Freud!

What is it, then, that woman wants? And where do we go from here? Ought we now to tangle with the thorny question of 'the subject'? Ought we to plunge headlong into Lacan and Jacques Derrida? This lies outside my competence, since their thinking is not (? yet) within the scope of my experience. Perhaps I am like a cow that needs to chew its earlier cud before grazing once again. This shall not be cause for shame. It is how some are constituted.

I have throughout preferred to use the terms 'sentient being' and 'authenticity', in their straight dictionary meaning. It seems to me that for the present we have not yet exhausted all their nuances. Is it not difficult enough in the everyday mêlée to obtain rigorous bearings of when we are and when we are not being true to ourselves, living within the field of our own energies without short-changing ourselves or those whom we claim to love?

What is it that woman wants? Where do we stand today in full authenticity of our highly complex being? There is a

natural temptation to escape if we can, to close the door behind us on this despised realm which threatens to engulf all women, whether as mothers, or in marriage, or as the invisible, ill-paid sustainers of the professionals and social institutions. There is a natural fear that if we do not enter the common world of men, as asexual beings or as 'exceptional' women, . . . we will be sucked back into the realm of servitude, whatever our temporary class status or privileges. (Rich, A., 1980, pp. 206–7)

The fear is certainly well founded, but what does it demand of us? How can we be exceptional without first being ordinary? How can we be men, if our authenticity is rooted in being women? Not on the obvious ground of our anatomy, of the gender we were allocated with our very first pink ribbons, but by personal conviction where this happens to apply; even if it is fraught at times and we are shaken to the very core by these momentous current issues hammering at our intellect.

I know from personal experience that I was utterly wretched as a young, new-baked doctor until I came to recognize that it was safe to work from home, from its privacy and heartland. That my surgery or consulting room could adjoin the nursery or kitchen. That between seeing patients I could listen to a child home for lunch from nursery school, or put a casserole in the oven or adjust its seasoning. And this was not because I was still under the thumb of 'the angel of the house'. It was, I felt, my way of living in the inner and the outer world, in accordance with my needs, with my authenticity. It was the freedom of my choice.

Free choice remains dangerous, for the woman as for the man. If our sojourn within the dyad imprints that knowledge on our being, later life will confirm it. What is it that woman wants? The freedom to make a choice and live her life accordingly. A century and a half ago the niece of Emily Dickinson 'told of visiting her in her corner bedroom on the second floor at 280 Main Street, Amherst, and how Emily Dickinson made as if to lock the door with an imaginary key, turned, and said: "Matty: here's freedom." ' (Rich, A., 1980, p. 158).

A recent biographer, a classical Freudian and stickler for that discipline, takes up 500 pages to define the poet as 'an anxiety-ridden personality' (Cody, J., 1971, p. 12) who was 'contorted and grotesque' (p. 13) in many aspects of her life. He writes her off as 'agoraphobic' and suffering, among other things, from an obvious 'crisis of sexual identity' (p. 143).

But the poet herself made this precocious reply, anticipating such a one:

> *Much madness is divinest sense –*
> *To a discerning Eye –*
> *Much Sense – the starkest Madness –*
> *'Tis the Majority*

> *In this, as All prevail –*
> *Assent and you are sane –*
> *Demur – you're straightway dangerous –*
> *And handled with a Chain –*
> (Rich, A., 1980, p. 175, quoting Emily Dickinson)

Adrienne Rich shares with us her visit to that corner room:

Here, at a small table with one drawer, she wrote most of her poems. Here she read Elizabet Barrett's Aurora Leigh *... also George Eliot; Emerson; Carlyle; Shakespeare; Charlotte and Emily Brontë ... Here she wrote poems about volcanoes, deserts, eternity, suicide, physical passion, wild beasts, rape, power, madness, separation, the daemon, the grave. Here, with a darning needle, she bound these poems – ... into booklets, secured with darning thread, to be found and read after her death ... It was a life deliberately organized on her terms. The terms she had been handed by Society ... could spell insanity to a woman of genius. (Rich, A., 1980, p. 161)*

Not only of genius – but can it not spell madness to the ordinary woman still? What is it that woman wants? Has anyone yet posed that question as relevant to man? We have not reached that moment yet in our human history, although it is overdue if the species shall survive. Does he really want to pose as ruler and as provider, to struggle with that lonely role? And if not, what does he want? And what does woman want of him as a wife and as a daughter in the late twentieth century?

Here is certainly a subject for yet another book, even if we have touched on some of the salient answers. It is

through the intense mother–daughter relationship [that] women come into a deep and richer inner life than men, and, even when heterosexual, tend to be more deeply attached to women than to men, and more capable than men of relationship. (Rich, A., 1980, p. 91)

The poet carries conviction because we sense how all she says is born of her own deep experience. But how can we generalize concerning such momentous issues? There are mother's girls and father's girls. There are women who drank deeply from the spirit of their father, whose inner world was fertilized through that momentous contact either with or without mother's benevolent permission. In such a case we can conceive that it is relatively easy for the girl to change her object, to transfer deep-coursing passions from her mother to a man, a husband, in her later years. There cannot be a simple answer since in psychoanalytic thought, in its conflict with biology, woman is not born but instead is constituted in the crucible of her formative experience, one of whose main components is that montage of transactions, both liberating and constraining, within the mother–daughter dyad. Another is her experience of the third party, of the male: of the potency and poetry he may reach out and offer her, or on the other hand withhold. Again, we must not forget that this nuclear drama is enacted on the stage of the wider family with its complex circumstances, while that in turn is subject to prevailing cultural norms and political conundrums. The totality is somewhat like a set of Russian dolls where one is found within the other, down to the tiniest of all.

Certainly at this moment the resounding clarion call of the women's liberation movement is as irresistible as the call to the swallow when the time comes to migrate:

We have come from many pasts: out of the Left, out of the ghetto, out of the holocaust, out of the churches, out of marriage, out of the 'gay' movement, out of the closet, out of the darker closet of longterm suffocation of our love of women . . . to a view of society whose goal is not equality but utter transformation. (Rich, A., 1980, p. 229)

But transformation is envisaged only when its component parts are already in existence – when all they require is an intelligent assembly, or in certain instances the location of some missing links:

4 January 1979

Dear Mother . . . For me, courage means being able to change the pattern of our lives, recognizing the faults and the beauty in our lives and always going beyond the limitations that others have imposed upon us . . . The possibilities for women's lives have expanded in the past decade as they never have before . . . I am aware of my own power as a woman, as a human being; I am aware of my potential to change the patterns around me; I am aware of my capacity to love, to nurture, to act. As Adrienne Rich has written, speaking of what a mother can do for a daughter, 'The most important thing one woman can do for another is to illuminate and expand her sense of actual possibilities . . . It means that the mother herself is trying to expand the limits of her life. To refuse to be a victim: and then go on from there.' It hurts me, it pains me, to see you give up sometimes. It hurts because I know it must hurt you . . . I am learning to understand you, to love you, without having to BECOME you . . . I must be myself. And that means acknowledging what I have inherited from you, and acknowledging what I have inherited from others . . . There are times, like the last night when you were here, that I wanted to crawl out of my bed and into yours, to lie next to your body, feel its warmth, as I did when I was a child.

Mother, this is a new age for both of us. For the first time, we can be proud of being women, we can define ourselves any way we want. We can struggle together. We have a long history behind us of grandmothers, and great-grandmothers and great-great-grandmothers . . . we are beautiful. We are strong.

Mother, I love you, and may we always be able to acknowledge the mother and the daughter in each of us . . . (Payne, K., 1984, p. 305)

This letter from the treasure chest of Karen Payne's anthology leaves little more to be said concerning present vantage ground at its most lofty. To love you without having to BECOME you and at the same time to expand each for herself and for the other, her actual possibilities, while acutely conscious of the tug of symbiotic yearning. As for maternal growth, did the biologist not find that even in older rats a stimulus-rich environment improved certain features of nerve cells in the brain?

We have had a bird's-eye view of how the component parts of this gradual transformation of possibilities for a freer, richer life, within the context of the dyad, have age by age come into being. At the same time we are aware of the constant pull back into the tellurian era of enwrapment in the swamp: of how difficult it is to live a freedom day by day. How difficult, invariably, for a mother and daughter both to become aware of their own power as women, to exercise it lovingly without hostile competition, without the need for one to triumph or seek to triumph over the other, while constantly aware of envy, the parameter of death and lifelong vulnerability: the swing of the pendulum between helplessness and strength, near defeat and tasks accomplished: the prospect for womanness.

We no longer require, we are wary of a goddess as we hear an Anzia say: 'I'd give my life but I cannot stop studying' – growing to become myself; while a mother at the ironing board pleads in her troubled heart: 'Help her to know that she is more than this dress on the ironing board, helpless before the iron.'

I would like to end our journey with a letter from a mother, written in the 1930s, to her daughter, who was then approaching the age of fifty:

You can't imagine how empty it grew yesterday, after you left, nor is there a moment when I don't miss you . . . I am only afraid that you will feel an obligation to 'please' me in my last years, and that is so far from the case . . . You not only have the right, you have the duty to follow your own way . . . It would be a fine thing for a parent, having nurtured a child, to demand that she give up her future to live with a more or less dried up wreck. When I know that you are well and happy, I . . . will be made happy; so sits the while at home the mother well content. Your two rooms stand as if you had just left them, ready to be used at whatever time, and you know that my arms will be around you at the same instant you appear, and with the same warmth that they held you yesterday, my beloved. (Thurman, J., 1984, p. 305)

The daughter, Karen Blixen, opened her autobiography, *Out of Africa*, with that unforgettable sentence uttered by a free spirit: 'I had a farm in Africa, at the foot of the Ngong Hills' (Blixen, K., 1980, p. 13). Yet during the seventeen years that she lived in the hills of Kenya, for long stretches on her own, far from others of her kind, she would inveigle her mother time and again to make the endless journey to where the coffee grew on the Karen Plantation. When her mother prevaricated that she could not at this moment leave her orphaned granddaughter, whose sole care she had assumed, Karen countered that 'the farm was like a grandchild too, just as deserving of her blessing and solicitude' (Thurman, J., 1984, p. 189).

Is not a woman's every project her mother's grandchild in that sense, requiring the maternal blessing?

Perhaps in ending here I stand in the place of the aged Moses as he surveys the land which is the site of the future that he himself is not to reach; not just in terms of geography, but of that formative experience which sets the older generation rearward from the coming one. I am certainly aware that there comes a moment when experience can be the lie at a certain frontier post where the future meets the past. I believe that where our thinking about woman is concerned we are approaching such a frontier – but we have not crossed it yet.

BIBLIOGRAPHY

(The place of publication is London unless otherwise specified)

Abelard and Héloïse (1974) *Letters*. Harmondsworth: Penguin.

Aeschylus (1977) *The Oresteia*, Robert Fagles, trans. Wildwood.

—— (1981) *The Oresteia*, Tony Harrison, trans. Rex Collings.

Austen, J. (1986) *Pride and Prejudice*. Harmondsworth: Penguin.

Bachofen, J.J. (1967) *Myth, Religion and Mother Right. Selected Writings of J.J. Bachofen*, trans from the German by Ralph Manheim. Routledge & Kegan Paul.

Baker, D., ed. (1924) *Medieval Women. Studies in Church History*. Oxford: Basil Blackwell.

de Beauvoir, S. (1969) *A Very Easy Death*. Harmondsworth: Penguin.

—— (1977) *The Second Sex*. Harmondsworth: Penguin.

Bell, S., ed. (1973) *Women from the Greeks to the French Revolution*. Belmont, CA: The Wadsworth Company.

Bigland, E. (1959) *Mary Shelley*. Cassell.

Blixen, K. (1980) *Out of Africa*. Harmondsworth: Penguin.

Brown, N. (1959) *Life Against Death*. Middletown, CT: Wesleyan University Press.

Burney, S. (1893) *Introduction to Diaries and Letters of Madame D'Arblay*, vol. 1, 1778–84. Swann & Sonnerschein.

Cardinal, M. (1984) *The Words to Say it*. Picador.

Chasseguet-Smirgel, J. (1970) *Female Sexuality. New Psychoanalytic Views*. Maresfield Library.

Chodorow, N. (1978) *The Reproduction of Mothering*. University of California Press.

Clifford, Lady A. (1923) *The Diary of Lady Anne Clifford*, introduced by Vita Sackville-West. Heinemann.

Cody, J. (1971) *After Great Pain. The Inner Life of Emily Dickinson*. Cambridge, MA: Harvard University Press.

Colette (1966) *My Mother's House and Sido*. Harmondsworth: Penguin.

Derrida, J. (1976) *Of Grammatology*. Trans and Preface by Gayatri Chakravorty Spivak. Baltimore, MD/London: Johns Hopkins University Press.

Dinnerstein, D. (1987) *The Rocking of the Cradle and the Ruling of the World*. Souvenir Press, The Women's Press.

Ernst, S. and Maguire, M., eds (1987) *Living with the Sphinx. Papers from the Women's Therapy Centre*. The Women's Press.

Euripides (1963) *Medea. Hecabe. Electra. Heracles*. Philip Vellacott, trans. Harmondsworth: Penguin Classics.

Fanshawe, Lady A. (1829) *Memoirs Written by Herself*. Henry Colburn.

Forrester-Brown, G. (1919) *The Importance of Women in Anglo-Saxon Times*. The Society for the Promotion of Christian Knowledge.

Freud, S. (1905) *Three Essays on the Theory of Sexuality*, in James Strachey, ed. *The Standard Edition of the Complete Psychological Works of Sigmund Freud*, 24 vols. Hogarth, 1953–73, vol. 7.

—— (1913) *Totem and Taboo*. *S.E.* 13.

—— (1915a) 'The unconscious'. *S.E.* 14, pp. 159–216.

—— (1915b) 'A case of paranoia'. *S.E.* 14, pp. 261–72.

—— (1915c) 'Observations on transference-love'. *S.E.* 12, pp. 157–71.

—— (1919) 'The "uncanny" '. *S.E.* 17, pp. 219–56.

—— (1931) 'Female sexuality'. *S.E.* 21, pp. 225–43.

—— (1933) 'Femininity'. *S.E.* 22, pp. 112–35.

—— (1938) 'An example of psychoanalytic work'. *S.E.* 23, pp. 183–94.

—— (1940) *An Outline of Psycho-Analysis*. *S.E.* 23.

Fromm, E. (1984) *The Fear of Freedom*. London/Melbourne/Henley: Ark Paperback.

Garrett Anderson, L. (1939) *Elizabeth Garrett Anderson*. Methuen.

Gaskell, E. (1973) *North and South*. Oxford University Press: The World's Classics.

Goldsmith, M. (1938) *Sappho of Lesbos*. Rich & Cowan.

Goulianos, J., ed. (1973) *By a Woman Writ. Literature from Six Centuries by and about Women*. Baltimore, MD: Penguin.

Grant, D. (1957) *Margaret the First*. Rupert Hart-Davis.

Graves, R. (1959) *Introduction to Larousse Encyclopaedia of Mythology*. Batchworth.

—— (1981) *The White Goddess*. Faber & Faber.

Hall, N. (1980) *The Moon and the Virgin*. The Women's Press.

H.D. (1981) 'The master', *Feminist Studies* 7.

Herman, N. (1985) *My Kleinian Home*. Quartet; Free Association Books, 1988.

Holmes, M. (1975) *Proud Northern Lady*. Phillmore.

Hutchinson, L. (1973) *Memoirs of the Life of Colonel Hutchinson, including The Life of Mrs Lucy Hutchinson by Herself*, J. Sutherland, ed. Oxford University Press.

Jameson, S. (1984) *Journey from the North*, vol. 1. Virago.

Jenkins, H.A. (1982) *Three Classical Poets. Sappho, Catullus and Juvenal*. Duckworth.

Jones, E. (1967 [1953]) *The Life and Work of Sigmund Freud*, abridged edn. Harmondsworth: Penguin.

Jung, C.G. (1952) Foreword to White, C. *God and the Unconscious*. Dallas, TX: Spring Publications.

Jung, C.G. and Kerenyi, C. (1949) *Essays on a Science of Mythology*, R.F.C. Hull, trans. Pantheon: Bollingen Series, 22.

Kemp-Welch, A. (1913) *Of Six Mediaeval Women*. Macmillan.

Kerenyi, C. (1962) *Die Mysterien von Eleusis*. Zurich: Rhein Verlag.

King-Rugg, W. (1930) *Unafraid. A Life of Anne Hutchinson*. Cambridge/Boston/New York: Houghton Mifflin, The Riverside Press.

Klein, M. (1963) 'Some reflections on the *Oresteia*', in *The Writings of Melanie Klein*, vol. 3. Hogarth/Institute of Psycho-Analysis, pp. 275–99.

—— (1937) 'Love, guilt and reparation', *The Writings of Melanie Klein*, vol. 1. Hogarth/Institute of Psycho-Analysis, pp. 306–43.

Kohon, G. (1984) 'Reflections on Dora: the case of hysteria', *Int. J. Psycho-Anal.* 65: 73–84.

Konner, M. (1984) *The Tangled Wing. Biological Constraints on the Human Spirit.* Harmondsworth: Pelican.

Labalme, P.H., ed. (1972) *Beyond Their Sex. Learned Women of the European Past.* New York University Press.

Laing, R.D. (1965) *The Divided Self.* Harmondsworth: Pelican.

—— and Esterson, A. (1970) *Sanity, Madness and the Family.* Harmondsworth: Pelican.

Larousse (1959) *Encyclopaedia of Mythology.* Batchworth.

Lehmann, R. (1967) *The Swan in the Evening.* Collins.

Lessing, D. (1972) *Landlocked.* Panther.

—— (1978) *The Four-Gated City.* Panther.

—— (1985) *A Proper Marriage.* Grafton.

Lester, E.P. (1985) 'The female analyst and the erotized transference', *Int. J. Psycho-Anal.* 66: 283–95.

Liddington, J. (1984) *Respectable Rebel. The Life and Times of Selina Cooper, 1864–1946.* Virago.

Lieberman, E.J. (1985) *Acts of Will. The Life and Work of Otto Rank.* New York: Free Press.

Lincoln, E. (1809) *The Countess of Lincoln's Nurseries.* The Harleian Miscellany, vol. 55.

Lloyd Mayer, E. (1985) 'Everybody must be just like me: observations on female castration anxiety', *Int. J. Psycho-Anal.* 66: 331–490.

Mahl, M. and Koon, H., eds (1977) *The Female Spectator. English Women Writers before 1800.* New York: The Feminist Press.

Mann Kulish, N. (1986) 'Gender and transference: the screen of the phallic mother', *Int. J. Psycho-Anal.* 13: 393–405.

Mann, T. (1984) *Joseph and his Brothers.* Harmondsworth: Penguin.

Manton, J. (1965) *Elizabeth Garrett Anderson.* Methuen.

Martineau, H. (1877) *Autobiography in Three Volumes.* Smith, Elder & Co.

Milner, M. (1969) *The Hands of the Living God. An Account of a Psycho-Analytic Treatment.* Hogarth/Institute of Psycho-Analysis.

Mitchell, J. and Rose, J., eds (1982) *Feminine Sexuality. Jacques Lacan and the École Freudienne*, Jacqueline Rose, trans. Macmillan.

Modersohn-Becker, P. (1979) *In Briefen und Tagebüchern.* Frankfurt am Main: S. Fischer.

Morgan, F. (1981) *The Female Wits. Women Playwrights of the Restoration.* Virago.

Neumann, E. (1974) *The Great Mother. An Analysis of the Archetype*, R. Manheim, trans. Princeton, NJ: Princeton University Press. Bollingen Series, 47.

Newman, C., ed. (1970) *The Art of Sylvia Plath. A Symposium.* Faber & Faber.

Nixon, E. (1971) *Mary Wollstonecraft, her Life and Times.* J.M. Dent.

Oakley, A. (1985) *Taking it like a Woman.* Flamingo.

Olsen, T. (1980) *Tell Me a Riddle.* Virago.

—— (1985) *Mother to Daughter, Daughter to Mother. A Reader and Diary.* Virago.

Opie, A., Mrs (1986 [1804]) *Adelaine Mowbray. The Mother and Daughter.* Pandora.

Orbach, S. and Eichenbaum, L. (1987) *Bittersweet. Facing up to Feelings of Love, Envy and Competition in Women Friendships.* Century Hutchinson.

Pagels, E. (1980) *The Gnostic Gospels.* Weidenfeld & Nicolson.

Pankhurst, C., Dame (1959) *Unshackled. The Story of how we Won the Vote.* Hutchinson.

Pankhurst, E. (1914) *The Pankhursts' Own Story.* Eveleigh Nash.

Paracelsus (1969) *Selected Writings*, Jolande Jacobson, ed. Princeton, NJ: Princeton University Press. Bollingen Series, 33.

Paston, G. (1907) *Lady Mary Montagu and her Times.* Methuen.

Payne, K., ed. (1984) *Between Ourselves. Letters between Mothers and Daughters.* Picador.

Pinchbeck, I. (1981) *Women Workers and the Industrial Revolution.* Virago.

de Pizan, C. (1983) *The Book of the City of Ladies.* Picador.

Plath, A.S. ed. (1976) *Letters Home. Correspondence 1950–1963.* Faber & Faber; New York: Harper & Row.

Plath, S. (1963) *The Bell Jar.* Faber & Faber; New York: Harper & Row.

—— (1965) *Ariel. Poems by Sylvia Plath.* Faber & Faber.

Power, E. (1975) *Mediaeval Women*, Margaret Postan, ed. Cambridge University Press.

Prior, M., ed. (1985) *Women in English Society 1500–1800.* Methuen.

Rhode, E. (1987) 'Life before words. Coleridge as psychotherapist', *Encounter*, March, pp. 43–8.

Rich, A. (1977) *Of Woman Born.* Virago.

—— (1980) *On Lies, Secrets and Silence.* Virago.

de Riencourt, A. (1983) *Woman and Power in History.* Honeyglen.

Roethke, T. (1937) *Collected Poems.* New York: Doubleday.

Ross, I. (1949) *Margaret Fell, the Mother of Quakerism.* London/New York/Toronto: Longmans, Green.

Sackville-West, V. (1923) *The Diary of Lady Anne Clifford.* Heinemann.

Sand, G. and Flaubert, G. (1979) *Letters.* Chicago: Academy Chicago.

Sarde, M. (1981) *Colette Free and Fettered.* Michael Joseph.

Saxton, M. (1928) *Louisa May.* André Deutsch.

Schwarzer, A. (1985) *Simone de Beauvoir Today.* Chatto & Windus.

Segal, H. (1981) *The Work of Hanna Segal.* New York: Jason Aronson.

Seltman, C. (1956) *Women in Antiquity.* Thames & Hudson.

Sexton, A. (1975) *The Awful Rowing Towards God.* Boston, MA: Houghton Mifflin.

Shahar, S. (1983) *The Fourth Estate. A History of Women in the Middle Ages.* London/New York: Methuen.

Slater, M. (1983) *Dickens and Women.* London/Melbourne/Toronto: J.M. Dent.

Sophocles (1953) *Electra and Other Plays*, E.F. Watling, trans. Harmondsworth: Penguin Classics.

Spender, D. (1985) *Mothers of the Novel.* Pandora.

Steedman, C. (1986) *Landscape for a Good Woman. A Study of Two Lives.* Virago.

Stelzer, J. (1986) 'The formation and deformation of identity during psychoanalytic training', *Free Assns* 7: 59–75.

Stiller, N. (1980) *Eve's Orphans. Mothers and Daughters in Mediaeval English Literature.* Westport, CT/London: Greenwood.

Stoller, J. (1974) *The Sense of Femaleness in Psychoanalysis and Women.* Harmondsworth: Penguin.

Stone, L. (1985) 'Only women', *New York Review of Books*, 11 April 1985.

Swidler, L. (1976) *Women in Judaism.* Metuchen, NJ: Scarecrow.

Tagore, R. (1985) *Personality.* Macmillan.

Thornton, A. (1875) *The Autobiography of Mrs Alice Thornton.* The Surtees Society, Andrews, Durham; Whitaker, London; Blackwood, Edinburgh.

Thurman, J. (1984) *Isak Dinesen. The Life of Karen Blixen.* Harmondsworth: Penguin.

Warner, M. (1985) *Alone of All her Sex.* Picador.

Weigall, A. (1932) *Sappho of Lesbos.* Thornton Butterworth.

Whitmont, E.C. (1983) *The Return of the Goddess.* Arkana.

Williamson, Dr G. (1922) *Lady Anne Clifford, Countess of Dorset and Pembroke.* Edinburgh: Kendal, Titus, Wilson.

Winnicott, D.W. (1975) 'Hate in the countertransference', in *Through Paediatrics to Psycho-Analysis.* Hogarth/Institute of Psycho-Analysis, pp. 194–203.

Wiseman, A. (1987) *Memoirs of a Book Molesting Childhood and Other Essays.* Oxford University Press.

Woodbridge, L. (1984) *Women and the English Renaissance.* Brighton: Harvester.

Woodham-Smith, C. (1950) *Florence Nightingale.* Constable.

Wollstonecraft, M. (1792) *A Vindication of the Rights of Woman.* Fisher & Unwin.

Yezierska, A. (1984) *Bread Givers.* The Women's Press.

Zak de Goldstein, R. (1984) 'The dark continent and its enigmas', *Int. J. Psycho-Anal.* 65: 179–90.

Zeman, S.A. (1977) *Presumptuous Girls. Six Women and their World in the Serious Woman's Novel.* Weidenfeld & Nicolson.

Zuntz, G. (1971) *Persephone.* Oxford: Clarendon.

INDEX

Most references to women in this index also include references to their mothers and/or daughters.

TOO LONG A CHILD